Sep. 2020

W9-BKF-610

# Fodor's

# PRAGUE

# Welcome to Prague

Little did we realize that the emergence of a novel coronavirus in early 2020 would abruptly bring almost all travel to a halt. Although our Fodor's writers around the world have continued working to bring you the best of the destinations they cover, we still anticipate that more than the usual number of businesses will close permanently in the coming months, perhaps with little advance notice. We don't expect things to return to "normal" for some time. As you plan your upcoming travels to Prague, please confirm that places are still open and let us know when we need to make updates by writing to us at editors@fodors.com.

## TOP REASONS TO GO

★ **Historic architecture:** Gothic, baroque, Renaissance, art nouveau—it's all here.

★ **Prague Castle:** This Gothic fortress and soaring cathedral were Kafka's inspiration.

★ **Jewish heritage:** Historic synagogues and sights reflect an 800-year-old legacy.

★ **Old Town Square:** The city's pulsing heart fans out below the twin-spired Týn church.

★ **Excellent beer:** Czechs brew the best pilsner, and Prague pubs know how to pour it.

★ **Classical music:** Musicians from Dvořák to Mozart made their mark in Prague.

# Contents

## MAPS

Chapter 1

# EXPERIENCE PRAGUE

# 20 ULTIMATE EXPERIENCES

Prague offers terrific experiences that should be on every traveler's list. Here are Fodor's top picks for a memorable trip.

## 1 Prague Castle

Prague Castle is the largest ancient castle in the world, so don't be surprised if you need a full day to enjoy it. Built on a hill overlooking the city, it's one of the oldest, too—the structure dates back to AD 880. *(Ch. 5)*

## 2 Moravian Wine

On the Moravian Wine Trail, you can bike 11 different trails spread over 750 miles, and enjoy stops at wine-making towns on the Austrian border. *(Ch. 14)*

## 3 Pancava Falls

Krkonose National Park offers alpine meadows, dramatic granite outcrops speckled with wildflowers, and Pancava Falls, the country's tallest waterfall. *(Ch. 14)*

## 4 Czech Dumplings

Dumplings play a starring role in Czech cuisine, and they can come in many forms. Look for fruit-filled švestkové knedlíky—made even tastier when topped with melted butter and sprinkled sugar. *(Ch. 3)*

## 5 Brno Bar-Hopping

With the Czech Republic's largest student population, Brno has a lively nightlife scene and cool bars that redefine the typical Czech beer-drinking experience. *(Ch. 14)*

## 6 Litomyšl

Popular with classical music fans as the home of Bedřich Smetana, a famous Czech composer, this delightful small town has Renaissance arcades, rows of pastel homes, and monastery gardens. *(Ch. 11)*

## 7 Prague's Trendy Art District

The edgy-cool twin neighborhoods of Letná and Holešovice (collectively known as Prague 7), are home to the Fine Arts Academy and the Foundation for Contemporary Arts. *(Ch. 10)*

# 8 Olomouc

Often called "Little Prague," Southern Moravia's Olomouc has colorful baroque buildings, ornamental fountains, and a thriving arts scene. *(Ch. 14)*

# 9 A Vltava River Cruise

One of the best ways to soak up the Vltava's unspoiled beauty is via a scenic boat tour. Options include steamboats and vintage-style canal boats with music and food. *(Ch. 3)*

## 10 The Birthplace of Pilsner Beer

Take a tour of the Pilsner Urquell Brewery, where Pilsner Urquell beer was first created in 1842, for an exclusive tasting of unpasteurized pilsner, poured straight from an oak lager cask. *(Ch. 13)*

## 11 Find Kafka

Traces of Prague's famous author can be found all over the city, from house No. 22 in Prague Castle, where Kafka lived from 1916 to 1917 to a statue of him in Josefov. *(Chs. 3, 5)*

## 12 Kladruby Horses

A UNESCO World Heritage Site, the royal stables at Kladruby were once used to breed horses for Emperor Rudolf II. Tour the stables and learn about one of the oldest breeds of horses in the world. *(Ch. 11)*

## 13 A Night at the Theater

Try for a seat at the opulent Stavovské divadlo, where Mozart premiered his Don Giovanni in 1787, or the ornate Národní divadlo, Prague's main venue for opera, dance, and drama. *(Ch. 3)*

# 14 The Clock in Old Town Square

Hundreds of people gather under the clock every hour from 9 am to 11 pm, when statues of the 12 apostles move around the giant clockface and a skeleton rings his bell. *(Ch. 3)*

## 15 David Černý's Art

Controversial Czech artist David Černý's work can be found in the most unlikely of places in Prague: one installation features statues of babies crawling up Prague's Žižkov TV Tower. *(Ch. 9)*

## 16 Klementium

This former Jesuit university houses a clock tower that was once used by astronomers in the 15th centurie to observe the skies and a library that hasn't changed since 1727. *(Ch. 3)*

## 17 Europe's Oldest Synagogue

Though the Jewish Quarter only spans a few city blocks, its history dates to the 10th century. The Staronová synagoga built in 1270, is the oldest active synagogue in Europe. *(Ch. 3)*

## 18 The Healing Waters in Karlovy Vary

Drinking fountains are dotted throughout this historic spa town, and visitors are encouraged to sip the mineral-rich water using special porcelain mugs—which also make nifty souvenirs. *(Ch. 13)*

# 19 Prague's Most Beautiful Garden

The Valdštejnska zahrada (Wallenstein Palace Gardens), designed by Italian gardeners in 1621, offers reflection ponds, outdoor concerts, and a flock of resident peacocks. *(Ch. 4)*

# 20 The Charles Bridge at Sunset

Visit Prague's most congested landmark in the late afternoon, when crowds thin and the setting sun provides a more scenic backdrop. *(Ch. 3)*

# WHAT'S WHERE

**1** **Staré Město and Josefov (Old Town and Jewish Quarter).** Prague's historic heart is "tourist central," so it's often jam-packed with people. Most gather in Old Town Square to marvel at the architecture and watch the astronomical clock strike, then wander the narrow streets.

**2** **Malá Strana (Lesser Quarter).** This neighborhood is filled with hilly cobblestoned streets edged with baroque buildings. The stunning Kostel sv. Mikuláše (Church of St. Nicholas) dominates the district.

**3** **Prague Castle and Hradčany.** The highlight here is the Prague Castle complex, which shelters a Romanesque basilica, a Gothic cathedral, a Renaissance garden, and a baroque palace.

**4** **Nové Město (New Town).** Prague's so-called New Town was, in fact, laid out in the 14th century. Its focal point is Václavské náměstí (Wenceslas Square): a grand boulevard lined with shops, restaurants, and hotels.

**5** **Smíchov and Vyšehrad.** Smíchov is one of Prague's best entertainment

districts, home to a dizzying array of great restaurants, trendy bars, historic theaters, and multiplex cinemas. Across the river lies compact Vyšehrad, with the remains of Prague's "other castle" as well as a cemetery for famed Czech artists.

**6 Vinohrady and Vršovice.** As its name implies, Vinohrady began as a wine-producing region, and the lovely, leafy neighborhood is still intoxicating. Neighboring Vršovice is home to arguably Prague's coolest street.

**7 Žižkov and Karlín.** Žižkov retains its counterculture reputation despite increasing gentrification. Meanwhile, the former industrial district of Karlín is a now a hipster paradise.

**8 Letná, Holešovice, and Troja.** Known for its park, Letná is where some of the largest Velvet Revolution marches took place. Major redevelopment continues in Holešovice, where the chief attraction is the National Gallery's collection of art. Troja, with its zoo, botanical garden, and eponymous château, feels like a day-trip destination inside the city.

# WHAT'S WHERE

**9 Day-Trips from Prague.** From fairy-tale hilltop castles to human-bone-decorated churches, medieval Gothic cathedrals to chilling Holocaust memorials, there are all manner of fascinating attractions within easy reach of the Czech capital.

**10 Southern Bohemia.** A landscape lover's paradise, Southern Bohemia is one of the country's favorite hiking, cycling, and kayaking destinations. Dotted among the rolling hills and snaking rivers are several lovely towns and cities, not least the impossibly pretty Český Krumlov.

POLAND

Náchod

Hradec
Králové

Pardubice

Chrudim

Havlíčkův
Brod

Jihlava

Svitavy

MORAVIA

Olomouc

Prostejov

Opava

Ostrava

Novy Jicín

Přerov

Karviná

Česky
Tesín

Frydek-
Mistek

Vsetín

Brno

12

Otrokovice

Zlín

Znojmo

Mikulov

Uherské
Hradiste

Breclav

SLOVAKIA

Donau (Danube)

0        60 miles

0        90 km

**11 Western Bohemia.**
This is a region dominated by charming spa towns, from the pretty, park-filled Františkovy Lázně (Franzensbad) to the perennially popular Karlovy Vary (Carlsbad)—famed for its annual film festival. Come to take to the waters or enjoy a massage, but stay for the beautiful Empire architecture.

**12 Moravia.** It may be less visited than Bohemia, but the Czech Republic's eastern element has plenty of charms of its own, including the excellent locally grown wine, the regular folk music and dance shows, and the gorgeous town squares of Telč and Olomouc. It also has the country's second city, Brno.

# What's New in Prague

The "City of a Hundred Spires" is as staggeringly beautiful as ever, attracting record numbers of visitors to see its array of historical, architectural, and cultural gems. But over the last decade or so, this much-cherished heritage and tradition has been allied with a more modern, internationalist outlook. The 2011 death of former president Václav Havel—a global icon and hero of the 1989 Velvet Revolution—seemed to jolt Czechs into the realization that nothing stands still, and Prague has since been on a relentless drive to catch up with Western trends and sensibilities. A walk around the city center reveals some of these transformations, from long-term renovations of landmark buildings to an increased choice of international restaurants. But for those who really want to see what modern Prague has to offer, head a little farther afield to neighborhoods like Karlín, Smíchov, and Vršovice, where contemporary art galleries, cool coffee shops, art house cinemas, craft beer bars, and independent boutiques await.

### THE RISE OF CRAFT
When it comes to beer, the Czech Republic rules the roost. After all, the world's first lager, Pilsner Urquell, was brewed here, and the country still has the highest beer consumption per capita in the world. However, this grand brewing tradition meant a resistance to change and a glacially slow adoption of the microbrewing craze. Luckily, Prague has now more than caught up, with its expert brewers producing an impressive array of pale ales, porters, and saisons— along with classic pilsner lagers, of course. Taste the revolution for yourself at one of the city's many excellent microbreweries, from the fast-expanding Vinohradský Pivovar to the boat-based Loď Pivovar.

As well as beer, Prague's gone all crafty with coffee, too. Since the fall of communism, coffee in the city has slowly evolved from a cup of low-quality grind doused with hot water to Italian imports like Illy and Lavazza and big-name chains like Starbucks and Costa. Today, it's all about aeropresses and vacuum pots. For a taste of the current craft coffee craze, head to the Vietnamese-influenced and vegan-friendly Cafefin in Vinohrady, or the shabby-chic hipster haven Vnitroblock in Holešovice.

### STICKING WITH KORUNY
The Czech Republic was admitted into the European Union way back in 2004, but—despite innumerable promises and passed deadlines—the country has yet to adopt the euro. What gives? Well, mostly, the euro crisis of the early 2010s greatly dented the currency's prestige. With the Czechs all but recovered from the economic crisis, there's no great push to join the common currency. And with prices stable and the country's accounts solid, there's no pressing need.

### PACK YOUR APPETITE
Since 2008, when Prague gained the first Michelin star of anywhere in the former Eastern Bloc, the city has built on its success to become the undisputed culinary king of the region. Today, fine-dining restaurants abound, from the 19th-century-inspired Czech fare of La Degustation Bohême Bourgeoise to the Scandinavian-slanted contemporary cooking of Field.

However, it's not all about formal, high-end dining. Fresh food, slow food, locally grown, seasonal, organic... call it what you want, Praguers have fully embraced the notion that food should be local, tasty, and sustainable. Weekend farmers' markets are all over town, bringing fresh, locally sourced fruits, vegetables, meats, and cheeses to the urban masses. Pubs and restaurants have gotten in on the act, too, rewriting menus to embrace domestic ingredients and old-fashioned Czech cooking.

## WORK IN PROGRESS

Deep down, Prague must have some kind of inferiority complex. What else could explain the perpetual need to make a beautiful city even more beautiful? In the last few years, there have been major, multiyear renovations of the Charles Bridge, Prague Castle's Zlatá ulička (Golden Lane), the Národní muzeum (National Museum), and even the main train station (Hlavní nádraží). While it's wonderful to see many long-neglected buildings dazzling once more, it does feel as though the grand city project will never end. Be prepared that you may have to crop construction equipment out of your favorite vacation snaps.

## WATCH OUT!

Watch out for that scooter! Segways may have been banned from the city center in 2016, but there are still plenty of two-wheeled hazards to avoid. Prague residents have taken to city cycling in greater and greater numbers—credit Berlin and Vienna for showing how cycling can work as a viable urban transport model—while Lime's dockless rent-as-you-go e-scooters can make the sidewalks just as dangerous as the roads. The real bane of locals' lives, however, are the "beer bikes"; pedal-powered vehicles with seating for up to 15 beer-swilling driver-passengers arranged around a bar.

## LIMITING AIRBNB

In the last five years, Airbnb rentals have soared in Prague, contributing to record numbers of city tourists (eight million in 2018) and, some believe, a detrimental effect on the city's residential neighborhoods. To try and combat this, Prague's mayor Zdeněk Hřib proposed a ban on residents leasing out entire apartments. By limiting Airbnb renters to single rooms in accommodation where the owner also lives, he believes this will reduce overall accommodation capacity and help to curb tourist numbers. Time will tell if the proposals are approved and, if so, what impact they have.

## BREXIT HOMECOMING

If you're annoyed by the crowds in your Charles Bridge selfie, don't (just) blame tourists. Prague is also experiencing a large influx of Czech residents. According to official data, there are 45,000 Czechs currently living in Britain – although some estimates put it at more than 100,000. With the UK having left the European Union, it's anticipated that many of these are returning or will return to the country following the end of the transition period.

# The Best Castles in Prague and the Czech Republic

### PRAGUE CASTLE

From jousting and defenestrations (literally, chucking one's enemies out of the window—it happened several times in the history of Bohemia) to more modern moments like the arrival of Adolf Hitler in Prague or the inauguration of President Václav Havel, Prague Castle has seen it all, and it remains the official residence of the Czech president. Sightswise, it boasts the dazzling St. Vitus Cathedral, several palaces, ancient treasure, historic courtyards, stunning, hilly gardens and the bewitching Golden Lane.

### KARLŠTEJN CASTLE

Karlštejn, a large castle close to Prague, was built to house the crown jewels and was once Charles IV's summer palace. It's a steep climb up to see it, mind you, on a path lined with tacky souvenir stalls, but it's worth it for the battlements, turrets, and towers that reward you at the top.

### KONOPIŠTĚ CASTLE

Konopiště, a château in a huge, beautiful park, traded hands between nobles in the centuries following its construction around the 13th century, but it is best known for its supporting role in a piece of modern history: it was the country residence for the doomed Archduke Franz Ferdinand, whose 1914 assassination sparked World War I. In World War II, it housed some units of the German SS.

### KŘIVOKLÁT

This romantic 12th-century château is a favorite with Czechs because of its appearances in various works of literature. Its monumental tower steals the glory, but the atmospheric chapel, library, and dungeons are worth a visit, too.

### VYŠEHRAD CITADEL

Prague's "second castle" is much less visited but it has an awesome history, fascinating buildings, and lovely views over the Vltava River. The hourly tour of the casemates, which house some of the original baroque statues from the Charles Bridge, is not to be missed.

### LOUČEŇ CASTLE

You can stay overnight at this romantic baroque château in central Bohemia, and we don't just mean inadvertently if you get stuck in one of the many garden mazes. Tours around the castle can be taken with a costumed prince, princess, their valet, or even a forester, and the 11 garden labyrinths in the castle's large English-style park enhance the vibe.

Zamek Loučeň

There are three suites in the castle itself for those who really want to take the whole "king for a day" fantasy to the max, and the Maximilian hotel on-site is housed in a building dating from 1834 but boasts modern amenities like a swimming pool in a nearby annex.

**ARCHBISHOPS' CHÂTEAU**
The entire town is an attractive stop in Moravia, but the real draw here is the Archbishops' Château, a spectacular residence designed for the powerful archbishops of Olomouc in 1260. The gardens are beautiful and UNESCO listed, too. The château's Assembly Hall is considered to be one of the most jaw-dropping rococo halls in the Czech Republic.

**STATE CHÂTEAU HLUBOKÁ**
Possibly the most beautiful and romantic castle in the country, located in Southern Bohemia, Hluboká has roots in the 13th century but really came into its own in the hands of a wealthy family in the 19th, who took their inspiration from Britain's Windsor Castle, which gives you an idea of the grandeur on offer here.

**LEDNICE-VALTICE CULTURAL LANDSCAPE**
Two châteaus for the price of one, with vineyards and a gorgeous park to boot. This absolutely immense complex in southern Moravia was transformed between the 17th and 20th centuries into the striking 200-km (124-mile) landscape visitors find today.

**ČESKÝ KRUMLOV CASTLE**
There is a reason the entire historic center of this town in Southern Bohemia, including its 13th-century castle, has been a UNESCO World Heritage Site since 1992: it is storybook perfect. Oh, and there's a bear in the castle moat.

# Best Beer Experiences in the Czech Republic

## BEER SPA

It's a beer lover's dream: bathe in water made from the same ingredients used to make the brew, while drinking ice-cold beer straight from the tap at the Czech Republic's original beer spa in Chodovar.

## LOKÁL DLOUHÁÁÁ

Pilsner Urquell as fresh as it comes at this modern take on an old-school Czech pub in Prague's Staré Město draws the crowds all day and all year, so arrive early. The beer itself comes straight from the tanks that you can see at one end of the bar, guaranteeing its taste and purity. The traditional Czech food on offer is as good as the beer, from the fried cheese to the goulash with traditional bread and potato dumplings. Once you've secured your table, settle in for a long session. It's a little more expensive than some of the authentic old venues farther out of town, but it's worth it.

## ČESKÉ BUDĚJOVICE

Take a deep dive (not literally) into the beer-making process at the original home of Budvar, České Budějovice, the town housing the famous brewery. The vast Budějovický Budvar complex was founded in 1895, but the 125-year old, state-owned brewery is showing no signs of slowing down. And as for the beer? Well, it's hard to doubt the quality of a beer made from 984-foot-deep artesian wells in the brewery that pump up water from a lake dating back to the Ice Age. The brewery tours are fantastic and run at 2 daily.

## KLÁŠTERNÍ PIVOVAR STRAHOV

At this monastery/brewery, where monks have been brewing beer since the turn of the 14th century, guests can now sample a variety of brews made on-site with traditional methods. Sadly, the monks themselves aren't involved in the brewing anymore, but that doesn't make the atmosphere any less fun, the history any less quirky, or the beers any less good: in particular, the dark St. Norbert has a good reputation, although the seasonal wheat beer is also delicious.

## U SLOVANSKÉ LÍPY

Sometimes you don't need all the bells and whistles; this is just a classic Czech pub in Prague's Žižkov district, an area rumored to have more pubs per square kilometer than anywhere else in the world. The beer is good, the atmosphere is fantastic, and there's robust Czech food on offer, too. It claims to be the oldest pub in the neighborhood, too, but that heritage is likely less of a draw than the fantastic and ever-changing range of artisan beers it offers on tap.

## BEER GARDENS

For views with your brews, join the rest of Prague in summer at one of the city's lively outdoor drinking spots. Letná Park's river and Staré Město views, the gentle hum of conversation, and dappled shade from the trees above make this the best place to drink in the warmer months, bar none.

České Budějovice

## VINOHRADSKÝ PIVOVAR
The craft beer revolution of recent years has seen hyperlocal neighborhood breweries spring up in many of Prague's districts, from Vinohrady to Anděl. Vinohradský pivovar is one of the breakout successes of the trend, and its brews can be found at a number of other bars around town. Its HQ is a modern, chill spot, too, down some steps on a main street at the border of Vinohrady and Vršovice, with classic Czech grub, several varieties of the in-house beer, and portholes to glimpse the beer tanks and pipes.

## BEER FESTIVALS
Predictably and wonderfully, there are beer festivals all over the Czech Republic. Pilsner Fest in Plzeň in October, celebrating the first ever brewing of a pilsner-style lager and also featuring bands, is one of the biggest and best. The Řečkovice festival

on the grounds of an old brewery in Brno showcases microbreweries, and an annual shindig at Prague Castle—offering around 140 different kinds of beer brewed by small outfits—is another standout.

## CUSTOMS
As beer is the Czech Republic's national drink, the customs and traditions surrounding it are enshrined in every Czech's heart. Passing the citizenship exam for immigrants who want to become permanent residents even requires some beer knowledge. Win hearts by saying "Na zdraví" (cheers) before you take your first sip, and find yourself a beer mat quickly to avoid spilling the frothy head onto the table. Those ordering a malý pivo (small beer), particularly men, can expect a little ribbing: the phrase is a gentle insult in Czech. One of the best (and riskiest) traditions is still upheld

in the more authentic bars and involves bringing more beers as soon as a patron's glass is empty, unless they have signaled that they are finished by placing their beer mat on the glass.

## U FLEKŮ
Dating back to 1499, this boisterous, touristy, giant beer hall is still fantastic fun and a great place to try dark beer. While the service at the venerable U Fleků can be downright rude, that's all part of the atmosphere, and clinking glasses (and elbows) with the hundreds of other patrons is part of it, too. Vast, ancient, and a bit kitschy, there are eight separate dining halls and a beer garden in the summer. There are cabaret shows on a Friday and beers can also be bought to take away.

# What to Buy

### BOHEMIA CRYSTAL
For centuries, Czech-made glassware, known as Bohemia crystal or Bohemian glass, has been internationally recognized for its quality and beauty. Czech crystal chandeliers hang, for example, in Milan's La Scala, in Rome's Teatro dell'Opera, in Versailles, in the Hermitage Museum in St. Petersburg and in the royal palace in Riyadh. Nowadays, shoppers can go traditional at emporia like Moser Crystal, or opt for more unusual pieces at Artěl.

### BEER
It's the Czech Republic's most famous export and you can easily take a bottle or two home. Get them direct from source at the Staropramen Brewery in Anděl or go deliciously niche by hunting down a small Czech brewer with the help of the staff at a beer shop like Pivní Mozaika in Karlín. As well as generally making you feel good, Czech beer can also make you look good. Hop promotes healthy hair growth, reduces scalp irritations, and adds strength and shine, so be sure to look for organic shampoos and shower gels in the beauty aisles. Brands to look for include Manufaktura, Ryor, and Saela.

### GARNET JEWELRY
Czech garnets (also known as Prague garnets or Bohemian garnets) are usually deep red, but can also be black or clear. Garnets have been mined in the Czech Republic since the early 17th century. In modern-day Prague and the Czech Republic, garnet prices vary according to their quality, quantity, and size. Today, garnet is used to make everything from paperweights to fine jewelry, so there is something for every budget and taste. However, all that glitters here may not be gold (or garnet)—watch out for the touristy shops promising real garnets in Old Town, and make sure to get a certificate of authenticity upon purchasing. The beautiful deep red glint of Bohemian garnet is best showcased by Wollem in Old Town, and Halada and Granat Turnov which have several locations in Prague.

### COMMUNIST MEMORABILIA
Browse junk shops to pick up eerie reminders of Prague's dark past, from signs and posters to badges emblazoned with the red Communist star. The standout is Bric a Brac, right by Old Town Square: talk to the owner, who speaks good English, about his fascinating treasure trove.

### CZECH DESIGN
Modern design in the Czech Republic is thriving, and there are lots of studios and ateliers where you can grab something unique and, often, even meet the designer. Try the Chemistry Design Store or the amazing Vnitroblock in a former factory, both in hip Holešovice.

### MARIONETTES AND WOODEN TOYS
Puppetry has UNESCO-heritage status in Czechia and Slovakia, and the traditional wooden marionettes are wonderful souvenirs. There are figures from folklore as well as more modern characters, from robots to politicians,

Manufaktura

plus puppetry courses, DIY lessons, and kits. The Centre for Contemporary Puppetry sits right next to a puppet shop on the main route up to the castle in Malá Strana.

## NATURAL COSMETICS
Botanicus and Manufaktura, among others, have been pioneering natural, organic cosmetics made from local plant-based ingredients, using traditional methods, for years. Look for Bohemian lavender and Czech beer products.

## KOH-I-NOOR PENCILS
This historic brand pretty much invented the first pencil in the 1790s and has been making top-end stationery and art supplies ever since. Its shops are iconic in Prague, with a huge gorilla made entirely out of pencils in one of them, and its stationery top-notch; the best buy is one of the pencils that made the company's name.

## OPLATKY (SPA WAFERS)
You might wish you could take the restorative spa water of Karlovy Vary home with you, but you can in a way, because the spa wafer treats you nibble on during spa visits are made with it. They are also protected by the European Union as unique geographical products (like Champagne or feta cheese), so stock up! You can find Czech wafers in supermarkets and grocery stores or at the outdoor Havelská market in Old Town.

## KAFKA
There's something special about buying one of 20th-century visionary author Franz Kafka's books in the city where he grew up, after strolling the streets he walked as a boy in the Jewish Quarter or visiting the museum dedicated to his work and memory. Or, even better, from the atmospheric bookshop bearing his name on Široká.

## CLASSICAL MUSIC
The Czech Republic has produced many famous classical music composers: Bedrich Smetana, Antonin Dvorak, Leos Janacek, and Bohuslav Martinu, to name just the most famous ones, so classical music CDs and records are a great souvenir. Music fans should check out Supraphon Musicpoint, from the distinguished Czech music label, located in Nové Město. The store has a classical music section and hosts readings, listening sessions, concerts, and autograph sessions.

# Under-the-Radar Prague

### PRAGUE'S SECRET GARDENS
The abundance of charming, sanctuary-like gardens hidden around Prague includes the Vrtbovská zahrada (Vrtba Garden), a gorgeous baroque terraced garden that's concealed in the back of the Aria Hotel.

### CONTEMPORARY ART
Officially known as Prague 7, the neighboring districts of Letná and Holešovice are home to Vnitroblock, an old factory that's been turned into a multifaceted performance space that also comprises a café, art gallery, vinyl shop, and even a small cinema; The Chemistry, a cutting-edge gallery focused solely on works by young Czech artists today; and DOX, one of Prague's main contemporary art galleries.

### PRAGUE'S COOLEST CINEMA
Bio Oko is a refurbished cinema from the 1950s that wouldn't be out of place in Brooklyn. On the program is a mix of current and classic films, including everything from Star Wars to obscure European animated features. Show up early to nab a seat in the vintage 1987 Trabant limousine that's parked in the front row.

### AN UNDERGROUND PUB
Celetná, a student's club at Charles University, is a favorite haunt of college students, though everyone's welcome. The vaulted ceilings and lack of windows make you feel like you're in a cave. Check the calendar for frequent music and art performances.

### A TUNNEL OF BOOKS
Located inside the lobby (no entrance fee required) of the Prague Municipal Library, the Infinite Book Tunnel, by Slovak artist Matej Kren, is a cylindrical tower of books that mimics the way an inspiring,

### STEFANIK OBSERVATORY
This hilltop working observatory dedicated to Slovak astronomer Milan Rastislav Stefanik has amateur guides to explain what you're seeing through the viewfinder and an exhibit room with sundials, lunar globes, and an octant from the 18th century.

### DIVADLO ALFRED VE DVOŘE
Look for imaginative storytelling by independent artists from all over Europe, all for the reasonable price of $10. Even the space is arresting: a pavilion theater with an eye-catching geometric design, built in the courtyard of an old apartment building.

Klementinum

hard-to-put-down novel can feel; mirrors are inserted, so when you poke your head in the tunnel, it appears to travel upward forever.

### THE KLEMENTINUM

Hidden among the *trdelník* stands and souvenir shops on Karlova ulice is an old library that remains unchanged since the 1700s. To reach it, you have to sign up for a guided tour, which costs $10. Ascending the narrow spiral staircase, you're brought to a hushed gallery filled with old-world mechanical globes, ceiling frescoes above, and ancient texts. Continue on the tour to reach the top of the tower, and you'll be rewarded with one of the prettiest views in Prague.

### BEER-MAKING AT U MEDVÍDKŮ

One of the best ways to tap into one of the city's oldest pubs' history is by signing up for a beer-making class. The nine-hour course walks you through the entire beer-making process, from mashing to cooling. As a reward for your full day's work, the ticket ($353 USD) includes refreshments, lunch, and a tasting in the bar.

### CZECH VENICE

Book a Venice-style gondola tour of the Vltava River and the Čertovka Canal and you'll be cruising in an original Venetian gondola built in 1858. The guides provide Italian sparkling wine in summer and mulled wine in winter.

### TAKE A UNIQUE STREET TOUR

"Street tour" takes on a whole new meaning with the guys at Pragulic, who employ current or formerly homeless people as tour guides. Part social experiment, part immersive study, the two-hour tours offer a candid look at a side of Prague rarely seen by tourists.

# What to Eat and Drink

Trdelnik

### TRDELNÍK

This crusty, sugar-coated morsel proves that Prague is a paradise for sweets lovers. Despite its Hungarian origin, a trdelník is the most ubiquitous Czech treat—a hollow pastry cone cooked over an open flame, rolled in sugar, and often filled with ice cream.

### VĚNEČEK

Věneček has been compared to a cruller doughnut, though since this is Eastern Europe, expect more dough and a healthy dollop of cream. It comes sliced in half with a layer of cold custard in the middle, making it a bit like a doughnut sandwich. It's best eaten cold with a strong, hot coffee.

### SVÍČKOVÁ

Like a Slavic Thanksgiving on a plate, this entrée consists of larded sirloin beef slathered in a creamy root-vegetable sauce and served with knedlíky, or bread dumplings (and sometimes, cranberry sauce). The beef is braised directly with the vegetables and copious amounts of butter, while the dumplings soak up all the meaty goodness.

Svickova

### SCHNITZEL

Meat connoisseurs could spend hours weighing the virtues of traditional Czech schnitzel, which is made with pork, against the Austrian version, which uses veal. For the rest of us, suffice to say, this a perfectly breaded, delicately fried, and incredibly tasty piece of meat, almost always accompanied by a heaping serving of mashed potatoes.

### FRUIT DUMPLINGS

Fruit dumplings, or *ovocné knedlíky*, are an instantly recognizable Czech specialty. And they are just what they say on the box: hot, sweet, jammy fruit-filled steamed dumplings, served with a side of melted butter, poppy seeds, or farmer cheese.

### SAUERKRAUT SOUP

Nothing says Czech comfort food like a bowl of hot sauerkraut soup. Traditionally a vegetarian breakfast eaten by forest workers to brace for a long day outside, the recipe was gradually expanded to include smoked sausage. Luckily, you won't have to trek into the woods to find it for yourself.

### GOULASH

Flavored with paprika (a nod to its Hungarian heritage), this deceptively simple stew is the cornerstone of any Czech menu. The recipe marries beef, onions, and peppers, which simmer in a single pot for two hours. The spongy, addictive bread dumplings that accompany the stew are something of a delicacy themselves.

### PICKLED CHEESE

Pickled cheese is a little like the Charles Bridge: Overhyped? Perhaps. But you're going to remember it. Best enjoyed spread on dark Czech bread.

### PILSNER

Known for its light, hoppy flavor, pilsner is not only a necessary refresher during the warmer months—it's also a major point of pride for Czechs across the country. Originating in Plzeň, just 40 miles south of Prague, the most popular version comes from Pilsner Urquell, the largest brewery in the country.

### BECHEROVKA

This Czech digestif makes a potent palate cleanser at the end of a heavy meal. Bestowed with an herb-like flavor, the liquor has been produced the same way—in the same town—since 1807.

# What to Watch and Read

### THE TRIAL AND THE METAMORPHOSIS BY FRANZ KAFKA

Seize this opportunity to read the masterpieces of Prague's most famous literary son, Franz Kafka. Kafka wasn't considered Czech during his life, as a German-speaking Jew in Prague, but he's been reclaimed since, often by tourist touts selling Kafka-themed junk. His books, however, are far more substantial: haunting and visionary, disturbing and dystopian, they remain darkly enjoyable and shouldn't be seen as daunting. Kafka's prose is elegant but accessible, and the stories are short.

### PRAGUE SPRING BY SIMON MAWER

This book is a tremendously evocative depiction, told through the eyes of outsiders, of the events of 1968, when Russian troops crushed the flowering of freedom in communist Czechoslovakia. The book is packed full of historical and geographical detail that readers will easily place in modern-day Prague, as well as identifiable characters whose lives and loves keep the story from feeling too dense.

### THE GOLEM BY GUSTAV MEYRINK

This modern European classic is an expressionist horror story set in Prague's Jewish ghetto. It's astonishingly creepy and atmospheric, and a little bit mad, too. But for a slice of fantastika deeply rooted in the Czech capital, it's a great read.

### THE UNBEARABLE LIGHTNESS OF BEING BY MILAN KUNDERA

Perhaps the most famous work of Czech literature globally, this postmodern classic is a love story at heart, although don't expect happy endings. Also set at the time of the Prague Spring in 1968, the philosophical work follows Tomas, a surgeon in Prague who sleeps around, and traces the repercussions of both his actions and the wider societal upheaval at the time.

### THE GOOD SOLDIER ŠVEJK BY JAROSLAV HAŠEK

A black satire set in World War II, this classic will give you an insight into the Czech sense of humor, but it might be best to get it as an e-book rather than in print, as it's quite the tome. Genuinely funny, provocative, and progressive, it's one of those books whose fame has been eclipsed by those it inspired: notably, Joseph Heller's *Catch-22*.

### BÁBA Z LEDU (ICE MOTHER)

This 2017 Tribeca Film Festival favorite set in modern-day Prague tells the story of a modest widow, love, and winter swimming. Beautifully shot and intensely evocative—particularly of the intense cold that open-water swimming in the Czech Republic entails—it's a moving portrait of love in the third act of life, directed by Bohdan Sláma.

### AMADEUS

This 1984 Oscar winner from renowned Czech director Miloš Forman was partly filmed in Prague's historically relevant locations and in other suitably stunning places around the country. It follows the life of Wolfgang Amadeus Mozart, and is epic, ostentatious, over the top, and fun, with (obviously) a fantastic score, and plenty of darkness, too.

### ANTHROPOID

Based on historical events, this film directed by Sean Ellis covers the astonishing story of the Czech paratroopers who assassinated the Butcher of Prague, Reinhard Heydrich, in World War II. After watching, visit the church where they died in Prague, St. Cyril and Methodius Cathedral, to really bring their stories to life.

# Chapter 2

# TRAVEL SMART

Updated by
Raymond Johnson,
Jennifer Rigby

★ **CAPITAL:**
Prague

👥 **POPULATION:**
1.3 million

💬 **LANGUAGE:**
Czech

$ **CURRENCY:**
Koruna (crown)

☎ **COUNTRY CODE:**
420

⚠ **EMERGENCIES:**
112

🚗 **DRIVING:**
On the right

⚡ **ELECTRICITY:**
230 c/50 cycle, plugs have two round pins, or two pins and a hole.

🕐 **TIME:**
6 hours ahead of New York

🌐 **WEB RESOURCES:**
www.czechtourism.cz
www.prague.eu
www.praguecitytourism.cz

✈ **AIRPORT:**
PRG

# Know Before You Go

What should you pack? How can you get a good photo of the Charles Bridge? Is English widely spoken? Is it Czechia or the Czech Republic? And *is* beer really cheaper than water? Plus tips on using the ATM, dodging the crowds, tipping, and taxis.

## HELLO, MY NAME IS CZECHIA

The country recently changed its name from the Czech Republic to Czechia. Why? Who knows? Certainly not its inhabitants: two-thirds of Czechs polled by a newspaper when the name changed said they didn't like the new moniker, which was suddenly imposed by the government without any real explanation. The official reasoning is that it makes it easier for English speakers to pronounce, and easier for companies and sports teams to use on branding, although critics said it makes foreigners even more likely to confuse it with Chechnya. Fun fact: it's actually just the short name for the country, as France is for the official "The French Republic" (who knew). And as for the Czechs themselves? Most of them couldn't care less what you call their homeland; they call it Česko, anyway.

## PSA: IT'S COLD IN WINTER AND HOT IN SUMMER!

It gets cold in winter, with temperatures regularly well below freezing. Make sure you have a serious coat, hat, gloves, and most importantly, boots (the cobbles in the snow or frost are extremely slippery, and nobody wants cold feet while sightseeing). Build time in your schedule to dip into warm pubs or cafés (not really a hardship), and bear in mind that lots of the more outdoorsy sights are closed in winter. At the opposite end of the scale, the height of summer can get very hot; pack sunscreen and cover-up hats, and like all warm-weather destinations, avoid the hottest parts of the day for serious pavement pounding. Luckily, the beer gardens are shady and many hotels and restaurants have air-conditioning. There are also a host of outdoor pools and even lakes and ponds within easy reach of the city for a cooling dip, including at the Podolí complex by the river.

## YOU'LL NEED TO DUCK THE CROWDS

Prague is one of the most visited cities in the world, so be prepared for hordes, and rise early to avoid them. Plus, get off the beaten track in Staré Město (especially the main route to the Charles Bridge) and you'll find some surprisingly quiet streets; in particular, the streets around Konvikstka and the lower end of Karoliny Světlé can be quite calm. And if you want to take that perfect picture of the view from the bridge itself, here's a tip: go to the next bridge up in either direction (Mánesův most, or Mánes Bridge, to the north, and Most Legií, or Legion Bridge, to the south), where the crowds are much smaller and your picture of the gorgeous vista beyond will include the famous bridge, too. Alternatively, head out to neighborhoods like Vršovice and Vinohrady to gaze at some of Prague's stately signature architecture (and find some great cafés and bars). Lastly, if you hate bachelor parties (known as "stag parties" in Europe), perhaps try to avoid the biggest bars in Staré Město and Nové Město on a Saturday night.

## AVOID STREET TAXIS

Taxis in Prague are notorious rip-offs, so try to avoid flagging one down on the street. This is easy to do these days, as ridesharing apps like Uber and Bolt are as omnipresent here as they are in most major global cities. One word of warning though: don't rely on them in the middle of the night for a ride to the airport, for example; there just aren't enough drivers working at 3 am in the city to make it guaranteed that there will be a car for you. Instead, there are some reliable taxi services you can call or book online, such as the reasonably priced Modrý Anděl, which has English-speaking operators.

### MOST PEOPLE SPEAK SOME ENGLISH

English is widely spoken, and with astonishing fluency by a lot of the younger generation working in hotels and restaurants, but a bit of Czech (ahoj—pronounced ahoy—for hello, dekuji for thank you) goes down very well.

### PART OF THE EU WITHOUT THE EUROS PART

Czech crowns, not euros, are the order of the day, and they are usually in the region of 20–22 koruny (Kč) to the dollar depending on the current exchange rate. Try not to get huge bills from the ATM, as they can be hard to change or spend: while the machine will try to dispense notes in the 1,000 or even 2,000 denomination, try to withdraw multiples of 100 instead so that you can break the note more easily.

### TIPPING IS APPRECIATED

The tradition is just to round up to the nearest whole number, but the international 10% standard is fine, too. It's really up to you, but the gesture is appreciated (and the ferocity of the glare that will greet you if you force your server to fumble around with 1 Kč coins is best avoided).

### DON'T FALL FOR THE RUSSIAN DOLLS

Don't get taken in by the gaudy Russian dolls sold everywhere, particularly in the Jewish Quarter and around Old Town Square. These souvenirs have nothing to do with Czech culture but are a throwback to the 1990s, when Prague was one of the first former Soviet Bloc places that tourists started to visit. If you're looking for traditional Czech gifts, consider beer, wooden puppets, Koh-i-noor pencils, or Bohemian crystal instead.

### BEER IS NOT ALWAYS CHEAPER THAN WATER, SORRY

Beer is a way of life in the Czech Republic, where citizens drink more per head than anywhere else in the world. But the rumors about it being cheaper than water are sadly exaggerated; while it is true that in some pubs it can occasionally be cheaper than bottled water (and it's certainly cheaper than coffee or soft drinks like Coca-Cola in many locales), it's not quite the unbelievable bargain it used to be. And more importantly, most places now will provide you with tap water entirely gratis, too.

# Getting Here and Around

Prague is divided into 10 major administrative districts (with numbers above 10 being used for administrative purposes for some of the larger public housing developments and outlying areas). Most visitors spend their time in "Prague 1," which encompasses Staré Město (Old Town), Malá Strana (Lesser Quarter), part of Nové Město (New Town), and Hradčany (Castle Area). Residents in conversation will often refer to the districts by number to orient themselves geographically ("x is in Prague 1" or "y is in Prague 7"). These district numbers correspond roughly to the city's traditional neighborhoods. The neighborhood of Vinohrady, which lies just to the east of Václavské náměstí (Wenceslas Square), for example, is mostly in Prague 2. Other common neighborhoods and district numbers include Žižkov, Prague 3; Smíchov, Prague 5; and Holešovice, Prague 7. These names—along with the district numbers—appear on street signs.

## ✈ Air

Prague is served by a growing number of budget carriers, which connect the Czech capital to several cities in the United Kingdom and across the European continent. These airlines are a great and cheap way to travel within Europe—though since the flights are popular, be sure to book well in advance. Budget carriers, however, are usually not much help in cutting costs when traveling from North America. Most of these carriers operate out of secondary airports (for example, Stansted in London instead of Heathrow, where most transatlantic flights land; or Orly in Paris instead of the larger Charles de Gaulle airport). This means travelers must change not only airlines but also airports, which can add frustration and expense. Also, consider limits on both carry-on and checked baggage, which are often more stringent on budget carriers than on large international carriers. For flights within Europe, low-cost airlines are sometimes a viable alternative to bus and train travel.

The nonstop flight from New York to Prague takes about eight hours, but the entire journey will take longer (12–15 hours) if you have to change planes at a European hub. The flight from London to Prague takes about two hours; the flight from Vienna to Prague takes less than an hour.

### AIRPORT

Prague's Václav Havel Airport (formerly Ruzyně Airport) is the country's main international airport and lies about 15 km (10 miles) northwest of the city center. The airport has two main terminals— Terminal 1 (T1) and Terminal 2 (T2)—so make sure to read your ticket carefully to see where you are arriving and departing from. There is also a Terminal 3 for private and charter flights. The trip from the airport to the downtown area by car or taxi will take about 30 minutes—add another 20 minutes during rush hour (7–9 am and 4–6 pm).

### AIRLINES

Delta Airlines offers nonstop flights from the United States (from New York's JFK airport) to Prague in the summer (daily flights during the busiest season). No carrier offers direct service in the winter. Most major U.S.-based airlines fly to Prague through code-share arrangements with their European counterparts. However, nearly all the major European airlines fly there, so it's usually easy to connect through a major European airport (such as London–Heathrow, Paris, Amsterdam, or Vienna) and continue to Prague; indeed, flights between the United Kingdom and Prague are numerous and frequent, including some on cheap discount airlines, though in London most of these leave from Gatwick or Stansted airports rather than Heathrow, making them less attractive options for Americans. Fares from the United States tend to rise dramatically during the busy summer season, particularly from June through August or September. There are many discounts during the slow winter months.

## 🚌 Bus

The Czech complex of regional bus lines known collectively as ČSAD operates its dense network from the sprawling Florenc station. For information about routes and schedules, consult the confusingly displayed timetables posted at the station or visit the information window in the lower-level lobby, which is open daily from 6 am to 9 pm. The company's website will give you bus and train information in English (click on the British flag).

There are also private bus companies servicing routes between Czech towns and cities. Many of these have newer buses with added services and comfort, as well as competitive prices and seasonal deals.

Most, but not all, buses use the Florenc station. Some buses—primarily those heading to smaller destinations in the south of the country—depart from above Roztyly Metro station (Line C [red]). You won't know beforehand which buses leave from Roztyly or from one of several other hubs, so you will have to ask first at Florenc or check the website. There's no central information center at most other hubs; you simply have to sort out the timetables at the bus stops or ask someone.

Buses offer an easier and quicker alternative to trains for many destinations. The Western Bohemian spa town of Karlovy Vary, for example, is an easy two-hour bus ride away. The same journey by train—because of the circuitous rail route—often takes 3½ hours.

##  Car

Traveling by car has some obvious advantages: it offers much more flexibility and is often quicker than a bus or train. But these advantages can be outweighed by the costs of the rental and gasoline, as well as the general hassles of driving in the Czech Republic. Most roads in the country are of the two-lane variety and are often jammed with trucks. And then there's parking. It's impossible in Prague and often difficult in the larger cities and towns outside the capital.

A special permit is required to drive on expressways and other four-lane highways. Rental cars should already have a permit affixed to the windshield. Temporary permits—for 10 days (310 Kč) or one month (440 Kč)—are available at border crossings, post offices, and service stations.

### PARKING

Finding a parking spot in Prague can be next to impossible. Most of the spaces in the city center, Prague 1, 2, 3, 5, 6, 7, 8, and 10, are reserved for residents, so you'll have to look for public lots with machines that issue temporary permits (look for the big blue P on machines). To use the machines, insert the required amount of change—usually 20–30 Kč an hour—or use a debit card, then place the ticket in a visible spot on the dashboard. Violators will find their cars towed away or immobilized by a "boot" on the tire. Some hotels offer parking—and this is a

# Getting Here and Around

real advantage—though you may have to pay extra. A few streets also have meter parking that sells tickets to put in your window, but finding a spot is a virtual impossibility. Changes in the parking policy are pending, due to complaints from local businesses.

Parking is generally unrestricted in the outer areas of the city, though vacant spots can still be hard to find. There's an underground lot at Náměstí Jana Palacha, near Old Town Square. There are also park-and-ride (p+r) lots at distant suburban Metro stations, including Skalka (Line A), Zličín and Černý Most (Line B), and Nádraží Holešovice and Opatov (Line C). These charge as little as 20 Kč per day and 140 Kč overnight, substantially cheaper than downtown parking.

## RULES OF THE ROAD

The Czech Republic follows the usual continental rules of the road. A right turn on red is permitted *only* when indicated by a green arrow. Signposts with yellow diamonds indicate a main road where drivers have the right of way. The speed limit is 130 kph (78 mph) on four-lane highways, 90 kph (56 mph) on open roads, and 50 kph (30 mph) in built-up areas and villages. Passengers under 12 years of age or less than 5 feet in height must ride in the back seat.

## CAR RENTAL

Drivers from the United States need no international driving permit to rent a car in the Czech Republic, only a valid domestic license, along with the vehicle registration. If you intend to drive across a border, ask about restrictions on driving into other countries. The minimum age required for renting is usually 21 or older, and some companies also have maximum ages; be sure to inquire when making your arrangements. The Czech Republic requires that you have held your driver's license for at least a year before you can rent a car.

# Metro

Prague has an excellent public transit system, which includes a clean and reliable underground subway system—called the Metro—as well as an extensive tram and bus network. Metro stations are marked with an inconspicuous M sign. A refurbished old tram (No. 41) travels through Staré Město and Malá Strana on summer weekends. Beware of pickpockets, who often operate in large groups on crowded trams and Metro cars and all other forms of transportation, including intercity buses.

The basic Metro, bus, and tram ticket costs 32 Kč. It permits 90 minutes of travel throughout the Metro, tram, and bus network. Short-term tickets cost 24 Kč and allow 30 minutes' ride on a tram, bus, or Metro. If you're carrying a big bag, you need to buy an additional 16 Kč ticket. Most local people have monthly or annual passes, so while it may look like almost everyone is riding for free, they do have tickets. A matter of politeness: Czechs keep to the right side of escalators, leaving the left side free to people who want to walk up or down.

Tickets (*jízdenky*) can be bought at dispensing machines in Metro stations and at some newsstands. If you have a SIM card from a Czech service provider, tickets can also be purchased by texting ☎ *902–06–26*. If you send an SMS that says DPT24 or DPT32 to the number, you will receive a virtual ticket for 24 Kč or 32 Kč. Trams now also allow people to buy tickets with a contactless payment card from an orange dispenser. English instructions can be selected from a menu by touching the British flag icon.

You can buy a one-day pass allowing unlimited use of the system for 110 Kč or a three-day pass for 310 Kč. Validated one- or three-day passes allow traveling

...ars old for free. The passes can be purchased at main Metro stations, from ticket machines, and at some newsstands in the center. A pass is not valid until stamped in the yellow machines in a Metro station or aboard a tram.

The trams and Metro shut down around midnight, but special night trams (Nos. 91–99) and some buses run all night. Night trams run at 20- to 30-minute intervals, and all routes intersect at the corner of Lazarská and Spálená ulice in Nové Město, near the Národní třída Metro station. Schedules and regulations in English are on the transportation department's official website. Travel information centers provide all substantial information about public transport operation, routes, timetables, and so on. They are at major Metro stations and at both terminals at the airport.

Validate your Metro ticket at a yellow stamping machine before descending the escalator. Trains are patrolled often; the fine for riding without a valid ticket is 1,500 Kč, but the fine is reduced to 800 Kč if you pay on the spot or within 15 days. Tickets for buses are the same as those used for the Metro, although you validate them at machines inside the bus or tram. Information about tickets, route changes, and fines is on the city transit company website.

# 🚗 Taxi

Taxis are a convenient way of getting around town, particularly in the evening, when the number of trams and Metro trains starts to thin out. But be on the lookout for dishonest drivers, especially if you hail a taxi on the street or from one of the taxi stands at heavily touristed areas like Wenceslas Square. Typical scams include drivers doctoring the meter or failing to turn the meter on and then demanding an exorbitant sum at the end of the ride. In an honest cab, the meter starts at 60 Kč and increases by 36 Kč per km (½ mile) or 7 Kč per minute at rest. Most rides within town should cost no more than 150 Kč–250 Kč. Separate slightly higher rates have also been set for electric taxis. The best way to avoid getting ripped off is to ask your hotel or restaurant to call a cab for you. If you have to hail a taxi on the street, agree with the driver on a fare before getting in. (If the driver says he can't tell you what the approximate fare will be, that's almost a sure sign he's giving you a line.) If you have access to a phone, a better bet is to call one of the many radio-operated companies, like AAA Taxi. The drivers are honest, and the dispatchers speak English.

Smartphone-based ridesharing services like Uber, Liftago, and Bolt are also available in Prague. A new legal framework allows then to use an app instead of a meter.

# 🚆 Train

Prague is serviced by two international train stations, so always make certain you know which station your train is using. The main station, Hlavní nádraží, is about 500 yards east of Wenceslas Square via Washingtonova ulice. The other international station is Nádraží Holešovice, in a suburban area about 2 km (1 mile) north of the city center along Metro Line C (red). Nádraží Holešovice is frequently the point of departure for trains heading to Berlin, Vienna, and Budapest. Two other large stations in Prague service mostly local destinations. Smíchovské nádraží—southwest of the city center across the Vltava (on Metro

# Getting Here and Around

Line B [yellow]—services destinations to the west, including trains to Karlštejn. Masarykovo nádraží, near Náměstí Republiky in the center of the city, services mostly suburban destinations.

For train times, consult the timetables posted at the stations. On timetables, departures (*odjezd*) appear on a yellow background; arrivals (*příjezd*) are on white. There are two information desks at the main station, Hlavní nádraží. The main Čedok office downtown can advise on train times and schedules.

On arriving at Hlavní nádraží, the best way to get to the center of town is by Metro. The station lies on Metro Line C (red) and is just one stop from the top of Wenceslas Square (Muzeum station)—travel in the direction of Haje station. You can also walk the 500 yards or so to the square, though the walk is not advisable late at night. A taxi ride from the main station to the center should cost about 100 Kč. To reach the city center from Nádraží Holešovice, take the Metro Line C (red) four stops to Muzeum; a taxi ride should cost roughly 200 Kč–250 Kč.

The state-run rail system is called České dráhy (ČD). On longer runs, it's not really worth taking anything less than an express (*rychlík*) train, marked in red on the timetable. Tickets are inexpensive: a second-class ticket from Prague to Brno (a distance of 200 km [124 miles]) costs about 205 Kč. A 40 Kč–60 Kč supplement is charged for the excellent international expresses, EuroCity (EC) and InterCity (IC), and for domestic SuperCity (SC) schedules. Seats can be reserved online or over a mobile app for free on domestic journeys, but cost from 35 Kč up to 200 Kč for the high-speed Pendolino train, which goes to Plzeň, Pardubice, Olomouc, and Ostrava. If you haven't bought a ticket in advance, you can buy one aboard the train but for an extra fee.

It's possible to book sleepers (*lůžkový*) or the less-roomy couchettes (*lehátkový*) on most overnight trains. You do not need to validate your train ticket before boarding.

Private firms have been allowed to operate trains. Two companies, Leo Express and RegioJet, have routes from Prague to other major cities and also some international destinations. Tickets are not interchangable between companies.

The Eurail Pass and the Eurail Youthpass are valid for travel within the Czech Republic, and if you're traveling through to neighboring countries like Hungary, Austria, or Poland, it can be an economic way to bounce between the regions. (A pass for three days of second-class travel in one month starts at $220 for adults or $171 for students.) The European East Pass is also a good option for first-class travel on the national railroads of the Czech Republic, Austria, Hungary, Poland, and Slovakia. The pass allows five days of unlimited travel within a one-month period for €266 for first class and €183 for second class, and it must be purchased from Rail Europe before your departure. The many Czech rail passes available are useful chiefly by regular travelers. A discount applies to any group of 2–30 people traveling second class (*sleva pro skupiny*). It's always cheaper to buy a return ticket. Foreign visitors will find it easiest to inquire at the international booking offices of major stations for the latest discounts and passes that will apply to them. Rail schedules are available at ⊕ *www.idos.cz*.

# Essentials

##  Activities

Czechs are avid sportsmen and sportswomen. In the summertime, Prague empties out as residents head to their country cottages to hike or bike in clean air. In winter the action shifts to the mountains, a few hours to the north and east of the city, for decent downhill and cross-country skiing. City districts and private entities operate pop-up skating rinks and ski trails in the winter.

The most popular spectator sport, bar none, is ice hockey. Czechs are world hockey champions, and the Czech gold medal at the Nagano Winter Olympics in 1998 is held up as a national achievement practically on par with the 1989 Velvet Revolution. If you're here in wintertime, witness the fervor by seeking out tickets to an Extraliga game. The main Prague teams are Sparta and Slavia.

Soccer plays a perennial second fiddle to hockey, although the Czech national soccer team ranks among the best in the world. Prague's main professional team, Sparta, plays its home games at Toyota Arena near Letná.

### BICYCLING

Much of the Czech Republic is a cyclist's dream of gently sloping tracks for pedalers. The capital, however, can be unkind to bicyclers. Prague's ubiquitous tram tracks and cobblestones make for hazardous conditions—as do the legions of tourist groups clogging the streets. Nevertheless, cycling is increasingly popular, and there are now several adequate yellow-marked cycling trails that crisscross the city. From April to October two bike-rental companies provide decent bikes—as well as locks, helmets, and maps. There are also several bike-sharing programs that can be used via phone apps. Instructions can be found on the bikes.

### City Bike

BICYCLING | City Bike runs guided tours leaving at 10:30, 1:30, and 4:30. Your English-speaking guides offer fun tidbits of history and point out architecture but do not offer a full tour. The ride's pace is comfortable for those who haven't taken a spin in a while. ⚠ **Be warned, Prague is not a bike-friendly city.** ✉ *Králodvorská 5, Staré Město* ☎ *776–180–284* ⊕ *www.citybike-prague.com* Ⓜ *Line B: Náměstí Republiky.*

### Praha Bike

BICYCLING | One of the multicultural teams from Praha Bike can casually guide you around several routes. The "classic" and "panoramic" are the most popular. There are also beer-garden and pub tours, a ride out of Prague to Karlštejn, and night tours. ✉ *Dlouhá 24, Staré Město* ☎ *732–388–880* ⊕ *www.prahabike.cz* Ⓜ *Line B: Náměstí Republiky.*

### HOCKEY

A feverish national fixation, ice hockey becomes a full-blown obsession during the World Championships (held every year in late spring) and the Winter Olympics.

The Czech national hockey league, Extraliga, is one of the most competitive in the world, and the best players regularly move on to the North American National Hockey League. Slavia Praha and Sparta are the two best teams, both in Prague. Hockey season runs from September to March. Tickets cost 160 Kč–900 Kč and are reasonably easy to get.

### HC Slavia Praha

HOCKEY | Although a relative giant in the Czech Republic, HC Slavia Praha usually finds itself chasing the leaders of the pack in international matches. ✉ *Zimní stadion Eden, Vladivostocká 1460/10, Vršovice* ☎ *267–311–417* ⊕ *www.hc-slavia.cz.*

# Essentials

### HC Sparta Praha

**HOCKEY** | HC Sparta Praha is routinely regarded as the premier team in an excellent local league—until players are lured across the Atlantic. Come to spot the next Jágr or Hašek. ⊠ *O2 Arena, Českomoravská 2345/17, Karlín* ☎ *266–727–443* ⊕ *www.hcsparta.cz* Ⓜ *Line B: Českomoravská.*

## PARKS AND PLAYGROUNDS

Praguers are gluttons for·a sunny day in the park. A pleasant weekend afternoon brings out plenty of sun worshippers and Frisbee tossers, with their blankets, books, and dogs. Two of the city's best beer gardens can be found at Letenské sady (Letná Park) and Riegrovy sady (Rieger Park).

### Kampa

**PARK—SPORTS-OUTDOORS** | Under the noses of the throng on the Charles Bridge, take the steps off the bridge onto Na Kampě and follow the wide cobbled street to the end; Kampa is a diminutive gem hidden in the heart of Malá Strana. It's a location for lazing in the sunshine and resting your eyes from all the busy baroque architecture, with a playground for when the kids grow restless from the endless palaces and churches. ⊠ *Malá Strana* Ⓜ *Tram 15 to Malostranské náměstí.*

### Letenské sady (*Letná Park*)

**PARK—SPORTS-OUTDOORS** | With killer views of the city across the river, this park is eternally busy. It has a huge restaurant and beer garden, for chilling like a local, located around Letenský zámeček, near the intersection of Kostelní and Muzejní. The large grassy northern plateau is also a great place to throw a Frisbee or kick a soccer ball. An excellent playground sits in the center near the tennis courts, just to the west of Letenský zámeček. Long-term construction projects in the area often hinder the tram routes. ⊠ *Holešovice* Ⓜ *Tram 12, 17 to Sparta.*

### Riegrovy sady (*Rieger Park*)

**PARK—SPORTS-OUTDOORS** | This lush park climbs sharply up the slopes of Vinohrady. On the east side of the park, lovely landscaping surrounds a large beer garden and playground. A smaller and cozier beer stand with rooftop seating is in the center. It offers lavish views of Prague Castle on the distant horizon. It has become popular with exchange students and other English-speaking people. ⊠ *Vinohrady* Ⓜ *Line A: Jiřího z Poděbrad.*

### Stromovka

**PARK—SPORTS-OUTDOORS** | King of all Prague parks, these lands were formerly royal hunting grounds. Today the deer have been usurped by horse riders and dog lovers. Remarkably rustic for a city-based park, it's primarily a place for walking rather than loafing about. Many of the paths and ponds were recently renovated. There are a few places to stop for a beverage or a snack. ⊠ *Holešovice* Ⓜ *Tram to Výstaviště.*

## SKIING

Czechs are enthusiastic and gifted skiers, and the country's northern border regions with Germany and Poland hold many small ski resorts. Czechs generally acknowledge the Krkonoše Mountains, which straddle a border with Poland, to be the best. Experienced skiers may find the hills here a little small and the facilities not quite up to international standards. (Hard-core Czech skiers usually head to Austria or France.) Nevertheless, if you're here in midwinter and you get a good snowfall, the Czech resorts can make for a fun overnight trip from the capital. All the area ski resorts are regularly served by buses leaving from Florenc.

### Černá Hora

SKIING/SNOWBOARDING | Černá Hora is 180 km (112 miles, about a four-hour drive) east of Prague. The resort has a cable car, one chairlift, and a couple of drag lifts. The "Black Mountain" is not the biggest of ski resorts but is often fairly quiet, meaning less waiting and a nice unofficial run, with plenty of forest to explore, directly under the cable car. ⊠ Cernohorská 265, Janské Lázne ☎ 840–888–229 ⊕ www.skiresort.cz/en.

### Harrachov

SKIING/SNOWBOARDING | On weekends, when you want to take in some crisp mountain air and clap on a pair of skis, head for Harrachov. In the west of the Krkonoše, around 120 km (74 miles, a three-hour drive) from the capital, the resort offers red and blue runs served by two chairlifts and 11 rope tows. This small and friendly resort is ideal for beginners and intermediates. ⊠ Harrachov ☎ 481–529–600 for town info center ⊕ www.harrachov.cz.

### Skiareal Špindlerův Mlýn

SKIING/SNOWBOARDING | The biggest and most popular ski resort in the Czech Republic is Skiareal Špindlerův Mlýn, which is 160 km (99 miles, about a 3½-hour drive) from Prague. The twin slopes, Svatý Petr and Medvedín, gaze at each other over the small village and offer blue, red, and black runs served by four chairlifts and numerous rope tows. Weekends here are mobbed to a point well past frustration. ⊠ Špindleruv Mlýn ☎ 499–467–101 ⊕ www.skiarealspindl.cz.

## SOCCER

Games for the domestic Czech league, the Fortuna liga, run from August to May with a break in December and January. The games and the fans tend to be somewhat lackluster. Tickets are plentiful enough on match days (except for tournaments). International matches are hosted at Sparta's stadium.

### AC Sparta Praha

SOCCER | AC Sparta Praha has an enthusiastic fan base, with the stadium roar to match. Although it has seen its fortunes dip a little recently, the team remains a domestic Goliath and a stone-slinging David in European competition. ⊠ Generali arena, Milady Horákové 98, Letná ☎ 296–111–400 ⊕ www.sparta.cz Ⓜ Line A: Sparta.

### Bohemians 1905

SOCCER | Bohemians 1905 are back in the top league after a few difficult years. Fans are highly enthusiastic. ⊠ Doliček stadion, Vršovická 31, Vršovice ☎ 245–005–014 ⊕ www.bohemians.cz Ⓜ Tram 22 to Vršovice Nám.

### SK Slavia Praha

SOCCER | Sparta's success is much to the chagrin of its bitter rival, SK Slavia Praha, which now plays in the modern Sinobo Arena, though most fans still refer to it by its old name, Eden. ⊠ Sinobo Stadium, Vladivostocká 1460/10, Vršovice ☎ 272–118–311 ⊕ www.slavia.cz Ⓜ Tram 4, 7, 22, or 24 to Slavia.

## TENNIS

Tennis is one of the favorite local sports, but the national passion remains at a simmer instead of a rolling boil. The best-known Czech players have been Ivan Lendl and, by ethnicity at least, Martina Navratilova. But there is a crop of younger players out there trying to crowd into the top 10. Prague is blessed with several public tennis courts; most are cinder or clay surface.

### Český Lawn Tennis Klub

TENNIS | Some of the city's best tennis courts can be found right next door to the tennis stadium, Český Lawn Tennis Klub, which in its time has hosted ATP events. Open to the public for 350

# Essentials

Kč–660 Kč per hour are 10 outdoor courts and 6 indoor courts, all hard surface or clay, despite the name. ✉ *Ostrov Štvanice 38, Holešovice* ☎ *222–316–317* ⊕ *cltk. cz* Ⓜ *Line C: Vltavská.*

**SK Hradčany**

**TENNIS** | At SK Hradčany outdoor courts cost 290 Kč–490 Kč per hour. ✉ *Diskařská 1, Hradčany* ☎ *603–509–950* ⊕ *tenispraha.cz* Ⓜ *Tram 22 or 25 to Malovanka.*

## 🍴 Dining

### DISCOUNTS AND DEALS

Most pubs and restaurants, especially near office buildings, serve good lunch specials of Czech cuisine standards for a very reasonable price from 11 to 3. Some places still also distinguish between *hotová jídla* (ready meals) and *minutky* (meals that require preparation). Ready meals, heavy on gravy and dumplings, are cheaper.

### PAYING

Most restaurants take credit cards, but some smaller places do not. It's worth asking. Servers in the center are starting to expect Western-style tips, but in general 10% is standard, with more only for exceptional service. Outside the city center, rounding the bill up to the closest 10 Kč is still common. Restaurants are required to give printed receipts, and it is a good idea to check them for items that weren't ordered, surprise service charges, or precalculated tips. Unless stated on the menu, service charges and tips can't be added automatically.

### RESERVATIONS AND DRESS

Reservations are recommended for some of the top upscale restaurants in the center, but most others can accommodate walk-ins. Business casual is fine in most cases for high-end places, while jeans will pass muster in most other venues. Shorts and T-shirts are fine for outdoor dining in the summer. If you have doubts, call the restaurant and ask.

### MEALS AND MEALTIMES

Late-night dining hasn't really caught on, and it's difficult to find a good place that serves after 11, though fast food is available around the clock. Some high-end restaurants close between lunch and dinner. Many places have a lunch special until 3. Places outside the center tend to close at 10 or earlier and may be closed Sunday or Monday.

### SMOKING

Smoking is banned in all restaurants and bars, with a few exceptions for water pipes and vaping.

| WHAT IT COSTS in Koruny | | | |
|---|---|---|---|
| $ | $$ | $$$ | $$$$ |
| **AT DINNER** | | | |
| under 150 Kč | 150 Kč–400 Kč | 401 Kč–700 Kč | over 700 Kč |

## ➕ Health

Pharmacies in Prague are well stocked with prescription and nonprescription drugs, though you may have trouble persuading a pharmacist to fill a foreign prescription. Pharmacies are generally open during regular business hours, from 9 to 6, with some offering night and weekend service. A law requires a standard 30 Kč fee per prescription. During off-hours, pharmacies will often post the name and address of the nearest open pharmacy on their doors. Pharmacies not only sell prescription medicines but are the only licensed dealers of typical over-the-counter products like pain relievers and cough medicines. Most standard U.S. over-the-counter products have Czech equivalents. Aspirin is widely available. However, items such as aspirin cannot be found outside pharmacies. The most common nonaspirin pain reliever is Ibalgin (ibuprofen), sold in 200 mg and 400 mg doses.

■ TIP→ **Pharmacists may not speak English or know a drug's non-Czech brand name but will certainly know the drug's generic name ("acetaminophen" for Tylenol, for example). Be sure to call a drug by its generic name when asking for it.**

#  Lodging

## PRICES

Summer is the main season, but spring and fall have been catching up. Significant rate drops are only seen in the winter. Pricing is still very competitive, especially among three- and four-star hotels. Some big hotels outside of the historical area are cheaper and less crowded, but some lack good public transit connections.

## RESERVATIONS

Prague is one of Europe's top destinations, so hotels tend to be near capacity. Reservations in the summer are essential if you want to stay in the center for a reasonable rate. New Year's Eve and the time around Christmas can also book up months in advance; otherwise, last-minute bookings can be found in winter.

### WHAT IT COSTS in Koruny

| $ | $$ | $$$ | $$$$ |
|---|----|-----|------|
| **FOR TWO PEOPLE** | | | |
| under 2,500 Kč | 2,501 Kč–4,500 Kč | 4,501 Kč–8,000 Kč | over 8,000 Kč |

# $ Money

The Czech koruna has been maintained at a level to promote foreign trade and tourism, though prices for some items are close to those of Western Europe. Many hotel prices are more realistic thanks to tough competition, and it's easy to find last-minute bargains. Prices at tourist resorts outside the capital are lower and, in the outlying areas and off the beaten track, very low. The story is similar for restaurants, with Prague being comparable to the United States and Western Europe, whereas outlying towns are much more reasonable. The prices for castles, museums, and other sights are rising but still low by outside standards.

ATMs are common in Prague and most towns in the Czech Republic and more often than not are part of the Cirrus and Plus networks, meaning you can get cash easily. Outside of urban areas, machines can be scarce, and you should plan to carry enough cash to meet your needs.

In Czech an ATM is called a *bankomat,* and a PIN is also a PIN, just as in English.

Prices throughout this guide are given for adults. Substantially reduced fees are almost always available for children, students, and senior citizens.

Banks in the United States never have every foreign currency on hand, and it may take as long as a week to order. If you're planning to exchange funds before leaving home, don't wait until the last minute.

## TIPPING

Service is not usually included in restaurant bills. In pubs or ordinary places, simply round up the bill to the next multiple of 10 (if the bill comes to 83 Kč, for example, give the waiter 90 Kč); in nicer places, 10% is considered appropriate for good food and service. Tip porters

## Where Should I Stay?

| | NEIGHBORHOOD VIBE | PROS | CONS |
|---|---|---|---|
| Staré Město (Old Town) | Most tourist attractions are in Staré Město, which is filled with historical buildings. | Easy access to all the main sights, many lovely places to take photos. Some hotels have wonderful views. | Noisy, crowded, expensive, and few locals, as many flats are now short-term rentals. Parking is almost impossible. |
| Nové Město (New Town) | "New" means 1348, when Nové Město was established. It's more relaxed than Staré Město, with a mix of modern and historical architecture. | Less crowded than Staré Město but still near the main attractions. | Still on the expensive side and filled with late-night noise. |
| Vinohrady | The former royal vineyard has art nouveau buildings, upscale eateries, and relaxing parks. | Still close to tourist attractions but with a warm and friendly ambience. | Some smaller pubs and stores have limited English. New restaurants can be hit or miss in quality. |
| Karlín | Rebuilt after floods in 2003, the former industrial area is now home to modern offices and new nightlife but still has some derelict buildings. | Good public transit makes it just minutes from the center. Some good restaurants that cater to the office crowd. | Parts can get a bit desolate after dark, and some streets are a bit seedy. |
| Smíchov | The district is a colorful blend of people and places. Modern housing developments are slowly filling in abandoned lots. | Cinema multiplexes, bars, and shopping centers make it a center of nightlife. | Some side streets are still very run down and best avoided. Rail tracks and busy roads make walking around a bit difficult. |
| Žižkov | A lively middle-class neighborhood used to be an independent city and still marches to its own beat. | Prague's Brooklyn has old-school pubs and restaurants with very affordable prices. | Groups of people making lots of noise at all hours of the night are common. Some sections are iffy, even in the daytime. |
| Holešovice | Abandoned factories have been redeveloped into art centers, attracting a new generation to the area. | Lots of international cuisine and quirky cafés plus easy access to two huge parks. | Parts still have an industrial feel and are a bit far from public transit. |
| Vršovice | The least touristy of the central districts gives a real feel of Czech life. | The area around Krymská ulice has become a hipster paradise with modern architecture landmarks. | Large parts of the area still haven't gotten the memo about becoming trendy. Only a few small hotels. |

who bring bags to your rooms 40 Kč–50 Kč total. For room service, a 20 Kč tip is enough. In taxis, add 10%. Give tour guides and helpful concierges 50 Kč–100 Kč for services rendered.

# 📖 Packing

Prague's climate is continental, so in summer plan on relatively warm days and cool nights. Spring tends to be wet and cool; fall is drier but also on the chilly side. In winter, pack plenty of warm clothes and plan to use them. An umbrella is a good idea any time of year. Note that areas in higher elevations tend to stay very cool even in midsummer.

In general, pack for comfort rather than for style. Casual dress is the norm for everyday wear, including at most restaurants. Men will need a sport coat for an evening out at a concert or the opera.

Many areas are best seen on foot, so take a pair of sturdy walking shoes and be prepared to use them. High heels can present considerable problems on the cobblestoned streets of Prague.

# 🌐 Passports

Citizens of the United States need only a valid passport to enter the Czech Republic and can stay for as long as 90 days without a visa. It's a good idea to make sure your passport is valid for at least six months on entry. If you plan on living or working in the Czech Republic, be advised that long-term and work visas must be obtained outside the country. Contact the Czech embassy or consulate in your home country well in advance of your trip. The Czech Republic is part of the Schengen area, meaning that once a visitor enters one of the countries in the zone, which covers most of Europe, he or she will not have to show a passport at each border; a visitor's three-month stay begins upon the first point of entry into the Schengen area. Travelers are still required to have a valid passport, and spot checks still occur.

# 💲 Taxes

Taxes are usually included in the prices of hotel rooms, restaurant meals, and items purchased in shops. The price on the tag is what you'll pay at the register.

The Czech value-added tax (V.A.T.) is called DPH (*daň z přidané hodnoty*), and there are two rates. The higher one (21%) covers nearly everything—gifts, souvenirs, clothing, and food in restaurants. Food in grocery stores and books are taxed 15%. Exported goods are exempt from the tax, which can be refunded. All tourists outside the European Union are entitled to claim the tax back if they spend more than 2,000 Kč in one shop on the same day. Global Blue processes V.A.T. refunds in the Czech Republic and will give you your refund in cash (U.S. dollars or euros) from a booth at the airport; be aware that the Czech Republic does *not* provide a postage-paid mailer for V.A.T. refund forms, unlike most other European countries.

# Tours

Major U.S. agencies often plan trips covering Prague and the Czech Republic. Abercrombie & Kent, Inc., is one agency that offers package tours to the area. The largest Czech agency, Čedok, also offers package tours.

You can take a 30- to 60-minute boat trip along the Vltava year-round with several boat companies that are based on the quays near the Malá Strana side of the Charles Bridge. It's not really necessary to buy tickets in advance, though you can; boats leave as they fill up. One of the cruise companies stands out, and it's on the Staré Město side of the bridge. Prague-Venice Cruises operates restored, classic canal boats from the late 19th century; the company operates one larger boat that holds 35 passengers and eight smaller boats that hold 12 passengers.

■ TIP→ **Take one of the smaller boats—particularly one of the uncovered ones—if you can, for a more intimate narrated cruise of about 45 minutes along the Vltava and nearby canals.**

Refreshments are included in all cruises. You actually set sail from beneath the last remaining span of Judith's Bridge (the Roman-built precursor to the Charles Bridge). Look for the touts in sailor suits right before the bridge; they will direct you to the ticket office. Cruises are offered daily 10:30–6 from November through February, until 8 from March through June and September through October, and until 11 in July and August. Cruises cost 460 Kč.

**CONTACTS Prague-Venice Cruises.** ✉ *Křižovnické nám. 3, Staré Mesto* ☎ *776–776–779* ⊕ *www.prague-venice. cz.*

Čedok offers a 3½-hour "Prague Castle in Detail" tour, a combination bus and walking venture that covers the castle and major sights around town in English. The price is about 1,000 Kč. Stop by the main office for information on other tours and tour departure points. You can also arrange a personalized walking tour. Times and itineraries are negotiable; prices start at around 400 Kč per hour.

Very similar tours by other operators also depart daily from Náměstí Republiky, Národní třída near Jungmannovo náměstí, and Wenceslas Square. Prices are generally a couple of hundred crowns less than for Čedok's tours.

**CONTACTS Čedok.** ☎ *221–447–256* ⊕ *www.cedok.cz.* **Martin Tours.** ☎ *777–318–198* ⊕ *www.martintour.cz.* **Premiant City Tour.** ☎ *606–600–123* ⊕ *www.premiant.cz.* **Wittmann Tours.** ☎ *222–252–472* ⊕ *www.wittmann-tours.com.*

Tours of Prague come under the supervision of Prague Information Service, which is reliable and always informative. The partly city-funded company organizes walking tours in Prague's city center and in the outskirts, including excursions from Prague. Many tailor-made tours can be arranged. Nonregistered guides can also be found, but unless they come with a personal recommendation from someone you trust, their services cannot be guaranteed. Due to a loophole in the law, many guides offer so-called free tours but ask for "tips" at the end so they can avoid regulation.

Czech Tourism has a free app for Android and iPhone called Czech Republic Land of Stories, with suggested trips, maps, and other information for Prague and other cities. The app uses GPS to help people stay on track.

One small private company that does an excellent tour of the city is Custom Travel Services, operated by Jaroslav Pesta. The service offers a wide range of touring options. A full-day private walking tour of Prague with a boat ride for two or three people is 4,000 Kč, or 5,000 Kč for five to six people. The firm offers 100 different tours across the country and also will customize a tour according to your interests.

**CONTACTS Custom Travel Services.**
☎ 773–103–102 ⊕ www.private-prague-guide.com. **Prague City Tourism.** ☎ 221–714 –14 ⊕ www.praguecitytourism.cz/en.

One reason visitors come to the Czech Republic is to connect with their Jewish heritage. Wittmann Tours provides not only coverage of the main sights in Prague but excursions to smaller Czech towns and to Trebíč.

**CONTACTS Čedok.** ☎ 221–447–256 ⊕ www.cedok.com. **Wittmann Tours.** ☎ 222–252–472 ⊕ www.wittmann-tours.com.

Themed walking tours are popular in Prague. You can choose from tours on medieval architecture, Velvet Revolution walks, visits to communist monuments, and any number of pub crawls. Each year, four or five small operators do these tours, which generally last a couple of hours and cost from 150 Kč to more than 1,000 Kč. Inquire at Prague Information Service or a major ticket agency for the current season's offerings. Most walks start at the clock tower on Old Town Square.

A special guide service is available in the Czech Republic designed to examine and explain the country's Jewish history. The company, Wittmann Tours, offers several different tours within Prague and also outside, including the Terezín concentration camp.

For gourmands, Prague has upped its food game in recent years. Several different food tours can be booked that showcase Czech cuisine, craft beer, and small bistros with wine.

**CONTACTS Eating Prague Food Tours.**
☎ 228–885–011 ⊕ www.eatingeurope.com/prague. **Wittmann Tours.** ☎ 222–252–472 ⊕ www.wittmann-tours.com.

# Czech Helpful Phrases

## BASICS

| | | |
|---|---|---|
| Hello | Ahoj | ah-hoy |
| Yes/No | Ano/ne | ah-no/nay |
| Please | Prosím | pro-seem |
| Thank you | Děkuju | dyek-oo-yoo |
| You're welcome | Není zač! | nah-nee zatch |
| I'm Sorry (apology) | Omlouvám se | oh-mloo-vam say |
| Sorry (Excuse me) | Promiňte | pro-min-tye |
| Good morning | Dobrý ráno | doh-bree rah-no |
| Good day | Dobrý den | doh-bree den |
| Good evening | Dobrý večer | doh-bree veh-chair |
| Goodbye | Na shledanou | nah sklad-en-owe |
| Mr. (Sir) | Pan | pahn |
| Mrs. | Paní | pahn-nee |
| Miss | Slečna | stetch-nah |
| Pleased to meet you | Těší mě! | teh-shee-mye |
| How are you? | Jak se máš | yahk say mahsh |

## NUMBERS

| | | |
|---|---|---|
| one-half | Půl | puhl |
| one | Jeden/jedna/jedno | jeh-den/jeh-dnah/jeh-dnoh |
| two | Dva/dvě | dvah/dvyay |
| three | Tři | trzhee |
| four | Čtyři | sht-ear-zhee |
| five | Pět | pyet |
| six | Šest | shest |
| seven | Sedm | sed-uhm |
| eight | Osm | aw-suhm |
| nine | Devět | dehv-yet |
| ten | Deset | deh-set |
| eleven | Jedenáct | jeh-den-atst |
| twelve | Dvanáct | dvah-natst |
| thirteen | Třináct | trzhee-natst |
| fourteen | Čtrnáct | shter-natst |
| fifteen | Patnáct | paht-natst |
| sixteen | Šestnáct | shest-natst |
| seventeen | Sedmnáct | sed-uhm-natst |
| eighteen | Osmnáct | aw-suhm-natst |
| nineteen | Devatenáct | dehv-aht-ay-natst |
| twenty | Dvacet | dva-test |
| twenty-one | Dvacet jeden/jedna/jedno | dvah-tset jeh-den/jeh-dnah/jeh-dnoh |
| thirty | Třicet | trzhee-tset |
| forty | Čtyřicet | shteer-ee-tset |
| fifty | Padesát | pah -deh-saht |
| sixty | Šedesát | sheh-deh-sat |
| seventy | Sedmdesát | seh-dum-deh-sat |
| eighty | Osmdesát | aw-suhm-deh-sat |
| ninety | Devadesát | deh-vah-deh-sat |
| one hundred | Sto | stow |
| one thousand | Tisíc | rih-seets |
| one million | Milión | Mih-lee-yon |

## COLORS

| | | |
|---|---|---|
| black | Černý/černá/černé | cher-nee/cher-nah/cher-nay |
| blue | Modrý/modrá/modrá | moh-dree/moh-drah/moh-dray |
| brown | Hnědý/hnědá/hnědé | hned-ee/hned-ah/hned-ay |
| green | Zelený/Zzlená/zelené | zehl-en-ee/zehl-en-ah/zehl-en-ay |
| orange | Oranžový/oranžoáý/oranžové | ahr-ahn-zho-vee/ahr-ahn-zho-vah/ahr-ahn-zho-vay |
| red | Červený/červená/červené | cher-veh-nee/cher-veh-nah/cher-veh-nay |
| white | Bílý/bílá/bílé | bil-ee/bil-ah/bil-ay |
| yellow | Žlutý/žlutá/žluté | zhlooh-tee/zhlooh-tah/zhlooh-tay |

## DAYS OF THE WEEK

| | | |
|---|---|---|
| Sunday | Neděle | neh-dyeh-leh |
| Monday | Pondělí | pon-dye-lee |
| Tuesday | Úterý | ooh-teh-ree |
| Wednesday | Středa | strzeh-dah |
| Thursday | Čtvrtek | stver-tehk |
| Friday | Pátek | pah-tek |
| Saturday | Sobota | soh-boh-ta |

## MONTHS

| | | |
|---|---|---|
| January | Leden | leh-dehn |
| February | Únor | ooh-nor |
| March | Březen | brzeh-zen |
| April | duben | dooh-ben |
| May | Květen | kvyeh-ten |
| June | Červen | cher-ven |
| July | Červenec | cher-ven-ets |
| August | Srpen | sir-pen |
| September | Záři | zahr-zhee |
| October | Říjen | rzhee-jen |
| November | Listopad | lihs-to-pad |
| December | Prosinec | pro-see-nets |

## USEFUL WORDS AND PHRASES

| | | |
|---|---|---|
| Do you speak English? | Mluvíte anglicky? | nluh-viy-tey ang-lits-kee |
| I don't speak [Language]. | Nemluvím česky | nay-mlooh-veem ches-kee |
| I don't understand. | Nerozumím | neh-rohs-ooh-meem |
| I don't know. | Nevím | neh-veem |
| I understand. | Rozumím | rohs-ooh-meem |
| i'm American. | Jsem Američan/Američanka | sem ahm-er-itch-an/ahm-er-itch-an-ka |
| I'm British. | Jsem Brit/Britka | Sem vbit/btirt-ka |

| English | Czech | Pronunciation |
|---|---|---|
| What's your name. | Jak se jmenujete? | jahk say yum-ehn-ooh-jah-tay |
| My name is ... | Jmenuji se | yum-ehn-ooh-yee say |
| What time is it? | Kolik je hodin? | koh-lick yay hoe-deen |
| How? | Jak | yahk |
| When? | Kdy | ka-dee |
| Yesterday | Včera | va-chair-ah |
| Today | Dnes | da-ness |
| Tomorrow | Zítra | zee-tra |
| This morning | Toto ráno | tow-tow rah-no |
| This afternoon | Toto odpoledne | tow-tow od-poe-led-nay |
| Tonight | Dnes večer | da-ness veh-chair |
| What? | Co? | tso |
| What is it? | Co je to? | tso tow jay |
| Why? | Proč? | proach |
| Who? | Kdo? | k-doh |
| Where is ... | Kde je | k-day yay |
| ... the train station? | vlakové nádraží? | vlock-oh-vay nah-drah-zhee |
| ... the subway station? | stanice metra? | stahn-eet-say met-rah |
| ... the bus stop? | autobusová zastávka? | aut-oh-boos-oh-vah zah-stahv-ka |
| ... the airport? | letiště? | leht-ist-yay |
| ... the post office? | pošta? | poh-stah |
| ... the bank? | banka? | ban-kah |
| ... the hotel? | hotel? | hoh-tel |
| ... the museum? | muzeum? | mooh-zay-uhm |
| ... the hospital? | nemocnice? | nehm-ots-nee-tsa |
| ... the elevator? | výtah? | vee-tahk |
| Where are the restrooms? | Kde jsou toalety? | k-day soh toh-ah-let-ee |
| Here/there | Tady/tam | tah-dee.tahm |
| Left/right | Vlevo/vpravo | v-leh-voh/v-prah-voh |
| Is it near/far? | Je to blízko/daleko? | yay tow blee-zsko/dah-lehk-oh |
| I'd like ... | Chtěl bych | k-tel bick |
| ... a room | pokoj | poe-koy |
| ... the key | klíč | kleech |
| ... a newspaper | noviny | noh-vin-ee |
| ... a stamp | známku | znahm-kooh |
| I'd like to buy ... | Chtěl bych koupit | k-tel bick ko-peet |
| ... a city map | mapu města | mah-pooh myest-ah |
| ... a road map | cestovní mapu | tsest-oh-vahn-ee mah-pooh |
| ... a magaine | časopis | chas-owe-pis |
| ... envelopes | obálky | oh-bahl-kee |
| ... writing paper | papír na psaní | pah-peer nah psahn-ee |
| ... a postcard | pohlednici | pih-ledneets-ee |
| ... a ticket | lístek | lee-steck |
| How much is it? | Kolik to stojí? | ko-lick to stoy-ee |
| It's expensive/cheap | Je to drahé/levné | yay tow drah-ay/lev-nay |
| A little/a lot | Trochu/ hodně | trow-kew.hoed-nay |
| More/less | Více/méně | vitz-ay/men-ay |
| Enough/too (much) | Dost /příliš mnoho | doast/przee-leash m-no-hoe |
| I am ill/sick | Jsem nemocný/nemocná | sem neh-mots-nee/neh-mots-nah |
| Call a doctor | Zavolejte lékaře | zah-vol-ay-te lehk-arz-ay |
| Help! | Pomoc! | poh-mots |
| Stop! | Stop! | stop |

**DINING OUT**

| English | Czech | Pronunciation |
|---|---|---|
| A bottle of ... | Láhev | la-hev |
| A cup of ... | Šálek | sha-lehk |
| A glass of ... | Sklenice | sklen-ee-tse |
| Beer | Pivo | pee-voh |
| Bill/check | Účet | ooh-chet |
| Bread | Chléb | kh-lehb |
| Breakfast | Snídaně | snee-dah-nay |
| Butter | Máslo | mah-slow |
| Cocktail/aperatif | Koktejl/aperitiv | cock-tail/ap-er-teev |
| Coffee | Káva | kah-vah |
| Dinner | Večeře | vech-erzh-ay |
| Fixed-price menu | Nabídka s pevnou cenou | nah-mid-kah sa pev-noh sen-oh |
| Fork | Vidlička | vid-litch-kah |
| I am a vegetarian/I don't eat meat | Jsem vegetarián(ka)/ nejím maso | sem veg-et-air-ee-an(ka)/nay-jeem mah-so |
| I cannot eat ... | Nemohu jíst ... | nay-moh-oo jeest |
| I'd like to order ... | Chtěl bych objednat ... | k-tel bick o-byed-not |
| Is service included? | Je servis v ceně? | yay se-vis va tsen-ay |
| I'm hungry/thirsty | Mám hlad/žízeň | mom hlad.zee-zen |
| It's good/bad | Je to dobré/špatné | yay toe doh-brzay/shpat-nay |
| It's hot/cold | To je teplá/studená | tow yay tep-lah/stooh-den-ah |
| Knife | Nůž | noozh |
| Lunch | Oběd | oh-byed |
| Menu | Jídelní lístek | yih-del-nee lee-stek |
| Napkin | Ubrousek | ooh-bro-seck |
| Pepper | Pepř | pep-erzh |
| Plate | Talíř | tah-leerzh |
| Please give me ... | Prosím, dejte mi ... | ptoh-seem day-ty me |
| Salt | Sůl | soohl |
| Spoon | Lžíce | lzh-itz-ay |
| Tea | Čaj | chay |
| Water | Voda | voh-dah |
| Wine | Víno | vee-noh |

# Great Itineraries

## 7 Days in Prague

Seven days is barely time to scratch this beautiful city's surface.

### DAY 1: ARRIVAL, PRAŽSKÝ HRAD (PRAGUE CASTLE)

Even jet lag can't dampen the allure of Prague Castle, so it is a perfect place to hit on your first day in the city. The castle's ancient 17-acre property contains a slew of individual attractions conveniently linked by internal courtyards. The showstopper is Katedrála sv. Víta (St. Vitus Cathedral, wherein lie the remains of fabled Czechs like Charles IV and St. Wenceslas). But don't forget to hit the Starý Královský palác (Old Royal Palace) and Lobkovický palác (Lobkowicz Palace), too. Also worth a gander is Zlatá ulička (Golden Lane): a row of crooked cottages, one of which was once occupied by Kafka.

### DAY 2: JOSEFOV, STARÉ MĚSTO (OLD TOWN), AND NOVÉ MĚSTO (NEW TOWN)

Begin your day early in the Jewish Quarter. (Because it is best approached with a certain solemnity, arriving ahead of the tour groups is a definite advantage.) Here you will find Europe's oldest active synagogue—the Staronová synagóga (Old-New Synagogue), erected in 1270—as well as the Jewish Museum. Once you've seen the latter's evocative exhibits and paid your respects at the topsy-turvy Starý židovský hřbitov (Old Jewish Cemetery), saunter over to Staré Město to explore its centuries-old—and certifiably touristy—tangle of streets. Prepare to linger around Old Town Square, ideally timing your arrival to coincide with the striking of the newly restored astronomical clock. Later you can retrace the "Royal Way" (so named for the kings who trod it) that links the square with Prašná brána (the Powder Tower). Obecní dům (the Municipal House), an eye-popping 20th-century addition to Nové Město's medieval streetscape, is right beside it.

### DAY 3: MALÁ STRANA

You shouldn't be surprised if the neighborhood you visit today looks vaguely familiar: after all, it has been featured in a glut of period movies ranging from *Amadeus* to *Spider-Man: Far From Home*. Filmmakers come because its cobbled streets, beautifully preserved baroque buildings, and gorgeous formal gardens conjure up a long-ago time. Since the area seems to have a surprise at every turn, aimless wandering is Malá Strana's main pleasure; however, there is one site that deserves thorough investigation: Kostel sv. Mikuláše (Church of St. Nicholas)—an 18th-century beauty dedicated to Ol' Saint Nick. If you choose to climb the 215 steep steps of the church bell tower, you can reward your aching feet afterward by resting in Vrtbovská zahrada (Vrtba Garden) or taking an extended break in leafy Kampa Island Park before returning to Staré Město via the Charles Bridge.

### DAY 4: VYŠEHRAD

The "Higher Castle" can be reached by the C line Metro to the Vyšehrad station, just two stops from Muzeum station. Nonetheless, it is off the radar for most people, and much less crowded, offering a bit of a breather from the hectic pace of the center. The origins of the complex go back over 1,000 years. The massive neo-Gothic-style Bazilika sv. Petra a Pavla (Basilica of Sts. Peter and Paul), with an art nouveau interior, has a shoulder bone from St. Valentine among its collection of valuable religious items. Behind the church is a stone column that legend claims was placed there by a devil. A cemetery adjacent to the church has graves of several notable people, including composer Antonín Dvořák. In the park, four large statues depict characters from early Czech history. The tunnels in the fortified walls, accessible to the public, contain some of the original statues from the Charles Bridge. A walk on top of the walls offers a stunning view of the Vltava River and Prague Castle.

## DAY 5: HRADČANY AND STRAHOV

Hradčanské náměstí, the square in front of Prague Castle, is filled with palaces. Three are operated by the National Gallery. The Archbishop's Palace, still used by the Catholic Church, and Martinic Palace, in private hands, can be appreciated from the outside. Up the street, Loretánské náměstí has the imposing Černín Palace, now the Ministry of Foreign Affairs, and an attached public garden. Across from it is the Loreta, a baroque pilgrimage cloister with a rich collection of religious artifacts. Across the street from the nearby tram stop at Pohořelec, you can enter Strahov, a monastery complex with a beautifully preserved baroque library, a church where Mozart played the organ, and a microbrewery. On the way out, you can walk down through Petřín Park and stop at Petřín Tower, also called the Little Eiffel Tower.

## DAY 6: TROJA, PRAGUE ZOO, AND THE PRAGUE BOTANICAL GARDENS

In the northern part of the city, a vast red-and-white château called Troja, named after the ancient city, has a grand ballroom with an opulent ceiling mural, sculpted staircases, and a large art collection. The baroque garden, with fountains and statues, is accessible without a ticket. Next to the château is Prague Zoo, considered one of the world's finest. New, modern pavilions and a restaurant have been built since the 2003 floods. The zoo actively works to preserve several endangered species. Up the hill from the zoo is the Prague

Botanical Garden, with its Fata Morgana tropical greenhouse, St. Claire's vineyard, and Japanese meditation garden.

## DAY 7: DAY-TRIP TO KUTNÁ HORA

If you are ready for a break from the city. Kutná Hora—44 miles east of Prague—is a memorable destination for day-trippers. Rich deposits of silver put this town on the map in the 12th century, and the premier local attractions are still tied to them. Chances are you will start your visit at Chrám sv. Barbory (St. Barbara's Cathedral), a divine Gothic sanctuary that was built with miners' donations. Afterward you can get the lowdown on mineralogy at the Czech Museum of Silver, then tour portions of an original silver mine and restored mint. (For a real heavy-metal experience, try coming in late June, when the town relives its glory days during the annual Royal Silvering Festival.) When in the area, it is also worth making a detour to suburban Sedlec to see the somewhat spooky Kostnice Ossuary, a bizarre church decorated with human bones.

Depending on what time you get back to Prague, you might explore a new neighborhood or just rest up for a big night on the town. One tempting alternative is to indulge in some last-minute shopping, whether opting for upscale items on Pařížská ulice or folksy mementos in Havelské tržiště. (Admit it: you're *dying* to have one of those omnipresent Mozart marionettes!) Before bedding down, revisit the Charles Bridge for a final floodlit look at Golden Prague. Although you'll be hard pressed to take your eyes off the illuminated castle in the background, do take a moment to search among the many statues that decorate the span for the one depicting St. John Nepomuk. It's the eighth on the right, and—according to legend—travelers who rub it are bound to return.

# A Walk through Old Town's Greatest Hits

There's a reason the Old Town is congested with people practically every day of the week—it's stuffed with A-list attractions, surrounded with looping cobblestone streets, and bordered with eye-candy architecture from subtle *sgraffito* to bold baroque.

## THE "ROYAL WAY"

Start on the perimeter of the Old Town. From the bottom of Wenceslas Square, turning right onto **Na příkopě**. A short detour down the first street on your left, Havířská, takes you to the 18th-century **Stavovské divadlo** (Estates Theater).

Return to Na příkopě, turn left, and continue to the street's end, **náměstí Republiky** (Republic Square). Two stunning buildings, constructed hundreds of years apart, anchor the area. Centuries of grime have not diminished the majesty of the Gothic **Prašná brána** (Powder Tower), with its stately spires looming above the square. Adjacent to this tower, the rapturous art nouveau **Obecní dům** (Municipal Hall) looks like a brightly decorated confection.

Walk through the archway of the Powder Tower and down the formal **Celetná** street, the first leg of the "Royal Way." The cubist building at Celetná No. 34 is the **Dům U černé Matky boží** (House of the Black Madonna); look for the miniature Madonna placed on the corner of the building.

## THE HEART OF OLD TOWN

After a few blocks, Celetná opens onto the justly famous **Staroměstské náměstí** (Old Town Square), the beating heart of the Old Town with dazzling architecture on all sides. On the east side of the square, the double-spire church **Kostel Panny Marie před Týnem** (Týn Church) rises from behind a row of patrician houses. To the immediate left of this, at No. 13, is **Dům U Kamenného zvonu** (Stone Bell

## A Walk through Old Town's Greatest Hits

**WHERE TO START:**
The northern end of Wenceslas Square.

**TIME/LENGTH:**
Three to four hours.

**WHERE TO STOP:**
The Clementinum complex.

**BEST TIME TO GO:**
For fewer crowds, time your visit for early morning on the weekends. Hit the Astronomical Clock 10 minutes before the hour.

**WORST TIME TO GO:**
Saturday afternoon when crowds are at their peak. Evenings are also surprisingly busy.

**HIGHLIGHTS:**
Stavovské divadlo, Obecní dům, Staroměstské náměstí, Staroměstská radnice, Clementinum.

**WHERE TO REFUEL:**
Au Gourmand, just outside Old Town Square on Dlouhá street, offers a tranquil garden where you can enjoy pastries or a sandwich. Around the corner from Obecní dům, you'll also find the Hotel Paříž: its café serves up hearty omelets.

House), a baroque town house that has been stripped down to its original Gothic elements. Next door, at No. 12, stands the gorgeous pink-and-ocher **Palác Kinských** (Kinsky Palace), considered

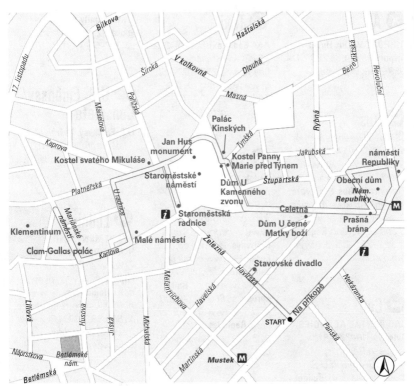

the most prominent example of late baroque–rococo in the area. At this end of the square, you can't help noticing the gigantic expressive **Jan Hus monument.**

Beyond this is the Gothic **Staroměstská radnice** (Old Town Hall) with its impressive 200-foot tower that gives the square gravitas. As the hour approaches, join the people milling below the tower's 15th-century Astronomical Clock for a brief but curiously compelling spectacle. The square's second church is the baroque **Kostel svatého Mikuláše** (St. Nicholas Church).

## TOWARD THE CLEMENTINUM

Turn left and continue along U Radnice proper a few yards until you come to **Malé náměstí,** a minisquare with arcades

on one side. Look for tiny Karlova street, which begins in the southwest corner of the square, and take another quick right to stay on it. This cobbled medieval street draws the attention with its quaint souvenir shops, restaurants, and theaters, but keep an eye on where you're going (it has a habit of confounding visitors). While strolling, you may find yourself lured away by the exotic **Clam-Gallas palác** at Husova 20.

A block north, the street opens onto Mariánské náměstí, where you'll discover the entrance to the **Clementinum,** a grouping of historic buildings once used as a Jesuit stronghold.

# Contacts

## ✈ Air

**AIRPORT Václav Havel Airport.** (*PRG*). ☎ *220–111–888* ⊕ *www.prg.aero.*

## 🚌 Bus

**ČSAD.** ✉ *Florenc station, Křižíkova 4, Karlín* ☎ *221–895–111* ⊕ *www. idos.cz* Ⓜ *Lines B and C: Florenc.* **Flixbus.** ✉ *Florenc station, Křižíkova 4, Karlín* ⊕ *www.flixbus.cz* Ⓜ *Lines B and C: Florenc.* **RegioJet.** ☎ *222–222–221* ⊕ *www. regiojet.cz.*

## 🚗 Car

**CAR RENTAL AGENCIES Avis.** ☎ *810–777–810 in Czech Republic, 800/230–4898 in U.S.* ⊕ *www.avis.com.* **Budget.** ☎ *800/472–3325 in U.S.* ⊕ *www.budget.com.* **Europcar.** ☎ *235–364–531 for reservations at Václav Havel Airport in Prague* ⊕ *www.europcar.com.* **Hertz.** ☎ *225–345–000 in Czech Republic* ⊕ *www. hertz.com.*

## 🚇 Metro

**METRO Dopravní Podnik.** ⊕ *www.dpp.cz.*

**LOST AND FOUND Lost and Found.** ✉ *Ztráty a nálezy, Karoliny Světlé 5, Staré Mesto* ☎ *224–235–085.*

## 🚕 Taxi

**AAA Radiotaxi.** ☎ *222–333–222* ⊕ *www.aaa-taxi.cz.* **City Taxi.** ☎ *257–257–257* ⊕ *www.citytaxi.cz.* **Tick Tack.** ☎ *721–300–300* ⊕ *www.ticktack.cz.*

## 🚆 Train

**Čedok.** ✉ *Na příkopě 18, Nové Mesto* ☎ *800–112–112 toll-free, 221–447–256 for incoming tourists* ⊕ *www.cedok.cz.* **Czech Railways.** ⊕ *www.cd.cz.* **Eurail.** ⊕ *www.eurail.com.* **Leo Express.** ☎ *220–311–700* ⊕ *www.le.cz.* **Rail Europe.** ☎ *800/622–8600 in U.S.* ⊕ *www.raileurope.com.* **RegioJet.** ☎ *222–222–221* ⊕ *www.regiojet.cz.*

## ➕ Emergencies

**Autoklub Bohemia Assistance.** ☎ *1240* ⊕ *www.aba.cz.* **Ambulance.** ☎ *155.* **Na Homolce Hospital.** ✉ *Roentgenova 2* ☎ *257–271–111* ⊕ *www.homolka.cz.* **Prague City Police.** ☎ *156.* **State Police.** ☎ *158* ⊕ *www.policie.cz.* **ÚAMK Emergency Roadside Assistance.** ☎ *261–104–333* ⊕ *www.uamk.cz.*

**DOCTORS AND DENTISTS American Dental.** ✉ *Hvězdova 33, Pankrác* ☎ *733–737–337* ⊕ *www.americandental.cz.* **Lékárna**

**U sv. Ludmily.** ✉ *Belgická 37, Nové Mesto* ☎ *222–519–731.*

## 🏛 U.S. Embassy/Consulate

**U.S. Embassy.** ✉ *Tržiště 15, Malá Strana* ☎ *257–022–000* ⊕ *www.usembassy.cz.*

## 🛏 Lodging

**APARTMENT AND HOUSE RENTALS Airbnb.** ⊕ *www.airbnb.com.* **Flipkey.** ⊕ *www.flipkey.com.* **HomeAway.** ⊕ *www.homeaway.com.* **Interhome.** ☎ *800/882–6864* ⊕ *www.interhome.us.* **Vrbo.** ⊕ *www.vrbo.com.*

## 📍 Visitor Information

**Czech Tourist Authority.** ⊕ *www.czechtourism.com.* **Prague City Tourism.** ✉ *Staroměstska radnice (Old Town Hall), Staroměstské nám., Staré Mesto* ☎ *221–714–714* ⊕ *www.prague.eu.*

Chapter 3

# STARÉ MĚSTO (OLD TOWN) AND JOSEFOV

3

Updated by
Jennifer Rigby

| ◉ Sights | 🍴 Restaurants | 🛏 Hotels | 🛍 Shopping | 🍸 Nightlife |
|:---:|:---:|:---:|:---:|:---:|
| ★★★★★ | ★★★★★ | ★★★★★ | ★★★☆☆ | ★★★★☆ |

# NEIGHBORHOOD SNAPSHOT

## TOP EXPERIENCES

■ **Old Town Square:** It's not described as one of the most beautiful squares in Europe for nothing. Get here early in the morning to beat the crowds.

■ **Lokál Dlouháááá:** Clink foaming mugs of fresh beer and enjoy modern takes on classic Czech cooking.

■ **Shopping:** Look for botanical cosmetics made from beer to cool designer clothing and antique treasure troves.

■ **Barokní knihovní sál:** One of the most beautiful concert halls in all of Prague is also home to one of its best classical music ensembles.

■ **Zlata Praha:** Toast stunning city views with Bohemia Sekt (Czech sparkling wine) from one of Prague's prettiest rooftop bars.

## GETTING HERE

There's little public transit in Staré Město, so walking is really the most practical way to get around. It takes about 15 minutes to walk from the Prašná brána (Powder Tower, one of the original city gates) across to the Staré Město end of the Charles Bridge, which leads you into Malá Strana (Lesser Quarter). If you're coming to Staré Město from another part of Prague, three metro stops circumscribe the area: Staroměstská on the west, Náměstí Republiky on the east, and Můstek on the south, at the point where Staré Město and Václavské náměstí (Wenceslas Square) meet.

## PLANNING YOUR TIME

Remember to be in Old Town Square just before the hour if you want to see the astronomical clock in action, and prepare for crowds. The best (read: less crowded) time to visit Josefov is early morning, when the museums and cemetery first open. The area itself is very compact, and a fairly thorough tour should take only half a day. Don't go on the Sabbath (Saturday), when all the museums are closed.

## QUICK BITES

■ **Burrito Loco.** While Prague isn't famous for its Mexican food, Burrito Loco is a notable exception: fresh, spicy takeout burritos and nachos, at affordable prices, right by Old Town Square. There are a few branches around the city. ⊠ *Masná 620/2, Staré Město* ⊕ *burritoloco.cz*

■ **Havelská Koruna.** This old-school canteen dishes up classic Czech grub very cheaply, and aims to do so within five minutes of getting the order, so unsurprisingly it can get very busy at lunchtime. The soups in particular are a bargain and very traditional. ⊠ *Havelská Koruna 21, Staré Město* ⊕ *www. havelska-koruna.com*

■ **Mansson's Bakery.** This little bakery was set up by a Danish chef in 1999, which means predictably good Danish pastries and brilliant breads, including the house special, rye bread with sunflower seeds. ⊠ *Bílkova 8, Staré Město* ⊕ *www. mansson-bakery.com*

Staré Město is usually, rightly, the first stop for any visitor to Prague. Old Town Square, its gorgeous houses and churches, and the astronomical clock are blockbuster attractions, and the winding streets around the main event are worth visiting in their own right, with shops, restaurants, and historic buildings galore, from Kafka's former apartment to the theater where Mozart premiered *Don Giovanni*.

For centuries Prague had an active, vital Jewish community that was an exuberant part of the city's culture. Much of that activity was concentrated in Josefov, the former Jewish ghetto, just a short walk north of Old Town Square and entirely enclosed by the rest of Staré Město. This area first became a Jewish settlement around the 12th century, but it didn't actually take on the physical aspects of a ghetto—walled off from the rest of the city—until much later.

## Staré Město (Old Town)

Founded in 1231 and dense with stellar examples of Gothic architecture, as well as many other styles, history still feels alive on the cobbled streets of Staré Město—that is, if you can ignore the sometimes intrusive crowds, brightly lit shop fronts, and assorted tourist paraphernalia. Approaching the district from the north of Wenceslas Square—its base, the opposite end from the statue and the museum—is a good place to begin a tour of the area, as this T-intersection marks the border between the old and new worlds in Prague. A quick glance around reveals the often jarring juxtaposition: centuries-old buildings sit side by side with modern retail names like Starbucks, but in the main, there are still, astonishingly, authentic places to eat, drink, and be merry, as well as some of the capital's hippest shops. Staying here puts you right in the heart of the action but comes with the caveat that it can be noisy. To drown it out, the classical concerts in some of the city's most beautiful concert halls and churches are a hauntingly beautiful experience, or if jazz is more your style, a handful of atmospheric cellar bars have you covered.

 **Sights**

**Betlémská kaple** (*Bethlehem Chapel*)
**RELIGIOUS SITE** | The original church was built at the end of the 14th century, and the Czech religious reformer Jan Hus was a regular preacher here from 1402 until his exile in 1412. Here he gave the mass in "vulgar" Czech—not in Latin as the church in Rome demanded. After the

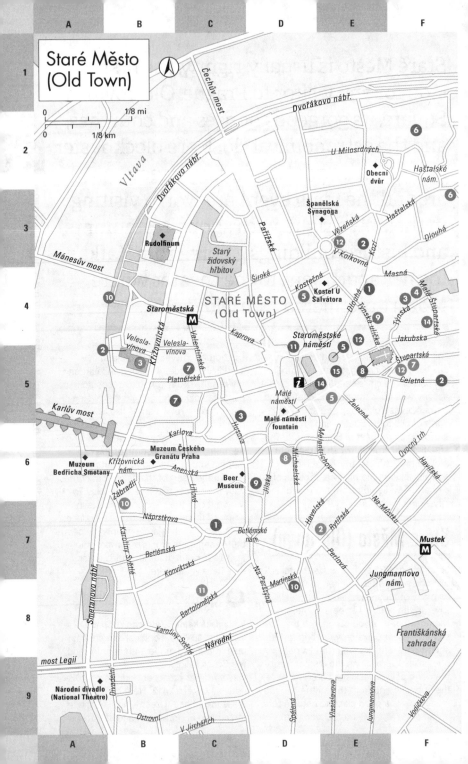

## Sights ▼

1 Betlémská kaple ......... **C7**
2 Celetná ulice ............. **F5**
3 Clam-Gallas palác ....... **C5**
4 Dům U černé
 Matky boží .............. **G5**
5 Jan Hus monument...... **E5**
6 Klášter sv. Anežky
 České.................... **F2**
7 Klementinum............. **B5**
8 Kostel Matky
 Boží před Týnem ........ **E5**
9 Kostel sv. Jiljí........... **D6**
10 Kostel sv.
 Martina ve zdi .......... **D8**
11 Kostel sv.
 Mikuláše ................ **D5**
12 Palác Kinských.......... **E4**
13 Prašná brána........... **H5**
14 Staroměstská radnice... **E5**
15 Staroměstské
 náměstí ................. **E5**

## Restaurants ▼

1 Bánh-mì-ba.............. **G3**
2 Cotto Crudo ............. **B5**
3 Dhaba Beas ............. **F4**
4 Divinis................... **F4**
5 Krčma .................. **D4**
6 La Degustation
 Bohême Bourgeoise .... **F3**
7 La Finestra in Cucina ... **C5**
8 Lokál Dlouhááá ......... **G3**
9 Maitrea .................. **E4**
10 Marina .................. **B4**
11 Naše Maso.............. **G3**
12 V Kolkovně.............. **E3**
13 Yami ..................... **G2**
14 Zdenek's Oyster Bar.... **F4**

## Quick Bites ▼

1 Au Gourmand ........... **E4**
2 Bakeshop Praha ......... **E3**
3 Piknik.................... **G3**

## Hotels ▼

1 Buddha-Bar Hotel ...... **G4**
2 Design Hotel Jewel
 Prague ................... **E7**
3 Four Seasons Hotel
 Prague .................. **B5**
4 Grand Hotel
 Bohemia ................ **G5**
5 Grand Hotel Praha....... **E5**
6 Hotel Residence
 Agnes ................... **G2**
7 Hotel U Zlatého
 Jelena ................... **F5**
8 Iron Gate Hotel
 and Suites .............. **D6**
9 Josef .................... **G3**
10 Smetana Hotel ......... **B7**
11 Unitas Hotel ............. **C8**
12 Ventana Hotel
 Prague ................... **F5**

**3**

**Staré Město (Old Town) and Josefov** STARÉ MĚSTO (OLD TOWN)

Thirty Years' War in the 17th century, the chapel fell into the hands of the Jesuits and was demolished in 1786. Excavations carried out after World War I uncovered the original portal and three windows; the entire church was reconstructed during the 1950s. Although little remains of the first church, some remnants of Hus's teachings can still be read on the inside walls. ☒ *Betlémské nám. 3, Staré Mesto* ☎ *224–248–595* ⊕ *www.bethlehemchapel.eu* ✉ *60 Kč* Ⓜ *Line A: Staroměstská.*

### Celetná ulice

NEIGHBORHOOD | This is the main thoroughfare connecting Old Town Square and Náměstí Republiky; it's packed day and (most of the) night. Many of the street's façades are styled in the classic 17th- or 18th-century manner, but appearances are deceiving: nearly all of the houses in fact have foundations that, astonishingly, date back to the 12th century. Be sure to look above the street-level storefronts to see the fine examples of baroque detail. ☒ *Staré Mesto* Ⓜ *Lines A and B: Můstek.*

### Clam-Gallas palác (*Clam-Gallas Palace*)

BUILDING | The work of Johann Bernhard Fischer von Erlach, the famed Viennese baroque virtuoso architect of the day, is showcased in this earth-tone palace. Construction began in 1713 and finished in 1729. Clam-Gallas Palace now serves as a state archive but is also occasionally used to house temporary art exhibitions and concerts. If the building is open, try walking in to glimpse the Italian frescoes depicting Apollo and the battered but intricately carved staircase, done by the master himself. ☒ *Husova 20, Staré Mesto* ✉ *Free* Ⓜ *Line A: Staroměstská.*

### Dům U černé Matky boží (*House at the Black Madonna*)

BUILDING | This building, designed by Josef Gočár, is a shining example of relatively modern Czech architecture amid Staré Město's historical splendor. In the second decade of the 20th century, young Czech architects boldly applied cubism's radical reworking of visual space to architecture and design, with the characteristic geometric lines and sharp angles of the building's exterior the result. There's a permanent Czech cubism exhibition inside and a café. ☒ *Ovocný trh 19, Staré Mesto* ☎ *776–623–016* ⊕ *www.czkubismus.cz/en/the-house-at-the-black-madonna* ✉ *150 Kč* ⊙ *Closed Mon.* Ⓜ *Line B: Náměstí Republiky.*

### Jan Hus monument

PUBLIC ART | Few memorials in Prague have consistently elicited as much controversy as this one, dedicated in July 1915, exactly 500 years after Hus was burned at the stake in Constance, Germany. Some maintain that the monument's secessionist style (the inscription seems to come right from turn-of-the-20th-century Vienna) clashes with the Gothic and baroque style of the square. Others dispute the romantic depiction of Hus, who appears here as tall and bearded in flowing garb, whereas the real Hus, as historians maintain, was short and had a baby face. Either way, the fiery preacher's influence is not in dispute. His ability to transform doctrinal disagreements, both literally and metaphorically, into the language of the common man made him into a religious and national symbol for the Czechs. ☒ *Staroměstské nám., Staré Mesto* Ⓜ *Line A: Staroměstská.*

### Klášter sv. Anežky České (*St. Agnes's Convent*)

MUSEUM | Near the river between Pařížská and Revoluční ulice, in the northeastern corner of Staré Město, this peaceful complex has Prague's first buildings in the Gothic style. Built between the 1230s and the 1280s, the convent provides a fitting home for the National Gallery's marvelous collection of Czech and Central European Gothic art, including altarpieces, portraits, and statues from the 13th to the 16th century. ☒ *U Milosrdných 17, Staré Mesto* ☎ *778–725–086* ⊕ *www.ngprague.cz* ✉ *220 Kč* ⊙ *Closed Mon.* Ⓜ *Line A: Staroměstská.*

The Klementium's Baroque Library houses more than 20,000 volumes of mostly foreign theological literature from the beginning of the 17th century until recent times.

### ⭐ Klementinum

**LIBRARY** | It's advertised as the most beautiful library in the world and delivers on the hype. The origins of this massive, ancient complex date back to the 12th and 13th centuries, but it's best known as the stronghold of the Jesuits, who occupied it for more than 200 years beginning in the early 1600s. Though many buildings are closed to the public, the resplendent **Baroque Library** feels like such a hidden gem featuring fabulous ceiling murals that portray the three levels of knowledge, with the "Dome of Wisdom" as a centerpiece. Next door, the **Mirror Chapel** is a symphony of reflective surfaces, with acoustics to match. Mozart played here, and the space still hosts chamber music concerts. The **Astronomical Tower** in the middle of the complex offers stunning 360-degree views of Staré Město and was once used by game-changing astronomer Johannes Kepler and afterward functioned as the "Prague Meridian," where the time was set each day. Nowadays, you can visit the complex only on guided tours, which run every half hour. ■TIP→ **There is no elevator** to the Astronomical Tower rooftop and the steps are steep, so you may want to avoid this section if you have walking difficulties. ✉ *Mariánské nám. 5, Staré Mesto* ☎ *222–220–879* ⊕ *www.klementinum.com* ✉ *300 Kč (incl. tour)* Ⓜ *Line A: Staroměstská.*

**Kostel Matky Boží před Týnem** (*Church of Our Lady Before Týn, or Týn Church*)
**RELIGIOUS SITE** | The twin-spired Týn Church is an Old Town Square landmark and one of the city's best examples of Gothic architecture. The church's exterior was in part the work of Peter Parler, the architect responsible for the Charles Bridge and Katedrála sv. Víta (St. Vitus Cathedral). Construction of the twin black-spire towers began a little later, in 1461, by King Jiří of Poděbrady, during the heyday of the Hussites. Jiří had a gilded chalice, the symbol of the Hussites, proudly displayed on the front gable between the two towers. Following the defeat of the Czech Protestants by the Catholic Habsburgs in the 17th century, the chalice was melted down and made into the Madonna's

glimmering halo (you can still see it resting between the spires). Much of the interior, including the tall nave, was rebuilt in the baroque style in the 17th century. Some Gothic pieces remain, however: look to the left of the main altar for a beautifully preserved set of early carvings. The main altar itself was painted by Karel Škréta, a luminary of the Czech baroque. The church also houses the tomb of renowned Danish (and Prague court) astronomer Tycho Brahe, who died in 1601. ⊠ *Staroměstské nám. between Celetná and Týnská, Staré Mesto* ☎ *222–318–186* ⊕ *www.tyn.cz* ✉ *Free* ⊘ *Closed Mon.* Ⓜ *Line A: Staroměstská.*

**Kostel sv. Jiljí** (*Church of St. Giles*)
**RELIGIOUS SITE** | Replete with buttresses and a characteristic portal, this church's exterior is a powerful and beautiful example of Gothic architecture—famed Czech director Miloš Forman certainly thought so, shooting some of his hit film *Amadeus* inside. An important outpost of Czech Protestantism in the 16th century, the church reflects baroque style inside, with a design by Johann Bernhard Fischer von Erlach and sweeping frescoes by Václav Reiner. The interior can be viewed during the day from the vestibule or at the evening concerts held several times a week. ⊠ *Husova 8, Staré Mesto* ☎ *602–339–881* ⊕ *praha.op.cz* ✉ *Free* Ⓜ *Line A: Staroměstská.*

**Kostel sv. Martina ve zdi** (*Church of St. Martin-in-the-Wall*)
**RELIGIOUS SITE** | It was here, in this humble-looking corner church, that Holy Communion was first given to the Bohemian laity in the form of both bread and wine, way back in 1414. (The Catholic custom of the time dictated only bread would be offered to the masses, with wine reserved for priests and clergy.) From then on, the chalice came to symbolize the Hussite movement. The church's interior doesn't rival other grander religious buildings in Staré Město, but neverthless it is open to the public for a quick peek

every afternoon. German- and Czech-language services are held, too, and evening concerts. ⊠ *Martinská 8, Staré Mesto* ☎ *734–767–335* ⊕ *www.martinvezdi. eu* ✉ *Free* ⊘ *Closed Sun. and mornings (excl. services)* Ⓜ *Lines A & B: Můstek.*

**Kostel sv. Mikuláše** (*Church of St. Nicholas*)
**RELIGIOUS SITE** | While there has been a site of worship at this location since the 13th century, the church still standing was designed in the 18th century by Prague's own master of late baroque, Kilian Ignaz Dientzenhofer. Overall, it's probably less successful in capturing the style's lyric exuberance than its name-twin across town, the Kostel sv. Mikulase (Church of St. Nicholas) in Mala Strana; but Dientzenhofer utilized the limited space to create a well-balanced structure, and it can offer a moment of peace from Staré Město crowds. The interior is compact, with a beautiful chandelier and an enormous black organ that overwhelms the rear of the church. Afternoon and evening concerts for visitors are held almost continuously—walk past and you're sure to get leafleted for one. ⊠ *Staroměstské nám., Staré*

*Mesto* ☎ *224–190–990* ⊕ *www.svmiku-las.cz* ✉ *Free, fee for concerts* Ⓜ *Line A: Staroměstská.*

**Palác Kinských** (*Kinský Palace*)

**MUSEUM** | This exuberant building, built in 1765 from Kilian Ignaz Dientzenhofer's design, is considered one of Prague's finest rococo, late baroque structures. With its exaggerated pink overlay and numerous statues, it looks extravagant when contrasted with the marginally more somber baroque elements of other nearby buildings. (The interior, alas, was "modernized" under communism.)

The palace once contained a German school—where Franz Kafka studied for nine misery-laden years—and now houses revolving temporary exhibitions. Communist leader Klement Gottwald, alongside comrade Vladimír Clementis, first addressed the crowds from this building after seizing power in February 1948—an event recounted in the first chapter of Milan Kundera's novel *The Book of Laughter and Forgetting.* ✉ *Staroměstské nám. 12, Staré Mesto* ☎ *224–301–122* ⊕ *www.ngprague.cz* ✉ *220 Kč* ☽ *Closed Mon.* Ⓜ *Line A: Staroměstská.*

**Prašná brána** (*Powder Tower or Powder Gate*)

**VIEWPOINT** | Once used as storage space for gunpowder, this dark, imposing tower, covered in a web of carvings, offers a striking view of Staré Město and Prague Castle from the top. King Vladislav II of Jagiello began construction—it replaced one of the city's 13 original gates—in 1475. At the time, kings of Bohemia maintained their royal residence next door, on the site now occupied by the Obecní dům (Municipal House). The tower was intended to be the grandest gate of all. Vladislav, however, was Polish and somewhat disliked by the rebellious Czech citizens of Prague. Nine years after he assumed power, and fearing for his life, he moved the royal court across the river to Prague Castle. Work on the tower was abandoned, and the half-finished

# Sgraffiti Is Not a Crime ◉

*Sgraffiti*, plural for *sgraffito*, is a process where two contrasting shades of plaster are used on the façade of a building. Often the *sgraffiti* serve to highlight the original architecture; other times they can produce an optical illusion, painting brickwork and balconies from thin air. Walls can also be covered with lively classical pictures, which make houses resemble enormous Grecian vases. One of the best examples of *sgraffiti* is on Kafka's former residence, U Minuty, just next to the clock tower on Old Town Square.

structure remained a depository for gunpowder until the end of the 17th century. The golden spires were not added until the end of the 19th century. The ticket office is on the first floor, after you go up the dizzyingly narrow stairwell. ✉ *Nám. Republiky 5/1090, Staré Mesto* ☎ *725–847–875* ⊕ *www.muzeumprahy.cz* ✉ *100 Kč* Ⓜ *Line B: Náměstí Republiky.*

★ **Staroměstská radnice** (*Old Town Hall*)

**BUILDING** | Hundreds of visitors gravitate here throughout the day to see the hour struck by the mechanical figures of the **astronomical clock**. At the top of the hour, look to the upper part of the clock, where a skeleton begins by tolling a death knell and turning an hourglass upside down. The 12 apostles promenade by, and then a cockerel flaps its wings and screeches as the hour finally strikes. This theatrical spectacle doesn't reveal the way this 15th-century marvel indicates the time—by the season, the zodiac sign, and the positions of the sun and moon. The calendar under the clock dates to the mid-19th century.

Old Town Hall served as the center of administration for Staré Město beginning in 1338, when King John of Luxembourg first granted the city council the right to a permanent location. The impressive 200-foot **Town Hall Tower,** where the clock is mounted, was first built in the 14th century. For a rare view of Staré Město and its maze of crooked streets and alleyways, climb the ramp or ride the elevator to the top of the tower.

Walking around the hall to the left, you can see it's actually a series of houses jutting into the square; they were purchased over the years and successively added to the complex. On the other side, jagged stonework reveals where a large, neo-Gothic wing once adjoined the tower until it was destroyed by fleeing Nazi troops in May 1945.

Tours of the interiors depart from the main desk inside (most guides speak English, and English texts are on hand). There's also a branch of the tourist information office here. Previously unseen parts of the tower have now been opened to the public, and you can now see the inside of the famous clock. ☒ *Staroměstské nám., Staré Mesto* ⊕ *www.staromestskaradnicepraha.cz* ☎ *250 Kč* Ⓜ *Line A: Staroměstská.*

★ **Staroměstské náměstí** (*Old Town Square*)

**PLAZA** | The hype about Old Town Square is completely justified. Picture a perimeter of colorful baroque houses contrasting with the sweeping old-Gothic style of the Týn Church in the background. As the heart of Staré Město, the majestic square grew to its present proportions when Prague's original marketplace moved away from the river in the 12th century. Its shape and appearance have changed little since that time. During the day the square pulses with activity. In summer the square's south end is dominated by sprawling outdoor restaurants; during the Easter and Christmas seasons it fills with wooden booths of holiday vendors. At night the brightly lighted towers of the Týn Church rise gloriously over the glowing baroque façades. The square's history has also seen violence, from defenestrations (throwing people from windows) in the 15th century to 27 Bohemian noblemen killed by Austrian Habsburgs in 1621; 27 white crosses embedded in the square's paving stones commemorate the spot. ☒ *Staré Mesto* Ⓜ *Line A: Staroměstská.*

## 🍴 Restaurants

Staré Město is where visitors spend most of their time and where most of the best (and worst) restaurants are found. Ironically, perhaps the worst place to have a meal is directly on Old Town Square. Sadly, pretty much all places here are tourist traps. Instead, try exploring the area around Dlouhá to the northeast of the square, which boasts lots of fine dining, wine bars, and new high-end Czech eateries. As for the other parts of Staré Město, it's probably a good area to stick closely to the recommendations in this book. If there's someone hustling for patrons outside or offering "traditional Czech food" via a blackboard with no sign of prices (worst case scenario: with pictures), go elsewhere.

### Banh–mi–ba

**$$** | **VIETNAMESE** | Fresh, zingy Vietnamese food is available at this small, trendy spot on Rybná, from the eponymous baguettes to rolls, salads, and pho. There are good Vietnamese joints all over Prague thanks to ties between formerly communist Czechoslovakia and Hanoi, but until recently Staré Město was lacking its own standout. **Known for:** perfect Vietnamese baguettes; no glutamate additions; cool Czech couples grabbing a bite. Ⓢ *Average main: 150 Kč* ☒ *Rybná 26, Staré Mesto* ☎ *734–487–324* ⊕ *banhmiba.cz* Ⓜ *Line B: Náměstí Republiky.*

### ★ Cotto Crudo

**$$$** | **ITALIAN** | Having settled into its role as a leading light on Prague's culinary scene, the kitchen here dwells on crafting definitive Italian fare, overseen by chef Leonardo di Clemente. The comfortable Four Seasons restaurant and terrace (which has fantastic river views) graciously serves some of the finest Mediterranean cuisine in Prague, themed as cooked or raw, the latter in the form of a decadent mozarella bar and salami and prosciutto tower. **Known for:** quality Italian food; faultless service; special-occasion feel. $ *Average main: 501 Kč* ✉ *Four Seasons Prague, Veleslavinova 21, Staré Mesto* ☎ *221–426–880* ⊕ *www. cottocrudo.cz* Ⓜ *Line A: Staroměstská.*

### Dhaba Beas

$ | VEGETARIAN | Right behind the soaring spires of Staré Město's Týn Church, Beas offers inexpensive, Indian-style vegetarian and vegan food just a short walk from Old Town Square. Don't expect upscale service—you're going to bus your own table—but these dishes are worth the extra work. **Known for:** tasty curries; bringing vegetables to Old Town Square's meat-heavy dining roster; relaxed DIY service. $ *Average main: 80 Kč* ✉ *Týnská 19, Staré Mesto* ☎ *608–035–727* ⊕ *www.beas-dhaba.cz* 🚫 *No credit cards* Ⓜ *Line B: Náměstí Republiky.*

### Divinis

$$$ | ITALIAN | The simple decor—white walls and plank floors—at this wine-centric Italian restaurant on a quiet street near the Týn Church belies the quality and complexity of its food. Whether you stick to a simpler beetroot carpaccio with goat cheese or try something more complex like calamari with eggplant and pea ragout, the dishes are skillfully prepared and attractively presented. **Known for:** complex Italian cooking; great wine; celeb chef Zdeněk Pohlreich. $ *Average main: 500 Kč* ✉ *Týnská 21, Staré Mesto* ☎ *770–682–105* ⊕ *www.divinis.cz* 🕙 *Closed Sun.* Ⓜ *Line A: Staroměstská.*

### Krčma

$$ | CZECH | There are lots of pub-restaurants in Staré Město like Krčma—all beer, hearty Czech classics. and brick-lined cellar—but this is the best of the bunch.

Staff are friendly, prices are reasonable, it's not usually mobbed, and it retains a whiff of authenticity. **Known for:** traditional Czech food; authentic feel; fresh brews. $ *Average main: 250 Kč* ✉ *Kostečná 4, Staré Mesto* ☎ *725–157–262* ⊕ *krcma.cz* Ⓜ *Line B: Staroměstská.*

### ★ La Degustation Bohême Bourgeoise

$$$$ | ECLECTIC | One of Prague's two Michelin star holders is this elegant tasting room, where diners are taken on a superlative culinary adventure via a Czech-inspired tasting menu over an extended evening. The menu roves around Czech and European cuisine playfully and stylishly, including classic local specialties with a twist, like Prague ham, pumpkin, and whipped cream or a dessert of dark beer, caramel, and nuts. **Known for:** probably Prague's best food and service; playful and inventive takes on classic dishes; wine-paired tasting menu. $ *Average main: 3000 Kč* ✉ *Haštalská 18, Staré Mesto* ☎ *222–311–234* ⊕ *www.ladegustation.cz* 🕙 *Closed Mon. No lunch* Ⓜ *Line A: Staroměstská.*

### ★ La Finestra in Cucina

$$$ | ITALIAN | One of Prague's hottest tables, La Finestra is the meaty counterpart to its sister restaurant, Aromi, right down to the wooden tables and brick walls. Catering to local gourmands and boldface names, this restaurant lives up to the hype. **Known for:** organic dry-aged meats, foccacia and fried chickpeas to nibble on, and expert al dente pastas like spaghetti with sea urchin; extensive Italian wine selection; cooking classes. $ *Average main: 500 Kč* ✉ *Platnéřská 13, Staré Mesto* ☎ *222–325–325* ⊕ *lafinestra. lacollezione.cz* Ⓜ *Line A: Staroměstská.*

### ★ Lokál Dlouháááá

$$ | CZECH | Sleek and relatively sophisticated, Lokál Dlouháááá takes the Czech pub concept to a new level with fresh local ingredients, perfectly poured beers, and friendly, efficient service. It makes for an idealized version of a corner restaurant out of another era, right down

## Did You Know?

Yes, the skyline is stunning, but also look down. Old Town Square is marked with 27 white crosses in the paving stones that commemorate the spot where 27 noblemen were killed by the Austrian Habsburgs in 1621.

# Hunting for Dumplings

The quality of Bohemian cooking declined precipitously during the communist period, and bad habits were hard to shake in the aftermath of the 1989 revolution. Consequently, Czech cuisine has gotten an undeserved bad rap. Thankfully, some restaurateurs have taken up the baton to right past wrongs, and if you know where to go, it's now possible to find excellent traditional cooking outside the home. And as for the famed dumplings? Well, both the bread and potato versions are a must-try. Note: they can be quite dense (perhaps to fuel locals to get through the notorious Czech winters).

The Ambiente group, in particular, sees it as a priority to revive historic recipes and cooking techniques. This chain's flagship **La** Degustation Bohême **Bourgeoise** (✉ Haštalská 18 ☎ 222–311–234) offers a multicourse tasting menu using recipes from the 19th century. It's a bit pricey at more than 3,000 Kč a head, but if you want Czech at its fine-dining best, this is where to go. The chain also runs the far cheaper **Lokál Dlouhááá** (✉ Dlouhá 33 ☎ 222–316–265), and for much less money you can taste excellent renditions of pub staples like guláš and fried pork cutlets in an old-school pub atmosphere.

Brewpubs are another alternative for finding well-done domestic cooking. Good examples are the Pilsner Urquell chain, which runs V **Kolkovně** (✉ V Kolkovně 8 ☎ 224–819–701) in Josefov, as well as other similar establishments at a few other locations around town, including **Kulat'ák** (✉ Vítězné nám. 12 ☎ 773–973–037) in Dejvice. Here you'll find high standards for traditional Czech cuisine in a sleek environment with good service and fresh beers.

to the stark white walls, waiters in vests, and bathrooms wallpapered with old pinups and airplane posters. **Known for:** high-quality Czech food; fast and friendly service; always being busy (and noisy). 🛈 Average main: 175 Kč ✉ Dlouhá 33, Staré Mesto ☎ 734–283–874 ⊕ lokal-dlouha.ambi.cz Ⓜ Line B: Náměstí Republiky.

### Maitrea

$$ | **VEGETARIAN** | Vegetarians, you're in luck: the Czech Republic's best vegetarian restaurant just happens to be a five-minute walk from Old Town Square. Here, veg food is not viewed as a radical departure from other cuisines; indeed, most of the dishes, like the chilis, burritos, and Czech classics svíčková and guláš (goulash), look and taste like the originals, only without the meat. **Known for:** veggie versions of Czech classics; Buddhist-inspired vibes; long waits for a table. 🛈 Average main: 150 Kč ✉ Týnská ulička 6, Staré Mesto ☎ 221–711–631 ⊕ www.restaurace-maitrea.cz Ⓜ Line A: Staroměstská.

### Marina

$$ | **ITALIAN** | You don't have to splurge at expensive places like Kampa Park for regal dining vistas over the Charles Bridge or Prague Castle. For the price of a pizza or pasta, you can sit on the deck of this marina, anchored off the Vltava River. **Known for:** unbeatable views to the castle; reasonable prices for well-executed Italian staples; dining on the water. 🛈 Average main: 280 Kč ✉ Alšovo nábř. 1, Staré Mesto ☎ 222–316–744 ⊕ marinaristorante.cz Ⓜ Line A: Staroměstská.

### Naše Maso

$$ | **CZECH** | Butcher shops are serious business in the Czech Republic and many have barely changed for generations, at least in terms of offerings. This newly updated version, with friendlier service

and a handy lunch counter, stocks dozens of sausage varieties, classic smoked meats, and delicate fillets of pork and beef. **Known for:** meat galore; standing room only; a glorious tatarák (beef tartare). $ *Average main: 150 Kč* ✉ *Dlouhá 39, Staré Mesto* ☎ *222–311–378* ⊕ *nase-maso.cz* ◷ *No dinner Thurs.–Sun.* ▭ *No credit cards* Ⓜ *Náměstí Republiky.*

### V Kolkovně

$$ | **CZECH** | For Czechs, this traditional bar-restaurant remains one of the most popular spots to take visitors for a taste of local cuisine without the stress of tourist rip-offs. And it's a solid choice. **Known for:** traditional Czech cuisine done well, like svíčková, roast duck, and fried pork cutlets; warm and welcoming interiors; fresh Pilsner Urquell beer. $ *Average main: 250 Kč* ✉ *V Kolkovně 8, Staré Mesto* ☎ *224–819–701* ⊕ *www.vkolkovne.cz* Ⓜ *Line A: Staroměstská.*

### Yami

$$ | **JAPANESE** | Yami is sushi without the pretension that often accompanies a sushi place in Prague, and while the prices have crept up in recent years, the sushi sets and rolls are still cheaper than much of the competition (without any compromise in quality). The soups and appetizers are excellent, too. **Known for:** the "Ruby Roll," with tuna, butterfish, avocado, cucumber, and ponzu sauce; good sharing sushi sets; potential crammed feel. $ *Average main: 320 Kč* ✉ *Masná 3, Staré Mesto* ☎ *222–312–756* ⊕ *www.yami.cz* Ⓜ *Line A: Staromětská.*

### Zdenek's Oyster Bar

$$$$ | **SEAFOOD** | Since it opened in 2011, Zdenek's Oyster Bar has established itself as the city's best seafood bar. Aside from the namesake oysters (more than a dozen different varieties), head chef David Vlášek has developed creative entrées around mussels, shrimp, crab, lobster, and various types of fish. **Known for:** superb seafood dishes; extensive champagne list; high prices. $ *Average main: 1000 Kč* ✉ *Malá Štupartská 5, Staré Mesto* ☎ *725–946–250* ⊕ *www.oysterbar.cz* Ⓜ *Line B: Náměstí Republiky.*

## ☕ Coffee and Quick Bites

### Au Gourmand

$$ | **BAKERY** | This sweet little café with tiled mosaic floors, globe lights, and green pastry case decor provides an inviting spot for a light lunch. It's similar to the nearby Bakeshop Praha, but with a certain Gallic flair. **Known for:** fresh breads; homemade ice cream; refined café vibes. $ *Average main: 150 Kč* ✉ *Dlouhá 10, Staré Mesto* ☎ *602–682–189* ⊕ *www.augourmand.cz* Ⓜ *Line A: Staroměstská.*

### Bakeshop Praha

$ | **BAKERY** | An American-style bakery and café counter, Bakeshop Praha sells familiar U.S. favorites, from avocado BLTs to entire pumpkin pies. Though it gets crowded during peak lunch hours, there is indoor seating, and the space, with penny-tiled floors and ceiling moldings, has a retro charm. **Known for:** proper New York–style cheesecake; homemade breads, including great sourdough; daily cream cheese spread mixes. $ *Average main: 140 Kč* ✉ *Kozi 1, Staré Mesto* ☎ *222–316–823* ⊕ *www.bakeshop.cz* Ⓜ *Line A: Staroměstská.*

### Piknik

$ | **BAKERY** | With its hip signage and location, you could be forgiven for assuming that Piknik is style over substance. But the lines to the counter would quickly set you right, as customers line up for delicious pastries, cakes, sandwiches, breakfasts, and coffee. **Known for:** flaky, fruity pastries; long lines at breakfast; takeaway treats. $ *Average main: 90 Kč* ✉ *Dlouhá 52, Staré Mesto* ☎ *605–052–331* ⊕ *www.facebook.com/Piknik.Dlouha* Ⓜ *Line B: Náměstí Republiky.*

The most significant square of historical Prague, Old Town Square was founded in the 12th century and has been witness to many historical events.

#  Hotels

Staré Město, Prague's Old Town, is a highly desirable neighborhood in which to stay. The mix of baroque and Gothic buildings provides a storybook feeling, and all of the city's major sights are within reach via a pleasant cobblestoned stroll. Hotels here are mainly of the old-made-new variety. Don't be surprised to be standing in a hotel lobby that was originally built in the 17th century—or earlier—but looks and smells like a fresh coat of plaster and paint was added a month ago. Trendy restaurants, cute cafés, superior clubs, and the city's best clothing boutiques are all in this area, too.

### Buddha-Bar Hotel

**$$$ | HOTEL** | The concept here is "Chinoiserie meets art nouveau," as best as we can tell, meshing the hotel's original 100-year-old structure with Asian script and Buddhas throughout. **Pros:** stylish design, if not particularly "Czech"; mecca for club-going hipsters; great in-house bar. **Cons:** room rates can go up fast if booked late; rooms seem dark; small spa. $ *Rooms from: 6000 Kč* ⊠ *Jakubská 8, Staré Mesto* ☎ *221–776–300* ⊕ *www.buddhabarhotelprague.com* 🛏 *38 rooms* ⃝ *No meals* Ⓜ *Line C: Náměstí Republiky.*

### Design Hotel Jewel Prague

**$$ | HOTEL** | A friendly jewel-theme hotel that's close to all the Staré Město action, the staff here go the extra mile, from the little afternoon tea cakes brought to your room to the bedtime-story cards distributed in the evening. **Pros:** cute touches; bright, individual rooms; well priced. **Cons:** buffet breakfast could be fresher; some street noise; rooms can feel cramped. $ *Rooms from: 3200 Kč* ⊠ *Rytířská 3, Staré Mesto* ☎ *224–211–699* ⊕ *hoteljewelprague.com* 🛏 *10 rooms* ⃝ *No meals* Ⓜ *Lines A and B: Můstek.*

### Four Seasons Hotel Prague

**$$$$ | HOTEL** | Though it has plenty of competition at the top end of the market, the Prague outpost of the Four Seasons luxury chain keeps up, not least because it simply has one of the best locations in the city: right on the river, close to the

Charles Bridge, giving guests beautiful views from many of the rooms and a general fairy-tale feel. **Pros:** sumptuous beds; incredible views; perfect service. **Cons:** pricey breakfast; conservative styling; some tram noise from one side of the hotel (but this is Prague). [$] *Rooms from: 10500 Kč* ✉ *Veleslavinova 2A, Staré Mesto* ☎ *221–427–000* 🌐 *www.fourseasons.com/prague* 🛏 *157 rooms* 🍴 *No meals* [M] *Line A: Staroměstská.*

**Grand Hotel Bohemia**

**$$$** | **HOTEL** | This comfortable, stately old art nouveau *palais* dominates a picturesque corner near the Powder Tower and Náměstí Republiky. **Pros:** city-center location; fascinating history, with glittering surprise in the basement; comfortable rooms. **Cons:** a few nickel-and-dime charges (breakfast costs extra in cheaper rooms); pricier than comparable hotels in the area; old-fashioned lobby and bar, cozy in winter but less appealing in summer. [$] *Rooms from: 4500 Kč* ✉ *Králodvorská 4, Staré Mesto* ☎ *234–608–111* 🌐 *www.grandhotelbohemia.cz* 🛏 *78 rooms* 🍴 *Free Breakfast* [M] *Line B: Náměstí Republiky.*

**Grand Hotel Praha**

**$$** | **HOTEL** | The main selling point here is the amazing location (practically on top of one of Prague's most famous sights, the astronomical clock) but this has its downside: with the wonderful views comes a big tourist scrum from the moment you venture outside. **Pros:** can't get closer to the astronomical clock unless you sleep in its tower; good price, with breakfast included, for location; baroque Cafe Mozart is a nice place for afternoon tea or cocktails. **Cons:** obviously rooms with the best views of the clock are considerably pricier; Mitteleuropa-style decor is a little tired; can feel a bit hectic. [$] *Rooms from: 3200 Kč* ✉ *Staroměstské nám. 481/22, Staré Mesto* ☎ *221–632–556* 🌐 *www.grandhotelpraha.cz* 🛏 *38 rooms* 🍴 *Breakfast* 💳 *No credit cards* [M] *Line A: Staroměstská.*

★ **Hotel Residence Agnes**

**$$** | **HOTEL** | This gorgeous hotel, with a chic courtyard and atrium, is tucked away on a quiet alley in Staré Město and is a comfortable haven from the hustle and bustle of Prague. **Pros:** fantastic staff—nothing is too much trouble; homey feel, with welcome wine; tasty breakfast included. **Cons:** rooms sell out quickly; decor perhaps a little simple, although stylish; lacking extras: no spa, restaurant, or garden. [$] *Rooms from: 4000 Kč* ✉ *Haštalská 19, Staré Mesto* ☎ *222–312–417* 🌐 *www.residenceagnes.cz* 🛏 *22 rooms* 🍴 *Breakfast* [M] *Line B: Náměstí Republiky.*

**Hotel U Zlatého Jelena**

**$** | **HOTEL** | Authentically austere, what U Zlatého Jelena lacks in personality and amenities it makes up for with a killer location off Old Town Square. **Pros:** prime city-center location; large rooms with some typically Czech touches, like parquet floors; good breakfast buffet. **Cons:** no a/c; street noise in noncourtyard rooms; lacking in coziness. [$] *Rooms from: 2000 Kč* ✉ *Celetná 11, Staré Mesto* ☎ *257–531–925* 🌐 *www.goldendeer.cz* 🛏 *19 rooms* 🍴 *Free Breakfast* [M] *Line B: Náměstí Republiky.*

**Iron Gate Hotel and Suites**

**$$** | **HOTEL** | If you're looking for history, the Iron Gate has it in spades—the original building dates to the 14th century, and the architectural details are fascinating (ask to see a room with painted ceiling beams). **Pros:** real historical pedigree; each room is unique; located on a gorgeous cobblestoned street. **Cons:** hard beds; old building means architectural quirks—stairs, low ceilings—make access challenging; shower/baths don't appeal to everyone. [$] *Rooms from: 4100 Kč* ✉ *Michalská 19, Staré Mesto* ☎ *225–777–777* 🌐 *www.irongatehotel.com* 🛏 *43 rooms* 🍴 *Breakfast* [M] *Line A: Staroměstská.*

**Josef**

**$$$** | **HOTEL** | Cool, clean, white lines dominate the decor of this ultrahip modern boutique hotel designed by

London-based Czech architect Eva Jiricna. **Pros:** large patio for breakfast in the courtyard; some rooms have amazing views of Staré Město—try 801 for the best; great on-site bakery. **Cons:** the minimalist design might not be for everyone; glass dividers in some bathrooms give no privacy; rooms are not large. [$] *Rooms from: 4900 Kč* ✉ *Rybná 20, Staré Mesto* ☎ *221–700–111* 🌐 *www.hoteljosef.com* 🛏 *109 rooms* 🍴 *Breakfast* [M] *Line B: Náměstí Republiky.*

**★ Smetana Hotel**

**$$$** | **HOTEL** | Made from four structures—a baroque palace, two medieval houses, and a neoclassical building from 1836—Smetana Hotel, right by the river and the Charles Bridge, can't be matched for authenticity. **Pros:** friendly service; giant rooms with decadent details, like springy beds and chandeliers; fascinating centuries-long history including Mozart being locked in a room here until he wrote six sonatas for the owner. **Cons:** some street noise; staff can be disorganized at times; breakfast underwhelming. [$] *Rooms from: 6000 Kč* ✉ *Karoliny Světlé 34, Staré Mesto* ☎ *234–705–111* 🌐 *www.smetana-hotel.com* 🛏 *48 rooms* 🍴 *Free Breakfast* [M] *Line A: Staroměstská.*

**Unitas Hotel**

**$$$** | **HOTEL** | The rooms in this former convent once served as interrogation cells for the communist secret police, and the late president Václav Havel was once even a guest here[?]—though fortunately, the lobby and rooms betray nothing of this gloomy past. **Pros:** clean, airy, large and modern rooms; great location on a quiet street; historical wow factor can't be beat. **Cons:** few amenities; not exactly a bargain; no on-site restaurant. [$] *Rooms from: 5400 Kč* ✉ *Bartolomějská 9, Staré Mesto* ☎ *224–230–533* 🌐 *www.unitas.cz* 🛏 *22 rooms* 🍴 *Breakfast* [M] *Line B: Národní třída.*

**Ventana Hotel Prague**

**$$$** | **HOTEL** | Surprisingly quiet considering its location just steps from Old Town Square, the Ventana delivers old-school style and charm in spades. **Pros:** calm and cozy retreat; good location with a swanky bar; staff have old-school charm. **Cons:** pricey; rooms vary in terms of individuality and view quality, so check them out carefully; some access issues, for example, beds on mezzanine layers in loft rooms. [$] *Rooms from: 5400 Kč* ✉ *Celetná 7, Staré Mesto* ☎ *221–776–600* 🌐 *www.ventana-hotel.net* 🛏 *29 rooms* 🍴 *Breakfast* [M] *Lines A & B: Můstek.*

## Nightlife

Prague's historical heart is also the heart of its nightlife. It's packed with jazz bars, old pubs, and high-end cocktail bars. Be warned though: on the weekend this area can get a bit party-heavy, and at some of the fancier bars it might be a good idea to book a table.

### BARS AND PUBS

**Bar and Books**

**BARS/PUBS** | Just off Old Town Square, but worlds away from the raucous touristy venues nearby in terms of atmosphere, sophistication, and quiet, Bar and Books is a grown-up place for a cocktail. Try the martini, made as you like it; it's predictably good. ✉ *Týnská 19, Staré Mesto* 🌐 *www.barandbooks.cz* [M] *Lines A and B: Můstek.*

**★ Bokovka**

**WINE BARS—NIGHTLIFE** | Pretty much a fairy-tale dream of a European wine bar, established by a group of artsy Praguers: located in a crumbling courtyard and cellar-style cozy archway (check), serving up personally recommended wines to your taste (check), which you sup by candlelight on barrel tables either inside or outside, wrapped in blankets in the winter if you like (check). It's a little hidden: keep an eye out for the wine droplet sign, leading you into the courtyard, and it's on the right. Closed Sunday. ✉ *Dlouhá 37, Staré Mesto* 🌐 *www.bokovka.com* [M] *Line B: Náměstí Republiky.*

AghaRTA Jazz club opened the day after jazz legend Miles Davis died in 1991, and is named for his 1970s album.

## Champagneria

**PIANO BARS/LOUNGES** | If you like your champagne bars relaxed, located in ancient buildings with shutters and crumbling exterior walls that are covered with graffiti, this little joint is for you. A cool and welcoming spot, with candles scattered around as the sun sets, Champagneria offers a range of drinks from the fizz of its title to Matuška, a craft brew that many Prague hipsters consider the champagne of beers anyway. Great acoustics for cheerful conversation, proper champagne glasses, a tasty snack menu, and a piano in the corner and regular musical performances only add to the promise. ⊠ *Průchodní 4, Staré Mesto* ⊕ *champagneria.cz* Ⓜ *Line B: Národní třída.*

## Hemingway Bar

**BARS/PUBS** | Absinthe is all over Prague, and if you want to dabble in the green fairy's magic, there are worse places than the sophisticated cocktail bar Hemingway, which is named after the man himself. You won't find any flaming absinthe here, but you will find a range of interesting cocktails, alongside champagne and 200 varieties of rum—the famous writer's drinks of choice. It's worth reserving a table on weekends. ⊠ *Karolíny Světlé 26, Staré Mesto* ☎ *773–974–764* ⊕ *www.hemingwaybar. cz/bar-prague* Ⓜ *Lines A & B: Můstek.*

## Kristian Marco (river bar)

**BREWPUBS/BEER GARDENS** | As you walk by in summer, you'll be drawn in by the gentle guitar playing of the brilliant resident musicians, or the smell of the barbecue, or the lively hum of conversation and clink of glasses. There are some downers—a small entrance charge (apparently to pay the musician), steep beer prices, and occasionally surly staff— but it's worth it for the location, right on the water's edge near the Narodní divadlo (National Theater), with the castle looming over you on the other side of the river. Beware: you could lose hours of your vacation here if the weather's good, with the water lapping gently beside you and a never-ending stream of foaming beer mugs arriving at your table.

✉ *Smetanovo nábř. 198/1, Staré Mesto* ☎ *No phone* 🕒 *Closed Nov.–Apr.* Ⓜ *Line B: Národní třída.*

**Pivní lázně Bernard** (*Beer Spa Bernard*)
**THEMED ENTERTAINMENT** | A beer spa might sound a bit gimmicky, but this charming cellar space offers an unusual but intensely relaxing evening, with serious spa pedigree: it was a winner in the World Luxury Spa Awards in 2019. Baths are filled with beer-inspired waters, while taps on the sides pour out ice-cold Bernard to drink while you soak. A massage is included, too, and other treatments are available. ✉ *Týn 10 (courtyard Ungelt), Staré Mesto* ⊕ *www.pivnilaznebernard. cz* Ⓜ *Line B: Můstek.*

**Pohostinec Monarch**
**WINE BARS—NIGHTLIFE** | A classy wine bar and restaurant, with high ceilings, soft lighting, and a vast selection of vintages, including some particularly fine wines from the Czech Republic. Great steak here, too. ✉ *Na Perštýně 15, Staré Mesto* ⊕ *monarch.cz* Ⓜ *Line B: Národní třída.*

**Prague Beer Museum**
**BARS/PUBS** | With 30 Czech craft beers on tap, this is the place to go in Staré Město if you're hunting for an unusual brew in a fun environment. The owners scoured the countryside for their beers, and one is apparently available only as long as a friend of the brewer's doesn't break up with his girlfriend (he delivers the beer on the way to visiting her in Prague). Try a flight of beers to taste a few different brews. There's a second location in Vinohrady. ✉ *Smetanovo nábř. 22, Staré Mesto* ☎ *732–330–912* ⊕ *www.praguebeermuseum.cz* Ⓜ *Line B: Náměstí Republiky.*

**★ U Medvídků**
**BREWPUBS/BEER GARDENS** | A former brewery dating as far back as the 15th century, U Medvídků now serves draft Budvar shipped directly from České Budějovice, as well as its own superstrong X Beer 33, which is brewed on-site. It's perhaps the most authentic of the city-center Czech

pubs, which also means that it's often pretty busy and service can be correspondingly slow. However, it's also big enough that you've got a good chance of finding a seat. The interior, including the taps, has a turn-of-the-20th-century feel. Occasionally, the bar offers exclusive Budvar brews available only at this location. There's a hotel on-site, too. ✉ *Na Perštýně 7, Staré Mesto* ☎ *224–211–916* ⊕ *www. umedvidku.cz* Ⓜ *Line B: Národní třída.*

**★ U Zlatého tygra**
**BARS/PUBS** | The last of the old, smoky, surly pubs in Staré Město, the "Golden Tiger" is famous for being one of the best Prague pubs for Pilsner Urquell. It's also renowned as a former hangout of one of the country's best-known and beloved writers, Bohumil Hrabal, who died in 1997, as well as Velvet Revolution hero and then president Václav Havel. Reservations are not accepted; one option is to show up when the pub opens at 3 pm, with the rest of the early birds, and settle in for the rest of the night. You won't be disappointed. ✉ *Husova 17, Staré Mesto* ☎ *222–221–111* ⊕ *www.uzlatehotygra.cz* Ⓜ *Line A: Staroměstská.*

## JAZZ CLUBS
**★ AghaRTA**
**MUSIC CLUBS** | Bearing the name of an old Miles Davis album, this small but charming vaulted basement is home base for many local jazz acts. The management also runs a jazz record label and sells its CDs at the club's store. The historic place can't handle big acts, so the club's ongoing jazz festival often puts those who will draw larger crowds into Lucerna Music Bar. Music starts around 9, but come an hour earlier to get a seat. ✉ *Železná 16, Staré Mesto* ☎ *222–211–275* ⊕ *www. agharta.cz* Ⓜ *Lines A and C: Můstek.*

**Ungelt**
**MUSIC CLUBS** | Hidden in the side streets behind Old Town Square, this basement has been around since the 15th century and has been a cozy club with good music since 2000. The house

bands are decent and play jazz, blues, or fusion, depending on the night. Its central location means there's mainly an international crowd, but you can still see some classic Czech sights—a sleeping dachshund perched on a bar stool, unaware of and unimpressed by the stage acts, for example. ⊠ *Týn 2, Staré Mesto* ☎ *224–895–787* ⊕ *www.jazzungelt.cz* Ⓜ *Line A: Staroměstská.*

### LGBTQ
**Friends**

**BARS/PUBS** | This (appropriately named) friendly bar in Staré Město serves reasonably priced beer—and Western-priced mixed drinks—in a roomy cellar space. There's plenty of seating most weeknights, but it does get busy on weekends. It opens at 7 pm (and stays open until 6 am!), videos play every night, happy hour starts at 9, and a DJ spins after 10 on weekends, luring people onto a small dance floor—try karaoke on Tuesday. There's no cover. ⊠ *Bartolomějská 11, Staré Mesto* ☎ *734–304–183* ⊕ *www.friendsprague.cz* Ⓜ *Lines A and B: Můstek.*

### LIVE MUSIC CLUBS
**Roxy**

**MUSIC CLUBS** | Part nightclub, part performance space, the Roxy doubles as a residence for DJs and as a popular venue for electronica and touring cult bands. The large former theater has a comfortable, lived-in feel that borders on warehouse chic. All exits from the club are final, and patrons are encouraged not to hang around the area. Upstairs, the NoD space has all manner of bizarre acts. Monday is free. ⊠ *Dlouhá 33, Staré Mesto* ☎ *608–060–745 (SMS is best)* Ⓜ *Line B: Náměstí Republiky.*

## ⚙ Performing Arts

Prague is a fantastically cultured city: from classical music to theater, there are options for visitors right at the top end of the scale (internationally renowned orchestra performances) down to more experimental, try-anything theater. We've listed some of the best classical music ensembles to watch out for below, with a whistlestop tour of the most impressive venues (and what kinds of things they offer) to follow.

### CLASSICAL MUSIC
**Česká filharmonie** (*Czech Philharmonic*)

**MUSIC** | The big daddy in town: Antonín Dvořák conducted the orchestra's first performance back in 1896, and guest conductors have included Gustav Mahler and Leonard Bernstein. Performances are of a consistently high quality, and most programs include some works by Czech composers. ⊠ *Rudolfinum, Nám. Jana Palacha, Staré Mesto* ☎ *227–059–227* ⊕ *www.ceskafilharmonie.cz* Ⓜ *Line A: Staroměstská.*

**Collegium Marianum**

**MUSIC** | One of the most well-respected ensembles in town, Collegium Marianum is your best bet if you are looking to explore baroque music. They often revive seldom-heard works from archives and perform them on period instruments. Performances are usually organized around a historical or geographical theme. ⊠ *Vodičkova 700/32, Staré Mesto* ☎ *224–229–462* ⊕ *www.collegiummarianum.cz* Ⓜ *Line A: Staroměstská.*

**★ Prague Symphony Orchestra** (*FOK*)

**MUSIC** | The group's nickname stands for Film-Opera-Koncert. They started in 1934, but it wasn't until 1952 that they became the official city orchestra. In the 1930s they did music for many Czech films, although they don't do much opera and film anymore. The ensemble tours extensively and has a large back catalog of recordings. Programs tend to be quite diverse, from Beethoven to Bruckner. They also offer public rehearsals for a mere 160 Kč (book early though, because they are an understandably popular bargain). ⊠ *Obecní dům, Nám. Republiky 5, Staré Mesto* ☎ *222–002–336* ⊕ *www.fok.cz* Ⓜ *Line B: Náměstí Republiky.*

**3**

**Staré Město (Old Town) and Josefov** STARÉ MĚSTO (OLD TOWN)

## CHURCH CONCERTS

**Barokní knihovní sál** (*Baroque Library Hall*)
CONCERTS | Beautiful 18th-century frescoes and colorful stuccowork in a monastery library hall make for one of the more charming concert halls in a city with no shortage of charming concert halls. This is usually a good bet for a quality performance, as it is effectively home to the Collegium Marianum ensemble. ✉ *Melantrichova 971/19, Staré Město* ☎ *224–229–462* ⊕ *www.klementinum. com/prohlidky/barokni-knihovna* Ⓜ *Line A: Staroměstská.*

**Bazilika sv. Jakuba** (*Basilica of St. James*)
CONCERTS | This is an excellent venue for organ concerts thanks to the church's organ, which was finished in 1709 and restored in the early 1980s to its original tone structure. All those years later, it's still one of the best in town. ✉ *Malá Štupartská 6, Staré Město* ☎ *604–208–490* ⊕ *auditeorganum.cz* Ⓜ *Line A: Staroměstská.*

**Kostel sv. Mikuláše** (*Church of St. Nicholas*)
CONCERTS | The impressive chandelier inside this baroque landmark was a gift from the Russian czar. Private companies rent out the church for concerts by professional ensembles and visiting amateur choirs and orchestras. The quality and prices vary, but the location—right on the edge of Old Town Square—always delivers, as does the beauty of the church's interior. ✉ *Staroměstské nám., Staré Město* ☎ *224–190–990* ⊕ *www. svmikulas.cz* Ⓜ *Line A: Staroměstská.*

★ **Zrcadlová kaple Klementina** (*Mirrored Chapel of the Klementinum*)
CONCERTS | Now part of the National Library, this beautifully ornate little chapel in the middle of the Klementinum complex is worth a peek. Concerts are held almost daily and the music features the usual suspects—Mozart, Bach, and Vivaldi. Different concert companies program the space; signs nearby usually have the day's schedule. ✉ *Marianské nám. 5, Staré Město* ☎ *221–663–331* ⊕ *www. nkp.cz* Ⓜ *Line A: Staroměstská.*

## VENUES

★ **Rudolfinum**
ARTS CENTERS | Austrian Crown Prince Rudolf lent his name to this neo-Renaissance concert space and exhibition gallery built in 1884; it's only been open to the public since 1992. The impressive building has an interesting history: after 1918 it was converted into the parliament of the newly independent Czechoslovakia, until German invaders reinstated it as a space for music in 1939. The large concert hall, named for Antonín Dvořák, who conducted here, hosts concerts by the Czech Philharmonic. The smaller Josef Suk Hall, on the opposite side of the building, is used for chamber concerts. Rival theaters may have richer interiors, but the acoustics here are excellent (and the exterior is also pretty fancy, with some of the cleanest, brightest stonework in the city). To see the hall, you must attend a concert. ✉ *Alšovo nábř. 12, Staré Město* ☎ *227–059–227* ⊕ *www. rudolfinum.cz* Ⓜ *Line A: Staroměstská.*

★ **Stavovské divadlo** (*Estates Theater*)
ARTS VENUE | Built in the 1780s in the classical style, this opulent, green *palais* hosted the world premiere of Mozart's opera *Don Giovanni* in October 1787 with the composer himself conducting. Savvy Prague audiences were quick to acknowledge Mozart's genius: the opera was an instant hit here, though it flopped nearly everywhere else in Europe. Mozart wrote some of the opera's second act in Prague at the Villa Bertramka (in Smíchov), where he was a frequent guest. The program these days is mixed, incorporating demanding Czech drama alongside opera, ballet, and musical performances. You must attend a performance to see inside, although the interior, the history, and the quality of the shows here combined make it absolutely worth it; buy tickets via the National Theater. ✉ *Ovocný trh 1, Staré Město* ☎ *224–901–448* box office ⊕ *www.narodni-divadlo.cz* Ⓜ *Lines A and B: Můstek.*

# 🛍 Shopping

A jumble of funky boutiques, bookshops, antiques stores, jewelry dens, and souvenir shops converge in what is arguably Prague's prettiest district.

## ANTIQUES

### Antik Mucha

ANTIQUES/COLLECTIBLES | A charming antiques shop that has so many wares, and such friendly owners, that it has more of the feel of a museum than a store. It focuses on objects from the beginning of the 20th century and, as such, has some lovely art nouveau pieces, from inkstands to lamps. It also has a "mascot," bulldog Adamek. ⊠ *Liliová 12, Staré Mesto* ☎ *602–316–285* ⊕ *pokus-112.webnode.cz* Ⓜ *Line B: Můstek.*

### Art Deco Galerie

ANTIQUES/COLLECTIBLES | This cute antiques shop just off Old Town Square is pleasantly cluttered with art deco–era sculptures and furnishings, but specializes in Czech garnet and jewelry. Those with eclectic style will love the intricate brooches, turban-style headbands, and silk scarves here. ⊠ *Michalská 21, Staré Mesto* ☎ *606–904–604* ⊕ *artdecogalerie. cz* Ⓜ *Lines A and B: Můstek.*

### ★ Bric a Brac

ANTIQUES/COLLECTIBLES | If you like the sensation of unearthing your treasure, this wonderfully cluttered antiques store is the ticket. About the size of a closet, this shop uses every nook to display a mix of communist-era badges, tin Pilsner Urquell signs, charming old typewriters, and more. Memorable gifts can be found among the clutter, although some prices are high—that colorful Czech tobacco tin could make a great jewelry box, though. Ask the friendly English-speaking shopkeeper for tips, and pop round the corner to find his slightly larger cave of riches. ⊠ *Týnská 7, Staré Mesto* ☎ *606–873–955* Ⓜ *Line A: Staroměstská.*

### Starožítností Ungelt

ANTIQUES/COLLECTIBLES | Tucked away beneath an archway behind Týn Church, this elegant shop features a selection of art nouveau and art deco items. Beautiful and unusual glass vases from Czech designers sit alongside furniture, glittering brooches, and delicate porcelain butterflies. ⊠ *Týn 1, Staré Mesto* ☎ *224–895–454* ⊕ *www.antiqueungelt.cz* Ⓜ *Line A: Staroměstská.*

## ART GALLERIES

### AD Galerie

ART GALLERIES | A bright, interesting room packed with everything from puppets to paintings, jewelry to wire sculptures, this family-run gallery showcasing modern Czech creativity is worth a look for an interesting and unique souvenir. ⊠ *Uhelný trh 11, Staré Mesto* ☎ *732–160–647* ⊕ *www.adgalerie.cz* Ⓜ *Lines A and B: Můstek.*

### Galerie NoD

ART GALLERIES | Above the Roxy music club on Dlouhá ulice, this gallery space is filled with youthful energy. Exhibits feature edgy work by up-and-coming artists focusing on anything from puppets to photography. The gallery also hosts experimental theater, music, and comedy nights and touts an adjacent bar and café sprinkled with twentysomethings on laptops. ⊠ *Dlouhá 33, Staré Mesto* ☎ *733–307–600* ⊕ *nod.roxy.cz* Ⓜ *Line B: Náměstí Republiky.*

### Galerie U Betlémské kaple

ART GALLERIES | Specializing in postwar surrealism, this airy gallery features work from many of the leading Czech artists present and past, including globally significant painter Josef Šíma. If artwork prices are too many koruny for your comfort, a good alternative is picking up a book on the artist's exhibition, also for sale here. ⊠ *Betlémské nám. 8, Staré Mesto* ☎ *222–220–689* ⊕ *www.galerieubetlemskekaple.cz* Ⓜ *Line B: Národní třída.*

## BEAUTY

### Botanicus

**PERFUME/COSMETICS** | Organic body and bath products here, like "lettuce and olive oil" soap, are crafted from fresh fruits, vegetables, and herbs on a rural Czech farm. Inside the spacious and fragrant store there are myriad other all-natural products that make charming gifts for those back home, including tempting chutneys and condiments. ⊠ *Týnsky Dvůr 3, Staré Mesto* ☎ *234–767–446* ⊕ *www.botanicus.cz* Ⓜ *Line B: Náměstí Republiky.*

### Kosmetické delikatesy Madeleine

**PERFUME/COSMETICS** | Like a perfume delicatessen, this lovely shop has flowers in the window and perfumes lining the walls; it's a calming presence near Old Town Square. The friendly staff will help you choose the scent that suits you best. ⊠ *Dlouhá 10, Staré Mesto* ☎ *721–110–716* ⊕ *www.madeleine.cz* Ⓜ *Line A: Staroměstská.*

### ★ Manufaktura

**CRAFTS** | Established in 1991 in a bid to preserve traditional Czech and Moravian crafts, Manufaktura is now a thriving business with branches across the country. At this centrally located outpost, home-spa products like bath salts and creams are arranged in a pleasant, folksy manner, as are cosmetics made with Czech beer—yes, beer. ⊠ *Celetná 12, Staré Mesto* ☎ *601–310–608* ⊕ *www.manufaktura.cz* Ⓜ *Line B: Staroměstská.*

### Perfumed Prague

**SPA/BEAUTY** | It looks like a magician's workshop, accessed through a curved door into a rustic tunnel-style interior, full of potions and bottles, and the truth is not that far off: a perfume studio where customers can conjure up (with the expert help of staff) their own personalized fragrances, in the first outfit of its kind in Prague. There are also off-the-shelf perfumes and candles, and all products are eco-friendly. ⊠ *Karolíny Světlé 20, Staré Mesto* ☎ *607–800–307* ⊕ *www.perfumedprague.cz* ⊘ *Closed Sun. and Mon.* Ⓜ *Line B: Národní třída.*

## BOOKS AND PRINTS

### Galerie Antikvariat Ztichlá klika

**BOOKS/STATIONERY** | Rare books, old books, new books, art—this place is cavernous, but it has something for everyone. It's partly underground too, which only adds to the appeal. Be warned: you might lose hours browsing the shelves and shelves of books and walls of photographs and paintings, all of which are for sale. Be sure to take a moment to appreciate the quirky signage as well—the shop is also known as the "blue tiger," for reasons that will become obvious. It's only open Tuesday–Friday 1–7 pm. ⊠ *Betlémská 10–14, Staré Mesto* ☎ *222–222–079* ⊕ *www.ztichlaklika.cz* ⊘ *Closed Sat.–Mon.* Ⓜ *Line B: Národní třída.*

### Kavka Book

**BOOKS/STATIONERY** | This attractive store on a quiet Staré Město corner is pretty much a temple dedicated to art books. It's a pleasant place to browse, and while many of the books are in the Czech language, there's a foreign section and art available to buy, too. Some of the photography books are fantastic: Tomáš Princ's *Humans of Prague,* pictures of people walking the city streets who respond yes when he asks if he can take their picture, is a particular highlight. ⊠ *Krocínova 5, Staré Mesto* ☎ *606–030–202* ⊕ *www.kavkaartbooks.com* ⊘ *Closed Sun.* Ⓜ *Line B: Národní třída.*

## CLOTHING

### Beata Rajska

**CLOTHING** | The shop is imposing, and the sales assistants are positively forbidding, but don't let that deter you, because the clothes are worth it. Many of the pieces would make fantastic special-occasion outfits, so it's not surprising to learn that this eponymous Slovak-run designer shop dressed contestants for the Miss Czech Republic, Miss Europe, and Miss World pageants throughout the early 2000s (although the clothes are less ostentatious than that might suggest). If nothing else, it's fun to try a few items on and think, "Someday... " ⊠ *Dlouhá 3, Staré Mesto* ☏ *731–412–288* ⊕ *www.beatarajska.com* 🕘 *Closed Sun.* Ⓜ *Line B: Staroměstská.*

### Boheme

**CLOTHING** | The understated clothes and decor here tend toward creamy tones, muted grays, and warm browns. Czech designer Hana Stocklassa's garments are classics with unexpected elements—modern takes on knitwear or a shirt with a collar that's cut like a paper chain. Trying things on is a pleasure beneath the golden lighting from round overhead lamps. ⊠ *Dušní 8, Staré Mesto* ☏ *224–813–840* ⊕ *www.boheme.cz* Ⓜ *Line B: Náměstí Republiky.*

### Denim Heads

**CLOTHING** | Half of the world's population wears jeans every day, reasoned the bloke-y team behind this hip denim shop, so surely there is a gap in the market for a funky, quality denim brand in Prague's Staré Město. They weren't wrong, and it doesn't hurt that their shop—and the team behind it—is pretty cool; they're often found sipping a beer on the street underneath the horse's head mounted by the shop entrance at 6 pm, as the evening shoppers approach. ⊠ *Konviktská 30, Staré Mesto* ☏ *224–283–974* ⊕ *denimheads.cz* 🕘 *Closed Sun.* Ⓜ *Line B: Národní třída.*

### DNB

**CLOTHING** | Inside her chic studio close to the river, Czech designer Denisa Nova shows off carelessly sexy clothing that is both wearable and luxurious. Slouchy dresses, extra-long silk T-shirts, and an occasional pop of color (think electric-blue skirts) seal the effortless deal. You can get a personal consultation with the designer if you book ahead. ⊠ *Naprstkova 4, Staré Mesto* ☏ *222–221–342* ⊕ *www.denisanova.cz* 🕘 *Closed Sun.* Ⓜ *Line B: Národní třída.*

### Klára Nademlýnská

**CLOTHING** | If there's one word that describes this boutique—just off Old

# Pop-up Prague

The fad for "pop-up" shops has not passed Prague by—so make sure to explore if you see a promising-looking, hastily scrawled sign in Staré Město. Half the fun is getting lost down the alleyways and making your own discoveries anyway.

Town Square—and the wares within, it's "funky." Catering to moneyed but carefree hipsters (and hippies), this Czech designer excels in the little details—unusual draping, old-fashioned linen dresses, an unexpected giraffe print—that make each item unique and original. ⊠ *Dlouhá 3, Staré Mesto* ☏ *224–818–769* ⊕ *www.klaranademlynska.cz* 🕘 *Closed Sun.* Ⓜ *Line B: Náměstí Republiky.*

### ★ Leeda

**CLOTHING** | This artistic-minded shop is chic, original, and just a little bit mad. Stocked with genuine and original Czech designs, items range from painted dresses to billowing silk skirts. The designer collaborates with graphic designers, photographers, and musicians, which makes the little store feel all the more like a great embodiment of Czech style. ⊠ *Bartolomějská 1, Staré Mesto* ☏ *775–601–185* ⊕ *www.leeda.cz* 🕘 *Closed Sun.* Ⓜ *Line B: Národní třída.*

### Parazit Fashion Store

**CLOTHING** | A cool, graffiti-chic space that champions Czech and Slovak fashion students and young designers making limited-edition clothes, accessories, and gifts. The owners take their fashion seriously, adopting their motto from Nicholas Cage's character in the David Lynch film *Wild at Heart*: "This snakeskin jacket represents a symbol of my individuality and a belief in personal freedom." ⊠ *Karlova 25, Staré Mesto* ☏ *731–171–517* ⊕ *www.parazit.cz* Ⓜ *Line B: Staroměstská.*

### Šatna

**CLOTHING** | This cool little shop specializes in vintage and secondhand finds. If you can face a bit of rummaging, think extremely promising attic (the name means "cloakroom"), with cut-price pieces for men and women from designers like Ralph Lauren, as well as more random bits and pieces. The store also stocks interesting jewelry, including earrings made of headphones and scissors. ⊠ Konviktská 13, Staré Mesto ⊕ prevlikarna.cz Ⓜ Line B: Staroměstská.

## FOOD AND WINE

### Absintherie

**GIFTS/SOUVENIRS** | Absinthe is everywhere in Prague. It's a bit of a tourist cliché, but even if you aren't a fan of the "green fairy," it can be a fun gift for folks back home. This shop is the real deal for the fiery spirit—try a wee nip at the bar while you're there if you're brave enough! There's also an on-site museum with old advertisement posters, bottles, and absinthe spoons. ⊠ Jilská 7, Staré Mesto ☎ 774–229–172 ⊕ www.absintherie.cz Ⓜ Line A: Staroměstská.

## GLASS

### ★ Artěl

**CERAMICS/GLASSWARE** | This American company, led by designer Karen Feldman, merges modern style with traditional Czech techniques, using mouth-blown molten crystal and hand-painted glassware, for instance. Items are so painstakingly crafted that they're bound to become family heirlooms, but all are far from prim. The company also makes handbags to order and has a couple of other shops around town. ⊠ Celetná 29, entrance on Rybna, Staré Mesto ☎ 224–815–085 ⊕ www.artelglass.com Ⓜ Line B: Náměstí Republiky.

### Material

**CERAMICS/GLASSWARE** | The light dancing on the incredibly eye-catching glassware in this elegant boutique makes it almost impossible to walk on by. But the unusual jewelry, stunning brightly colored chandeliers, and an array of beads and Bohemia crystal will make you want to stay and shop. The prices are not for the fainthearted, but the pieces are worth it if you want to bring home something truly original. ⊠ Týn 1 (courtyard Ungelt), Staré Mesto ☎ 608–664–766 ⊕ www.i-material.com Ⓜ Line A: Staroměstská.

### Preciosa

**CERAMICS/GLASSWARE** | A genuine Czech glass success story, Preciosa has its headquarters just outside Prague and is now a global manufacturer, melting 40 tons of glass every day. In this sparkling shop in Staré Město, you can buy the chandeliers, glass sculptures, and jewelry the company is famous for. ⊠ Rytířská 29, Staré Mesto ☎ 488–118–106 ⊕ www.preciosa.com Ⓜ Line B: Můstek.

## HOME AND DESIGN

### Art Shop Prague

**ANTIQUES/COLLECTIBLES** | In this store, the city's famous astronomical clock is old news. The walls are lined with numerous new clock designs from a number of different Czech designers. Some are ceramic and some just totally wacky—from melting timepieces to a clock made out of a baseball glove. ⊠ Malá Štupartská 5, Staré Mesto ☎ 222–313–108 ⊕ www.artshopprague.cz Ⓜ Line A: Staroměstská.

### Deelive Design Store

**GIFTS/SOUVENIRS** | Located inside the SmetanaQ building, a gallery-cum-café-cum–design space right on the river, this fashion and interior design shop showcases the best of Czech design. Some of the artists work in the building's Bottega project on the second floor, and others are located elsewhere, but if you're looking for the most up-to-the-minute Czech design work out there—anything from chic leather backpacks to modernist posters and angular earrings—get it right from the source here. There's a great assortment of ubercool vases, in particular: much better than an "I love Prague" sweater. ⊠ SmetanaQ, Smetanovo nábř.

4, Staré Mesto ☎ 222–263–526 ⊕ deel-ive.cz Ⓜ Line B: Národní třída.

### Fajans Magolika Ungelt

**CERAMICS/GLASSWARE** | Handmade and hand-painted ceramic jugs, plates, and ornaments, from bells to birds, are on offer at this cute little workshop just behind Old Town Square. Made by Juraj Vanya and his sons, the faience pot-tery (high-quality glazed earthenware), covered with traditional Central European designs, is a lovely little souvenir if you can brave putting it in your suitcase. In a sign of the artisanal, authentic nature of this workshop, the potters have another on the historic Zlatá ulička (Golden Lane) in the Prague Castle complex. ✉ Týn 4, Staré Mesto Ⓜ Lines A and B: Můstek.

### ★ Kubista

**HOUSEHOLD ITEMS/FURNITURE** | Located in the stunning House at the Black Madonna, this gorgeous museum shop brings original and replica cubist and art deco pieces into the real world. Marvel at angular black-and-white vases by Vlas-tislav Hofman, and let your eyes linger on the lines of a 1930s tubular armchair. Maps of Prague's art deco, cubist, and modern architecture are also sold here. ✉ Ovocný trh 19, Staré Mesto ☎ 224–236–378 ⊕ www.kubista.cz ⊗ Closed Mon. Ⓜ Line B: Náměstí Republiky.

### Nobis Studio

**HOUSEHOLD ITEMS/FURNITURE** | Want to make over your home? This is interior design of the "whole kitchen" rather than the "one attractive vase" variety, so you won't be able to fit it all into your suitcase, but the sleek store could help unleash your creative potential and provide some inspiration in the form of classic and mod-ern styles. It's a pretty gorgeous place to browse, too, located in a palatial building on trendy Dlouhá. ✉ Dlouhá 32, Staré Mesto ☎ 222–212–859 ⊕ www.nobis.cz Ⓜ Line B: Náměstí Republiky.

### ★ Qubus Design

**GIFTS/SOUVENIRS** | Tucked away on a nar-row stretch of Rámová, this great home-wares shop is made even better by its friendly staff, who might just offer you a cup of coffee. The lure of what's for sale is really the draw here though—a fetch-ing pair of gold ceramic Wellington boots as well as funky home accessories from nonconformist Czech designers, such as some sleek glass shelves bisected by a floor lamp, cabinet, and vase. ✉ Rámová 3, Staré Mesto ☎ 737–921–377 ⊕ www.qubus.cz ⊗ Closed weekends Ⓜ Line B: Náměstí Republiky.

## JEWELRY

### ★ Granát Turnov

**JEWELRY/ACCESSORIES** | You will see signs all over Staré Město advertising authentic Czech garnet, but this is the real deal, complete with certificates of authenticity. This store is part of the Granát Co-op, the world's most prolific producer of Bohemian garnet jewelry. The elegant Dlouhá branch has two separate rooms. Gold and silver jewelry, including an especially nice selec-tion of brooches, is to the right. Pricier dia-mond-clad pieces are to the left. ✉ Dlouhá 28, Staré Mesto ☎ 222–315–612 ⊕ www.granat.cz Ⓜ Line B: Náměstí Republiky.

### Swarovksi Bohemia

**JEWELRY/ACCESSORIES** | There's no avoiding the allure of the crystal on offer from this brand, founded by a Bohemian jeweler living in Austria in 1895. This store, right by Old Town Square, is an attractive out-post, complete with some spectacular crystal pillars. Pick up a playful key-ring charm or glittering bauble at relatively affordable prices. It's worth spending some time reveling in the window-filled space, as shoppers outside point excited-ly at the displays. ✉ Celetná 7, Staré Mes-to ☎ 222–315–585 ⊕ www.swarovski.com Ⓜ Lines A and B: Můstek.

### Wollem

**JEWELRY/ACCESSORIES** | If you are really looking to make a statement, the garnets here are authentic, the designs delicate and attractive (set in rose gold), and the shopping experience very approachable, despite the suitably high price tags. ⊠ *Štupartská 11, Staré Mesto* ⊕ *www.wollem.com* Ⓜ *Lines A and B: Můstek.*

## MARKETS
### Havelská
**OUTDOOR/FLEA/GREEN MARKETS** | Havelská is a charming open-air market, centrally located in Staré Město, featuring touristy kitsch, seasonal trinkets, and handmade jewelry alongside fresh fruits and vegetables. The market is open daily. ⊠ *Havelská, Staré Mesto* Ⓜ *Lines A and B: Můstek.*

## MUSIC
### Music Antiquariat
**MUSIC STORES** | CDs, books, and records are lovingly curated at this music shop tucked behind Old Town Square. The owner lived in West Berlin, where his friend, an autograph hunter, snapped celebrities in their heyday. Now the negatives and pictures decorate the store, alongside old rock-and-roll photographs and postcards that are for sale. It's a delightful throwback to a pre-digital-music era. ⊠ *Týnská ulička 8, Staré Mesto* ☎ *281–865–781* ⊕ *www.musicantiquariat.cz* ⊘ *Closed Sun.* Ⓜ *Line B: Staroměstská.*

## SHOES
### ★ Botas 66
**SHOES/LUGGAGE/LEATHER GOODS** | A revival of an old Czech brand once so iconic that it was not only worn by Czechoslovak Olympians but actually became the word for any sports shoe (*botasky*), these cool sneakers still look the part. Originally restarted as a school project in 2008, the graphic-design pedigree of the team behind the brand is obvious, from the clean lines of the shoes themselves to the bright yellow of the shop. As well as trying on the shoes, you can also look into the brand's history while you're in the store. ⊠ *Skořepka 4, Staré Mesto* ☎ *776–892–069* ⊕ *www.bteam.cz* Ⓜ *Line B: Národní třída.*

## SOUVENIRS
### Lípa
**GIFTS/SOUVENIRS** | Forget the overpriced junk available on every corner, and bag yourself some quality souvenirs here, from Czech designers and producers, in a chic minimalist store. There's an impressive variety of products available, too, from jam and soap to soft toys and wooden bowls. ⊠ *Železná 12, Staré Mesto* ☎ *603–524–782* ⊕ *lipastore.cz* Ⓜ *Lines A and B: Můstek.*

## SPORTING GOODS
### Hudy Sport
**SPORTING GOODS** | Czechs love getting out into nature, so if you are planning to join them or just want to feel like a local, head here, where the two floors overflow with hiking, camping, and rock-climbing equipment from top outdoor brands. This store is also a good place to pick up a backpack, laptop bag, or water bottle. Look for end-of-season sale bins. ⊠ *Na Perštýně 14, Staré Mesto* ☎ *224–218–600* ⊕ *www.hudy.cz/praha.perstyn* Ⓜ *Line B: Náměstí Republiky.*

## TOYS
### ★ Pohádka
**GIFTS/SOUVENIRS | FAMILY** | You'll be drawn in by the amazing window display, which features anything and everything from puppets climbing trees to wooden airplanes. However, you'll stay to be a part of the sheer joy that bursts out of this two-floor toy shop. Packed with attractive wooden toys, stuffed animals, puzzles, and games, it harks back to a more innocent age. There's also a good selection of marionettes if you have your heart set on taking one of these traditional Czech items home. ⊠ *Celetná 32, Staré Mesto* ☎ *224–239–469* ⊕ *www.czechtoys.cz* Ⓜ *Line B: Náměstí Republiky.*

# Josefov

The history of Prague's Jews, like those of much of Europe, is mostly a sad one. There were horrible pogroms in the late Middle Ages, followed by a period of relative prosperity under Rudolf II in the late 16th century, though the freedoms of Jews were still tightly restricted. It was Austrian emperor Josef II—the ghetto's namesake—who did the most to improve the conditions of the city's Jews. His "Edict of Tolerance" in 1781 removed dress codes for Jews and paved the way for them to finally live in other parts of the city.

The prosperity of the 19th century lifted the Jews out of poverty, and many of them chose to leave the ghetto. By the end of the century the number of poor gentiles, drunks, and prostitutes in the ghetto was growing, and the number of actual Jews was declining. At this time, city officials decided to clear the slum and raze the buildings. In their place they built many of the gorgeous turn-of-the-20th-century and art nouveau town houses you see today. Only a handful of the synagogues, the town hall, and the cemetery were preserved.

World War II and the Nazi occupation brought profound tragedy to the city's Jews. A staggering percentage were deported—many to Terezín concentration camp, north of Prague, and then later to German Nazi death camps in Poland. Of the 40,000 Jews living in Prague before World War II, only about 1,200 returned after the war, and merely a handful live in the ghetto today.

The Nazi occupation contains a historic irony. Many of the treasures stored away in the Židovské muzeum v Praze (Prague Jewish Museum) were brought here from across Central Europe on Hitler's orders. His idea was to form a museum dedicated to the soon-to-be extinct Jewish race.

Today, even with the crowds, the former ghetto is a must-see. The Starý židovský hřbitov (Old Jewish Cemetery) alone, with its incredibly forlorn overlay of headstone upon headstone going back centuries, merits the steep admission price the Jewish Museum charges to see its treasures. Don't feel compelled to linger long right at the heart of the ghetto after visiting, though—much of it is tourist-trap territory, filled with overpriced T-shirt, trinket, and toy shops, the same lousy souvenirs found everywhere in Prague. However, the streets around and on the edge of the quarter offer some of the city's best—and weirdly, considering the crush nearby, quietest—bars, shops, and restaurants. Plus, fans of Prague's most famous literary son, Franz Kafka, should spend some time wandering in this area as the writer himself did back in the day. A Czech Jew, he was born in Josefov in 1883, and there are traces of him all over the area, from the houses he lived in to kitschy cafés bearing his name. ■ TIP→ **Take a fantastically informative and evocative tour of Kafka's Prague with the Franz Kafka Society (150 Kč for a 90-minute tour; Široká 14, 224–227–452, www.franz-kafka-soc.cz). The Kafka museum in Malá Strana (260 Kč, Cihelná 2B, 257–535–373, kafkamuseum.cz) is worth a visit, too.**

A ticket to the Prague Jewish Museum includes admission to the Old Jewish Cemetery and collections installed in four surviving synagogues and the Obřadní síň (Ceremony Hall). The Staronová synagóga (Old-New Synagogue), a functioning house of worship, does not technically belong to the museum and requires a separate admission ticket. Alternatively, you can buy a slightly pricier combined ticket, which includes all of the Jewish Museum attractions, plus the Old-New Synagogue. It's called the Pražské Židovské město (Prague Jewish Town) ticket.

#  Sights

### Franz Kafka Monument

**MEMORIAL** | It is fitting that the monument to Franz Kafka in Prague, located close to his birthplace, has a suitably surreal, Kafkaesque feel, depicting a small Kafka-like figure riding on the shoulders of a giant, empty suit. It was inspired by one of his short stories and created by sculptor Jaroslav Róna in 2003, and it now stands proudly on the corner of Dušní. Check out the base for the tiny tribute to arguably his most famous work, *The Metamorphosis*. There are other highlights for Kafka fans in Josefov, too—for example, his birthplace, on the corner of Maiselova and Kaprova, is marked with a bust. ⊠ *Dušní, Josefov* Ⓜ *Line A: Staroměstská.*

### Klausová synagóga (*Klausen Synagogue*)

**RELIGIOUS SITE** | This baroque synagogue, right by the entrance to the Old Jewish Cemetery, displays objects from Czech Jewish traditions, with an emphasis on celebrations and daily life. The synagogue was built at the end of the 17th century in place of three small buildings (a synagogue, a school, and a ritual bath) that were destroyed in a fire that devastated the ghetto in 1689. In the more recent **Ceremony Hall** that adjoins the Klausen Synagogue, the focus is more staid. You'll find a variety of Jewish funeral paraphernalia, including old gravestones, and medical instruments. Special attention is paid to the activities of the Jewish Burial Society through many fine objects and paintings. ⊠ *U starého hřbitova 3A, Josefov* ☎ *222–749–211* ⊕ *www. jewishmuseum.cz* ▣ *Jewish Museum combination ticket 350 Kč (excl. Old-New Synagogue) or 500 Kč (incl. Old-New Synagogue)* ⊘ *Closed Sat. and Jewish holidays* Ⓜ *Line A: Staroměstská.*

### Maiselova synagóga

**RELIGIOUS SITE** | The history of Czech Jews from the 10th to the 18th century is illustrated, accompanied by some of the Prague Jewish Museum's most precious objects. The collection includes silver Torah shields and pointers, spice boxes, and candelabras; historic tombstones; and fine ceremonial textiles—some donated by Mordechai Maisel to the very synagogue he founded. The glitziest items come from the late 16th and early 17th centuries, a prosperous era for Prague's Jews. ⊠ *Maiselova 10, Josefov* ☎ *222–749–211* ⊕ *www.jewishmuseum. cz* ▣ *Jewish Museum combination ticket 350 Kč (excl. Old-New Synagogue) or 500 Kč (incl. Old-New Synagogue)* ⊘ *Closed Sat. and Jewish holidays* Ⓜ *Line A: Staroměstská.*

### Pinkasova synagóga (*Pinkas Synagogue*)

**RELIGIOUS SITE** | Here you'll find two moving testimonies to the appalling crimes perpetrated against the Jews during World War II. One astounds by sheer numbers: the walls are covered with nearly 80,000 names of Bohemian and Moravian Jews murdered by the Nazis. Among them are the names of the paternal grandparents of former U.S. secretary of state Madeleine Albright. The second is an exhibition of drawings made by children at the Nazi concentration camp Terezín, north of Prague. The Nazis used the camp for propaganda purposes to demonstrate their "humanity" toward Jews, and for a time the prisoners were given relative freedom to lead "normal" lives. However, transports to death camps in Poland began in earnest in 1944, and many thousands of Terezín prisoners, including most of these children, eventually perished. The entrance to the Old Jewish Cemetery is through this synagogue. ⊠ *Široká 3, Josefov* ☎ *222–749–211* ⊕ *www. jewishmuseum.cz* ▣ *Jewish Museum combination ticket 350 Kč (excl. Old-New Synagogue) or 500 Kč (incl. Old-New Synagogue)* ⊘ *Closed Sat. and Jewish holidays* Ⓜ *Line A: Staroměstská.*

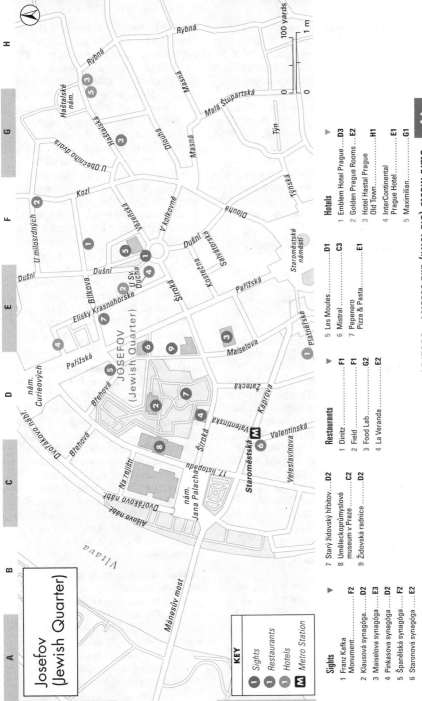

**3**

**Staré Město (Old Town) and Josefov** JOSEFOV

Josefov (Jewish Quarter)

**KEY**
- ① Sights
- ① Restaurants
- ① Hotels
- **M** Metro Station

**Sights** ▶
1 Franz Kafka Monument ..... **F2**
2 Klausová synagóga ..... **D2**
3 Maiselova synagóga ..... **E3**
4 Pinkasova synagóga ..... **D2**
5 Španělská synagóga ..... **F2**
6 Staronová synagóga ..... **E2**
7 Starý židovský hřbitov ..... **D2**
8 Uměleckoprůmyslové museum v Praze ..... **C2**
9 Židovská radnice ..... **D2**

**Restaurants** ▶
1 Dinitz ..... **F1**
2 Field ..... **F1**
3 Food Lab ..... **G2**
4 La Veranda ..... **E2**
5 Les Moules ..... **D1**
6 Mistral ..... **C3**
7 Pepenero Pizza & Pasta ..... **E1**

**Hotels** ▶
1 Emblem Hotel Prague ..... **D3**
2 Golden Prague Rooms ..... **E2**
3 Hotel Hastal Prague Old Town ..... **H1**
4 InterContinental Prague Hotel ..... **E1**
5 Maximilian ..... **G1**

**Španělská synagóga** (*Spanish Synagogue*)
RELIGIOUS SITE | This domed, Moorish-style synagogue was built in 1868 on the site of an older synagogue, the Altschul. Here the historical exposition that begins in the Maisel Synagogue continues to the post–World War II period. The attached Robert Guttmann Gallery has historic and well-curated art exhibitions. The building's painstakingly restored interior is also worth experiencing. ✉ *Vězeňská 1, Josefov* ☎ *222–749–211* ⊕ *www.jewishmuseum.cz* ✉ *Jewish Museum combination ticket 350 Kč (excl. Old-New Synagogue) or 500 Kč (incl. Old-New Synagogue)* ⊘ *Closed Sat. and Jewish holidays.*

**Staronová synagóga** (*Old-New Synagogue, or Altneuschul*)
RELIGIOUS SITE | Dating to the mid-13th century, this is the oldest functioning synagogue in Europe and one of the most important works of early Gothic architecture in Prague. The name refers to the legend that the synagogue was built on the site of an ancient Jewish temple, and the temple's stones were used to build the present structure. Amazingly, the synagogue has survived fires, the razing of the ghetto, and the Nazi occupation intact; it's still in use. The entrance, with its vault supported by two pillars, is the oldest part of the synagogue. Note that men are required to cover their heads inside, and during services men and women sit apart. ✉ *Červená 2, Josefov* ☎ *222–749–211* ⊕ *www.jewishmuseum.cz* ✉ *From 200 Kč* ⊘ *Closed Sat. and Jewish holidays* Ⓜ *Line A: Staroměstská.*

★ **Starý židovský hřbitov** (*Old Jewish Cemetery*)
CEMETERY | An unforgettable sight, this cemetery is where all Jews living in Prague from the 15th century to 1787 were laid to rest. The lack of any space in the tiny ghetto forced graves to be piled on top of one another. Tilted at crazy angles, the 12,000 visible tombstones are but a fraction of countless thousands more buried below. Walk the path amid the gravestones; the relief symbols you see represent the names and professions of the deceased. The oldest marked grave belongs to the poet Avigdor Kara, who died in 1439; the grave is not accessible from the pathway, but the original tombstone can be seen in the Maisel Synagogue. The best-known marker belongs to Jehuda ben Bezalel, the famed Rabbi Loew (died 1609), a chief rabbi of Prague and a profound scholar, credited with creating the mythical golem. Even today, small scraps of paper bearing wishes are stuffed into the cracks of the rabbi's tomb with the hope that he will grant them. Loew's grave lies near the exit. ✉ *Široká 3, entrance through Pinkas Synagogue, Josefov* ☎ *222–749–211* ⊕ *www.jewishmuseum. cz* ✉ *Jewish Museum combination ticket 350 Kč (excl. Old-New Synagogue) or 500 Kč (incl. Old-New Synagogue)* ⊘ *Closed Sat. and Jewish holidays* Ⓜ *Line A: Staroměstská.*

**Uměleckoprůmyslové museum v Praze** (*Museum of Decorative Arts, or U(P)M*)
MUSEUM | In a custom-built art nouveau building from 1897, this wonderfully laid-out museum of exquisite local prints, books, ceramics, textiles, clocks, and furniture will please anyone from the biggest decorative arts expert to those who just appreciate a little *Antiques Roadshow* on the weekend. Superb rotating exhibits, too, and a fantastic design-led gift shop. ✉ *17. listopadu 2, Josefov* ☎ *778–543–900* ⊕ *www.upm. cz* ✉ *300 Kč* ⊘ *Closed Mon.* Ⓜ *Line A: Staroměstská.*

**Židovská radnice** (*Jewish Town Hall*)
BUILDING | You can't just wander into this building as a member of the public, but while you're in the area, it's worth paying attention to the outside. The hall was the creation of Mordechai Maisel, an influential Jewish leader at the end of the 16th century. Restored in the 18th century, it was given a clock and bell tower at

**Thousands of graves, some dating to the 15th century, are layered on top of each other in the Old Jewish Cemetery.**

that time. A second clock, with Hebrew numbers, keeps time counterclockwise. Now a Jewish Community Center, the building also houses Shalom, a kosher restaurant. The restaurant is open to the public for walk-ins during the week, and for Shabbat lunch or dinner if you book, but there are probably better options for dining in this quarter if you don't keep kosher. ✉ *Maiselova 18, Josefov* ☎ *224–800–808* 🌐 *www.kehilaprag.cz* [M] *Line A: Staroměstská.*

## 🍴 Restaurants

Josefov occupies a quiet corner of Staré Město and it can get almost eerie at night. But there are a few good restaurants scattered in and around the neighborhood, and the setting can be magnificent.

### Dinitz

**$$ | MIDDLE EASTERN** | As you would expect, Josefov has some solid kosher options for Jewish travelers. Of these, Dinitz is probably the most welcoming to both Jews and non-Jews and is a relaxed, often buzzing spot for Middle Eastern–inspired food and good grilled meat. **Known for:** reasonably priced kosher food; large portions; tasty hummus and schnitzel sandwiches. [$] *Average main: 300 Kč* ✉ *Bílkova 12, Josefov* ☎ *222–244–000* 🌐 *www.dinitz.cz* 🕒 *No dinner Fri. No lunch Sat.* [M] *Line A: Staroměstská.*

### Field

**$$$ | SCANDINAVIAN** | A relative newcomer to Prague's fine-dining scene, Field has made a splash quickly, grabbing a Michelin star for its locally sourced, Scandi-style seasonal food. While its tasting menu is astronomically expensive, there are cheats: the shorter weekday lunch tasting menu is much more reasonable, at 1,300 Kč, and with a la carte entrées around the 600 Kč mark, it's actually one of the world's more affordably priced Michelin-starred restaurants. **Known for:** sensational seasonal food; an affordable lunchtime tasting menu; stripped-back decor with an eye-catching ceiling.

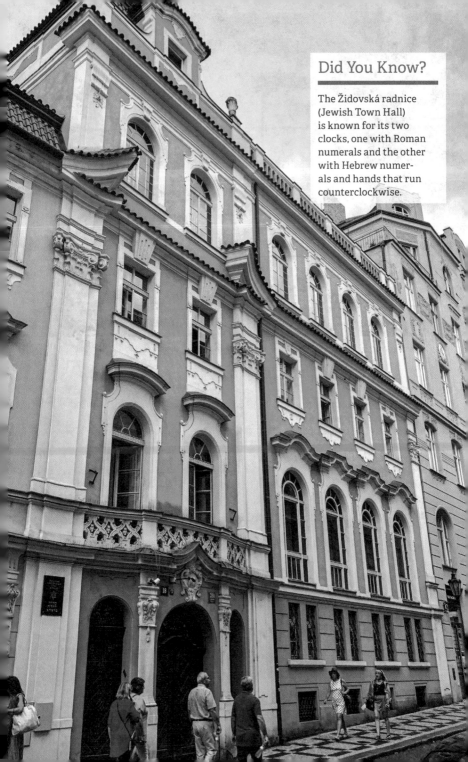

[$] *Average main: 600 Kč* ✉ *U Milosrdných 12, Josefov* ☎ *222–316–999* 🌐 *fieldrestaurant.cz* [M] *Line A: Staroměstská.*

**Food Lab**

$$ | **ECLECTIC** | At last! A huge, hip, all-day dining space on the edge of Staré Město's Jewish quarter. **Known for:** one of Prague's best brunches; well-priced lunch menu; beautiful, plant-filled interior. [$] *Average main: 200 Kč* ✉ *Haštalská 4, Josefov* ☎ *257–310–713* 🌐 *food-lab.cz* [M] *Line A: Haštalská.*

**★ La Veranda**

$$$ | **MODERN EUROPEAN** | Despite the quality of the cooking, La Veranda remains somewhat overlooked by visitors (though popular with locals), making a visit to this stylish, softly lighted room feel like you've been let in on a wonderful secret. The food is top-notch, with seasonal specials and a keenly priced six-course tasting menu showcasing the restaurant's greatest hits, like an incredibly rich beef tartare with egg yolk and black truffle. **Known for:** delicious, seasonal food; non-touristy vibe; reasonable six-course tasting menu. [$] *Average main: 450 Kč* ✉ *Elišky Krásnohorské 2, Josefov* ☎ *224–814–733* 🌐 *www.laveranda.cz* [M] *Line A: Staroměstská.*

**Les Moules**

$$ | **BELGIAN** | Staré Město can sometimes feel relentlessly "olde-worlde" Czech, and Belgian-styled bistro Les Moules represents part of the appeal of dining in Josefov instead, with a more international, modern vibe. There's a nice open terrace and a fine selection of mussels, as you'd expect from the name. **Known for:** mussels prepared 12 different ways; huge Belgian beer selection; brisk, bistro-like feel, overlooking Pařižská. [$] *Average main: 200 Kč* ✉ *Pařížská 19, Josefov* ☎ *222–315–022* 🌐 *www.lesmoules.cz* [M] *Line A: Staroměstská.*

**Mistral**

$$ | **EUROPEAN** | For travelers sick of heavy dumplings, rich fare, and dimly lit cellar pubs, Mistral is an oasis: light, bright, and modern, with a short international menu featuring fresh salads, soups, and pastas, with some Czech specials thrown in. Service is always friendly and somehow the place never seems to be too busy, despite its central location. **Known for:** a gentle hum of conversation in many different languages; fresh cakes; an unusual (in this part of town) focus on vegetables—particularly salads. [$] *Average main: 200 Kč* ✉ *Valentinská 11, Josefov* ☎ *222–317–737* 🌐 *www.mistralcafe.cz* [M] *Line A: Staroměstská.*

**Pepenero Pizza & Pasta**

$$ | **ITALIAN** | Whether Pepenero serves some of the best pizza in Prague is the source of constant debate among locals, but one thing is for sure: it has the city's best mozzarella. Tangy and creamy, the cheese is as authentic as can be. **Known for:** quick and easy food and service; delicious margherita pizza; lively spot. [$] *Average main: 230 Kč* ✉ *Bílkova 4, Josefov* ☎ *222–315–543* 🌐 *www.pepenero.cz* [M] *Line A: Staroměstská.*

## Hotels

**★ Emblem Hotel Prague**

$$$ | **HOTEL** | Rivaling the best design hotels in capital cities around the world, this unique retreat goes toe to toe with many of the city's grande dame hotels; it's smart, fresh, and funky, with a modern art deco theme created by a host of top-notch designers. **Pros:** major design chops; good restaurant; unique focus on modern art. **Cons:** rooms are a little small; rooftop Jacuzzi is an extra charge; underground hotel bar could have more atmosphere. [$] *Rooms from: 7100 Kč* ✉ *Platnéřská 19, Josefov* ☎ *226–202–500* 🌐 *emblemprague.com* 🛏 *59 rooms* 🍴 *No meals* [M] *Line A: Staroměstská.*

**Golden Prague Rooms**

$ | **HOTEL** | A quiet, affordable boutique hotel right in the heart of the Jewish Quarter, the entrance is so subtle you could almost walk past. **Pros:** chic, cubist-style decor; good location; great value. **Cons:** no elevator; some rooms are small; no air-conditioning. [$] *Rooms from: 1700 Kč* ✉ *Elišky Krásnohorské 11/4, Josefov* ☎ *703–147–073* 🌐 *golden-prague-rooms.com* 🛏 *38 rooms* 🍴 *No meals* [M] *Line A: Staroměstská.*

★ **Hotel Hastal Prague Old Town**

$$ | **HOTEL** | A brilliantly priced, charming, family-run hotel located in a quiet spot just a few minutes from Old Town Square, with welcoming touches including complimentary all-day coffee and wine in the lobby or courtyard—oh, and a golem statue out front. **Pros:** great location on a quiet street; pleasant rooms with a/c, some with views over the square; lovely welcome from family who have run the hotel for six generations. **Cons:** breakfast room can get busy; folksy feel might not appeal to everyone; rooms vary in size. [$] *Rooms from: 2500 Kč* ✉ *Haštalská 16, Josefov* ☎ *222–314–335* 🌐 *www.hotelhastalprague.com* 🛏 *31 rooms* 🍴 *Breakfast* [M] *Line A: Staroměstská.*

**InterContinental Prague Hotel**

$$$ | **HOTEL** | Built in the brutalist style in the late 1960s, this building can't really hold a candle to Prague's more ancient architectural treasures, but there are myriad compensations: views over the river, a fantastic roof bar, and an amazing salt-water pool. **Pros:** best swimming pool in central Prague; lovely Sunday brunch with views; great value. **Cons:** ugly exterior; can feel a little impersonal; slightly dated decor in the rooms. [$] *Rooms from: 5000 Kč* ✉ *Pařížská 30, Josefov* ☎ *296–631–111* 🌐 *www.ihg.com* 🛏 *372 rooms* 🍴 *Free Breakfast* [M] *Line B: Staroměstská.*

**Maximilian**

$$$ | **HOTEL** | This design hotel in the heart of Staré Město is a tasteful fusion of light, airy modernism, a look that works perfectly in the lobby, with chrome lamps and square armchairs, but is less successful in the rooms, which can be dark and gloomy. **Pros:** unique vibe: guests can even borrow a goldfish to keep them company; cozy library and honesty bar; relaxing on-site Planet Zen spa. **Cons:** upper-floor rooms could use more light; no in-house restaurant; breakfast is not extensive. [$] *Rooms from: 4900 Kč* ✉ *Haštalská 14, Josefov* ☎ *225–303–111* 🌐 *www.maximilianhotel.com* 🛏 *71 rooms* 🍴 *Breakfast* [M] *Line A: Staroměstská.*

## 🍸 Nightlife

Josefov specializes in the stylish cocktail crowd, plus it's the place to catch the boat for most of the evening cruises. This end of Staré Město also has a major plus: you'll rarely run into stag parties.

### BARS AND PUBS

**Bugsy's**

**BARS/PUBS** | A steel-and-glass, lights-in-the-bar design gives this popular American-style cocktail bar a modern look, and the bartenders, in bow ties and braces, lend a classic touch. The list of drinks has all the expected favorites, and sometimes there's live music. Check out the curio rack showing off one of the last Bacardi rum bottles to come from pre-Castro Cuba. ✉ *Pařížská 10, entrance on Kostečna, Josefov* ☎ *840–284–797* 🌐 *www.bugsysbar.cz* [M] *Line A: Staroměstská.*

**L'Fleur**

**BARS/PUBS** | One of a gaggle of swanky cocktail bars that have recently taken Prague by storm, L'Fleur mixes it with the best of them, blending old-school elegance—although arguably the decoration feels a little generic—and classic cocktails with local flavors (try the Parfum for a hit of traditional Czech spirit, Becherovka). The menu contains some unusual ingredients—so much so that it can be a bit incomprehensible—but friendly staff are happy to explain. It's open extraordinarily late (until 6 am some nights, 3 am others). ✉ *V Kolkovně 920/5, Josefov* ☎ *734–255–665* ⊕ *www.lfleur.cz* Ⓜ *Line A: Staroměstská.*

### Public Interest Bar

**BARS/PUBS** | With a cooler, more modern and stripped-back cocktail bar vibe than some of the others in this quarter, Public Interest has one of those drinks lists where everything is tempting, although the Garden Party is our current favorite (salted caramel makes an appearance, alongside champagne and calvados— what's not to like?). It also serves good coffee if you are looking for a slightly less decadent after-dinner drink. ✉ *U Milosrdných 12, Josefov* ☎ *725–821–878* ⊕ *www.publicinterest.cz* Ⓜ *Line A: Staroměstská.*

### Tretter's

**BARS/PUBS** | The lost elegance of the 1930s, with clean lines on dark wood, is re-created in a bar that serves Manhattans, martinis, and other classic cocktails, sometimes with live jazz in the background. This was a trendsetter in Prague when it first opened for classic cocktails, and it remains a great joint for a sophisticated tipple. Make sure to book in advance on weekends. ✉ *V Kolkovně 3, Josefov* ☎ *224–811–165* ⊕ *www.tretters.cz* Ⓜ *Line A: Staroměstská.*

### U Rudolfina

**BREWPUBS/BEER GARDENS** | Some people claim that the way the beer is tapped here makes it the best in town, which probably explains the constant crowds. This was one of the first places in the world to offer unpasteurized beer from tanks, rather than kegs. And the place still retains its old-fashioned charm, making it one of the best authentic Czech pubs in a heavily touristed area. Groups should make reservations—a free table is rare. ✉ *Křížovnická 10, Josefov* ☎ *222–328–758* ⊕ *www.urudolfina.cz* Ⓜ *Line A: Staroměstská.*

### ★ Zlatá Praha

**PIANO BARS/LOUNGES** | On the roof of this distinctly uninspiring building housing the InterContinental Prague Hotel is a bar with wonderful city views that make it worth the trip up in the lift. The ninth-floor Zlatá Praha restaurant and bar has an outdoor rooftop terrace that is perfect for an evening glass of Bohemia Sekt (Czech sparkling wine) while soaking up the gorgeous vista. Non-guests are welcome, and somehow, the large space retains a sense of clubby exclusivity. ✉ *InterContinental Prague Hotel, Pařížská 30, Josefov* ☎ *296–631–111* ⊕ *www.icprague.com/dining/zlata-praha* Ⓜ *Line A: Staroměstská.*

## EVENING BOAT TRIPS

### Boat Party Prague

**THEMED ENTERTAINMENT** | Join the floating party with a young international crowd for drinking and dancing on an outside deck or inside dance floor. A pre-party kicks off at 8:30, the boat sets sail at 11. The DJ spins pop and dance hits and the ticket includes booze and free entry to a nearby club at 1 am. Party reps sell tickets under the astronomical clock in Old Town Square. ✉ *Dvořákovo nábřeží, Josefov* ☎ *608–543–364* ⊕ *boatpartyprague.com* 💰 *380 Kč–730 Kč* Ⓜ *Line B: Nám. Republiky.*

### Dinner Cruise with Music

**THEMED ENTERTAINMENT** | This "dinner cruise" often degenerates into a sing-along once the beer kicks in, so be prepared for boisterous merriment. The boat is heated, and this cruise runs in both winter and summer. The relatively early departure hour (7 pm) means you can catch the sunset in summertime, and than dine by candlelight, which is lovely. Entry price includes a buffet dinner and welcome drink, but no additional beverages. ✉ *Dvořákovo nábř., under Čechův most, Josefov* ☎ *742–202–505* ⊕ *www.evd.cz* 💰 *1220 Kč* Ⓜ *Line A: Staroměstská.*

## Jazzboat

**THEMED ENTERTAINMENT** | Jazz, food, drinks, floating down the Vltava, and spectacular views of Prague—if you're a jazz fan (or a fan of river cruises), it doesn't get much better than this. The Jazzboat sails throughout the year; blankets are provided if it gets chilly for those sitting outside. The 690 Kč fee includes a welcome drink, but your food bill is separate and there's an extra 100 Kč fee for peak nights, and for window seats. ■ **TIP ➔ Be punctual, as the boat sails at 8:30 pm on the dot.** ✉ *Josefov ✛ Usually takes off from Pier 2, under Čechův most* ☎ *731–183–180* ⊕ *www.jazzboat.cz* Ⓜ *Line A: Staroměstská.*

#  Performing Arts

## CHURCH CONCERTS

**Kostel sv. Šimona a Judy** (*Church of Sts. Simon and Jude*)

**CONCERTS** | This decommissioned church with a restored organ and frescoes is used by the Prague Symphony Orchestra for chamber concerts and recitals, and it's also a popular venue for music festivals. The baroque altar is actually an elaborate painting on the wall. ✉ *Dušní ul., Josefov* ☎ *222–002–336* ⊕ *www.fok. cz/cs/kostel-sv-simona-judy* Ⓜ *Line A: Staroměstská.*

#  Shopping

Shopping in Josefov is a tale of two cities. Firstly, and most dramatically, it is bisected by Pařížská, Prague's swankiest shopping street. A long, straight boulevard from Old Town Square down to the river, Pařížská boasts all of the world's fanciest labels and parking spaces housing Bugattis and Bentleys, but not much in the way of a unique Czech vibe. It's a nice enough tree-lined stroll, though, if only to see how the other half lives. More interesting, however, are the side streets that wind around this ancient quarter, housing fantastic and unique boutiques of all hues, as well as bookshops and even an old-fashioned general store.

## ACCESSORIES

### ★ BackYard Boutique

**CLOTHING** | A large, extremely hip space that is more than just a shop; it's also a design collective where you can meet jewelers and fashion designers, see their work, hear lectures, or just have a coffee or a glass of wine. The neon sign glimpsed from across the street is enticing, and the light-filled interior does not disappoint: from Nastassia Aleinikava's modern baroque flower-stuffed necklaces and out-there specs to unique jackets made from recycled jeans from Restore by Acarin, these are some of the coolest modern design pieces in the city. ✉ *U Obecního dvora 2, Josefov* ☎ *605–894–096* ⊕ *www. back-yard.cz* Ⓜ *Line A: Staroměstská.*

### Kara

**CLOTHING** | It may not be for everyone, but if you are a fan of natural leather and fur products, Kara is probably the top Czech brand in this area. This small, high-quality boutique showcases butter-soft leather jackets, mink fur gloves, and handbags with raccoon-fur pom-poms, among many other items, all of which would provide more than adequate protection against the fierce Czech winter. ✉ *Maiselova 12, Josefov* ☎ *734–257–620* ⊕ *www. kara.cz* Ⓜ *Line A: Staroměstská.*

## BEAUTY

### Ingredients

**PERFUME/COSMETICS** | An extremely swanky beauty boutique run by two Czechs, with Sisley Boudoir, the on-site aromatherapy and treatment center. Rare perfumes, skin-care products, and candles are displayed amid contemporary Czech art in such a crisp display that it borders on clinical. ✉ *Maiselova 41/21, Josefov* ☎ *211–150–159* ⊕ *www.ingredients-store.cz* Ⓜ *Line A: Staroměstská.*

## BOOKS

### Franz Kafka Bookshop

BOOKS/STATIONERY | Franz Kafka is one of Prague's most famous sons, and he is celebrated throughout the city, but perhaps nowhere more gently and authentically than in this old-fashioned, atmospheric bookshop, run by the Franz Kafka Society. As well as Czech books, there are English versions of Kafka's works, as well as other classics and books about Prague. Talks and events like drawing workshops are held here, too, and there's a Kafka exhibition in the courtyard. Check out the lovely double-height bookshelves, accessed by a ladder on wheels. ⊠ *Široká 14, Josefov* ☎ *224–241–346* ⊕ *www.franzkafka-soc. cz/knihkupectvi* Ⓜ *Line A: Staroměstská.*

## CLOTHING

### La Sartoria

CLOTHING | Big, luxurious rugs, Frank Sinatra playing in the background, a set of whiskey glasses in the window, and the dartboard. Oh, right: there are clothes, too, such as beautifully made Neapolitan-style men's suits and jackets perfect for a weekend in the country. There's a tailoring service, too. ⊠ *Haštalska 9, Josefov* ☎ *606–788–878* ⊕ *www. lasartoria.cz* Ⓜ *Line A: Staroměstská.*

### Navarila

CLOTHING | Czech designer Martina Nevarilova offers a great line of relaxed and cozy knitwear, often in bold colors or stripes. The shops are worth a look if you're feeling the chill of the Prague winter or if you're on the hunt for a classy and unique cover-up for other occasions. There is another boutique on Vodičkova in Nové Město. ⊠ *Haštalska 8, Josefov* ☎ *222–311–748* ⊕ *www.navarila.cz* Ⓜ *Line B: Národní třída.*

### Space Praga

CLOTHING | One of the coolest shops in Prague, Space is usually teeming with funky young Czechs on the lookout for something new and different. The garments, from a mixture of local and global, new and established, fashion houses, are beautiful, from the distressed jackets to the bright shirts; browsing the racks makes you feel like you're looking through somebody's wonderful closet. This is the menswear branch; the women's shop, which collaborates with leading Czech leather and fur specialist Ivana Mentlova, is a few streets over at Rámová 1. ⊠ *Vězeňská 6, Josefov* ☎ *725–100–317* ⊕ *spacepraga.com* Ⓜ *Line A: Staroměstská.*

### Timoure et Group

CLOTHING | Led by two Czech designers, this label churns out sleek, minimalist career and casual wear like wrap dresses and trenches. The flagship Prague store is relaxed and welcoming, with elegant T-shirts neatly displayed. ⊠ *V Kolkovné 6, Josefov* ☎ *222–327–358* ⊕ *www. timoure.cz* Ⓜ *Line A: Staroměstská.*

### Tina Hollas

CLOTHING | This hidden-away little studio and shop offers organic clothing and accessories, following the designer Martina Hollasová's belief that the materials we have close to our bodies can have a real impact on our lives. The pieces are elegant, expensive, and simple, but never boring, from beige swing coats to loose cream dresses. Custom consultations are available. ⊠ *U Obecního dvora 4, Josefov* ☎ *602–325–125* ⊕ *www.tinahollas.com* Ⓜ *Line A: Staroměstská.*

### ★ Vidda

CLOTHING | Do not waste your time with the typical multinational brands stationed on Pařížská. Instead, pop round the corner to this lovely, minimalist clothing and lifestyle store, check out its roster of stylish Czech and Slovak fashion, and buy yourself a cup of coffee while you chat with the friendly owner, perched on one of the small tables by the entrance. A lovely place to while away half an hour or more, while also probably picking up some unique items to take home. ⊠ *Elišky Krásnohorské 9, Josefov* ☎ *739–333–444* ⊕ *lagallery.cz* ⊙ *Closed Sun.* Ⓜ *Line A: Staroměstská.*

## FOOD AND DRINK

### ★ Masna na Kozím plácku

**FOOD/CANDY** | This food shop on a quiet stretch of Kozí is like walking into a bygone era before supermarkets took over the high street. Think the best bread, meat, and cheese shop from the 18th century that you can possibly imagine, and you've just described this place. Shelves groan with fresh produce, the air is full of delicious smells, and friendly staff are ready to help tease your taste buds. ■ TIP→ **You can get freshly cooked meaty meals here, too—a worthy alternative to the extremely popular, and busy, Naše maso butcher's shop on Dlouhá. Dobrou chut'! (That's Czech for "Bon appétit!")** ⊠ Kozí 9, Josefov ☎ 255–795–404 Closed Sun. ⊕ www.masnakozi.cz Ⓜ Line B: Staroměstská.

### Tretter's Gallery Spirits Shop

**SPECIALTY STORES** | If you liked the sophisticated cocktail bar of the same name just round the corner, why not take a bit of it home with you? This little store, a spin-off of the bar, takes its alcohol seriously and offers tastings and many unique and rare bottles—and even offers to buy unusual spirits that customers may have in their collections. There are also some branded products and retro accessories. ⊠ Kozí 9, Josefov ☎ 224–815–848 ⊕ www.tretters-spirits.cz Ⓜ Line A: Staroměstská.

## HOME AND DESIGN

### Glassimo

**CERAMICS/GLASSWARE** | Josefov's answer to Staré Město's glass stores certainly holds its own. A bright space filled with amazing Czech glass sculptures, as well as porcelain pieces and contemporary art, Glassimo is a good option if you just have to take home some Bohemian glassware. The light fittings made by Kateřina Smolíková and Italy bowls and vases by Jiří Pačínek are unique to the store. ⊠ Elišky Krásnohorské 3, Josefov ☎ 702–181–804 ⊕ www.glassimo.eu Ⓜ Line A: Staroměstská.

## JEWELRY

### Antiques Cinolter

**ANTIQUES/COLLECTIBLES** | This traditional antiques store, with its wares displayed in cases and on dark wood tables, specializes in jewelry and gems but also has a great line in silverware of various kinds. There are some really unusual rings and brooches, as well as pieces like a vintage umbrella and a cobalt vase. Established in 1991 by gemologist Martin Cinolter, the store also makes bespoke pieces, including a miniature version of the Czech crown jewels for the Dalai Lama when he visited Prague. ⊠ Maiselova 9, Josefov ☎ 222–319–816 ⊕ antiquesprague.cz Ⓜ Line A: Staroměstská.

### Halada

**JEWELRY/ACCESSORIES** | This classy Czech-German jewelry company, set up by a couple in the 1970s, supplies trinkets by carefully chosen brands and produces its own pieces and is probably the only home-grown brand on swanky Pařížská. It holds its own against the international big hitters, offering stunning pearls in different shades, as well as gold, silver, and platinum items. This branch offers the most varied selection, while the serene shop on Na příkopě focuses on pearls. ⊠ Pařížská 7, Josefov ☎ 724–986–111 ⊕ www.halada.cz Ⓜ Line A: Staroměstská.

### Zlatnictví Miloslav Ráž

**JEWELRY/ACCESSORIES** | The real treat at this old-school jewelry store is getting a glimpse of the jeweler at work—he may even give you a wave if you're lucky. The store has a variety of items including rings and other jewels, some of which are displayed in the window, but you can also create your own unique piece with a designer. It can be expensive, but you're getting handcrafted items with real gems, after all. ⊠ V Kolkovně 8, Josefov ☎ 603–440–874 ⊕ www.zlatnictviraz.cz Ⓜ Line A: Staroměstská.

# Chapter 4

# MALÁ STRANA

4

Updated by
Jennifer Rigby

| ⊙ Sights | 🍴 Restaurants | 🛏 Hotels | 🛍 Shopping | 🍸 Nightlife |
|---|---|---|---|---|
| ★★★☆☆ | ★★★★☆ | ★★★★☆ | ★★★☆☆ | ★★☆☆☆ |

# CHARLES BRIDGE

This is Prague's signature monument. The view from the foot of the bridge on the Staré Město side, encompassing the towers and domes of Malá Strana and the soaring spires of Katedrála sv. Víta (St. Vitus Cathedral), is nothing short of breathtaking.

This heavenly vista subtly changes in perspective as you walk across the bridge, attended by a host of baroque saints that decorate the bridge's peaceful Gothic stones. At night its drama is spellbinding: St. Vitus Cathedral lit in a ghostly green, the castle in monumental yellow, and the Church of St. Nicholas in a voluptuous pink, all viewed through the menacing silhouettes of the bowed statues and the Gothic towers. Night is the best time to visit the bridge, which is choked with visitors and vendors by day. The later the hour, the thinner the crowds—though the bridge is never truly empty, even at daybreak. ■ TIP→ If you want a bit more space to appreciate the views, including of the Charles Bridge itself, head to Mánesův most (Mánes Bridge) a little up the river by the Rudolfinum in Josefov.

The bridge is open all day, every day, and entry is free. The easiest way to find the bridge from Staroměstské náměstí (Old Town Square) is to follow the narrow, winding Karlova lane, which begins on the western end of Malé náměstí, just next to Old Town Square, and takes you, twisting and turning, to the foot of the bridge. From the Malá Strana side, start from central Lesser Quarter Square and follow the street Mostecká directly to the bridge (you can't miss it).

## A BRIEF HISTORY OF THE BRIDGE

When the Přemyslid princes set up residence in Prague during the 10th century, there was a ford across the Vltava here—a vital link along one of Europe's major trading routes. After several wooden bridges and the first stone bridge washed away in floods, Charles IV appointed the 27-year-old German Peter Parler, the architect of St. Vitus Cathedral, to build a new structure in 1357. It became one of the wonders of the world in the Middle Ages.

After 1620, following the disastrous defeat of Czech Protestants by Catholic Habsburgs at the Battle of White Mountain, the bridge became a symbol of the Counter-Reformation's vigorous re-Catholicization efforts.

The religious conflict is less obvious nowadays, leaving behind only an artistic tension between baroque and Gothic that gives the bridge its allure.

## ABOUT THE TOWER

Staroměstská mostecká věž (Old Town Bridge Tower), at the bridge entrance on the Staré Město side, is where Peter Parler, the architect of the Charles Bridge, began his bridge building. The carved façades he designed for the sides of the tower were destroyed by Swedish soldiers in 1648, at the end of the Thirty Years' War. The sculptures facing Staré Město, however, are still intact (although some are recent copies). They depict an old and gout-ridden Charles IV with his son, who became Wenceslas IV. Above them are two of Bohemia's patron saints, Adalbert of Prague and Sigismund. The top of the tower offers a spectacular view of the city for 100 Kč; it's open daily from 10 to 10 in the summer, closing earlier in the winter.

## TOURING THE BRIDGE, STATUE BY STATUE

Take a closer look at some of the statues while walking toward Malá Strana. The third one on the right, a bronze crucifix from the mid-17th century, is the oldest of all. The fifth on the left, which shows St. Francis Xavier carrying four pagan princes (an Indian, Moor, Chinese, and Tartar) ready for conversion, represents an outstanding piece of baroque sculpture. Eighth on the right is the statue of St. John of Nepomuk, who according to legend was wrapped in chains and thrown to his death from this bridge. Touching the statue is supposed to bring good luck or, according to some versions of the story, a return visit to Prague.

# NEIGHBORHOOD SNAPSHOT

## TOP EXPERIENCES

■ **Charles Bridge:** Walk over very early in the morning to avoid the crowds and bathe in its beauty.

■ **Baráčnická rychta:** Pretend you're a local, supping beers with the authentic crowd at this joint.

■ **Shopping:** Nail shopping for souvenirs at Pragtique, some serious Czech design at the Chemistry Design Store, or the best Czech puppets in town at Marionety.

■ **Terasa U Zlaté studně:** Break the bank—it's worth it—here, with a swanky lunch accompanied by a drop-dead-gorgeous view.

■ **Kampa:** Soak up the riverside calm (don't miss the weird baby sculptures or the graffiti at the nearby John Lennon wall), or head up peaceful Petřín.

■ **Kostel sv. Mikuláše (Church of St. Nicholas):** One of the most beautiful examples of baroque church architecture in Prague (and that's really saying something).

## GETTING HERE

Metro Line A will lead you to Malá Strana (Lesser Quarter), with Malostranská station the most central stop (from here, you can either walk or take Tram 12, 20, or 26 one stop to Malostranské náměstí, or Lesser Quarter Square). Various other trams also come into the main square from all over town, including Trams 15, 22, and 23. But there's no better way to arrive at Malá Strana than a scenic downhill walk from the castle or a lovely stroll from Staré Město (Old Town) across the Charles Bridge.

## PLANNING YOUR TIME

Note that in summer, the heat builds up during the day in this area—as do the crowds—so it's best visited before noon or in the early evening, and allow at least a couple of hours to tick off the main sights. On pretty much every block there are plenty of cafés in which to stop, sip coffee or tea, and people-watch and a wealth of gardens and parks ideal for resting in the cool shade.

## QUICK BITES

■ **Roesel.** Craft beer and cake is a great refueling combination in this cute, family-run café in a historic building (check out the mini-exhibition on the way in). ✉ *Mostecká 20, Malá Strana* ⊕ *roesel-beer-cake. business.site*

■ **Bread Gap.** For a quick lunch on the go, walk smugly past the greasy international chains and come here for tasty fresh sandwiches, salads, and barista-brewed coffees. ✉ *Tržiště 3, Malá Strana* ⊕ *www.breadgap.cz*

■ **Angelato.** Across from the Újezd tram stop, this gelato gem offers delicious, homemade ice cream and gelato almost all year. ✉ *Újezd 24, Malá Strana* ⊕ *angelato.cz*

Established in 1257, this is Prague's most perfectly formed—yet totally asymmetrical—neighborhood. Translated as the "Lesser Quarter" and also known as "Little Town," it was originally home to the merchants and craftsmen who served the royal court, itself housed in the famous castle that sits just above this district. Don't let the diminutive moniker fool you, though; Malá Strana is small, but its charm more than stands up to the rest of the city center, and it can be less crowded, particularly off the main drag.

Though it is not nearly as confusing as the labyrinth that is Staré Město, the streets here can baffle, but they also bewitch, with hidden alleyways, uneven, ancient stone steps, and baroque gems on every corner. Originally a cluster of noble homes and palaces, today the area holds embassies, Czech government offices, historical attractions, and galleries, mixed in with the usual glut of pubs, restaurants, and souvenir shops. The neighborhood also boasts some pretty squares, gorgeous gardens, and the green spaces of Kampa and Petřín, giving it a sense of calm that's a welcome bonus, particularly after tackling the crowds that rightfully pack themselves onto Charles Bridge for some of the most arresting urban vistas in the world.

Other than the bridge, Malá Strana isn't as studded with "must-sees" as Staré Město, but take time to experience the architecture and the history of its streets. The shopping is an interesting mix, with some cool Czech design interspersed with more traditional tourist fare. Malá Strana also has a varied eating offer, including down-to-earth Czech joints as well as some of the city center's fanciest restaurants with views. The area is quiet at night, which can make for enchanting lamplit walks and a good option for those who prefer more chill accommodation, often featuring the historical quirks that make this centuries-old, architecturally rich neighborhood such a magical place to explore.

##  Sights

★ **Charles Bridge** (*Karlův most*)
**BUILDING** | This is Prague's most iconic and popular attraction, and rightly so. The view from the foot of the bridge on

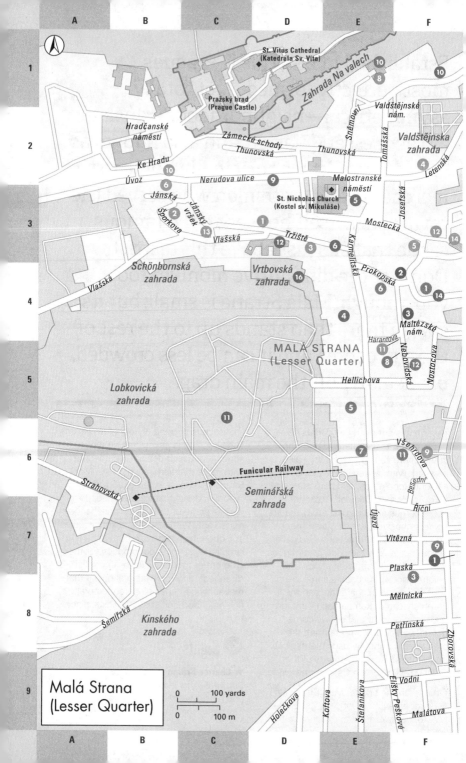

## Sights ▼

1 Charles Bridge .......... **H4**
2 Franz Kafka Museum... **H3**
3 Kampa ................... **G5**
4 Kostel Panny Marie
   vítězné ................... **E4**
5 Kostel sv.
   Mikuláše ................. **E3**
6 Malostranské
   náměstí ................... **E3**
7 Museum Kampa ........ **G5**
8 Na Kampě .............. **G4**
9 Nerudova ulice......... **D2**
10 Palácové zahrady
   pod Pražským
   hradem................... **F1**
11 Petřínské sady .......... **C5**
12 Schönbornský palác ... **D3**
13 Valdštejnska
   zahrada ................. **G1**
14 Velkopřevorské
   náměstí .................. **F4**
15 Vojanovy sady.......... **G2**
16 Vrtbovská zahrada...... **D4**

## Restaurants ▼

1 Café de Paris............. **F4**
2 Hergetova Cihelna...... **H3**
3 Ichnusa Botega
   & Bistro .................. **F8**
4 Kampa Park ............. **G5**
5 Luka Lu................... **E5**
6 The Mailroom
   & Bistro .................. **E4**
7 NOI ....................... **E6**
8 Spices Restaurant
   & Bar..................... **F5**
9 The Sushi Bar............ **F7**
10 Terasa U Zlaté
   studně.................... **E1**
11 Tlustá myš ............... **F6**
12 U Modré kachničky...... **F5**

## Quick Bites ▼

1 Café Savoy .............. **F7**
2 Cukrkávalimonáda....... **F4**
3 Kafíčko ................... **F4**

## Hotels ▼

1 Alchymist Grand Hotel
   and Spa ................. **D3**
2 Appia Hotel
   Residences.............. **B3**
3 Aria Hotel .............. **D3**
4 Augustine, a Luxury
   Collection Hotel,
   Prague ................... **F2**
5 Domus Balthasar ....... **F3**
6 Dům U
   Červeného Lva .......... **B2**
7 EA Residence
   U Bílé kuželky .......... **G3**
8 Golden Well Hotel ....... **E1**
9 Hotel Kampa Stará
   zbrojnice................. **F6**
10 Hotel Neruda ........... **B2**
11 Mandarin Oriental
   Prague ................... **F4**
12 Pod Věží.................. **F3**
13 Sax Vintage
   Design Hotel.............. **C3**
14 U Tří Pštrosů.............. **F3**

**4**

**Malá Strana**

### KEY

● Sights
● Restaurants
● Quick Bites
● Hotels

Klárov
Vojanovy sady
Chelná
U lužického semináře
Na Kampě
Hroznová
Vltava
U Sovových mlýnů
most Legii
Střelecký ostrov
Janáčkovo nábř.
Dětský ostrov

Stop at the Franz Kafka Museum to see a number of first edition Kafka books, original letters, diaries, and drawings created by Kafka.

the Staré Město side, encompassing the towers and domes of Malá Strana and the soaring spires of St. Vitus Cathedral, is breathtaking. After several wooden bridges and the first stone bridge washed away in floods, Charles IV appointed the 27-year-old German Peter Parler, the architect of St. Vitus Cathedral, to build a new structure in 1357. It became one of the wonders of the world in the Middle Ages. Its heavenly vista subtly changes in perspective as you walk across the bridge, attended by a host of baroque saints from the late 17th century (most now copies) that decorate the bridge's peaceful Gothic stones. Touching the statue of St. John of Nepomuk is thought to bring good luck or a return visit to Prague. Try to visit at night, the least busy time, and climb the **Staroměstská mostecká věž** (Old Town Bridge Tower) for a spectacular view. ☒ *Staré Mesto* Ⓜ Line A: *Staroměstská.*

### Franz Kafka Museum

MUSEUM | The great early-20th-century Jewish author Franz Kafka wasn't considered to be Czech and he wrote in German, but he lived in Prague nearly his entire life, so it's fitting that his shrine is here, too. The museum's designers have created exhibits true to Kafka's darkly paranoid and paradoxical work; though not for young children, they're fascinating to anyone familiar with Kafka's work. Facsimiles of manuscripts, documents, first editions, photographs, and newspaper obits are displayed in glass vitrines situated in "Kafkaesque" settings: huge open filing cabinets, stone gardens, piles of coal. The even freakier basement level features expressionistic representations of Kafka's work itself, including a model of the horrible torture machine from the "In the Penal Colony" story. Other Kafka sites include his home on Zlatá ulička (Golden Lane), his birthplace at Náměstí Franze Kafky 3, and Jaroslav Rona's bronze sculpture on Dušní street in Staré Město. The animatronic *Piss* statue in the Kafka Museum's courtyard is by local sculptor David Černý. ☒ *Cihelná 2B, Malá Strana* ☎ *257–535–507* ⊕ *www.kafkamuseum.cz* ▣ *260 Kč* Ⓜ Line A: *Malostranská.*

## Kampa

**CITY PARK | FAMILY |** Prague's largest "island" is cut off from the "mainland" by the narrow Čertovka streamlet. The name Čertovka, or "Devil's Stream," reputedly refers to a cranky old lady who once lived on Maltézské náměstí. During the historic 2002 floods, the well-kept lawns of the **Kampa Gardens,** which occupy much of the island, were underwater, as was much of the lower portion of Malá Strana. Evidence of flood damage occasionally marks the landscape, along with a sign indicating where the waters crested. These days, the green space is a lovely, calm place to avoid the crowds, even on the hottest days. Don't miss another of leading Czech public artist David Černý's works in the middle of the island, too: giant crawling babies with what look like barcodes in place of their faces. ⊠ *Malá Strana* Ⓜ *Line A: Malostranská.*

## Kostel Panny Marie vítězné (*Church of Our Lady Victorious*)

**RELIGIOUS SITE |** This aging, well-appointed church on Malá Strana's main street is the unlikely home of Prague's most famous religious artifact, the Pražské Jezulátko (Infant Jesus of Prague). Originally brought to Prague from Spain in the 16th century, the wax doll holds a reputation for bestowing miracles on many who have prayed for its help. A measure of its widespread attraction is reflected in the prayer books on the kneelers in front of the statue, which have prayers of intercession in 20 different languages. The Bambino, as he's known locally, has an enormous and incredibly ornate wardrobe, some of which is on display in a museum upstairs. Nuns from a nearby convent change the outfit on the statue regularly. Don't miss the souvenir shop (accessible via a doorway to the right of the main altar), where the Bambino's custodians flex their marketing skills. ⊠ *Karmelitská 9A, Malá Strana* ☎ *257–533–646* ⊕ *www.pragjesu.cz* 🕾 *Free* Ⓜ *Line A: Malostranská plus Tram 12, 20, or 22.*

## Kostel sv. Mikuláše (*Church of St. Nicholas*)

**RELIGIOUS SITE |** With its dynamic curves, this church is arguably the purest and most ambitious example of high baroque in Prague. The celebrated architect Christoph Dientzenhofer began the Jesuit church in 1704 on the site of one of the more active Hussite churches of 15th-century Prague. Work on the building was taken over by his son Kilian Ignaz Dientzenhofer, who built the dome and presbytery. Anselmo Lurago completed the whole thing in 1755 by adding the bell tower. The juxtaposition of the broad, full-bodied dome with the slender bell tower is one of the many striking architectural contrasts that mark the Prague skyline. Inside, the vast pink-and-green space is impossible to take in with a single glance. Every corner bristles with life, guiding the eye first to the dramatic statues, then to the hectic frescoes, and on to the shining faux-marble pillars. Many of the statues are the work of Ignaz Platzer and constitute his last blaze of success. Platzer's workshop was forced to declare bankruptcy when the centralizing and secularizing reforms of Joseph II toward the end of the 18th century brought an end to the flamboyant baroque era. The tower, with an entrance on the side of the church, is open in summer. The church also hosts chamber music concerts in summer, which complement this eye-popping setting but do not reflect the true caliber of classical music in Prague. For that, check the schedule posted across the street at **Líchtenštejnský palác** (Liechtenstein Palace), where the faculty of HAMU, the city's premier music academy, sometimes also gives performances. ⊠ *Malostranské nám., Malá Strana* ☎ *257–534–215* ⊕ *www.stnicholas.cz* 🕾 *100 Kč, concerts 490 Kč* Ⓜ *Line A: Malostranská plus Tram 12, 20, or 22 to Malostranské náměstí.*

## Did You Know?

According to popular superstition, touching the eighth statue on the right of the Charles Bridge, St. John of Nepomuk, is said to bring a return visit to Prague.

**Malostranské náměstí** (*Lesser Quarter Square*)

PLAZA | Another one of the many classic examples of Prague's charm, this square is flanked on the east and south sides by arcaded houses dating from the 16th and 17th centuries. The Czech Parliament resides partly in the gaudy yellow-and-green palace on the square's north side, partly in a building on Sněmovní ulice, behind the palace. The huge bulk of the Church of St. Nicholas divides the lower, busier section—buzzing with restaurants, street vendors, clubs, and shops, including an unfortunately prominent Starbucks—from the quieter upper part. There are plans under way to spruce up the centuries-old space and make it more pedestrian friendly. ⊠ *Malá Strana* Ⓜ *Line A: Malostranská.*

★ **Museum Kampa**

MUSEUM | Kampa Island's gem is a remodeled flour mill that displays the private collection of Jan and Meda Mládek, leading Czech exiles during the communist period who supported the then Czechoslovak nonconformist artists. There's a large collection of paintings by Czech artist František Kupka, considered one of the founders of modern abstract painting, and first-rate temporary exhibitions by both Czech and other Central European visual wizards. The aim of the museum is to showcase the work and the difficult circumstances under which it was created. The museum itself has had some tough times: it was hit hard by flooding in 2002 and 2013 but rebounded relatively quickly on both occasions. The outdoor terrace offers a splendid view of the river and historic buildings on the opposite bank. ⊠ *U Sovových mlýnů 2, Malá Strana* ☏ 257–286–144 ⊕ *www. museumkampa.cz* ⊡ *280 Kč* Ⓜ *Line A: Malostranská plus Tram 12, 20, or 22.*

**Na Kampě**

PLAZA | Take the stairs on the left of the Charles Bridge as you approach Malá Strana (making sure to peek at the lucky soul who has a balcony overlooking the bridge), and you will come upon one of the most picturesque little squares in Prague. This understated square has a few spots for a beer, a couple of hotels, a regular market, and a wonderfully chill, almost local feel considering how central it is. If you double back on yourself and go under the bridge, that vibe continues with a kid's playground with a stunning view directly onto the Charles Bridge. ⊠ *Malá Strana* Ⓜ *Line A: Malostranská plus Tram 12, 20, or 22.*

**Nerudova ulice**

NEIGHBORHOOD | This steep street used to be the last leg of the "Royal Way," the king's procession before his coronation (naturally, he rode a horse rather than climbing). It was named for 19th-century Czech journalist and poet Jan Neruda and has a historical quirk: until 18th-century reforms, house numbering was unknown in Prague. Before this, each house bore a name, depicted pictorially on the façade. Check out No. 6 here, U červeného orla (At the Red Eagle), and No. 12, U tří housliček (At the Three Fiddles), where the Edlinger violin-making family once lived. Two palaces designed by baroque architect Giovanni Santini (who lived at No. 14), are worth pausing at: the Morzin Palace, on the left at No. 5, has an allegorical "night and day" façade created in 1713 by Ferdinand Brokoff, of Charles Bridge statue fame. Across the street at No. 20 is the Thun-Hohenstein Palace, with its eagle gateway designed by the other great bridge statue sculptor, Mathias Braun. Keep an eye out for the winding passageway under the arch of No. 13, a typical feature of this quarter; note No. 33, the Bretfeld Palace, where Mozart and Casanova stayed when *Don Giovanni* had its world premiere in 1787. ⊠ *Prague.*

**Palácové zahrady pod Pražským hradem** (*Gardens below Prague Castle*)

GARDEN | A break in the houses along Valdštejnská ulice opens to a gate that leads to five beautifully manicured and terraced baroque gardens, which in season are open to the public. A combined-entry ticket allows you to wander at will, climbing up and down the steps and trying to find the little entryways that lead from one garden to the next. Each of the gardens bears the name of a noble family and includes the Kolovratská zahrada (Kolowrat Garden), Ledeburská zahrada (Ledeburg Garden), Malá a Velká Pálffyovská zahrada (Small and Large Palffy Gardens), and Furstenberská zahrada (Furstenberg Garden). ⊠ *Valdštejnská 12–14, Malá Strana* ☎ *257–214–817* ⊕ *www.palacove-zahrady.cz* 🎫 *80 Kč* Ⓜ *Line A: Malostranská.*

**Petřínské sady** (*Petřín Park or Petřín Gardens*)
**CITY PARK | FAMILY |** For a superb view of the city—from a slightly more solitary perch—the park on top of Petřín Hill includes a charming playground for children and adults alike, with a miniature (but still pretty big) Eiffel Tower. You'll also find a *bludiště* (mirror maze), as well as a working observatory and the seemingly abandoned Sv. Vavřinec (St. Lawrence) church, which does still hold Sunday Mass. To get here from Malá Strana, simply hike up Petřín Hill (from Karmelitská ulice or Újezd) or ride the funicular railway (which departs near the Újezd tram stop). Regular public-transportation tickets are valid on the funicular.

From Hradčany, you can also stroll over from Strahov klášter (Strahov Monastery), following a wide path that crosses above some fruit orchards and offers breathtaking views over the city below. ⊠ *Petřín Hill, Malá Strana* ⊕ *www.muzeumprahy.cz* 🎫 *Observatory 80 Kč, tower 150 Kč, maze 90 Kč* Ⓜ *Line A: Malostranská plus Tram 12, 20, or 22 to Újezd (plus funicular).*

**Schönbornský palác** (*Schönborn Palace*)
**BUILDING |** Franz Kafka had an apartment in this massive baroque building at the top of Tržiště ulice in mid-1917, after moving from Golden Lane. The U.S. Embassy and consular office now occupy this prime location. Although security

# Taking You for a Ride

Prague has a deserved reputation for dishonest taxi drivers. In an honest cab, the meter starts at 40 Kč and increases by 28 Kč per kilometer (½ mile) or 6 Kč per minute at rest. A typical ride around the center, depending on the distance, should cost no more than 280 Kč. The best way to avoid getting ripped off is to ask your hotel or restaurant to call a cab for you. (AAA Taxi is the most trustworthy company.) The good news is that improvements have been made and the chance of hailing an honest cab on the street has increased. The addition of ridesharing apps like Uber and Bolt has improved matters further.

has been stepped down compared with a few years ago, the many police, guards, and Jersey barriers don't offer much of an invitation to linger. ⊠ *Tržiště 15, at Vlašská, Malá Strana* Ⓜ *Line A: Malostranská plus Tram 12, 20, or 22.*

★ **Valdštejnska zahrada** (*Wallenstein Palace Gardens*)
**GARDEN |** With its idiosyncratic high-walled gardens and vaulted Renaissance *sala terrena* (room opening onto a garden), this palace displays superbly elegant grounds. Walking around the formal paths, you come across numerous fountains and statues depicting figures from classical mythology or warriors dispatching a variety of beasts. However, nothing beats the trippy "Grotto," a huge dripstone wall packed with imaginative rock formations, like little faces and animals hidden in the charcoal-color landscape, and what's billed as "illusory hints of secret corridors." Here, truly, staring at the wall is a form of entertainment. Albrecht von Wallenstein, onetime owner

**4**

**Malá Strana**

of the house and gardens, began a mete-oric military career in 1622, when the Austrian emperor Ferdinand II retained him to save the empire from the Swedes and Protestants during the Thirty Years' War. Wallenstein, wealthy by marriage, offered to raise an army of 20,000 men at his own cost and lead them personally. Ferdinand II accepted and showered Wallenstein with confiscated land and titles. Wallenstein's first acquisition was this enormous area. After knocking down 23 houses, a brick factory, and three gardens, in 1623 he began to build his magnificent palace. Most of the palace itself now serves the Czech Senate as meeting chamber and offices. The palace's cavernous former Jízdárna, or riding school, now hosts art exhibitions. ⊠ Letenská 10, Malá Strana ☎ 257–075–707 ⊕ www.senat.cz ⊠ Free ⊙ Closed Nov.–Mar. Ⓜ Line A: Malostranská.

### Velkopřevorské náměstí (Grand Priory Square)

PLAZA | This square is south and slightly west of the Charles Bridge, next to the Čertovka stream. The Grand Prior's Palace fronting the square is considered one of the finest baroque buildings in the area, though it's now part of the Embassy of the Sovereign Military Order of Malta—the contemporary (and very real) descendants of the Knights of Malta. Alas, it's closed to the public. Opposite is the flamboyant orange-and-white stucco façade of the Buquoy Palace, built in 1719 by Giovanni Santini and now the French Embassy. The nearby **John Lennon Peace Wall** was once a kind of monument to youthful rebellion, emblazoned with polit-ical slogans and the large painted head of the former Beatle during the communist era in Prague. Back then, it was regularly painted over by the authorities; nowa-days, Lennon's visage is seldom seen because it is usually covered instead with political and music-related graffiti. For now, you can still take a pen and add your own, but there's talk of regula-tions to prevent obscene daubings by

inebriated tourists. ⊠ Malá Strana Ⓜ Line A: Malostranská plus Tram 12, 20, or 22.

### Vojanovy sady (Vojan Park)

CITY PARK | FAMILY | Once the gardens of the Monastery of the Discalced Carmel-ites, later taken over by the Order of the English Virgins, this walled garden is now part of the Ministry of Finance. With its weeping willows, fruit trees, and bench-es, it provides another peaceful haven in summer. Exhibitions of modern sculpture are occasionally held here, contrasting sharply with the two baroque chapels and the graceful Ignaz Platzer statue of John of Nepomuk standing on a fish at the entrance. At the other end of the park you can find a terrace with a formal rose garden and a pair of peacocks that like to aggressively preen for visitors under the trellises. The park is surrounded by the high walls of the old monastery and new Ministry of Finance buildings, with only an occasional glimpse of a tower or spire to remind you of the world beyond. ⊠ U lužického semináře 17, between Leten-ská ul. and Míšeňská ul., Malá Strana ☎ 221–097–231 Ⓜ Line A: Malostranská.

### Vrtbovská zahrada (Vrtba Garden)

GARDEN | An unobtrusive door on noisy Karmelitská hides the entranceway to a fascinating sanctuary with one of the best views of Malá Strana. The street door opens onto the intimate courtyard of the Vrtbovský palác (Vrtba Palace). Two Renaissance wings flank the courtyard; the left one was built in 1575, the right one in 1591. The original owner of the latter house was one of the 27 Bohemian nobles executed by the Habsburgs in 1621. The house was given as confiscat-ed property to Count Sezima of Vrtba, who bought the neighboring property and turned the buildings into a late-Re-naissance palace. The Vrtba Garden was created a century later. Built in five levels rising behind the courtyard in a wave of statuary-bedecked staircases and formal terraces reaching toward a seashell-decorated pavilion at the top, it's a popular spot for weddings, receptions, and occasional concerts. (The fenced-off garden immediately behind and above belongs to the U.S. Embassy—hence the U.S. flag that often flies there.) The powerful stone figure of Atlas that caps the entranceway in the courtyard and most of the other statues of mythological figures are from the workshop of Mathias Braun, perhaps the best of the Czech baroque sculptors. ⊠ *Karmelitská 25, Malá Strana* ☎ *272–088–350* ⊕ *www.vrtbovska.cz* ⊴ *80 Kč* ◷ *Closed Nov.– Mar.* Ⓜ *Line A: Malostranská plus Tram 12, 20, or 22 to Hellichova.*

## ⊛ Restaurants

Malá Strana has come into its own as a dining scene of late. In the past it was either tourist central or high-end, with little in between, but today there is a wider spread of options to suit every palate and budget. The area around Lesser Quarter Square has several wonderful restaurants, including Mandarin Oriental's house restaurant. The eastern edge of Malá Strana along the Vltava River offers dining with amazing views, all for a price.

### Café de Paris

**$$ | FRENCH |** The twin stars of the show at this Gallic import are beef entrecote and french fries. Café de Paris even makes its own "special sauce" (think béarnaise with a hint of mustard). **Known for:** classic French bistro; house specials; steak frites. Ⓢ *Average main: 260 Kč* ⊠ *Maltézské nám. 4, Malá Strana* ☎ *603–160–718* ⊕ *www.cafedeparis.cz* ▭ *No credit cards* Ⓜ *Line A: Malostranská.*

### Hergetova Cihelna

**$$$ | ECLECTIC |** Between the attractive staff and sleek, minimalist interior, there's no shortage of glamour at Hergetova Cihelna. The most gorgeous thing, however, is the view of the Charles Bridge from the expansive terrace. **Known for:** views, views, views; reputation as the chiller sister of Kampa Park; high-quality

ingredients, from burrata to venison svíčková (cream sauce). Ⓢ *Average main: 500 Kč* ⊠ *Cihelná 2B, Malá Strana* ☎ *296–826–103* ⊕ *cihelna.com* Ⓜ *Line A: Malostranská.*

### Ichnusa Botega & Bistro

**$$ | ITALIAN |** On a side street between Malá Strana and Smíchov, the Ichnusa Botega & Bistro evokes the island of Sardinia, with Mediterranean-blue accents, rustic wall decor, and plenty of seafood and wines from Italy's southern reaches. The owners are Sardinian, so the experience is authentic overall. **Known for:** the grilled fish—it can't be beat; fresh and flavorful Italian specialties; sharing platters from seafood to prosciutto. Ⓢ *Average main: 350 Kč* ⊠ *Plaská 5, Malá Strana* ☎ *605–375–012* ⊕ *ichnusa.business.site* ◷ *Closed Sun. No lunch Sat.* Ⓜ *Line A: Malostranská plus Tram 12, 20, or 22 to Újezd.*

### Kampa Park

**$$$$ | EUROPEAN |** The zenith of riverside dining is offered at this legendary restaurant just off the Charles Bridge, known almost as much for its chic decor and celebrity guests as it is for its elegant continental cuisine and great wines—it's the kind of place where European royals and heads of state mingle with their head-of-studio counterparts from Hollywood. But the real star power arrives on the plate, with dishes like olive-oil-poached halibut with black truffles or rack of lamb with sheep cheese and chorizo. **Known for:** romantic riverside setting; some of Prague's finest food; incredibly attentive staff. Ⓢ *Average main: 900 Kč* ⊠ *Na Kampě 8B, Malá Strana* ☎ *296–826–112* ⊕ *www.kampapark.com* Ⓜ *Line A: Malostranská.*

### Luka Lu

**$$ | MEDITERRANEAN |** The decor is bright and eccentric—think cats in fake windows, Picasso-esque murals, and bells hanging from the ceiling—but the ambience is friendly at this pan-Balkan restaurant on a busy stretch of the Malá Strana.

**The John Lennon Peace Wall on the Kampa island continues to be marked with free-spirited, antiwar graffiti years after his death.**

Taking cues from Bosnian, Serbian, and Macedonian cuisine, the menu branches out to cover the best of the coasts and hill country plus hearty regional wines from family-run vineyards. **Known for:** authentic specialties like mincemeat sausages called čevapčiči; Balkan wines; garden at the foot of Petřín. [$] *Average main: 300 Kč* ✉ *Újezd 33, Malá Strana* ☎ *257–212–388* 🌐 *www.lukalu.cz* [M] *Line A: Malostranská.*

**The Mailroom & Bistro**

**$$** | **EUROPEAN** | A proper, French-style bistro, in the sense that you can eat delicious meals there all day from 7:30 am to 10 pm (6 on Sunday), the Mailroom & Bistro also has a quirky postal theme thanks to its location in the former royal post office of Prague. It ticks boxes across the board: good service, reasonable prices, quality ingredients, and a pleasant courtyard garden in summer. **Known for:** delicious brunches; all-day dining; old favorites, like Prague ham, given a modern twist. [$] *Average main: 300 Kč* ✉ *Maltézské nám. 8, Malá Strana* ☎ *775–068–752* 🌐 *www.mailroombistro.com* [M] *Line A: Malostranská.*

**★ NOI**

**$$** | **THAI** | A loungy spot on a well-trafficked stretch of Újezd, NOI delivers on the promise of its Zen interior by cooking excellent Thai classics. Lithe staff are quick to accommodate their hip clientele at low tables surrounded by Buddha statues. **Known for:** fried shrimp cakes; pleasant patio for summer dining; curt but efficient service. [$] *Average main: 250 Kč* ✉ *Újezd 19, Malá Strana* ☎ *257–311–411* 🌐 *www.noirestaurant.cz* [M] *Line A: Malostranská plus Tram 12, 20, or 22 to Újezd.*

**Spices Restaurant & Bar**

**$$$** | **ASIAN** | This ancient-made-modern space, with arched whitewashed ceilings, terrace, lounge, and tasteful gold accents, just keeps improving, as you'd expect from a cuisine shrine inside the majorly chic Mandarin Oriental hotel. Head chef Jiří Stift has created a menu that cunningly focuses on Asian dishes made with fresh, local ingredients from

Czech farmers. **Known for:** high-end versions of Asian classics like beef rendang; alluring "crossover" dishes featuring suckling pig and caramel; exquisite service and atmosphere. [$] *Average main: 500 Kč* ✉ *Mandarin Oriental Prague, Nebovidská 1, Malá Strana* ☎ *233–088–777* 🌐 *www.mandarinoriental.com* [M] *Line A: Malostranská.*

**The Sushi Bar**

$$$ | **JAPANESE** | This narrow little room across the river from the Narodní divadlo (National Theater) is home to some of the city's best sushi, courtesy of the fish market next door. It was the first sushi place to open in Prague, back in 1999, and the selection remains first-rate by Central European standards. **Known for:** great soft-shell crab maki and seaweed salad; tiny space, so advance reservations are needed; melt-in-the-mouth fish. [$] *Average main: 450 Kč* ✉ *Zborovská 49, Malá Strana* ☎ *603–244–882* 🌐 *www.sushi.cz* [M] *Line A: Malostranská.*

**★ Terasa U Zlaté studně**

$$$$ | **INTERNATIONAL** | On top of the boutique Golden Well Hotel, lunch or dinner, either inside or on the terrace of this Michelin-rated restaurant overlooking the city's rooftops, is a delicious experience that more than lives up to the views and prices. The menu runs the gamut from the full degustation (3,100 Kč) to the two-course seasonal lunch menu for 790 Kč. **Known for:** exceptional cooking of an inventive international menu; among the best views in Prague; feeling of exclusivity thanks to its slightly hidden location. [$] *Average main: 1000 Kč* ✉ *Golden Well Hotel, U Zlaté studně 4, Malá Strana* ☎ *257–533–322* 🌐 *www.terasauzlatestudne.cz* [M] *Line A: Malostranská.*

**Tlustá myš**

$$ | **CZECH** | With no-frills, well-priced, hearty Czech cooking in an atmospheric cellar, this is the kind of restaurant where tourists and locals happily intermingle. The menu boasts the big hitters of Czech cuisine at non-rip-off prices and hosts many happy patrons chowing down—with large mugs of pilsner, of course. **Known for:** satisfying goulash, schnitzel, and fried cheese; reputation as a popular local spot; good beer. [$] *Average main: 150 Kč* ✉ *Všehrdova 19, Malá Strana* ☎ *257–320–409* 🌐 *www.tlustamys.cz* [M] *Line A: Malostranská.*

## Scenic Spots

Prague's best rooftop views probably belong to the fantastic restaurant at the Golden Well Hotel, **Terasa U Zlaté studně,** (✉ *U Zlaté studně 4* ☎ *257–011–213*), although **Ginger & Fred,** on top of Frank Gehry's Tančící dům (Dancing House) across the river (✉ *Rašínovo nábř. 80* ☎ *221–984–160*), also makes a reasonable claim. If you're visiting in the summer months, sit on the terrace. If the Charles Bridge is your ideal vista, try the outdoor seating at **Hergetova Cihelna** (✉ *Cihelná 2B* ☎ *296–826–103*). The restaurant keeps blankets and heat lamps for when the nights get nippy.

**★ U Modré kachničky**

$$$ | **CZECH** | This old-fashioned tavern puts on airs, but if you're looking for the perfect Czech venue for a special occasion, it's hard to beat the "Blue Duckling." Dusty portraits hanging on the walls and lavish curtains and table settings impart a certain slightly frilly 19th-century look. The menu, filled with succulent duck and game choices, brings things down to earth a notch. **Known for:** gloriously gamey menu; beautiful old-world interior; friendly service staff. [$] *Average main: 500 Kč* ✉ *Nebovidská 6, Malá Strana* ☎ *257–320–308* 🌐 *www.umodrekachnicky.cz* [M] *Line A: Malostranská plus Tram 12, 20, or 22 to Hellichova.*

Cafe Savoy is known for its long lines but the spectacular art nouveau interior is worth the wait.

#  Coffee and Quick Bites

### ★ Café Savoy

**$ | ČZECH |** One of the best of Prague's traditional turn-of-the-century-style grand cafés, the Savoy is popular day and night for its brunches, coffees, Czech classics, and pastries. In particular, try the *větrník*, a Czech classic made of choux pastry with cream and caramel (it's far more authentic than the touristy *trdelník* (a type of rolled, spit cake) available everywhere, although if you need that sugar hit to get up up the hill to the castle, no judgment). **Known for:** lavish interior; coffee and cake; long lines. *$ Average main:* ☒ *Vítězná 5, Malá Strana* ☎ *731–136–144* ⊕ *cafesavoy.ambi.cz* Ⓜ *Tram 1, 9, 20, 22, 23, 25, 97, 98, or 99 to Újezd.*

### ★ Cukrkávalimonáda

**$$ | CAFÉ |** An excellent pit stop while exploring Malá Strana, this warm, inviting café and bakery serves freshly made soups, salads, sandwiches, and pasta dishes, making it a convenient oasis for lunch. Or just rest your feet with a coffee and a slice of pie or cake. **Known for:** unique heritage-hipster interior; delicious Viennese-style confections; great value for its location. *$ Average main: 190 Kč* ☒ *Lázeňská 7, Malá Strana* ☎ *257–225–396* ⊕ *www.cukrkavalimonada.com* ⊟ *No credit cards* Ⓜ *Line A: Malostranská plus Tram 12, 20, or 22 to Hellichova.*

### Kafíčko

**$ | CAFÉ |** The "Little Coffee" grinds freshly roasted beans from Brazil, Kenya, Colombia, and other renowned growing regions. Superlative strudel and small snacks in a peaceful setting make this a pleasant stop for refueling near Charles Bridge. *$ Average main: 50 Kč* ☒ *Maltézské náměstí 15, Malá Strana* ☎ *724–151–795* ⊟ *No credit cards* Ⓜ *Line A: Malostranská.*

# 🛏 Hotels

With a bewitching storybook suite of baroque palaces and Renaissance façades, Malá Strana—at the other end of the Charles Bridge from Staré

Město—is the darling of Prague. Mostly a quiet area, removed from the bustle across the river, it also has some good traditional restaurants and pubs. Malá Strana provides an excellent location for visiting Prague Castle just up the hill but may not be the best choice for people with mobility problems. Other cons: car access on the narrow cobblestoned streets is restricted, parking is difficult, and you'll spend a lot of your time walking on the Charles Bridge to get to Staré Město.

### ★ Alchymist Grand Hotel and Spa

$$$ | HOTEL | A baroque fever dream of Prague masterminded by an Italian developer, the Alchymist doesn't go the understated route. **Pros:** unique design; high-quality spa; central yet tucked away. **Cons:** steep uphill walk from the tram; loud a/c; underwhelming breakfast. $ *Rooms from: 6500 Kč* ⊠ *Tržiště 19, Malá Strana* ☎ *257–286–011* ⊕ *www. alchymisthotel.com* ⤴ *46 rooms* ⦿ *Free Breakfast* Ⓜ *Line A: Malostranská plus Tram 12, 20, or 22 to Malostranské náměstí.*

### Appia Hotel Residences

$$ | HOTEL | A stylish hotel comprised of rooms and apartments, in a slightly off-the-beaten-track location in Malá Strana. **Pros:** lovely courtyard and 12th-century hall; quiet and stylish; location allows for exploration of undervisited parts of Malá Strana. **Cons:** too quiet for some; staff professional but not warm; some may find the beds a little firm. $ *Rooms from: 4000 Kč* ⊠ *Šporkova 3/322, Malá Strana* ☎ *257–215–819* ⊕ *www.appiaresidenc-esprague.cz* ⤴ *21 rooms* ⦿ *Free Breakfast* Ⓜ *Line A: Malostranská.*

### Aria Hotel

$$$ | HOTEL | This charming music-themed property kicked off Prague's luxury hotel boom in the early 2000s and still holds up well against the competition. **Pros:** gorgeous gardens and rooftop bar make for a sophisticated escape; excellent restaurant and breakfast; Apple televisions

in all rooms, along with killer sound systems. **Cons:** proximity to the embassy can lead to tiresome security checks; some of the suites are small and might be better labeled as standard rooms; slightly standard-issue furniture in otherwise personality-filled hotel. $ *Rooms from: 6700 Kč* ⊠ *Tržiště 9, Malá Strana* ☎ *225–334–111* ⊕ *www.ariahotel.net* ⤴ *51 rooms* ⦿ *Free Breakfast* Ⓜ *Line A: Malostranská.*

### ★ Augustine, a Luxury Collection Hotel, Prague

$$$$ | HOTEL | There's plenty of competition in Prague's high-end hotel market, but the Augustine—now part of Marriott's Luxury Collection—continues to come out on top. **Pros:** impeccable service; clever design; impressive spa. **Cons:** breakfast not always included; noisy wood floors; no swimming pool. $ *Rooms from: 9200 Kč* ⊠ *Letenská 12, Malá Strana* ☎ *266–112–233* ⊕ *www. marriott.com/hotels/travel/prglc-augus-tine-a-luxury-collection-hotel-prague* ⤴ *101 rooms* ⦿ *No meals* Ⓜ *Line A: Malostranská.*

### Domus Balthasar

$ | HOTEL | This chic retreat is hidden in plain sight on one of the busiest streets in Prague, the road up from the Charles Bridge in Malá Strana. **Pros:** reasonably priced; modern decor and good Wi-Fi; friendly service from hip staff. **Cons:** very busy street; no elevator; ceilings in attractive loft rooms too low for anyone over 6 feet. $ *Rooms from: 2200 Kč* ⊠ *Mos-tecká 5, Malá Strana* ☎ *257–199–499* ⊕ *www.domus-balthasar.cz* ⤴ *8 rooms* ⦿ *No meals* Ⓜ *Line A: Malostranská.*

### Dům U Červeného Lva (*House at the Red Lion*)

$$ | B&B/INN | An intimate, immaculately kept baroque building dating to the 15th century, this hotel is right on the main thoroughfare in Malá Strana, a five-minute walk from Prague Castle's front gates. **Pros:** historic baroque building; beautiful location not far from Prague

Castle; rooms have parquet floors and 17th-century painted-beam ceilings. **Cons:** no elevator; no air-conditioning; no reception desk in the hotel. $ *Rooms from: 2500 Kč* ✉ *Nerudova 41, Malá Strana* ☎ *257–533–832* ⊕ *www.hotelredlion.cz* ⬎ *6 rooms* ⦿*◎* *Free Breakfast* Ⓜ *Line A: Malostranská.*

### ★ EA Residence U Bílé kuželky

$$ | **B&B/INN** | This 18th-century inn offers an unbeatable combination of location, ambience, and convenience. **Pros:** central location; historic surroundings; modern amenities. **Cons:** restaurant noise can reach rooms; a/c only in some rooms (and loud); no elevator. $ *Rooms from: 4000 Kč* ✉ *Míšeňská 12, Malá Strana* ☎ *257–014–800* ⊕ *www.ubilekuzelky.cz* ⬎ *14 rooms* ⦿*◎* *Free Breakfast* Ⓜ *Line A: Malostranská.*

### ★ Golden Well Hotel

$$$ | **HOTEL** | Consistently rated one of Prague's best boutique hotels, the Golden Well Hotel is hidden away at the top of a narrow side street in Malá Strana. **Pros:** great views at fantastic restaurant; always friendly service; spacious rooms. **Cons:** outlet shortage; far from the Metro and tram stops; wooden floors can be noisy. $ *Rooms from: 6600 Kč* ✉ *U Zlaté studně 4, Malá Strana* ☎ *257–011–213* ⊕ *www.goldenwell.cz* ⬎ *19 rooms* ⦿*◎* *No meals* Ⓜ *Line A: Malostranská.*

### Hotel Kampa Stará zbrojnice

$ | **HOTEL** | The secluded and picturesque location of this historic inn that once served as an armory is the main selling point here. **Pros:** location is gorgeously positioned by Kampa Park; live music at breakfast; interesting period details—suits of armor and all. **Cons:** the breakfasts could use more variety; uninspiring room decor and thin pillows; feels a little tired. $ *Rooms from: 2000 Kč* ✉ *Všehrdova 16, Malá Strana* ☎ *272–114–444* ⊕ *www.hotelkampa.cz* ⬎ *84 rooms* ⦿*◎* *Free Breakfast* Ⓜ *Line A: Malostranská.*

### Hotel Neruda

$$ | **HOTEL** | Built in 1348, this landmark—now a flashy boutique hotel with major design chops—is where the author Jan Neruda and his mother lived in 1860. **Pros:** designer rooms have lots of character; historic location; lots of unique flavor, from bathtubs enclosed in glass to rumors of a ghost. **Cons:** design can impinge on the livability of the hotel; no nearby Metro and an uphill walk from the nearest tram stop; some rooms face a wall. $ *Rooms from: 3000 Kč* ✉ *Nerudova 44, Malá Strana* ☎ *257–535–557* ⊕ *www.designhotelneruda.com* ⬎ *42 rooms* ⦿*◎* *Free Breakfast* Ⓜ *Line A: Malostranská.*

### ★ Mandarin Oriental Prague

$$$$ | **HOTEL** | Architects wisely chose to retain many of the Dominican monastery's original flourishes when it was restored, creating a peaceful, inspired backdrop for the Mandarin Oriental's luxurious offerings. **Pros:** historic building; lovely peaceful setting; attentive, personalized service. **Cons:** some rooms are small; a/c seriously underpowered; breakfast a little disappointing. $ *Rooms from: 10500 Kč* ✉ *Nebovidská 1, Malá Strana* ☎ *233–088–888* ⊕ *www.mandarinoriental.com/prague* ⬎ *99 rooms* ⦿*◎* *No meals* Ⓜ *Line A: Malostranská.*

### Pod Věží

$$ | **HOTEL** | The family-friendly Pod Věží is perched on the end of the famous Charles Bridge, so close you even get a free ticket to the tower if you stay here. **Pros:** nice touches like daily gifts for guests; couldn't be closer to one of Prague's main attractions; large rooms. **Cons:** can be loud; hectic location with constant stream of tourists outside the door; some of the beautiful beam rooms are accessible only by staircase. $ *Rooms from: 2500 Kč* ✉ *Mostecká 58/2, Malá Strana* ☎ *257–532–041* ⊕ *www.podvezi.com* ⬎ *12 rooms, plus 16 rooms in adjacent building* ⦿*◎* *Free Breakfast* Ⓜ *Line A: Malostranská.*

### Sax Vintage Design Hotel

**$ | HOTEL |** This bold, bright, and affordable hotel was favored by former secretary of state Madeleine Albright (there's a framed letter of thanks on the wall). **Pros:** good price and free happy hour; located on a quiet street; unique and lively decor. **Cons:** design might be too much for those with more conservative tastes; not convenient to Prague nightlife; some noise in rooms near communal areas. $ *Rooms from: 2000 Kč* ✉ *Jánský vršek 3, Malá Strana* ☎ *775–859–694* ⊕ *www.hotelsax.cz* ⤵ *22 rooms* ⅋ *Free Breakfast* Ⓜ *Line A: Malostranská.*

### U Tří Pštrosů (*At the Three Ostriches*)

**$$ | HOTEL |** This historic inn has taken a couple of licks—first it was flooded, then burned to the ground, then rebuilt, only to be taken by the communists, and finally restituted to the family owners. **Pros:** location, location, location; real sense of grandeur; huge buffet breakfasts. **Cons:** small rooms up top; no elevator; too in the thick of it for some. $ *Rooms from: 2600 Kč* ✉ *Dražického nám. 12, Malá Strana* ☎ *257–288–888* ⊕ *www.utrip-strosu.cz* ⤵ *18 rooms* ⅋ *Free Breakfast* Ⓜ *Line A: Malostranská.*

 ## Nightlife

A mix of tourist traps, café-bars, and authentic late-night haunts, Malá Strana is a beguiling place to drink, in the shadow of Prague Castle—although it's nowhere near as buzzy or varied as Staré Město, just across the river.

## BARS AND PUBS

### Baráčnická rychta

**BARS/PUBS |** This is an authentic Czech pub, with wooden benches and booths, great beers, and reasonable food; it even delivers on traditional service (i.e., not always that attentive). But that's part of the vibe—just ask the mix of tourists and locals supping on the Svijany and Malastrana brews. The courtyard beer garden is a nice spot in summer, too, and it's far enough off the main drag that it isn't

overly packed. ✉ *Tržiště 23, Malá Strana* ☎ *257–286–083* ⊕ *www.baracnickarych-ta.cz* Ⓜ *Line A: Malostranská.*

### Bluelight Bar

**BARS/PUBS |** Despite its location just off the main drag up from the Charles Bridge, the Bluelight Bar manages to remain a laid-back, grungy haunt for some dedicated late-night drinking. The rock walls of the cavelike space are covered in graffiti, and the clientele is a mixed bag, but somehow it works. This is the perfect destination for a nightcap—just don't blame us if you're still ensconced hours later. ✉ *Josefská 42/1, Malá Strana* ☎ *257–533–126* ⊕ *www.bluelightbar.cz* Ⓜ *Line A: Malostranská.*

### Café Club Míšeňská

**CAFES—NIGHTLIFE |** From morning until it closes at midnight, this relaxed, hip café-bar serves up decent drinks and cakes, but what it really trades on is its creative and cultural atmosphere. Open mike nights and an archway entrance, plus chill courtyard seating when the weather allows, complete the picture. ✉ *Míšeňská 3, Malá Strana* ☎ *723–380–950* ⊕ *www.facebook.com/misenskafe* Ⓜ *Line A: Malostranská.*

### Kellyxír

**BARS/PUBS |** An atmospheric haunt that calls itself an "alchemical pub" (probably thanks to its location in the same building as the Museum of Alchemists), this bar likely hasn't worked out how to turn base metals into gold or discovered the elixir of life yet, but it's a pretty fun gimmick nonetheless. Try the cocktails (complete with dry ice) and enjoy the drinks in flasks, pipes on the ceilings (allegedly full of said elixir), and drawings and diagrams on the walls. ✉ *Jánský vršek 8, Malá Strana* ⊕ *kellyxir.cz* Ⓜ *Line A: Malostranská.*

### ★ Olympia

**BARS/PUBS |** A hot spot from the 1930s returned to its former glory provides a somewhat romanticized but enjoyable take on a Czech pub. Part of the Kolkovna chain that has locations around the city, Olympia appeals to visitors and locals alike who like the special unpasteurized Pilsner Urquell. There's also a great menu of Czech classics to help soak up all that delicious beer. Try the schnitzel or the steak tartare. ⊠ *Vítežná 7, Malá Strana* ☎ *251–511–080* ⊕ *www. kolkovna.cz* Ⓜ *Line A: Malostranská.*

**U Hrocha**

BARS/PUBS | Probably the most authentic and atmospheric old bar in the touristy Hradčany, this traditional Czech pub is just below Prague Castle. U Hrocha (At the Hippo) is nothing fancy (quite the opposite: think wooden benches, smoke, and stone walls), but the pilsner is delicious and soon you'll feel right at home. The waiters can seem surly, but we don't think they mean it. ⊠ *Thunovská 10, Malá Strana* ☎ *257– 533–389* ⊕ *www.facebook.com/noreservationsonthispage* Ⓜ *Line A: Malostranská.*

**Vinograf Míšeňská**

WINE BARS—NIGHTLIFE | This is a charming wine bar that takes its tipple of choice seriously, with a great range of Czech wines from a mix of renowned vineyards and small family wine makers. Having said that, though, it's a lighthearted and unpretenious place to try some wines, with staff happy to help. There are some small bar snacks available and many wines available by the glass as well as the bottle, so it's perfect either for a quick one before heading for dinner or for a leisurely evening over a quality bottle. ⊠ *Míšeňská 8, Malá Strana* ☎ *604–705–730* ⊕ *vinograf. cz* Ⓜ *Line A: Malostranská.*

## JAZZ CLUBS

**U Malého Glena**

MUSIC CLUBS | Commonly known as "Little Glen," patrons are willing to cram in to hear solid house jazz and blues bands, as well as a few visiting acts. Get there early to stake out a seat near the stage; the tunnel-shape vault can be crowded but that only adds to the atmosphere. Upstairs they serve food until midnight. ⊠ *Karmelitská*

*23, Malá Strana* ☎ *257–531–717* ⊕ *www. malyglen.cz* Ⓜ *Line A: Malostranská.*

## LIVE MUSIC CLUBS

**Malostranská Beseda**

BARS/PUBS | Once the town hall, then a mecca for writers and artists, it's now a three-story music and theater club. Every level of this attractive building has something different going on—there's an art gallery under the roof, a "video café," a live music bar, a restaurant, a café, and a basement beer pub. ■TIP➔ The live acts are mostly popular Czech bands. ⊠ *Malostranské nám. 21, Malá Strana* ☎ *257–409–112* ⊕ *www.malostranska-beseda.cz* Ⓜ *Line A: Malostranská.*

#  Performing Arts

There are a couple of pleasant venues where visitors can catch some classical music in Malá Strana, although it isn't as stuffed with options as nearby Staré Město.

## CHURCH CONCERTS

★ **Kostel sv. Mikuláše** (*Church of St. Nicholas*)

CONCERTS | Ballroom scenes in the movie *Van Helsing* used the interior of this beautiful baroque church, probably the most famous of its kind in Prague. The building's dome was one of the last works finished by architect Kilian Ignaz Dientzenhofer before his death in 1751, and a memorial service to Mozart was held here after his death. Local ensembles play concerts of popular classics here throughout the year. ⊠ *Malostranské nám., Malá Strana* ☎ *257–534–215* ⊕ *www.stnicholas.cz* Ⓜ *Line A: Malostranská.*

## VENUES

**Lichtenštejnský palác** (*Liechtenstein Palace*)

CONCERTS | Home to the Czech music academy (HAMU), this baroque palace from the 1790s has the large Martinů Hall for professional concerts and a smaller gallery occasionally used for student recitals. The pleasant courtyard

Mozart once played the pipe-organ at the Church of St. Nicholas. Check the church's website for a program of classical music concerts.

sometimes has music in the summer months. ✉ *Malostranské nám. 13, Malá Strana* ☎ *774–427–600* ⊕ *tickets-ico.com* Ⓜ *Line A: Malostranská.*

## 🛍 Shopping

There are plenty of souvenir shops just off the Charles Bridge, one or two of which are worth your koruny, but explore the other streets for more unusual options.

### ANTIQUES
#### Antique Újezd
**ANTIQUES/COLLECTIBLES** | This dimly lit antiques shop fills bureau drawers with vintage accessories and trinkets as well as a selection of dainty 1930s pocketbooks, clutches, and bejeweled coin purses. There are also glass cases housing a pricey supply of diamonds, pearls, and gems, as well as a selection of paintings, furniture, and the odd cat porcelain piece. ✉ *Újezd 37, Malá Strana* ☎ *257–217–177* Ⓜ *Tram 9, 12, 15, 20, 22, or 23 to Újezd.*

### BOOKS AND PRINTS
#### Shakespeare & Sons
**BOOKS/STATIONERY** | The cozy Malá Strana store boasts two floors of books, mostly in English, and displays work by local and international artists. Bookworms will be intoxicated by the sheer choice and reverent attitude to the tomes; this is a real old-school bookshop. Everyone else can soak up the expat atmosphere and pretend that they, too, never have to leave the Golden City. ✉ *U Lužického semináře 10, Malá Strana* ☎ *257–531–894* ⊕ *www. shakes.cz* Ⓜ *Line A: Malostranská.*

### CAMERAS
#### Analogue
**CAMERAS/ELECTRONICS** | A photography and camera lover's paradise, Analogue offers a knowledgeable staff passionate about analog photography, Lomography cameras (the trend for which apparently began in Prague in 1991), Polaroids, and more. There's a public darkroom, exhibitions, and a lab, and you can also get passport photos done here (the U.S. Embassy is just down the road). ✉ *Vlašská 357/10,*

*Malá Strana* ☎ *603–530–035* ⊕ *www. analogue.cz* ⊗ *Closed weekends* Ⓜ *Line A: Malostranská.*

## HOME AND DESIGN

### Chemistry Design Store

**SPECIALTY STORES** | An airy Czech art and design palace, with a host of wonderful pieces from huge, brilliant posters to candles, bright notebooks, and sharp clothes. The store is curated by the gallery of the same name, so the quality of the products is to be expected, and the space itself is fittingly hip, too, with neon ceilings, a huge paper elephant, and a pop-up café in the courtyard. ✉ *U Lužického semináře 11, Malá Strana* ☎ *606–649–170* ⊕ *www. thechemistry.cz* Ⓜ *Line A: Malostranská.*

### Cihelna Concept Store

**HOUSEHOLD ITEMS/FURNITURE** | Attractively located by the river, this design concept shop near the gorgeous Hergetova Cihelna restaurant profiles the best in Czech design in a clean, unfussy space, from funky chairs to inventive lighting. ✉ *Cihelna 2B, Malá Strana* ☎ *257–317–318* ⊕ *www.cihelnaprague.com* Ⓜ *Line A: Malostranská.*

### Slavica Polish Pottery

**CERAMICS/GLASSWARE** | A nice change from the same old tourist shops, this authentic Polish pottery store offers beautiful, bright, traditional homeware. It will also ship your hand-decorated gifts back home (at an additional cost) if you have run out of space in your suitcase—or if you don't trust yourself or your airline with breakable souvenirs. ✉ *Vlašská 631/11A, Malá Strana* ☎ *735–015–848* ⊕ *www.slavicapottery. com* Ⓜ *Line A: Malostranská.*

## MARIONETTES

### Marionety

**CRAFTS** | A fresh wooded scent greets visitors to this pleasant puppet shop on steep Nerudova ulice, which is next door to Prague's Center of Contemporary Puppetry. Discover an array of linden-wood marionettes, including classic characters like Tinkerbell and Charlie Chaplin, eerily reptilian wizards, and princesses in pink—plus some modern politicians. Artist biographies are found alongside a few displays, and plaster puppets—cheaper but not quite as charming—are also on offer, as well as custom-made ones for those who have really signed on to this Czech tradition. ✉ *Nerudova 51, Malá Strana* ☎ *604–230–945* ⊕ *www.loutky.cz* Ⓜ *Line A: Malostranská.*

### Truhlář Marionety

**CRAFTS** | Among Prague's many marionette peddlers, this shop below the Charles Bridge stands out for its selection of unadorned linden-wood marionettes handmade by local and regional artisans. There's also a quirky stock of decorative wooden toys, such as rocking horses and giant mermaids, fit for a lucky child's bedroom. ✉ *U Lužického semináře 5, Malá Strana* ☎ *602–689–918* ⊕ *www. marionety.com* Ⓜ *Line A: Malostranská.*

## SOUVENIRS

### Galerie Nostalgie

**GIFTS/SOUVENIRS** | A small, vaguely hippieish store with loose-fitting linen clothes, mugs and other pottery, dried flowers, and some more traditionally touristy postcards and Kafka-themed gifts. The friendly owner is happy to chat with patrons, and the calm vibe of the space makes for a nice place to recoup after the mania of the Charles Bridge and its environs, even if nothing catches your eye (but it probably will). ✉ *U Lužického semináře 8, Malá Strana* ☎ *602–838–033* Ⓜ *Line A: Malostranská.*

### ★ Pragtique

**GIFTS/SOUVENIRS** | A souvenir shop right by the Charles Bridge that is so exemplary that we defy you to leave without buying just one thing, be it a witty postcard, beautiful book, or some other unique and delightful little item. Forget the junk available all over the city, this tiny, corridor-like shop (there's a bigger version in Nové Město) is lovingly curated and designed and absolutely the place to bag the best gifts to take home. Do not miss it. ✉ *Mostecká 20, Malá Strana* ⊕ *pragtique.cz* Ⓜ *Line A: Malostranská.*

# Chapter 5

# PRAGUE CASTLE AND HRADČANY

Updated by
Joseph Reaney

| ⊙ Sights | 🍴 Restaurants | 🛏 Hotels | 🛍 Shopping | 🍸 Nightlife |
|-----------|---------------|-----------|-------------|-------------|
| ★★★★★ | ★★★★☆ | ★★★★☆ | ★★☆☆☆ | ★★☆☆☆ |

# NEIGHBORHOOD SNAPSHOT

## TOP EXPERIENCES

■ **Last Judgment Mosaic:** Head to the south-facing side of Katedrála sv. Víta (St. Vitus Cathedral) to see this extraordinary triptych mosaic, which dates back to 1371.

■ **Holiday Shopping:** Visiting in December? Browse for gifts at the castle's festive market or pick up a retro wooden toy from the Rocking Horse Toy Shop.

■ **Golden Lane:** Poke your head into the cute, colorful cottages that line charming Zlatá ulička (Golden Lane) to read about the people that once lived in them.

■ **Classical Music:** Tune into one of the regular—and always excellent—classical concerts held in Prague Castle's Romanesque Bazilika sv. Jiří (St. George's Basilica).

## GETTING HERE

As with the neighboring environs, the best public transportation here is via Metro Line A to Malostranská and then continuing onward with Tram 22. Taxis work, too, of course, but they can be expensive. The castle is compact and easily navigated. But be forewarned: the castle, especially St. Vitus Cathedral, teems with huge crowds practically year-round.

## PLANNING YOUR TIME

The castle is at its best in early morning and late evening, when it holds an air of mystery and intrigue. The cathedral deserves an hour—but bear in mind that, as the number of visitors allowed inside is limited, the lines can be long. Another hour should be spent in the Starý Královský palác (Old Royal Palace). And you can spend several more hours taking in the museums, the views of the city, and the hidden nooks of the castle. Add in the many restaurants and shops of surrounding Hradčany (Castle Area), and you should budget a day for the whole experience.

## QUICK BITES

■ **Kavárna Nový Svět.** This cozy little café tucked away on one of the city's prettiest backstreets is a great stop for coffee and cake. ✉ Nový Svět 2, Hradčany ⊕ kavarna. novysvet.net Ⓜ Tram 22 to Brusnice

■ **Restaurace U Labutí.** Enjoy traditional, quality Czech pub grub without delay; you'll have a beer and menu in your hand within seconds of taking a seat. ✉ Hradčanské nám. 11, Hradčany ⊕ www.ulabuti. com Ⓜ Tram 22 to Pražský hrad

■ **Na Hubálce.** This is the place to come for big, meaty burgers served with fries and, of course, a frothy pilsner beer. ✉ Za Hládkovem 2, Hradčany ⊕ www. nahubalce.com Ⓜ Tram 22 to Hládkov

Despite its monolithic presence, Prague Castle is not a single structure but a collection of structures dating from the 10th to the 20th centuries, all linked by internal courtyards. The most important buildings with the castle complex are the St. Vitus Cathedral, a grand Gothic house of worship clearly visible soaring above the castle walls, and the Old Royal Palace, the official residence of kings and presidents and still the center of political power in the Czech Republic.

To the west of Prague Castle is the residential Hradčany, a town that emerged from a collection of monasteries and churches in the early 14th century. The concentration of history packed into Prague Castle and Hradčany challenges those not versed in the ups and downs of Bohemian kings, religious uprisings, wars, and oppression—but there's no shame in taking it all in on a purely aesthetic level.

## ◉ Sights

**Bazilika sv. Jiří** (*St. George's Basilica*)
**RELIGIOUS SITE** | Inside, this church looks more or less as it did in the 12th century; it's the best-preserved Romanesque relic in the country. The effect is at once barnlike and peaceful, as the warm golden yellow of the stone walls and the small arched windows exude a sense of enduring harmony. Prince Vratislav I originally built it in the 10th century,

though only the foundations remain from that time. The father of Prince Wenceslas (of Christmas carol fame) dedicated it to St. George (of dragon fame), a figure supposedly more agreeable to the still largely pagan people. The outside was remodeled during early baroque times, although the striking rusty-red color is in keeping with the look of the Romanesque edifice. The painted, house-shape tomb at the front of the church holds Vratislav's remains. Up the steps, in a chapel to the right, is the tomb Peter Parler designed for St. Ludmila, grandmother of St. Wenceslas. ✉ *Nám. U sv. Jiří, Pražský Hrad* ☎ *224-371-111* ⊕ *www.hrad.cz* 🎟 *Included in 2-day castle ticket (from 250 Kč)* Ⓜ *Line A: Malostranská plus Tram 22 to Pražský Hrad.*

**Druhé nádvoří** (*Second Courtyard*)
**PLAZA** | Built in the late 16th and early 17th centuries, the Second Courtyard was originally part of a reconstruction program commissioned by Rudolf II. He

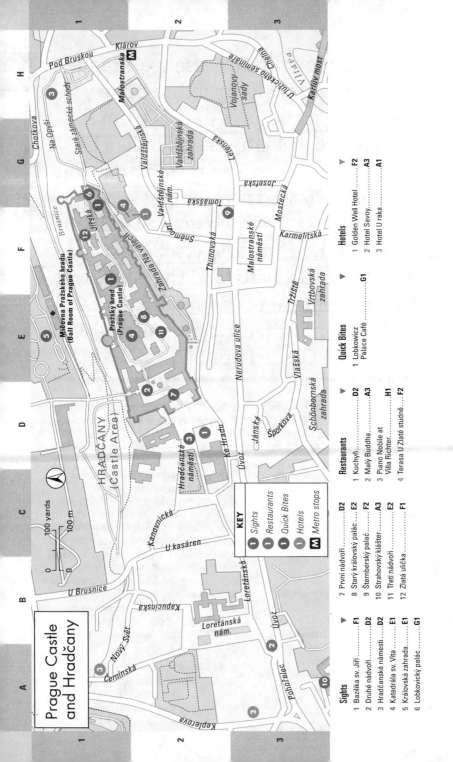

# Prague Castle and Hradčany

**Sights** ▶

1 Bazilika sv. Jiří .............. **F1**
2 Druhé nádvoří ............... **D2**
3 Hradčanské náměsti ....... **D2**
4 Katedrála sv. Víta .......... **E1**
5 Královská zahrada .......... **E1**
6 Lobkovický palác ........... **G1**

7 První nádvoří ................ **D2**
8 Starý královský palác ..... **E2**
9 Šternberský palác .......... **F2**
10 Strahovský klášter ........ **A3**
11 Třetí nádvoří ................ **E2**
12 Zlatá ulička ................. **F1**

**KEY**

1 Sights
1 Restaurants
1 Quick Bites
1 Hotels
M Metro stops

**Restaurants** ▶

1 Kuchyň ........................ **D2**
2 Malý Buddha ................. **A3**
3 Piano Nobile at
   Villa Richter ................. **H1**
4 Terasa U Zlaté studně ... **F2**

**Quick Bites** ▶

1 Lobkowicz
   Palace Café .................. **G1**

**Hotels** ▶

1 Golden Well Hotel .......... **F2**
2 Hotel Savoy .................. **A3**
3 Hotel U raka ................. **A1**

HRADČANY
(Castle Area)

Mičovna Pražského hradu
(Ball Room of Prague Castle)

Pražský hrad
(Prague Castle)

St. George's Basilica is the oldest church building within the Prague Castle complex.

amassed a large and famed collection of fine and decorative art, scientific instruments, philosophical and alchemical books, natural wonders, coins, and a hodgepodge of other treasures. The bulk of the collection was looted by the Swedes during the Thirty Years' War, removed to Vienna when the imperial capital returned there after Rudolf's death, or auctioned off during the 18th century. Artworks that survived the turmoil, for the most part acquired after Rudolf's time, are displayed in the **Obrazárna** (Picture Gallery) on the courtyard's left side as you face St. Vitus. In rooms redecorated by castle architect Bořek Šípek, there are good Renaissance, mannerist, and baroque paintings that demonstrate the luxurious tastes of Rudolf's court.

Except for the view of the spires of St. Vitus Cathedral, the exterior courtyard offers little for the eye to feast on. Empress Maria Theresa's court architect, Nicolò Pacassi, received imperial approval to remake the castle in the 1760s, as it

was badly damaged by Prussian shelling during the Seven Years' War in 1757. The Second Courtyard was the main victim of Pacassi's attempts at imparting classical grandeur to what had been a picturesque collection of Gothic and Renaissance styles. This courtyard also houses the rather gaudy **Kaple sv. Kříže** (Chapel of the Holy Cross), with decorations from the 18th and 19th centuries, which now serves as a souvenir and ticket stand.

Across the passageway by the gallery entrance is the **Císařská konírna** (Imperial Stable), where temporary exhibitions are held. The passageway at the northern end of the courtyard forms the northern entrance to the castle and leads out over a luxurious ravine known as the **Jelení příkop** (Stag Moat), which can be entered either here or at the lower end via the metal catwalk off Chotkova ulice, when it isn't closed for sporadic renovations. ✉ *Pražský Hrad* ☎ *224–372–423* ⊕ *www. hrad.cz* ✉ *Courtyard free, Picture Gallery 100 Kč or incl. in 2-day castle ticket (from*

*250 Kč)* Ⓜ *Line A: Malostranská plus Tram 22 to Pražský Hrad.*

**Hradčanské náměstí** (*Hradčany Square*)
**PLAZA** | With its fabulous mixture of Baroque and Renaissance houses, topped by Prague Castle itself, this square had a prominent role in the film *Amadeus* (as a substitute for Vienna). Czech director Miloš Forman used the house at No. 7 for Mozart's residence, where the composer was haunted by the masked figure he thought was his father. The flamboyant Rococo **Arcibiskupský palác,** on the left as you face the Castle, was the Viennese archbishop's palace. For a brief time after World War II, No. 11 was home to a little girl named Marie Jana Korbelová, better known as former U.S. Secretary of State Madeleine Albright. ⊠ *Hradčanské náměstí, Hradčany* Ⓜ *Line A: Malostranská plus Tram No. 22 to Pražský Hrad.*

**Královská zahrada** (*Royal Garden*)
**CITY PARK** | This peaceful swath of greenery affords lovely views of St. Vitus Cathedral and the castle's walls and bastions. Originally laid out in the 16th century, it endured devastation in war, neglect in times of peace, and many redesigns, reaching its present parklike form in the early 20th century. Luckily, its Renaissance treasures survived. One of these is the long, narrow **Míčovna** (Ball Game Hall), built by Bonifaz Wohlmut in 1568, its garden front completely covered by a dense tangle of allegorical *sgraffiti.*

The **Královský letohrádek** (Royal Summer Palace, aka Queen Anne's Summer Palace or Belvedere), at the garden's eastern end, deserves its unusual reputation as one of the most beautiful Renaissance structures north of the Alps. Italian architects began it and Wohlmut finished it off in the 1560s, complete with a copper roof like an upturned boat's keel riding above the graceful arcades of the ground floor. During the 18th and 19th centuries military engineers tested artillery in the interior, which had already

lost its rich furnishings to Swedish soldiers during their siege of the city in 1648. The Renaissance-style *giardinetto* (little garden) adjoining the summer palace centers on another masterwork, the Italian-designed, Czech-produced Singing Fountain, which resonates from the sound of falling water. ⊠ *U Prašného mostu ul. and Mariánské hradby ul. near Chotkovy Park, Pražský Hrad* ☏ *224–372–435* ⊕ *www.hrad.cz* ▨ *Free* Ⓜ *Line A: Malostranská plus Tram 22 to Pražský Hrad.*

★ **Katedrála sv. Víta** (*St. Vitus Cathedral*)
**RELIGIOUS SITE** | With its graceful, soaring towers, this Gothic cathedral—among the most beautiful in Europe—is the spiritual heart of Prague Castle and of the Czech Republic itself. The cathedral has a long and complicated history, beginning in the 10th century and continuing to its completion in 1929. It's possible to enter the cathedral for free to take in the splendor from the back, but for the full experience, buy a ticket and walk around. You'll get even more out of the visit with the audio guide, which is available at the castle information center. ⊠ *Hrad III. nádvoří 2, Pražský Hrad* ☏ *224–372–434* ⊕ *www.katedralasvatehovita.cz* ▨ *Included in 2-day castle ticket (from 250 Kč)* Ⓜ *Line A: Malostranská plus Tram 22 to Pražský Hrad.*

**Lobkovický palác** (*Lobkowicz Palace*)
**MUSEUM** | Greatly benefiting from a recent renovation, this palace is a showcase for baroque and rococo styling. Exhibits here trace the ancestry of the Lobkowicz family, who were great patrons of the arts in their heyday (Beethoven was just one of the artists who received their funding). The audio tour adds a personal touch: it's narrated by William Lobkowicz, the family scion who spearheaded the property's restitution and rehabilitation, and includes quite a few anecdotes about the family through the years. Although inside the Prague Castle complex, this museum has a

Queen Anne's Summer Palace was commissioned by Ferdinand I in 1538 for his loving wife, but she never stepped foot in it as she passed away while delivering her 15th child.

separate admission. ⊠ *Jiřská 3, Pražský Hrad* ☎ *233–312–925* ⊕ *www.lobkowicz. cz* ✉ *295 Kč* Ⓜ *Line A: Malostranská.*

### První nádvoří (*First Courtyard*)

**PLAZA** | The main entrance to Prague Castle from Hradčanské náměstí is certain to impress any first-time visitor. Going through the wrought-iron gate, guarded at ground level by uniformed Czech soldiers and from above by the ferocious *Battling Titans* (a copy of Ignaz Platzer's original 18th-century work), you enter this courtyard, built on the site of old moats and gates that once separated the castle from the surrounding buildings and thus protected the vulnerable western flank. The courtyard is one of the more recent additions to the castle, designed by Maria Theresa's court architect, Nicolò Pacassi, in the 1760s. Today it forms part of the presidential office complex. Pacassi's reconstruction was intended to unify the eclectic collection of buildings that made up the castle, but the effect of his work is somewhat flat.

At its eastern end of the courtyard is **Matyášova brána** (Matthias Gate). Built in 1614, this stone gate once stood alone in front of the moats and bridges that surrounded the castle. Under the Habsburgs, the gate survived by being grafted as a relief onto the palace building. As you go through it, notice the ceremonial white-marble entrance halls on either side that lead up to the Czech president's reception rooms (which are only rarely open to the public).

■ TIP→ **Try to arrive on the hour to witness the changing of the guard; the fanfare peaks at noon with a special flag ceremony in the First Courtyard.** ⊠ *Pražský Hrad* ☎ *224–372–434* ⊕ *www.hrad.cz* Ⓜ *Line A: Malostranská plus Tram 22 to Pražský Hrad.*

### Starý královský palác (*Old Royal Palace*)

**CASTLE/PALACE** | A jumble of styles and add-ons from different eras are gathered in this palace. The best way to grasp its size is from within the **Vladislavský sál** (Vladislav Hall), the largest secular Gothic interior space in Central Europe.

Benedikt Ried completed the hall in 1493 (he was to late Bohemian Gothic what Peter Parler was to the earlier version). The room imparts a sense of space and light, softened by the sensuous lines of the vaulted ceilings and brought to a dignified close by the simple oblong form of the early Renaissance windows. In its heyday, the hall held jousting tournaments, festive markets, banquets, and coronations. In more recent times, it has been used to inaugurate presidents, from the communist leader Klement Gottwald (in 1948) to modern-day leaders like Václav Havel and current president Miloš Zeman.

From the front of the hall, turn right into the rooms of the **Česká kancelář** (Bohemian Chancellery). This wing was built by Benedikt Ried only 10 years after the hall was completed, but it shows a much stronger Renaissance influence. Pass through the portal into the last chamber of the chancellery. In 1618 this room was the site of the second defenestration of Prague, an event that marked the beginning of the Bohemian rebellion and, ultimately, the Thirty Years' War throughout Europe. The square window used in this protest is on the left as you enter the room.

At the back of Vladislav Hall a staircase leads up to a gallery of the **Kaple všech svatých** (All Saints' Chapel). Little remains of Peter Parler's original work, but the church contains some fine works of art. The large room to the left of the staircase is the **Stará sněmovna** (Council Chamber), where the Bohemian nobles met with the king in a prototype parliament of sorts. The descent from Vladislav Hall toward what remains of the **Romanský palác** (Romanesque Palace) is by way of a wide, shallow set of steps. This **Jezdecké schody** (Riders' Staircase) was the entranceway for knights who came for the jousting tournaments. ⊠ Hrad III. nádvoří, Pražský Hrad ☎ 224–372–434 ⊕ www.hrad.cz ✉ Included in 2-day

castle ticket (from 250 Kč) Ⓜ Line A: Malostranská plus Tram 22 to Pražský Hrad.

★ **Strahovský klášter** (Strahov Monastery) RELIGIOUS SITE | Founded by the Premonstratensian order in 1140, the monastery remained theirs until 1952, when the Communists suppressed all religious orders and turned the entire complex into the **Památník národního písemnictví** (Museum of National Literature). The major building of interest is the **Strahov Library,** with its collection of early Czech manuscripts, the 10th-century Strahov New Testament, and the collected works of famed Danish astronomer Tycho Brahe. Also of note is the late-18th-century **Philosophical Hall.** Its ceilings are engulfed in a startling sky-blue fresco that depicts an unusual cast of characters, including Socrates' nagging wife Xanthippe; Greek astronomer Thales, with his trusty telescope; and a collection of Greek philosophers mingling with Descartes, Diderot, and Voltaire. ⊠ Strahovské nádvoří 1, Hradčany ☎ 233–107–704 ⊕ www. strahovskyklaster.cz ✉ 120 Kč library Ⓜ Line A: Malostranská plus Tram No. 22 to Pohořelec.

**Šternberský palác** (Sternberg Palace) MUSEUM | The 18th-century Šternberský palác houses the National Gallery's collection of antiquities and paintings by European masters from the 14th to the 18th century. Holdings include impressive works by El Greco, Rubens, and Rembrandt. ⊠ Hradčanské nám. 15, Hradčany ☎ 233–090–570 ⊕ www. ngprague.cz ✉ 220 Kč ⊗ Closed Mon. Ⓜ Line A: Malostranská plus Tram No. 22 to Pražský Hrad.

**Třetí nádvoří** (Third Courtyard) PLAZA | The contrast between the cool, dark interior of St. Vitus Cathedral and the brightly colored Pacassi façades of the Third Courtyard just outside is startling. Noted Slovenian architect Josip Plečnik created the courtyard's clean lines in the 1930s, but the modern look is a

deception. Plečnik's paving was intended to cover an underground world of house foundations, streets, and walls from the 9th through 12th centuries and was rediscovered when the cathedral was completed. (You can see a few archways through a grating in a wall of the cathedral.) Plečnik added a few features to catch the eye: a granite obelisk to commemorate the fallen of World War I, a black-marble pedestal for the Gothic statue of St. George (a copy of the National Gallery's original statue), an inconspicuous entrance to his Bull Staircase leading down to the south garden, and a peculiar golden ball topping the eagle fountain near the eastern end of the courtyard. ✉ *Pražský Hrad* ☎ *224–372–434* 🌐 *www.hrad.cz* [M] *Line A: Malostranská plus Tram 22 to Pražský Hrad.*

★ **Zlatá ulička** (*Golden Lane*)
**NEIGHBORHOOD** | A jumbled collection of tiny, ancient, brightly colored houses crouched under the fortification wall looks remarkably like a set for *Snow White and the Seven Dwarfs*. Purportedly, these were the lodgings for an international group of alchemists whom Rudolf II brought to the court to produce gold. But the truth is a little less romantic: the houses were built during the 16th century for the castle guards. By the early 20th century Golden Lane had become the home of poor artists and writers. Franz Kafka, who lived at No. 22 in 1916 and 1917, described the house on first sight as "so small, so dirty, impossible to live in, and lacking everything necessary." But he soon came to love the place. As he wrote to his fiancée, "Life here is something special, to close out the world not just by shutting the door to a room or apartment but to the whole house, to step out into the snow of the silent lane." The lane now holds tiny stores selling books, music, and crafts, as well as including some exhibitions on former residents and their professions. It has become so popular that an admission fee is charged. The houses are cute, but crowds can be uncomfortable, and the fact remains that you are paying money for the privilege of walking down a narrow street. Within the walls above Golden Lane, a timber-roof corridor (enter between No. 23 and No. 24) is lined with replica suits of armor and weapons (some of them for sale), mock torture chambers, and a shooting gallery.

As you exit Golden Lane, you will also have an opportunity to visit Daliborka on the same ticket. This round cannon tower dates back to 1496 and gained notoriety through the centuries for its use as a brutal prison. Some of the instruments of torture used on its inmates, including the knight Dalibor of Kozojedy (for whom the tower is named), are now on display. ✉ *Pražský Hrad* ☎ *224–372–423* 🌐 *www.hrad.cz* 🎫 *Included in 2-day castle ticket (from 250 Kč)* [M] *Line A: Malostranská.*

## 🍴 Restaurants

The streets surrounding main square Hradčanské náměstí have several restaurants and cafés open for lunch, as does the area around Strahov Monastery. But for dinner, with Prague Castle having closed down for the day and tourists having dissipated, you'll find the best dining options in the farther reaches of Hradčany.

★ **Kuchyň**
**$$** | **CZECH** | This novel, menu-less restaurant offers a stove covered in pots and pans and leaves it up to you to lift the lids, take a sniff, and choose your meal accordingly. The focus is on Czech cuisine but with a look back into its culinary past with dishes like beef cheeks in plum sauce. **Known for:** soft sourdough bread to dip in soups; wonderful location by the castle; drinks including unfiltered dark beer. [$] *Average main: 245 Kč* ✉ *Hradčanské nám. 1, Hradčany* ☎ *736–152–891* 🌐 *kuchyn.ambi.cz* [M] *Line A: Malostranská plus Tram 22 to Pražský hrad.*

### Malý Buddha

**$$ | ASIAN |** Bamboo, wood, paper, incense—and the random creepy mask on the wall—are all part of the decor at this earthy hilltop hideaway near Prague Castle. It's as much about the atmosphere as the food here, which isn't complex but is cooked with heart; expect spring rolls, vegetable and mixed stir-fries, and various fish and chicken dishes, all in generous portions. **Known for:** lovely candlelit setting; extensive tea menu; cash only. $ *Average main: 190 Kč* ⊠ *Úvoz 46, Hradčany* 🕾 *220–513–894* ⊕ *www.malybuddha.cz* 🚍 *No credit cards* 🕙 *Closed Mon.* Ⓜ *Line A: Hradčanská plus Tram 32 or 35 to Pohořelec.*

### ★ Terasa U Zlaté studně

**$$$$ | EUROPEAN |** This fine-dining establishment is widely considered to be one of the country's best restaurants—and for good reason. First and foremost, the food is simply superb; expect mouthwatering Czech and international dishes, created by head chef Pavel Sapík and cooked to perfection. **Known for:** the best from-the-table view in Prague; mouthwateringly tender fallow deer; slightly tricky location. $ *Average main: 950 Kč* ⊠ *Golden Well Hotel, U Zlaté studně 4, Hradčany* 🕾 *257–533–322* ⊕ *www.terasauzlatestudne.cz* Ⓜ *Line A: Malostranská.*

### Piano Nobile at Villa Richter

**$$$ | FRENCH |** Set within an 18th-century neoclassical villa on the steps up to the castle, the upmarket Piano Nobile restaurant in Villa Richter offers decadently saucy dishes, from escargots drowning in herb butter to guinea fowl slathered in paprika sauce. The floral-wallpapered interior is gorgeous, but it's the outdoor terrace that has the best views, with the red roofs of Malá Strana to the right and the church spires of Staré Město (Old Town) to the left. **Known for:** wonderful city panoramas; impressive selection of wines; steak tartare. $ *Average main: 600 Kč* ⊠ *Staré zámecké schody 6,* *Hradčany* 🕾 *702–205–108* ⊕ *www.villar-ichter.cz* Ⓜ *Line A: Malostranská.*

##  Coffee and Quick Bites

### Lobkowicz Palace Café

**$$ | CAFÉ |** When visiting the castle, break for a coffee, pastry, or even lunch and enjoy one of the loveliest views of the city from the outdoor terrace of the Lobkowicz Palace Café. The menu is a touch expensive but full of delicious sandwiches, including ham and cheese, tuna, and smoked salmon, plus beverages and desserts. **Known for:** wonderful city panoramas; simple snacks and Czech classics; closing for the evening. $ *Average main: 280 Kč* ⊠ *Lobkovický palác, Jiřská 3, Pražský Hrad* 🕾 *233–356–978* ⊕ *www.lobkowicz.cz* Ⓜ *Line A: Malostranská.*

## 🛏 Hotels

For some, Prague Castle and Hradčany is the romantic heart of this city. Though it is a hectic spot during the day with a lot of foot traffic, it completely empties in the evening, so staying in this area can feel like having Prague all to yourself.

### ★ Golden Well Hotel (*U Zlaté studně*)

**$$$ | HOTEL |** Consistently rated one of Prague's best boutique hotels, Golden Well offers luxurious rooms with stellar views, first-class service, and one of the city's finest restaurants. **Pros:** luxurious rooms with modern bathrooms; excellent restaurant; magnificent views. **Cons:** the excellent breakfast is not included; rooms are not soundproof; not family friendly. $ *Rooms from: 6500 Kč* ⊠ *U Zlaté studně 4, Hradčany* 🕾 *257–011–213* ⊕ *www.goldenwell.cz* 🛏 *19 rooms* 🍽 *No meals* Ⓜ *Line A: Malostranská.*

### Hotel Savoy

**$$$ | HOTEL |** A modest Jugendstil façade conceals one of the city's most luxurious small hotels. **Pros:** peaceful location above it all; small but well-stocked bar; refurbished sauna facilities. **Cons:** long (uphill) walk home; some noise from tram stop outside; expensive for the area. $ *Rooms from: 5250 Kč* ✉ *Keplerova 6, Hradčany* ☎ *224–302–430* ⊕ *www.hotelsavoyprague.com* ➷ *61 rooms* ⦿ *Breakfast* Ⓜ *Line A: Malostranská plus Tram 22 to Pohořelec.*

### ★ Hotel U raka

$$ | HOTEL | With the quaint look of a woodsman's cottage from a bedtime story, this private guesthouse is saturated with romance. **Pros:** near Prague Castle but feels secluded; in-room fireplaces in some rooms; has a peaceful garden. **Cons:** tiny size makes rooms hard to come by; private parking costs extra; no Metro station nearby. $ *Rooms from: 4250 Kč* ✉ *Černínská 10, Hradčany* ☎ *220–511–100* ⊕ *www.hoteluraka.cz* ➷ *6 rooms* ⦿ *Breakfast* Ⓜ *Line A: Malostranská plus Tram 22 to Brusnice.*

##  Nightlife

There are a few good bars dotted around Prague Castle and Hradčany. Head up the castle hill to quaff beers that were brewed in a 13th-century monastery.

### BARS AND PUBS

#### ★ Klášterní pivovar Strahov

BREWPUBS/BEER GARDENS | The first references to this gorgeous hilltop brewery inside a monastery are from the turn of the 14th century, and while we don't think the monks still actually make the beer, the tasty Pivo Sv. Norbert is brewed on the spot. There's a decent food menu and outdoor seating too. ✉ *Strahovské nádvoří 10, Hradčany* ☎ *233–353–155* ⊕ *www.klasterni-pivovar.cz* Ⓜ *Line A: Malostranská plus Tram 22 to Pohořelec.*

#### U Černého vola

BARS/PUBS | The last old-fashioned pub in Hradčany, this place has cheap beer and the classic long tables. It's almost impossible to find many seats together at any time, though. Terry Jones, of Monty Python fame, is known to be a fan. The name translates as "At the Black

Ox," and while it's a little run-down on the outside, and is sometimes mistaken for being closed, once you're inside you are unlikely to leave in a hurry. The menu is in Czech, but trot out the trusty phrase *"Jedno pivo, prosím"* (One beer, please) and you'll be fine. ✉ *Loretánské nám. 1, Hradčany* ☎ *606–626–929* ⊕ *facebook.com/ucernehovola* Ⓜ *Line A: Hradčandská.*

## ⬤ Performing Arts

### CHURCH CONCERTS

**Bazilika sv. Jiří** (*St. George's Basilica*)
CONCERTS | Listen to small ensembles playing well-known Vivaldi and other classical "greatest hits" in a Romanesque setting. Located in Prague Castle, the building—or parts of it at least—dates to the 11th century and holds the tombs of some very early princes. ✉ *Nám. U sv. Jiří, Pražský Hrad* ☎ *224–371–111* ⊕ *www.kulturanahrade.cz* Ⓜ *Line A: Malostranská.*

## ⬤ Shopping

It's more about the views than the shopping in Hradčany, but while you're checking out those views, check out the traditional craft shops as well.

### Rocking Horse Toy Shop

GIFTS/SOUVENIRS | FAMILY | Take a trip back in time to when toys were made from wood and model cars were cherished. Everything about this store will make you smile, from the friendly owner's greeting to the stock of cheerful wind-up music boxes and animal figurines. Look closely at those wood-carved rocking horses and three-headed dragons; many items are handmade by Czech craftsmen. The shop even sells kits with colored pencils and pastels for budding young artists. ✉ *Loretánské nám. 3, Hradčany* ☎ *603–515–745* Ⓜ *Line A: Malostranská plus Tram 22 to Pohořelec.*

# Chapter 6

# NOVÉ MĚSTO

Updated by
Jennifer Rigby

| ◉ Sights | 🍴 Restaurants | 🛏 Hotels | 🛍 Shopping | 🍸 Nightlife |
|----------|---------------|----------|-------------|-------------|
| ★★★☆☆ | ★★★★☆ | ★★★★☆ | ★★★★★ | ★★★☆☆ |

# NEIGHBORHOOD SNAPSHOT

## TOP EXPERIENCES

■ **Wencelas Square:** Stand at the top of this strip and feel the weight of history: this is where Czechs overthrew communism via the massive protests of the Velvet Revolution in 1989.

■ **Kantýna:** The Czechs know their meat, and that's particularly evident at recently opened Kantýna, a butcher-cum-restaurant with top-quality cuts and a convivial atmosphere in a former bank.

■ **Lucerna:** Whether you're looking for a grand hall, an underground music bar, a historic former palace, some cheeky modern art, a café, a cinema, or even a rooftop bar, this wonderful building has it all (and is a good example of the *pasáže*, or arcades, in this area).

■ **Náplavka:** All of Nové Město (New Town) has good shopping, but to really feel like a local, hit up Náplavka's farmers' market by the river on a Saturday.

■ **Café Culture:** Make like a turn-of-the-century intellectual at one of Prague's grand cafés; the best are at the Obecní dům (Municipal House) and Café Slavia.

■ **National Theater:** Book in advance for great prices for opera and ballet performances in a grand setting.

## GETTING HERE

The best Metro stops for this area are those at Karlovo náměstí (Line B), Muzeum (Lines A and C), and Můstek (Lines A and B). Various trams run around the neighborhood, too, particularly along Vodičkova and Národní.

## PLANNING YOUR TIME

Václavské náměstí (Wenceslas Square) is well connected by public transport, and a short walk from most of the city center hotels. From here, leave at least an hour to cover the surrounding area, and then head up to Karlovo náměstí (Charles Square) or down the main pedestrianized shopping street, Na příkopě, to Náměstí Republiky. Leave an hour or two for the museums, churches, or parks at either end of Nové Město.

## QUICK BITES

■ **Mamacoffee.** Top-quality coffee (the founders were inspired to start their business after a trip to Ethiopia) and good grub, too, at this large, light coffee shop and roastery. ⊠ *Vodičkova 6, Nové Město* ⊕ *www.mamacoffee.cz* Ⓜ Karlovo náměstí or Lazarská

■ **Lahůdky Zlatý kříž (Golden Cross Deli).** Choose from more than 50 varieties of *chlebíček* (Czech traditional open sandwich) here. ⊠ *Jungmannova 34, Nové Město* ⊕ *www.typicalczechdeli.cz* Ⓜ Můstek

■ **Cacao.** Tasty, fresh superfoods, smoothies, and bowls sit alongside rather more indulgent cakes and homemade ice creams at this café just off Náměstí Republiky. ⊠ *V Celnici 1031/4, Nové Město* ⊕ *www.cacaoprague.cz* Ⓜ Náměstí Republiky

Though Nové Město translates as "New Town," its origins go all the way back to the 14th century and Emperor Charles IV. As Prague outgrew its Staré Město (Old Town) parameters, Charles IV extended the city's fortifications. A high wall surrounded the newly developed 2½-square-km (1½-square-mile) area south and east of Staré Město, tripling the walled territory on the Vltava's right bank. The wall extended south to link with the fortifications of the citadel called Vyšehrad.

But don't come here looking for Staré Město charm; although there are still some beautiful spots and fantastic period architecture, the magical alleyway vibe of that part of the city is completely absent. This part of Prague was instead thoroughly rebuilt in the mid-19th century in the neoclassical and neo-Renaissance styles and today forms the modern heart of the capital, particularly around the two main squares: Wenceslas Square and Charles Square. The area is great for hotels and restaurants, but the number of traditional sights is relatively small, with just a handful of important museums and churches. It does feel more like a "proper" city here, though, and it gets less clogged with tourists, so it can be a good base for practical travelers.

##  Sights

**Františkánská zahrada** (*Franciscan Garden*)

**GARDEN** | A peaceful green space in the heart of the city, the Franciscan Garden was established by monks from the nearby Carmelite Monastery to grow herbs and spices back in the 14th century, around the same time as Nové Město itself was founded. It remains a small oasis, with benches shaded by rose bushes, low hedges, a playground, and fruit trees and herb gardens that refer back to its original function. There's also a very cute café in the corner, Truhlárna, which does excellent cakes. ⊠ *Jungmannovo nám., Nové Mesto* ☎ *221–097–231* 🎫 *Free* Ⓜ *Lines A and B: Můstek.*

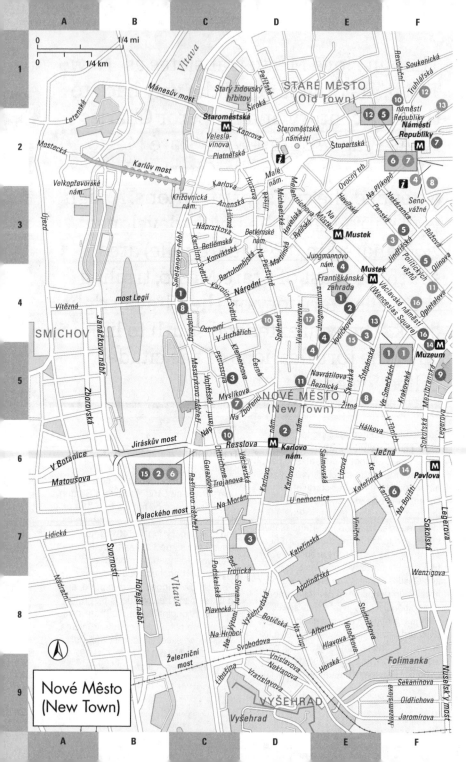

Nové Mêsto
(New Town)

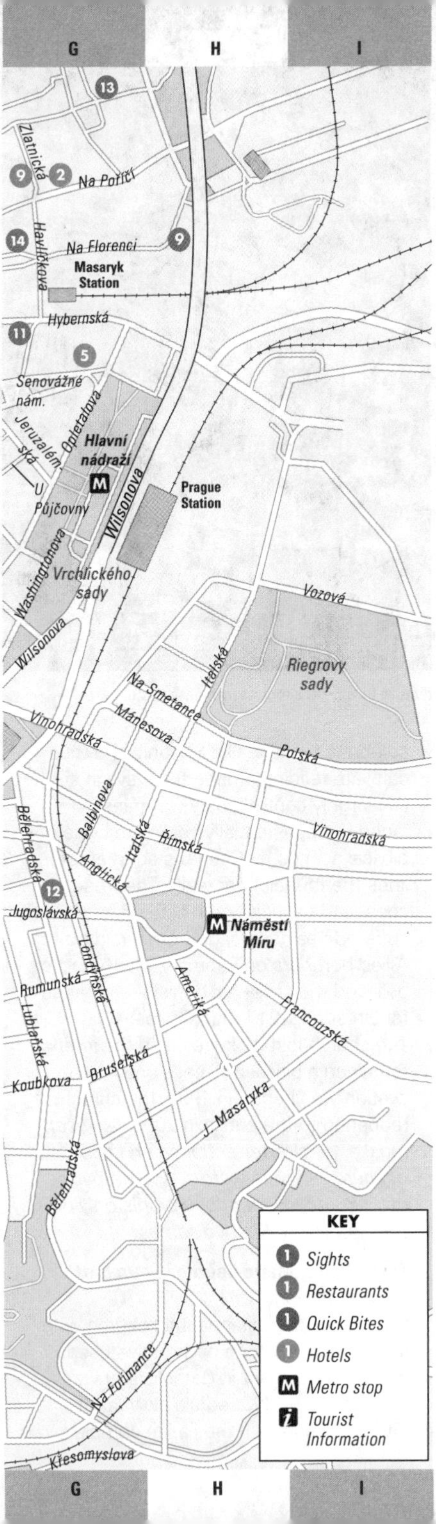

**6**

Nové Město

### Sights ▼

1 Františkánská zahrada ................... **E4**
2 Karlovo náměstí......... **D6**
3 Klášter Emauzy.......... **D7**
4 Kostel Panny Marie Sněžné ........... **E4**
5 Mucha Museum ......... **F3**
6 Muzeum Antonína Dvořáka................... **F6**
7 Muzeum Komunismu.... **F2**
8 Národní divadlo.......... **C4**
9 Národní muzeum ........ **F5**
10 Národní památník hrdinů heydrichiády.... **C6**
11 Novoměstská radnice.................. **D5**
12 Obecní dům.............. **F2**
13 Palác Lucerna........... **E4**
14 Statue of St. Wenceslas........... **F5**
15 Tančící dům ............. **C6**
16 Václavské náměstí...... **F4**

### Restaurants ▼

1 Alcron.................... **E4**
2 Ginger & Fred ........... **C6**
3 Jáma ..................... **E4**
4 Kafe Komedie .......... **D5**
5 Kantýna .................. **F3**
6 Le Grill................... **F2**
7 Lemon Leaf .............. **C5**
8 Levitate .................. **E5**
9 Manifesto Market ...... **H2**
10 Pizza Nuova ............. **F1**
11 Potrefená Husa ......... **G2**
12 Radost FX Café.......... **G6**
13 Sansho.................. **G1**
14 Zinc...................... **G2**

### Quick Bites ▼

1 Café Slavia .............. **C4**
2 Cukrárna Myšák ......... **E4**
3 Globe Bookstore & Café.................... **C5**
4 Home Kitchen............ **E4**
5 Kavárna Obecní dům.... **F2**

### Hotels ▼

1 Alcron Hotel.............. **E4**
2 Art Deco Imperial Hotel .......... **G1**
3 Art Nouveau Palace Hotel............. **F3**
4 Best Western Plus Hotel Meteor Plaza.... **F2**
5 Carlo IV, The Dedica Anthology, Autograph Collection............... **G2**
6 Dancing House Hotel.... **C6**
7 The Grand Mark ......... **F2**
8 Hotel Boho Prague ...... **F2**
9 Hotel Cosmopolitan..... **G1**
10 Hotel Élite Prague ...... **D4**
11 Hotel Grandium Prague ................... **F4**
12 Hotel Salvator............ **F1**
13 Ibis Old Town Hotel...... **F1**
14 Ibis Praha Wenceslas Square Hotel ............. **F6**
15 The ICON ................. **E5**
16 Jalta Boutique Hotel .... **F4**
17 Michelangelo Grand Hotel.............. **D4**

**KEY**

❶ Sights
❶ Restaurants
❶ Quick Bites
❶ Hotels
Ⓜ Metro stop
🛈 Tourist Information

Lovers of art nouveau can take in Obecní dům's architecture by day on a tour or by night at a concert.

**Karlovo náměstí** (*Charles Square*)

PLAZA | This square began life as a cattle market, a function chosen by Charles IV when he established Nové Město in 1348. The horse market (now Wenceslas Square) quickly overtook it as a live-stock-trading center, and an untidy collection of shacks accumulated here until the mid-1800s, when it became a green park named for its patron. Glassy, modern buildings clash with surrounding older architecture, but it's quite representative of Prague's past and present united in one spot. ⊠ *Nové Mesto* ✛ *Bounded by Řeznická on the north, U Nemocnice on the south, Karlovo nám. on the west, and Vodičkova on the east* Ⓜ *Line B: Karlovo náměstí.*

**Klášter Emauzy** (*Emmaus Monastery*)

RELIGIOUS SITE | Another of Charles IV's gifts to the city, the Benedictine monastery sits south of Charles Square. It's often called Na Slovanech (literally, "At the Slavs"), which refers to its purpose when it was established in 1347. The emperor invited Croatian monks here to celebrate mass in Old Slavonic and thus cultivate religion among the Slavs in a city largely controlled by Germans. A faded but substantially complete cycle of biblical scenes by Charles's court artists lines the four cloister walls. The frescoes, and especially the abbey church, suffered heavy damage from a raid by Allied bombers on February 14, 1945; it's believed they may have mistaken Prague for Dresden, 121 km (75 miles) away. The church lost its spires, and the interior remained a blackened shell until a renovation was begun in 1998; the church reopened to the public in 2003. ⊠ *Vyšehradská 49, cloister entrance on left at rear of church, Nové Mesto* ⊕ *www.emauzy. cz* ⊠ *60 Kč* ⊙ *Open for worship only on Sun.* Ⓜ *Line B: Karlovo náměstí.*

**Kostel Panny Marie Sněžné** (*Church of Our Lady of the Snows*)

RELIGIOUS SITE | This beautiful church with its poetic name (one of the titles used for the Virgin Mary in Catholicism) was intended to rival Katedrála sv. Víta (St. Vitus Cathedral), in the castle complex, for grandeur when Charles IV started building it in the 14th century; alas it was never finished and still has a slightly odd shape as a result of that today, taller than it is long. It has the highest vaults and column altar in the city. ⊠ *Jungmannovo nám. 753/18, Nové Mesto* ☎ *222–246–243* ⊕ *pms.ofm.cz* 🖸 *Free* Ⓜ *Lines A and B: Můstek.*

### Mucha Museum

MUSEUM | For decades it was almost impossible to find an Alfons Mucha original in his homeland, but in 1998 this private museum opened with nearly 100 works from this justly famous Czech artist's long career. Everything you expect to see from the man famed for his art nouveau style is here—the theater posters of actress Sarah Bernhardt, the eye-popping advertising posters, and the sinuous, intricate designs. Also exhibited are paintings, photographs taken in Mucha's studio (one shows Paul Gauguin playing the piano in his underwear), and even Czechoslovak banknotes designed by Mucha. ⊠ *Panská 7, Nové Mesto* ✛ *1 block off Václavské nám., across from Palace Hotel* ☎ *224–216–415* ⊕ *www. mucha.cz* 🖸 *300 Kč* Ⓜ *Lines A and B: Můstek.*

### Muzeum Antonína Dvořáka (*Antonín Dvořák Museum*)

MUSEUM | The stately red-and-yellow baroque villa housing this museum displays the 19th-century Czech composer's scores, photographs, viola, piano, and other memorabilia. The statues in the garden date to about 1735; the house is from 1720. Check the schedule for classical performances, as recitals are often held in the first floor of the two-story villa. ⊠ *Ke Karlovu 20, Nové Mesto* ☎ *224–918–013* ⊕ *www.antonin-dvorak.cz/muzea* 🖸 *50 Kč* ☽ *Closed Mon.* Ⓜ *Line C: I. P. Pavlova.*

### Muzeum komunismu (*Museum of Communism*)

MUSEUM | Formerly and perhaps ironically located in the Savarin Palace next to the

## Prague by Pedalo

There is no better way to see the beautiful riverside buildings of Staré Město and Nové Město on one side, and the magnificent vista of the castle on the other, than by boat. Specifically, a *pedalo*. Rent one from Slovanka boat rental on the island by the National Theater (⊠ *Slovanský ostrov, Nové Město*, ☎ *777–870–511*, ⊕ *www.slovanka.net*). And because this is beer-loving Prague, there's a pedal-up bar on the same island where you can get a drink to fuel your journey.

twin capitalist symbols of the yellow arches of a McDonald's and a casino, the Museum of Communism has relocated into a brightly lit and larger new space in V Celnici, albeit still next to a supermarket. The expanded museum offers a vivid look at life in Prague and then-Czechoslovakia under the totalitarian regime that held power from the coup in February 1948 through the Velvet Revolution in November 1989. Find works of social realist art, original texts and photos from the archives of the Security Services, film, and dozens of exhibits that explore the days of the ČSSR through sport, education, art, propaganda, and censorship. Exhibits tread the line between menacing and enlightening, showing aspects of daily life as well as the terrifying repercussions of noncompliance. ⊠ *V Celnici 4, Nové Mesto* ☎ *224–212–966* ⊕ *www. muzeumkomunismu.cz* 🖸 *380 Kč* Ⓜ *Line B: Náměstí Republiky.*

### Národní divadlo (*National Theater*)

ARTS VENUE | Statues representing Drama and Opera rise above the riverfront side entrances to this theater, and two gigantic chariots flank figures of Apollo and the nine Muses above the main façade.

The performance space lacks restraint as well: it's filled with gilding, voluptuous plaster figures, and plush upholstery. The idea for a Czech national theater began during the revolutionary decade of the 1840s. In a telling display of national pride, donations to fund the plan poured in from all over the country, from people of every socioeconomic stratum. The cornerstone was laid in 1868, and the "National Theater generation" who built the neo-Renaissance structure became the architectural and artistic establishment for decades to come. Its designer, Josef Zítek, was the leading neo-Renaissance architect in Bohemia. The nearly finished interior was gutted by a fire in 1881, and Zítek's onetime student Josef Schulz saw the reconstruction through to completion two years later. Today, it's still the country's leading dramatic stage. ■TIP➜ Guided tours in English (for groups only) can be arranged by phone or email in advance. ✉ Národní 2, Nové Mesto ☎ 224–901–448 for box office ⊕ www.narodni-divadlo.cz ☜ Tours 200 Kč Ⓜ Line B: Národní třída.

★ **Národní muzeum** (National Museum)
MUSEUM | Housed in a grandiose neo-Renaissance structure that dominates the top of Wenceslas Square, the National Museum was built between 1885 to 1890 as a symbol of the Czech national revival. Indeed, the building's exterior is so impressive that invading Soviet soldiers in 1968 mistook it for parliament. The holdings are a cross between natural history and ethnography and include dinosaur bones, minerals, textiles, coins, and many, many other things. The museum is gradually unveiling its vast collection after a long period of renovation, and there are rotating exhibitions, too, but the building remains a pretty spectacular draw in its own right while more and more exhibits are dusted off and brought out from storage. The gift shop has lots of treasures, too, including brooches made of the museum's original parquet flooring. ✉ Václavské nám. 68, Nové Mesto ☎ 224–497–111 ⊕ www.nm.cz ☜ 260 Kč, additional charge for some rotating exhibitions; dome tickets, only available on the day with the museum ticket, 50 Kč Ⓜ Lines A and C: Muzeum.

★ **Národní památník hrdinů heydrichiády** (National Monument to the Heroes of Heydrich)
MEMORIAL | This incredibly moving monument to the seven Czech and Slovak parachutists who assassinated the Nazi "Butcher of Prague," Reinhard Heydrich, in 1942, tells their astonishing story—the movie Anthropoid is based on what took place—and takes visitors into the crypt where they made their last, doomed stand against the occupying authorities, underneath the Church of Sts. Cyril and Methodius. ✉ Resslova 9A, Nové Mesto ☎ 222–540–718 ⊕ vhu.cz ☜ Free ☉ Closed Mon. Ⓜ Line B: Karlovo náměstí.

**Novoměstská radnice** (New Town Hall)
VIEWPOINT | At the northern edge of Charles Square, the New Town Hall has a late-Gothic tower similar to that of Staroměstská radnice (Old Town Hall), plus three tall Renaissance gables. The first defenestration in Prague occurred here on July 30, 1419, when a mob of townspeople, followers of the martyred religious reformer Jan Hus, hurled Catholic town councilors out the windows. Historical exhibitions and contemporary art shows are held regularly in the gallery, and you can climb the tower for a view of Nové Město. As in Staré Město, this town hall is a popular venue for weddings. ✉ Karlovo nám. 23, at Vodičkova, Nové Mesto ☎ 224–948–229 ⊕ www.nrpraha.cz ☜ Tower and exhibits on tower premises 60 Kč, gallery shows vary, combination ticket 350 Kč (incl. Old Town Hall) ☉ Closed Mon. and 30 min. between noon and 1 daily.

**Obecní dům** (Municipal House)
BUILDING | The city's art nouveau showpiece still fills the role it had when it was completed in 1911 as a center for

concerts, rotating art exhibits, and café society. The mature art nouveau style echoes the lengths the Czech middle class went to at the turn of the 20th century to imitate Paris. Much of the interior bears the work of Alfons Mucha, Max Švabinský, and other leading Czech artists. Mucha decorated the Hall of the Lord Mayor upstairs with impressive, magical frescoes depicting Czech history; unfortunately it's visible only as part of a guided tour. The beautiful Smetanova síň (Smetana Hall), which hosts concerts by the Prague Symphony Orchestra as well as international players, is on the second floor. The ground-floor restaurants are overcrowded with tourists but still impressive, with glimmering chandeliers and exquisite woodwork. There's also a beer hall in the cellar, with decent food and ceramic murals on the walls. Tours are normally held at two-hour intervals in the afternoons; check the website for details. ⊠ *Nám. Republiky 5, Staré Mesto* ☎ *222–002–101* ⊕ *www.obecnidum. cz* ⊠ *Guided tours 390 Kč* Ⓜ *Line B: Náměstí Republiky.*

★ **Palác Lucerna** (*Lucerna Palace*)
**BUILDING** | This art nouveau palace houses one of the city's many elegant pasáže , in this case a hallway studded with shops, restaurants, a beautiful grand hall, and a music club. It is also home to a gorgeous cinema and a cheeky David Černý sculpture referencing the statue of St. Wenceslas in the square outside (to give you a hint, it's often described as the hanging horse). Even better, in summer you can go onto the roof of the palace, which is a treat for two reasons: one, the makeshift bar at the top, with great views and a good vibe, and two, the chance to ride in an old-school, slightly terrifying paternoster lift to get up there. ⊠ *Štěpánská 61, Nové Mesto* ☎ *224–225–440* ⊕ *www. lucerna.cz* Ⓜ *Lines A and B: Můstek.*

**Statue of St. Wenceslas**
**PUBLIC ART** | "Let's meet at the horse" is the local expression referring to the traditional meeting place that is Josef Václav Myslbek's impressive equestrian representation of St. Wenceslas surrounded by other Czech patron saints. In 1939, Czechs gathered here to oppose Hitler's annexation of Bohemia and Moravia. In 1969, student Jan Palach set himself on fire near here to protest the Soviet-led invasion of the country a year earlier (there's a moving monument to him in the cobbles). And in 1989, many thousands successfully gathered here and all along the square to demand the end of the communist government. ⊠ *Václavské nám., Nové Mesto* Ⓜ *Lines A and C: Muzeum.*

★ **Tančící dům** (*Dancing House*)
**BUILDING** | This whimsical building, one of Prague's most popular modern structures, came to life in 1996 as a team effort from architect Frank Gehry (of Guggenheim Bilbao fame) and his Croatian-Czech collaborator Vlado Milunic. A wasp-waisted glass-and-steel tower sways into the main columned structure as though they were a couple on the dance floor—the "Fred and Ginger" effect gave the building its nickname. It's notable for a Gehry piece, as it's more grounded in the surrounding area than his larger projects. It now houses a hotel and top-floor restaurant, but even if you aren't staying or eating there, it's worth marveling at the building itself, either from the near side of the river or the far. ⊠ *Rašínovo nábř. 80, Nové Mesto.*

**Václavské náměstí**
**PLAZA** | This "square"—more of a very long, very thin rectangle—was first laid out by Charles IV in 1348, and began its existence as a horse market at the center of Nové Město. Today, it functions as the commercial heart of the city center and is far brasher and more modern than Staroměstské náměstí (Old Town Square). Throughout much of Czech history, Wenceslas Square has served as the focal point for public demonstrations and celebrations. It was here in the

heady days of November 1989 that some 500,000 people gathered to protest the policies of the then-communist regime. After a week of demonstrations, the government capitulated without a shot fired or the loss of a single life. After that, the first democratic government in 40 years (under playwright-president Václav Havel) was swept into office. This peaceful transfer of power is referred to as the "Velvet Revolution." (The subsequent "Velvet Divorce," when Czechoslovakia was peacefully divided into the Czech Republic and the Slovak Republic, took effect in 1993.) ■ TIP→ **Look up when you glimpse the Marks & Spencer shop sign—during the Velvet Revolution in 1989, Václav Havel addressed the crowds from this building's balcony.** ⊠ *Nové Mesto* Ⓜ *Lines A and C: Muzeum or Lines A and B: Můstek.*

## 🍴 Restaurants

The sprawling area of Nové Město, which surrounds Staré Město in a huge arc running from Charles Square in the south, through the Můstek area, and then on to Náměstí Republiky, holds hundreds of pubs and restaurants. There are clusters of good places to eat near all the quarter's main commercial centers, including Charles Square, the strip along Národní třída, Na příkopě, and Wenceslas Square. Important Metro stations include Náměstí Republiky and Karlovo náměstí on Line B, Můstek on Lines A and B, Muzeum on Lines A and C, and Florenc on Line C.

### Alcron

$$$$ | **SEAFOOD** | Michelin may have gotten it wrong when they took away Alcron's long-held star in 2018. Chefs Jakub Cerny and Roman Paulus still create an absolutely top-notch dining experience with delicious food (various tasting menus, starting from 1,800 Kč for dinner, showcase the kitchen's best work) and an intimate setting with just 24 seats, a 1930s fireplace, and a wraparound

dance-themed mural by Tamara de Lempicka. **Known for:** romantic setting; inventive menu; modern seafood like oyster tartare and lobster bisque with poached egg yolk. Ⓢ *Average main: 800 Kč* ⊠ *Alcron Hotel, Štěpánská 40, Nové Mesto* ☎ *222–820–000* ⊕ *www.alcron.cz* ⊘ *Closed Sun.* Ⓜ *Line A: Můstek.*

### Ginger & Fred

$$$ | **FRENCH** | Serving possibly Prague's most scenic meal, Ginger & Fred occupies the top floor of Frank Gehry's iconic Dancing House along the Vltava River, and the modern French-style food and service live up to the quality of the castle views. Of course, diners pay a premium for the view, and the wine list, though extensive, suffers from extreme markup. **Known for:** modern use of local ingredients; light-filled dining space; inventive dishes, from tonka bean duck to a "gastro-punk" dessert. Ⓢ *Average main: 550 Kč* ⊠ *Rašínovo nábř. 80, Nové Mesto* ☎ *221–984–160* ⊕ *www.dancinghouse-hotel.com* Ⓜ *Line B: Karlovo náměstí.*

### Jáma

$$ | **ECLECTIC** | American expatriates, Czech politicians, international consultants, and a constant crowd of students make this Czech-American hybrid pub feel like a place where everyone is welcome—especially when there's a big soccer game. **Known for:** relaxed international vibes; good pub food; inexpensive three-course lunch menus. Ⓢ *Average main: 180 Kč* ⊠ *V Jámě 7, Nové Mesto* ☎ *222–967–081* ⊕ *www.jamapub.cz* Ⓜ *Lines A and B: Můstek.*

### ★ Kantýna

$ | **STEAKHOUSE** | With a grand setting in a gorgeous former bank, you can bank on this cool butcher-shop-meets-meat-market-and-bar being packed when you arrive. There's a butcher's counter at the front where you can select the exact meat you want. **Known for:** the best burgers in town; excellent Czech meats, to either eat on-site or take away; cool vibes in a historic building. Ⓢ *Average*

The Dancing House or Fred and Ginger house was controversial when first built because the nontraditional design stands out among the baroque, Gothic, and art nouveau buildings for which Prague is famous.

main: 100 Kč ⊠ Politických vězňů 5, Nové Mesto ☎ No phone ⊕ www.kantyna. ambi.cz Ⓜ Lines A and C: Muzeum.

### Le Grill

$$$ | EUROPEAN | The main restaurant of the Grand Mark Hotel has established itself as one of the best restaurants in the country. Don't expect lots of innovation here, but dishes are skillfully prepared and presented, and the focus is on seasonal ingredients, with a monthly changing menu. **Known for:** good for business dinners; elevated versions of classics like duck and quince and spätzle; the "Grand Mark" cake, unique to the hotel. Ⓢ Average main: 600 Kč ⊠ Grand Mark Hotel, Hybernská 12, Nové Mesto ☎ 226–226–126 ⊕ www.grandmark.cz Ⓜ Line B: Náměstí Republiky.

### Lemon Leaf

$$ | THAI | Lemon Leaf serves a long list of Thai classics to an appreciative, dedicated clientele. Airy and luminous, with big pots of plants, tall windows, and funky lamps, this spot provides a solid alternative to European cuisine for lunch or dinner. **Known for:** crunchy spring rolls and traditional Thai soups; spicy curries; good for groups. Ⓢ Average main: 250 Kč ⊠ Myslíkova 14, Nové Mesto ☎ 224–919–056 ⊕ www.lemon.cz Ⓜ Line B: Karlovo Náměstí.

### Levitate

$$$$ | SCANDINAVIAN | The global trend for Nordic cuisine hasn't bypassed Prague, as evidenced by this hip basement restaurant with living plant walls, sounds of nature, and inventive, seasonal cooking delivered via tasting menus that are a blend of Scandinavian and Asian influences. There are only 22 seats, so reservations are advised. **Known for:** surprising tasting menus; fauna, flora, or aqua options; daily changing drinks. Ⓢ Average main: 1000 Kč ⊠ Štěpánská 611/14, Nové Mesto ☎ 724–516–996 ⊕ www.levita-terestaurant.cz ⊘ Closed Sun. and Mon. No lunch Ⓜ Lines A and B: Můstek.

### Manifesto Market

$$ | ECLECTIC | A trendy market with around 20 vendors based in shipping containers dishing up everything from

## Prague's Plaques

The famous, the forgotten, and the victims. Throughout the center of town a large number of plaques and even busts are attached to the sides of buildings marking the famous and sometimes not-so-famous people who lived or worked there. Composer Frederic Chopin can be found across from the Municipal House on the side of the Czech National Bank. Scientists like Albert Einstein—who was friends with author Franz Kafka, according to a marker on Old Town Square—also turn up. Some Czech figures like composer Bedřich Smetana or painter Josef Manés might be recognizable, while many plaques commemorate totally obscure teachers, civic organizers, or members of the 19th-century national awakening.

One set of plaques stands out from the rest—those marking the victims of the Prague Uprising that took place May 5–8, 1945. These mark where Prague citizens who tried to battle the German army at the end of World War II were killed. Many plaques depict a hand with two upraised fingers and the phrase *věrni zůstaneme*, meaning "remain faithful." Foil-covered wreaths are still regularly hung underneath them.

The area around Wenceslas Square has several, including one on the side of the main post office on Jindřišská ulice. Two plaques can even be found on the back of the plinth of the Jan Hus statue on Old Town Square.

Some of the more touching ones have black-and-white photographs of the victims, such as a marker for 23-year-old Viktorie Krupková, who was killed on Újezd near Říční ulice, just across from Petřín.

The area around Czech Radio headquarters on Vinohradská ulice in Vinohrady has many, as well as some plaques for victims of the 1968 Soviet-led invasion. Fighting for control of the radio station was fierce during the invasion.

Hawaiian poke bowls to hummus, fancy fries, and tasty burgers, Manifesto ups central Prague's cool stakes considerably. There are cocktails and beers on offer, too, and the chance to hang with Prague's hipsters on this formerly unused patch of land close to Masarykovo nádraží (Prague Masaryk railway station). **Known for:** global street food; no cash accepted, only cards; DJ sets while you eat. [$] *Average main: 250 Kč* ✉ *Na Florenci, Nové Mesto* ☎ *No phone* 🌐 *www.manifestomarket.com* 🕓 *Closed Jan. and Feb. Closed Mon. and Tues.* [M] *Lines B and C: Florenc.*

**Pizza Nuova**

**$$ | PIZZA | FAMILY** | Turning out tasty pies in true Neapolitan style, Pizza Nuova serves chewy pizzas that tend to get a bit soggy in the center—they're 100% authentic, if not the easiest to eat. The huge bilevel space, decked out in light and dark wood, also boasts a small outdoor eating area on Náměstí Republiky. **Known for:** good burrata cheese; crisp, thin pizzas; buzzing vibe and views over Náměstí Republiky. [$] *Average main: 260 Kč* ✉ *Revoluční 1, Nové Mesto* ☎ *221–803–308* 🌐 *pizzanuova.cz* [M] *Line B: Náměstí Republiky.*

**Potrefená Husa**

**$$ | CZECH** | The "Wounded Goose" is a local chain of casual restaurants and sports bars owned by the Prague-based Staropramen brewery, and besides having a great name, it's pretty good at

## Haute Czech 🍴

Czech cuisine isn't limited to the simpler dishes you'll find at pubs; it can also go upscale and experimental. Aside from **La Degustation Bohême Bourgeoise** (✉ *Haštalská 18,* ☎ *222–311–234*) in Staré Město, an excellent high-end Czech meal can be had at **U Modré kachničky** (✉ *Nebovidská 6,* ☎ *257–320–308*) in Malá Strana (Lesser Quarter). The specialty here, a restaurant whose name translates as the "Blue Duckling," is duck, naturally, and it's expertly prepared.

But don't be limited to restaurants that focus on Czech food; many high-end "continental" restaurants will spotlight a local dish or local ingredients, too. Among the best of these is the aerie atop the Frank Gehry building known as Dancing House, **Ginger & Fred** (✉ *Jiráskovo nám. 6,* ☎ *221–984–160*). The focus is French, but the restaurant works almost exclusively with local suppliers and there is a delicious take on veal tartare.

what it does: serving up bar staples and beer at a good value. This branch in Nové Město, in a historical house where writer Alois Jirásek lived, is one of several scattered throughout the city. **Known for:** great price-to-quality ratio; lively atmosphere for big sports games; full selection of Staropramen beers. [$] *Average main: 220 Kč* ✉ *Resslova 1, Nové Mesto* ☎ *224–918–691* 🌐 *www.staropramen.cz* [M] *Line B: Karlovo Náměstí.*

### Radost FX Café

**$$ | VEGETARIAN** | Still going strong after more than 20 years, this popular, hippieish vegetarian restaurant and café offers an eclectic assortment of salads, sandwiches, pizzas, and a smattering of Thai, Mexican, and American dishes. The clientele varies throughout the day. **Known for:** the ever-popular Popeye "burger," made from spinach, hazelnuts, and cheese; healthy, vegetable-packed lunches, which can be hard to find in Prague; brunch until 3 on weekends. [$] *Average main: 190 Kč* ✉ *Bělehradská 120, Nové Mesto* ☎ *603–193–711* 🌐 *www.radostfx.cz* 💳 *No credit cards* [M] *Line C: I. P. Pavlova.*

### ★ Sansho

**$$ | ASIAN FUSION** | When Sansho opened almost a decade ago, it radically redefined the local dining scene. Head chef Paul Day introduced many novel concepts to Prague's foodies, like pairing a simple, unadorned interior with highly intricate Asian-fusion cuisine, leaving the full focus on the plate. **Known for:** a nose-to-tail philosophy; impeccable unstuffy service; best quality-to-value ratio in Prague. [$] *Average main: 240 Kč* ✉ *Petrská 25, Nové Mesto* ☎ *222–317–425* 🌐 *www.sansho.cz* 🕒 *Closed Sun.* [M] *Lines B and C: Florenc.*

### Zinc

**$$$$ | EUROPEAN** | The story behind Zinc, the house restaurant of the Hilton Old Town hotel, is a comic case of culinary musical chairs. The site first held celeb-chef Gordon Ramsey's Maze restaurant, but after that shuttered, head chef Ari Munandar was quickly brought in from the Mandarin Oriental. [$] *Average main: 600 Kč* ✉ *V Celnici 7, Nové Mesto* ☎ *221–822–300* 🌐 *www.hiltonpragueoldtown.com* [M] *Line B: Náměstí Republiky.*

# ☕ Coffee and Quick Bites

### ★ Café Slavia

**$$ | EUROPEAN |** Overlooking the river and next to the National Theater, this old-school continental European-style café is one of a clutch in Prague where you can imagine playwright-turned–independence hero Václav Havel holding court or composer Bedřich Smetana winding down after a performance. Actually, you're not just imagining it: all sorts of Czech artistic luminaries have supped here, including the above, and Havel liked it so much he even lobbied for it to reopen when it closed for reconstruction in the 1990s. **Known for:** historical setting; affordable daily menu; Czech-style café culture. $ *Average main: 200 Kč* ⊠ *Smetanovo nábř. 2, Nové Mesto* ☎ *224–218–493* ⊕ *www.cafeslavia.cz* Ⓜ *Line B: Národní třída.*

### Cukrárna Myšák

**$ | BAKERY |** Visitors with a sweet tooth should not miss this historic pastry shop in Nové Město, where Czech desserts, cakes, sweets, and treats are showcased over two floors. Opened in 1911 by František Myšák, the First Republic feel has been faithfully reconstructed. **Known for:** classic Czech kremrole (cream-filled pastry roll); the famous ice-cream cup, served for generations; display cases filled with pastries. $ *Average main: 80 Kč* ⊠ *Vodičkova 31, Nové Mesto* ☎ *730–589–249* ⊕ *www.mysak.ambi.cz* Ⓜ *Lines A and B: Můstek.*

### Globe Bookstore & Café

**$$ | CAFÉ |** Prague's first English-language bookstore with a café continues to draw both foreigners and Czechs for its large selection of novels, regional nonfiction, popular brunches, and memories of the go-go '90s. The recently upgraded menu includes an excellent burger, good salads, and pastas. **Known for:** U.S.-style food—and portion sizes; English-language quiz night; decadent desserts including New York cheesecake. $ *Average main:* *190 Kč* ⊠ *Pštrossova 6, Nové Mesto* ☎ *224–934–203* ⊕ *www.globebookstore. cz* Ⓜ *Line B: Karlovo Náměstí.*

### Home Kitchen

**$$ | BAKERY |** A popular, teeny little café-bistro with a homey feel (per its name), the menu here changes daily, taking inspiration from a mix of the owners' grandmothers and U.K. superchef Gordon Ramsay. There are four branches now across the city, but this is the original. **Known for:** crusty home-baked bread and fluffy pancakes; lively spot, often packed; catering only to the morning and lunch crowd. $ *Average main: 150 Kč* ⊠ *Jungmannova 8, Nové Mesto* ☎ *734–714–227* ⊕ *www.homekitchen. cz* ⊙ *Closed weekends* Ⓜ *Lines A and B: Můstek.*

### Kavárna Obecní dům

**$$ | CAFÉ |** The magnificent art nouveau Municipal House has this ground-floor café that's every bit as opulent on the inside as the building is grand on the outside. Step through the doors and into another era—the first decade of the 20th century to be specific—when the practice of coffee drinking was given white-glove treatment. **Known for:** gorgeous interior; sweet treats; historical appeal. $ *Average main: 200 Kč* ⊠ *Obecní dům, Nám. Republiky 5, Nové Mesto* ☎ *222–002–763* ⊕ *www.kavarnaod.cz* Ⓜ *Line B: Náměstí Republiky.*

## 🛏 Hotels

Not exactly "new," this district dates back to the 14th century and includes bustling Wenceslas Square. Nové Město isn't as clean and architecturally fragile as Staré Město, but what it loses in baroque curls it makes up for in good location at slightly cheaper prices.

### Alcron Hotel

**$$ | HOTEL |** Opened in 1932, the Alcron was one of Prague's first luxury hotels; a major renovation of the building at the end of the '90s modernized the look but restored the art deco building and the crystal chandeliers—and kept the charm. **Pros:** good value and location; elegant art deco building; excellent restaurant. **Cons:** rooms vary in size; conservatively styled rooms compared with the public spaces; corporate feel. $ *Rooms from: 4000 Kč* ✉ *Štěpánská 40, Nové Město* ☎ *222–820–000* ⊕ *alcronhotel.com* ⇨ *204 rooms* ⏐◉⏐ *Breakfast* Ⓜ *Line A: Můstek.*

### Art Deco Imperial Hotel

$$ | HOTEL | The real sell here is the hotel's Café Imperial, one of Prague's "grand cafés," with its astonishing mosaic ceiling and ceramic wall tiles, formerly frequented by writer Franz Kafka, among others, and now run by celebrity chef Zdeněk Pohlreich; but the newly renovated hotel rooms don't let the side down either. **Pros:** perhaps one of the most attractive hotel breakfast rooms in Prague; newly renovated rooms with modern comforts and art deco charm; mosaic-walled fitness and wellness center with sauna and steam bath. **Cons:** Café Imperial is very popular, so can be hard to secure a reservation; some street noise; some rooms have no real view. $ *Rooms from: 3500 Kč* ✉ *Na Poříčí 15, Nové Město* ☎ *246–011–600* ⊕ *www.hotel-imperial. cz* ⇨ *126 rooms* ⏐◉⏐ *No meals* Ⓜ *Line B: Náměstí Republiky.*

### Art Nouveau Palace Hotel

$$ | HOTEL | Perched on a busy corner in the city center, this stately but reasonably priced pistachio-green art nouveau building trumpets its Victorian origins. **Pros:** good deals available; great location; a certain faded-grandeur charm. **Cons:** a little old-fashioned; gilded style not for everyone; some street noise. $ *Rooms from: 3200 Kč* ✉ *Panská 12, Nové Město* ☎ *224–093–111* ⊕ *www.palacehotel. cz* ⇨ *124 rooms* ⏐◉⏐ *Breakfast* Ⓜ *Line A: Můstek.*

### Best Western Plus Hotel Meteor Plaza

$$ | HOTEL | Though this hotel shares a street with the fancy-pants Grand Mark, and also occupies a baroque town

palace, it's a step down in terms of atmosphere and quality (but also, fortunately, price). **Pros:** just a few steps from the Municipal House and five minutes on foot from Staré Město; some historical details; 14th-century wine cellar. **Cons:** interior not very inspiring; breakfast room can fill up quickly; tiny elevator. $ *Rooms from: 2500 Kč* ✉ *Hybernská 6, Nové Město* ☎ *224–192–111* ⊕ *www.hotel-meteor.cz* ⇨ *88 rooms* ⏐◉⏐ *Breakfast* Ⓜ *Line B: Náměstí Republiky.*

### Carlo IV, The Dedica Anthology, Autograph Collection

$$$ | HOTEL | Dripping with glamour, this mammoth 19th-century neoclassical palace is part of the Marriott Hotel's high-end Autograph Collection. **Pros:** luxurious and historic vibe; beautiful spa; cool bar in a former bank vault. **Cons:** sometimes rude staff; expensive breakfast not always included in the room rate; room sizes vary. $ *Rooms from: 6000 Kč* ✉ *Senovážné nám. 13, Nové Město* ☎ *224–593–111* ⊕ *www.marriott.com/ hotels/hotel-deals/prgak-carlo-iv-the-dedica-anthology-autograph-collection* ⇨ *152 rooms* ⏐◉⏐ *No meals* Ⓜ *Line B: Náměstí Republiky.*

### Dancing House Hotel

$$ | HOTEL | The owners of this stylish riverside hotel have sensibly encompassed its biggest selling point in its name: the chance to sleep in arguably Prague's most iconic piece of modern architecture, the Frank Gehry–designed Dancing House. **Pros:** stylish rooms; stone bathrooms feel luxurious; fantastic views from the rooftop bar. **Cons:** rooftop attracts crowds and can delay elevators; small reception area; staff could be friendlier. $ *Rooms from: 3850 Kč* ✉ *Jiráskovo nám. 1981/6, Nové Město* ☎ *720–983–172* ⊕ *www.dancinghousehotel.com* ⇨ *21 rooms* ⏐◉⏐ *Free Breakfast* Ⓜ *Line B: Karlovo náměstí.*

### The Grand Mark

$$$ | HOTEL | This shiny new hotel and spa in an imposing 15th-century

palace—steps from Náměstí Repub-liky—brings a high level of service and attention to detail to a still-scruffy part of the center. **Pros:** big, beautiful garden; excellent service and fantastic restaurant; great bathrooms and possibly Prague's best beds. **Cons:** only a small gym; the street is not especially attractive; functions held at the hotel can be noisy or restrict access to some areas. $ *Rooms from: 6800 Kč* ✉ *Hybernská 12, Nové Mesto* ☎ *226–226–111* ⊕ *www.grand-mark.cz* ↴ *75 rooms* ❚◯❙ *No meals* Ⓜ *Line B: Náměstí Republiky.*

### Hotel Boho Prague
$$ | HOTEL | This isn't the flowing hippie boho vibe that the name implies: Hotel Boho is chic, sleek, cool, and located on a fairly uninspiring but quiet street not far from bustling Náměstí Republiky. **Pros:** trendy mid-20th-century-style bar; gorgeous gold-tiled spa and softly lit small pool; comfortable modern rooms in neutral tones with some stylish retro furnishing. **Cons:** a little impersonal decor-wise, although little extra touches from staff help; located on an uninspiring street; mirrored glass doors in bathrooms can feel a bit much. $ *Rooms from: 4000 Kč* ✉ *Senovázná 1254/4, Nové Mesto* ☎ *234–622–600* ⊕ *www.hotelbohop-rague.com* ↴ *57 rooms* ❚◯❙ *No meals* 🖃 *No credit cards* Ⓜ *Line B: Náměstí Republiky.*

### Hotel Cosmopolitan
$$ | HOTEL | This art nouveau proper-ty—sister hotel of the Imperial, almost next door—shares the same sophisti-cated vibe and even the same big-draw celebrity chef in its restaurant (Zdeněk Pohlreich), but it has a more intimate, low-key feel. **Pros:** classy feel throughout, with great service; contemporary-el-egant rooms; top-notch restaurant. **Cons:** only a small fitness studio and sauna, but guests can use the Imperi-al's wellness facilities; no bar; can get expensive in high season. $ *Rooms from: 3200 Kč* ✉ *Zlatnická 3, Nové Mesto*

☎ *295–563–000* ⊕ *www.hotel-cosmopol-itan.cz* ↴ *106 rooms* ❚◯❙ *No meals* Ⓜ *Line B: Náměstí Republiky.*

### Hotel Élite Prague
$ | HOTEL | A 14th-century Gothic façade and many poetic architectural details have been preserved in this affordable hotel, thanks to an extensive renovation. **Pros:** historic feel with modern comforts; close to the National Theater; good amenities. **Cons:** the neighborhood can get overrun with partygoers at night; smoking is allowed in the courtyard; some rooms can be noisy. $ *Rooms from: 2100 Kč* ✉ *Ostrovní 32, Nové Mes-to* ☎ *211–156–530* ⊕ *www.hotel-elite.cz* ↴ *78 rooms* ❚◯❙ *Breakfast* Ⓜ *Line B: Karlovo náměstí.*

### Hotel Grandium Prague
$$ | HOTEL | A sprightly presence on an imperious street (think communist-era blocks), the Hotel Grandium offers mod-ern design at good prices. **Pros:** close to Wenceslas Square; good breakfast spread; free access to sauna and gym. **Cons:** bland rooms; slow, overworked elevator; rooms are not huge. $ *Rooms from: 3000 Kč* ✉ *Politických vězňů 12, Nové Mesto* ☎ *234–100–111* ⊕ *www.hotel-grandium.cz* ↴ *196 rooms* ❚◯❙ *Breakfast* Ⓜ *Line A: Můstek.*

### Hotel Salvator
$ | HOTEL | This efficiently run establish-ment just outside Staré Město offers more comforts than most in its class, as well as a pretty setting arranged around a central courtyard and plant-filled balconies. **Pros:** lovely Spanish-themed restaurant and courtyard; in-house tourist office; good value. **Cons:** courtyard-facing rooms can be noisy at mealtimes; bland room decor; not all rooms have a/c. $ *Rooms from: 1500 Kč* ✉ *Truhlářská 10, Nové Mesto* ☎ *222–312–234* ⊕ *www.salvator.cz* ↴ *39 rooms* ❚◯❙ *Some meals* Ⓜ *Line B: Náměstí Republiky.*

**Ibis Praha Old Town Hotel**
$ | **HOTEL** | Reliable quality and low prices, and a location pretty much across the street from the Municipal House, win the day for this chain hotel. the modern rooms, done out in browns and beiges, are small and dark and lack views. **Pros:** within easy walking distance of Old Town Square; good value for money; for an added fee, guests can use the pool at a nearby property. **Cons:** expensive buffet breakfast; rooms are small and can be dark; no restaurant. [$] *Rooms from: 1900 Kč* ✉ *Na Poříčí 5, Nové Mesto* ☎ *266–000–999* 🌐 *www.accorhotels.com/gb/hotel-5477-ibis-praha-old-town/index.shtml* 🛏 *271 rooms* 🍴 *Breakfast* [M] *Line B: Náměstí Republiky.*

**Ibis Praha Wenceslas Square Hotel**
$ | **HOTEL** | Despite its name, this hotel isn't actually on the square itself, but a few minutes' walk away; regardless of this dodgy geography, it is still probably the cheapest modern air-conditioned place you can find this close to the city center. Rooms are without frills but have everything you would expect from an international chain hotel. **Pros:** comfortable and clean; quality beds; guests can use wellness center at Novotel next door. **Cons:** very little nightlife in the area; except for corner locations, rooms are rather small; price does not include breakfast, which is an additional charge. [$] *Rooms from: 1800 Kč* ✉ *Kateřinská 36, Nové Mesto* ☎ *222–865–777* 🌐 *www.accorhotels.com/gb/hotel-3195-ibis-praha-wenceslas-square/index.shtml* 🛏 *181 rooms* 🍴 *No meals* [M] *Line C: I. P. Pavlova.*

★ **The ICON**
$$ | **HOTEL** | From the fashionable staff to its plush, all-natural bedding, this hotel is dressed to impress. **Pros:** youthful, exuberant staff; all-day breakfast spread; good Metro and tram connections. **Cons:** small spa; street-facing rooms are loud; busy urban locale won't appeal to all. [$] *Rooms from: 4000 Kč* ✉ *V Jámě 6, Nové Mesto* ☎ *221–634–100* 🌐 *www.iconhotel.eu* 🛏 *31 rooms* 🍴 *Free Breakfast* [M] *Lines A and B: Můstek.*

**Jalta Boutique Hotel**
$$ | **HOTEL** | The Jalta is arguably the smartest, most interesting hotel on central Wenceslas Square, with a historically protected façade that dates to the 1950s in the socialist realist style first developed in the Soviet Union. **Pros:** underground nuclear shelter and museum; sleek, modern rooms; some rooms have balconies facing the square and National Museum. **Cons:** may be too close to the action for some; the cheaper rooms are small; some street noise although windows are good at blocking it. [$] *Rooms from: 3500 Kč* ✉ *Václavské nám. 45, Nové Mesto* ☎ *222–822–111* 🌐 *www.hoteljalta.com* 🛏 *94 rooms* 🍴 *Breakfast* [M] *Lines A and C: Muzeum.*

**Michelangelo Grand Hotel**
$$ | **HOTEL** | Large, airy, and located inside an attractive, 19th-century building that used to be a municipal meeting hall, this serviceable but still stylish hotel (lots of modern lilac tones) is based in an interesting part of Nové Město that manages to be both quiet and close to a lot of nightlife. **Pros:** pleasant lounge area and garden; good deals in off-season; Nespresso machines and Botanica cosmetics in all rooms. **Cons:** less touristy location may not appeal to everyone; spotty service; rooms are spacious but not particularly individual. [$] *Rooms from: 3000 Kč* ✉ *Vladislavova 1477/20, Nové Mesto* ☎ *222–500–177* 🌐 *www.michelangelograndhotel.com* 🛏 *134 rooms* 🍴 *Breakfast* [M] *Line B: Národní třída.*

## 🍸 Nightlife

Some areas of the neighborhood, particularly around Wenceslas Square, are still dealing with the aftereffects of the stag-party craze, but others have embraced funky, alternative evening offerings.

Náplavka is home to a popular weekly farmer's market but is at peak popularity in summer when its barge bars are the place to be.

## BARS AND PUBS

### Gin and Tonic Club

**BARS/PUBS** | With 6,400 combinations, this stylish gin palace offers everything from a perfect traditional tipple with ice and a slice to a G&T with sun-dried tomatoes or even bacon. Small plates complement the gin-heavy menu and there's a gorgeous little candlelit garden for mild nights. ⊠ *Navrátilova 11, Nové Mesto* ☎ *777–669–557* ⊕ *www.gintonic-club.com* Ⓜ *Lines A and B: Můstek.*

### ★ Náplavka

**BREWPUBS/BEER GARDENS** | One of the coolest places to drink and hang in Prague just got cooler (and considerably more appealing during the chilly winter months than it previously was). This riverside promenade near the Dancing House began with little more than pop-up pubs on benches and boats, but newly reclaimed former storage pods inside the waterfront walls offer cafés, galleries, and even a branch of the municipal library. Don't worry, sunset beers are still central to the vibe, with plenty of pop-up pubs still present as well as more permanent fixtures like hip bike repair shop-bar Bajkazyl. ⊠ *Náplavka, Nové Mesto* Ⓜ *Line B: Karlovo náměstí.*

### ★ Pivovarský dům

**BARS/PUBS** | This brewpub, which opened in 1998, may be short on history, but it makes up for that with outstanding beer. The dark, light, and seasonal microbrew beers are stellar. (Fermenting beer can be viewed through a window.) The food is good but a slight letdown when compared with the drinks, which include sour-cherry beer and even a champagne beer for the more adventurous. Take heed: there is often a line to get in. ⊠ *Lípová 15, Nové Mesto* ☎ *296–216–666* ⊕ *www.pivovarskydum.com* Ⓜ *Lines A and B: Můstek.*

### U Fleků

**BREWPUBS/BEER GARDENS** | The oldest brewpub in Europe—open since 1499—makes a tasty, if overpriced, dark beer and serves around 2,000 pints of it every day. But the steady stream of tours means it can be hard to find a seat (in the evenings, at least), even though the place is cavernous, spread over eight halls and a garden. There's also a brewery museum and cabaret shows. ⚠ **Beware of waiters putting unordered shots of liquor on your table.** If you don't insist they remove them right away, they'll be on your bill, and service can be indifferent to rude. But the raucous, beer-swilling, mug-clinking bonhomie makes up for that. ⊠ *Křemencova 11, Nové Mesto* ☎ *224–934–019* ⊕ *www.ufleku.cz* Ⓜ *Line B: Karlovo náměstí.*

### Vinárna U Sudu

**WINE BARS—NIGHTLIFE** | Although Prague is beer territory, this pays homage to that other camp: wine. A mazelike, multilevel cellar forms the large wine bar in a baroque building, and there's a garden too. Make note of where your traveling companions are or you might never find them again—the interior is that labyrinthine. But this also makes for a cozy drinking hole in the cold winter months, and it's open extremely late. ■**TIP→ This is usually one of the first places during the year to crack open burčák, tasty new wine served shortly after harvest.** ⊠ *Vodičkova 10, Nové Mesto* ☎ *222–232–207* ⊕ *www. usudu.cz* Ⓜ *Line B: Karlovo náměstí.*

### ★ Výtopna

**BARS/PUBS** | **FAMILY** | Located on the very touristy Wenceslas Square, the drinks here are delivered by miniature train. It's gimmicky but great fun when the drinks pull up to the table. ⊠ *Václavské nám. 56, Nové Mesto* ☎ *777–444–554* ⊕ *vytopna. cz* Ⓜ *Line C: Muzeum.*

### Vzorkovna

**BARS/PUBS** | Currently the holder of the unofficial title of Prague's most alternative city-center pub, Vzorkovna operates a confusing chip system for payment (you get the change back at the end of the night, but don't lose the chip, they'll charge you). It's an acquired taste, with a rough pop-up feel of bars in metropolises like London or New York, plus that uniquely Prague

junkyard vibe, with dusty floors, and a giant dog wandering around. The beers on tap are from the award-winning Únětický Pivovar brewery, and reasonably priced for such a centrally located bar. ⊠ *Národní 339/11, Nové Mesto* ☎ *No phone* Ⓜ *Line B: Národní třída.*

## CLUBS

### Duplex

**DANCE CLUBS** | While Duplex is effectively an all-nighter, strobe-heavy superclub in the center of Prague, it also boasts a gorgeous roof terrace right on Wenceslas Square and a restaurant. Prices can be high and it is obviously touristy, but the location makes up for it, and if you do feel like hitting the dance floor afterward, this is where the biggest global dance names perform. ⊠ *Václavské nám. 21, Nové Mesto* ☎ *732–221–111* ⊕ *www. duplex.cz* Ⓜ *Lines A and B: Můstek.*

### Nebe

**DANCE CLUBS** | Sometimes all you want is some guaranteed good pop tunes, a friendly vibe, and a packed dance floor. If that's what you're after, Nebe will never let you down. Plus there's no cover charge. There are a couple of branches, but this slightly hidden one on Křemencova is the best of the bunch. ⊠ *Křemencova, Nové Mesto* ☎ *608–644–784* ⊕ *www. nebepraha.cz* Ⓜ *Line B: Můstek.*

## LGBTQ

### Q Café

**CAFES—NIGHTLIFE** | This friendly and pretty hip LGBTQ café-bar opens at 3 every day and dishes up small bites, decent coffee, and reasonable beer and cocktails over two floors. This is one of the places in Prague to embrace Kofola—Czech communist-era Coca-Cola—which is worth a try. There's a library, too. ⊠ *Opatovická 166/12, Nové Mesto* ☎ *776–856–361* ⊕ *q-cafe.cz* Ⓜ *Line B: Národní třída.*

## LIVE MUSIC CLUBS

### ★ Lucerna Music Bar

**MUSIC CLUBS** | Rock bands on the comeback trail, touring bluesmen, and other solid performers across many different musical genres, including some Czech acts, make up the live schedule of this basement music venue in the historic pasáž. The crowds are always friendly and up for it, and the acoustics are good, making it a solid place to see some live music in the city center. Book tickets in advance for the bigger acts. Another big draw are the nights—usually Saturday—of 1980s or '90s music videos. The nostalgia-fest will have you dancing your socks off until the wee hours, alongside what feels like half of Prague and much of the rest of Europe as well. It's good fun. ⊠ *Vodičkova 36, Nové Mesto* ☎ *224–217–108* ⊕ *www.musicbar.cz* Ⓜ *Lines A and B: Můstek.*

### ★ Reduta

**MUSIC CLUBS** | This jazz club is where President Bill Clinton jammed with Czech president Václav Havel in 1994, and lots of pictures of that night are still hanging around the joint. Reduta was one of the bigger clubs in the 1960s and '70s, and it still feels a little like a dated museum of those glory days (or like a funky retro tribute to that era, depending on your persuasion). The coat-check person can be pretty aggressive, which is another throwback to the pre-1989 era, but the jazz is worth any aggravation. ■**TIP**➔ **If you go on a quiet weeknight, staff might upgrade you to the VIP seats, where Bill and Václav sat back in the day.** ⊠ *Národní 20, Nové Mesto* ☎ *224–933–487* ⊕ *www. redutajazzclub.cz* Ⓜ *Line B: Národní třída.*

##  Performing Arts

### VENUES

### ★ Národní divadlo (*National Theater*)

**ARTS CENTERS** | This is the main stage in the Czech Republic for drama, dance, and opera. The interior, with its ornate and etched ceilings, is worth the visit alone.

# A Night at the Opera

Opera has a long and strong tradition in the Czech Republic, and fans of it are rewarded with quality productions almost every night of the week for very reasonable prices. The imposing National Theater and the Stavovské divadlo (Estates Theater) in Staré Město are the best venues to see opera, as well as, of course, the beautiful Statní opera Praha (Prague State Opera), which reopened in 2020 after several years of renovations. Branch out from the usual composers with a Czech composer like Janaček, Dvořák, or Smetana.

Most of the theater performances are in Czech, but some operas have English supertitles, and ballet is an international language—right? Book the opera online ahead of time for fantastic discounts; you'll get to see top-quality performances in sumptuous surroundings at a snip of the price you could pay in other European capitals. The New Stage, next door, as well as the Estates Theater and Prague State Opera are all part of the National Theater system. ⊠ *Národní 2, Nové Mesto* ☎ *224–901–448* ⊕ *www.narodni-divadlo.cz* Ⓜ *Line B: Národní třída.*

### Obecní dům (*Municipal House*)

**ARTS CENTERS** | The main concert hall, a true art nouveau gem named after composer Bedřich Smetana, is home to the Prague Symphony Orchestra and many music festivals. A few smaller halls, all named for famous figures, host chamber concerts. Tours of the building are also offered. It's well worth a visit, even if you only pop your head in. ⊠ *Nám. Republiky 5, Staré Mesto* ☎ *222–002–101* ⊕ *www.obecnidum.cz* Ⓜ *Line B: Náměstí Republiky.*

**Statní opera Praha** (*Prague State Opera*)
**OPERA** | With the most ornate interior of any venue in Prague, this theater has more than a touch of *Phantom of the Opera*. Marble sculptures support the loges, and a fresco adorns the ceiling. The building started life as the German Theater in 1887 and has undergone several name changes since, and recently reemerged, like a butterfly from its chrysalis, from several years of renovations. It's a spectacular place to see quality opera, despite its slightly unfortunate position overlooking one of Prague's busiest roads. ⊠ *Wilsonova 4, Nové Mesto* ☎ *224–227–266* ⊕ *www. narodni-divadlo.cz/en/state-opera* Ⓜ *Lines A and C: Muzeum.*

**Velký sál, Lucerna** (*Great Hall, Lucerna*)
**ARTS CENTERS** | Part of the fascinating Lucerna complex, the Great Hall is a beautiful art nouveau ballroom with a big main floor and some loges. It hosts everything from swing dances to graduation balls, Czech and international rock and pop stars to Christmas concerts, and even the occasional boxing match, in wonderful historic surroundings. Everyone from Ray Charles to Maurice Chevalier has played here, so soak up the history as you sway to the beat. ⊠ *Štěpánská 61, Nové Mesto* ☎ *224–225–440* ⊕ *lucpra.com* Ⓜ *Lines A and B: Můstek.*

## PUPPET SHOWS AND BLACK-LIGHT THEATER

★ **Nová Scená** (*The New Stage*)
**DANCE** | The cool glass-block façade of the New Stage, which opened in 1983, stands out among the ornate 19th-century buildings in the area. Black-light theater company Laterna Magika (which takes its name from the original black-light presentation at Expo '58) performs here, and the rest of the program schedule is handled through the National Theater. Contemporary dance pieces and other language-free performances dominate the calendar. ⊠ *Národní 4, Nové Mesto*

☎ *224–901–111* ⊕ *www.novascena.cz* Ⓜ *Line B: Národní třída.*

#  Shopping

Prague's Nové Město is home to all the big department stores and international brands, which are located in two main shopping areas—Wenceslas Square and Na příkopě. But don't miss the various covered arcades, or "passages," around the city, because they are home to a few interesting boutiques as well as nail bars and wine shops.

## ANTIQUES

**JHB Starožitnosti**
**ANTIQUES/COLLECTIBLES** | This shop has beautiful art deco and art nouveau diamond rings, porcelain and brass decorative objects, and furniture. But the company's specialty is clocks from the 18th and 19th centuries hailing from Austria, the Czech Republic, France, and Germany. Antique pocket watches featured in the window displays also draw longing stares from knowing collectors and passing tourists alike. ⊠ *Panská 1, Nové Mesto* ☎ *222–245–836* ⊕ *www. jhbantique.cz* Ⓜ *Lines A and B: Můstek.*

## BOOKS AND PRINTS

**Antikvariát Karel Křenek**
**BOOKS/STATIONERY** | Despite the extensive collection of antique maps, prints, and engravings dating from the 16th century, this shop is refreshingly bright and clean. Among the shop's treasures: beautiful Japanese woodblocks and a well-known map depicting Asia as the winged horse Pegasus. The shop also mounts and frames works on request. ⊠ *Národní 20, Nové Mesto* ☎ *222–314–734* ⊕ *www. karelkrenek.com* Ⓜ *Line B: Národní třída.*

**Globe Bookstore & Café**
**BOOKS/STATIONERY** | A fine place to peruse the shelves of English-language titles, this friendly store leads to a café down the hall, where lattes, laptops, and expats are de rigueur. If you're hoping to attend English-language literary, film,

or arts events while in Prague, check out the wall of fliers near the front desk. ✉ *Pštrossova 6, Nové Mesto* ☎ *224–934–203* ⊕ *www.globebookstore.cz* Ⓜ *Line B: Národní třída.*

### Kiwi Travel Bookshop

**BOOKS/STATIONERY** | With more than 17,000 items in stock (including those featured on the online store), you'll find English-language travel guides, useful local maps, books about travel, and even a few globes scattered around the premises—but in keeping with the adventurous spirit, you might need to hunt them down a bit in this cavernous store. Sales associates are quite helpful, and most speak some English. ✉ *Jungmannova 23, Nové Mesto* ☎ *224–948–455* ⊕ *www.mapykiwi.cz* Ⓜ *Line B: Národní třída.*

### ★ Koh-i-noor

**BOOKS/STATIONERY** | This iconic Czech stationery and art supplies brand has two outposts in Nové Město—one on Na příkopě and the other here on Vodičkova—and both are pleasant, airy places to nab a bit of history. The brand, established in 1790, was the first to patent modern pencil lead and pioneered colored pencils, too, and it now sells all of the art kits you would expect as well as cute kids' drawing equipment, along with an unexpected gorilla made of drawing pencils. ✉ *Vodičkova 710/31, Nové Mesto* ☎ *734–799–551* ⊕ *www.koh-i-noor.cz* Ⓜ *Line B: Národní třída.*

### Luxor

**BOOKS/STATIONERY** | With its four floors, music section, and coffee shop, this bookstore is the biggest in the Czech Republic, reminiscent of major American chains and known as "the palace." Only a small area in the basement is set aside for English-language books, but the store is an excellent source for maps of the Czech Republic and other European cities and countries and has some travel guidebooks in English.

With its four floors, music section, and coffee shop, this bookstore is the biggest in the Czech Republic, reminiscent of major American chains and known as "the palace." Only a small area in the basement is set aside for English-language books, but the store is an excellent source for maps of the Czech Republic and other European cities and countries and has some travel guidebooks in English. ✉ *Václavské nám. 41, Nové Mesto* ☎ *296–110–370* ⊕ *www.luxor.cz* Ⓜ *Line A: Muzeum.*

### Mucha Museum shop

**GIFTS/SOUVENIRS** | The perfect place for your art nouveau or Alfons Mucha fix (the world-famous Czech artist who made his name painting Sarah Bernhardt in fin de siècle Paris), this charming shop is located in a museum dedicated to the artist. You'll find posters, postcards, calendars, glass, jewelry, scarves, books, lamps, and more, all with the signature Mucha motifs. ✉ *Mucha Museum, Panská 7, Nové Mesto* ☎ *224–216–415* ⊕ *www.mucha.cz* Ⓜ *Lines A and B: Můstek.*

## CLOTHING

### Alice Abraham

**CLOTHING** | Inside her eye-catching boutique, this Czech designer with an eye for the dramatic shows off her wares. Clearly fond of animal prints, glitz, and daring cuts, Abraham is unafraid of pushing the fashion envelope, and her styles are anything but demure. ✉ *Na příkopě 12, Nové Mesto* ☎ *604–531–020* Ⓜ *Line A: Staroměstská.*

### Cvrk

**CLOTHING** | A hodgepodge of jewelry, clothing, and bags gives this design-led Czech store a slight jumble-sale feel, and it's none the worse for that. Finding the unexpected, like robot faces on a skirt, is all part of the fun. There are a few branches around the capital. ✉ *U Stýblů passage, Václavské nám. 28, Nové Mesto* ☎ *777–999–788 Lines A and B: Můstek* ⊕ *www.cvrk.cz* Ⓜ *Lines A and B: Můstek.*

### Ivana Follová

**CLOTHING** | Ivana Follová's little boutique and atelier at the top of Wenceslas Square showcases her wares in a chic, green space in central Prague. The designer specializes in silk, which she dyes in bold patterns and shapes into gauzy, graffitied garments, from wedding dresses to coats. She also stocks distinctive accessories like chunky costume jewelry by other Czech designers. ⊠ *Mezibranská 9, Nové Mesto* ☎ *222–211–357* ⊕ *www.ivanafollova.cz* Ⓜ *Lines A and B: Muzeum.*

### Onvi & Onavi

**CLOTHING** | Boasting various urbane brands and occupying several residences on a posh street, Onvi & Onavi is great fun to browse in for both men and women. From Luisa Cerano's soft knits and chic coats to Jacob Cohen's handmade jeans, always with that extra decorative detail, there are plenty of options to tempt you to part with your koruny. ⊠ *Obecní dům, Nám. Republiky 5, Staré Mesto* ☎ *222–002–313* ⊕ *www.onvi.cz* Ⓜ *Line B: Náměstí Republiky.*

### Pietro Filipi

**CLOTHING** | Taking its inspiration from the elegance and quality of Italian couture, this Czech brand makes timeless clothing for style-conscious professionals. Classic styles, bright colors, and quality design and materials are the watchwords here. ⊠ *Národní 31, Nové Mesto* ☎ *724–346–793* ⊕ *www.pietro-filipi.com* Ⓜ *Line B: Národní třída.*

### The Room

**CLOTHING** | The Room stocks creative European brands for fashion-conscious men, from cool Chinese-French Three Animals to Alex Monhart's swanky Czech-made black backpacks. ⊠ *Školská 7, Nové Mesto* ☎ *222–967–770* ⊕ *www.basmatee.cz* ✆ *Closed Sun.* Ⓜ *Lines A and B: Můstek.*

## FOOD AND WINE

### Cellarius

**WINE/SPIRITS** | Try out acclaimed Moravian wines, or pick up a select imported bottle at one of two locations: in the lovely, historic Lucerna passage, or at the Budečská ulice store, which also features a wine cellar and garden restaurant. Both stores offer tastings. ⊠ *Lucerna passage, Štěpánská 61, Nové Mesto* ☎ *224–210–979* ⊕ *www.cellarius.cz* Ⓜ *Lines A and B: Můstek.*

### Oxalis

**FOOD/CANDY** | Located in the beautiful U Nováku building, a former department store, with its art nouveau entrance and decorated façade, this Czech tea and coffee company offers tastings, gift sets, teapots, and lots of different teas and blends in a high-ceilinged, airy store. ⊠ *Vodičkova 30, Nové Mesto* ☎ *733–182–413* ⊕ *oxalis.cz* Ⓜ *Lines A and B: Můstek.*

## GLASS

### Moser

**CERAMICS/GLASSWARE** | Elegant glass stemware and decorative bowls and candlesticks are hand-blown or-cut and gorgeous enough to outfit the dining tables of Europe's aristocratic elite. This historic Czech company, established in Karlovy Vary in 1857, maintains two Prague locations—here and on Old Town Square. Both stores are breathtaking (although this location is a bit less hectic), boasting chandeliers, tea sets, and porcelain figurines on multiple floors, in addition to all that graceful glass. ⊠ *Na příkopě 12, Nové Mesto* ☎ *224–211–293* ⊕ *www.moser-glass.com* Ⓜ *Line B: Náměstí Republiky.*

## HOME

### Le Patio

**HOUSEHOLD ITEMS/FURNITURE** | This properly chic Czech lifestyle and furniture boutique gives a glimpse of how the most stylish Prague locals live. From the fact that their pieces are often rented out to filmmakers, to the fact that the shop itself is in the Mozarteum Palace, designed in 1913 by Czech architect Jan Kotěra; it's worth a visit; plus, they ship globally. ⊠ *Jungmannova 748/30, Nové Mesto* ☎ *224–934–402* ⊕ *www.lepatio.cz* Ⓜ *Line B: Můstek.*

### Modernista
**HOUSEHOLD ITEMS/FURNITURE** | Innovation is revered at this store inside the Municipal House, a magnet for fans of cubist and modernist furniture and decor. Originals, reproductions, and work by new Czech designers are available, making it nearly impossible to leave without something distinctive—a streamlined steel liquor cabinet or a cool cubist vase, perhaps. There are other branches in Vinohrady and in the Museum of Decorative Arts; this store focuses on ceramics and porcelain. ⊠ *Obecní dům, Nám. Republiky 5, Nové Mesto* ☎ *222–002–102* ⊕ *www. modernista.cz* Ⓜ *Line B: Náměstí Republiky.*

## JEWELRY AND ACCESSORIES
### Belda Shop
**JEWELRY/ACCESSORIES** | This jewelry shop feels more like a gallery than a shop, with its statement pieces gleaming in the light. But don't be put off; it's a family-run business and the staff are friendly. The carefully curated sculptures and accessories are typified by an amazing use of metal and precious stone. ⊠ *Mikulandská 10, Nové Mesto* ☎ *224–933–052* ⊕ *www. belda.cz* ⊙ *Closed weekends* Ⓜ *Line B: Národní třída.*

## MARKETS
### ★ Náplavka
**FOOD/CANDY** | Every Saturday sees the hipster riverside hangout of Náplavka transformed into a farmers' market selling staples like potatoes and apples as well as more artisanal products like traditional Czech dumplings and honey wine, smoked meats, and tortellini. ⊠ *Náplavka, Nové Mesto* ⊕ *www.farmarsketrziste.cz* ⊙ *Closed Jan.* Ⓜ *Line B: Karlovo Náměstí.*

## SHOES
### Baťa
**SHOES/LUGGAGE/LEATHER GOODS** | Shoes, glorious shoes! Five floors of them, to be exact, are housed in this shoe giant that has locations around the world but got its start right here in the Czech Republic. ■**TIP**→ **There's a clearance section on the top floor for bargain hunters.** ⊠ *Václavské nám. 6, Nové Mesto* ☎ *221–088–478* ⊕ *www.bata.cz* Ⓜ *Lines A and B: Můstek.*

## TOYS
### Hugo chodí bos
**TOYS** | This almost impossibly cute toy store was founded in the last few years by a parent-led team who wanted to bring traditional Czech toys back to Czech children. Its name means "Hugo goes barefoot," and it sells a range of lovely toys and gifts, many wooden, which hark back to a more innocent age. ⊠ *Řeznická 12, Nové Mesto* ☎ *602–834–930* ⊕ *www. hugochodibos.cz* Ⓜ *Line B: Karlovo náměstí.*

### Sparkys
**GIFTS/SOUVENIRS** | **FAMILY** | This is Prague's preeminent toy store, with goodies for babies, toddlers, and older children. Let the little ones run wild among three floors of Legos, puzzles, and games. Sparkys also stocks an adorable array of stuffed animals, including Krtek, the cute Czech cartoon character whose popularity spread across the communist world in the second half of the 20th century. ⊠ *Havířská 2, Nové Mesto* ☎ *224–239–309* ⊕ *www.sparkys.cz* Ⓜ *Line B: Náměstí Republiky.*

Chapter 7

# SMÍCHOV AND VYŠEHRAD

Updated by
Joseph Reaney

| 👁 Sights | 🍴 Restaurants | 🛏 Hotels | 🛍 Shopping | 🍸 Nightlife |
|---|---|---|---|---|
| ★★★★☆ | ★★★★☆ | ★★★★☆ | ★★★☆☆ | ★★★★☆ |

# NEIGHBORHOOD SNAPSHOT

## TOP EXPERIENCES

■ **Vyšehrad Cemetery:** Spot famous names like Antonín Dvořák and Alfons Mucha on the tombs and headstones in this historical burial place.

■ **Live Theater:** Take in a show (with English subtitles) at the superb Švandovo divadlo (Švanda Theater), or catch an alternative art performance at Meet Factory.

■ **Gorlice Hall:** Navigate through Vyšehrad's tunnels to reach this barrel-vaulted hall, home to the original baroque statues from the Charles Bridge.

■ *Brown-Nosers:* Interact with art as never before by enjoying a unique rear view of local enfant terrible David Černý's infamous sculpture.

■ **Sky-High Swimming:** Practice your breaststroke while enjoying stunning city panoramas at the Corinthia Hotel Prague's 24th-floor pool.

## GETTING HERE

Smíchov is a major transport hub. All attractions are within walking distance of one of two Metro stations—Smíchovské nádraží and Anděl (both Line B)—while there are regular tram connections to Malá Strana (Lesser Quarter) and Nové Město (New Town). The neighborhood is also home to Praha-Smíchov railway station, which offers easy train connections to Karlstejn and Western Bohemia. Vyšehrad is easily accessible by the Metro station of the same name (Line C)—though expect a 15-minute walk from here to the main attractions—or by climbing the steep staircase up from the riverside near Výtoň tram stop. There's also parking available just outside Táborská brána (the entrance gate into the fortress).

## PLANNING YOUR TIME

Vyšehrad's main attractions are open only during the day, and you should plan at least four hours to see them all. However, the park can be visited at any time, and the view down the river to the castle is spectacular day or night. Due to its array of excellent restaurants, cinemas, and theaters, Smíchov is best visited after dark.

## QUICK BITES

■ **Artic Bakehouse.** The home-baked sourdough bread, the huge selection of delicious pastries, and the lovingly brewed coffee make this café-bakery a local favorite. ⊠ *Újezd 11, Smíchov* ⊕ *facebook.com/ articBakehouse* Ⓜ Tram 9 to Újezd

■ **Hospůdka Na hradbách.** This large beer garden is one of Prague's most popular after-work hangouts during the summer months, and it's no wonder with those stunning city views. ⊠ *V Pevnosti 2, Vyšehrad* ⊕ *facebook.com/hospud-kanahradbach* Ⓜ Line C: Vyšehrad

■ **Kavárna co hledá jméno.** Literally translated as "A Coffee Shop Looking for a Name," this achingly hip café-cum-gallery serves a wonderful weekend brunch. You can't reserve, so come early. ⊠ *Stroupežnického 10, Smíchov* ⊕ *kavarnacohledaj-meno.cz* Ⓜ Line B: Anděl

Separated by the Vltava River, Smíchov and Vyšehrad are like night and day. In fact, that's when these two neighborhoods are best experienced: spend a morning and afternoon exploring Vyšehrad, then head to Smíchov for your evening entertainment.

The high-top Vyšehrad Citadel once rivaled Prague Castle in size and importance, but much of its historic architecture was leveled during the Hussite wars of the 15th century. The area got a new lease on life in the 18th century as a military fortress, and the casements remain one of the leading attractions. There's also a grand neo-Gothic cathedral and the country's most important cemetery. For many Prague residents, a trip here means simply a chance to enjoy the fresh air and stunning views of Prague Castle in the distance.

Smíchov, meanwhile, really comes to life after the sun goes down. When the city had walls, the neighborhood was on the outside, and all manner of people could live there, making it a colorful, cosmopolitan area. Today, it's known for its top-drawer dining options, excellent craft beer and cocktail bars, and world-class theaters and live music venues. There are also plenty of good hotels, allowing you to enjoy all Smíchov has to offer at a more leisurely pace. Connections from here to the city center are regular, quick, and easy.

# Smíchov

##  Sights

Smíchov is less about sightseeing and more about food, drink, and entertainment. Nevertheless, there are a couple of sights worth seeing, including the Staropramen Brewery, which has been sitting proudly on the river since 1869.

**Chrám sv. archanděla Michaela** (*Church of St. Michael the Archangel*)
**RELIGIOUS SITE** | At the southern end of Petřínské sady (Petřín Gardens) lies an unusual, folk baroque wooden building. This is the Orthodox Church of St. Michael the Archangel. Originally built in 1793 in the Ukrainian village of Velyki Luchky, the building was donated to Prague in 1929 to celebrate the 10th anniversary of Carpathian Ruthenia's unification with Czechoslovakia (the region is today split between Ukraine, Poland, and Slovakia). It was duly dismantled and shipped over piece by piece to Prague, where it was reassembled on this site. Visitors today can stroll around the exterior or head inside for one of the twice-weekly services, held at 10 am on Sunday and 8 am on Monday. To get here, cross the road from tram stop Švandovo divadlo and enter Kinského zahrada (Kinsky Garden). Follow the

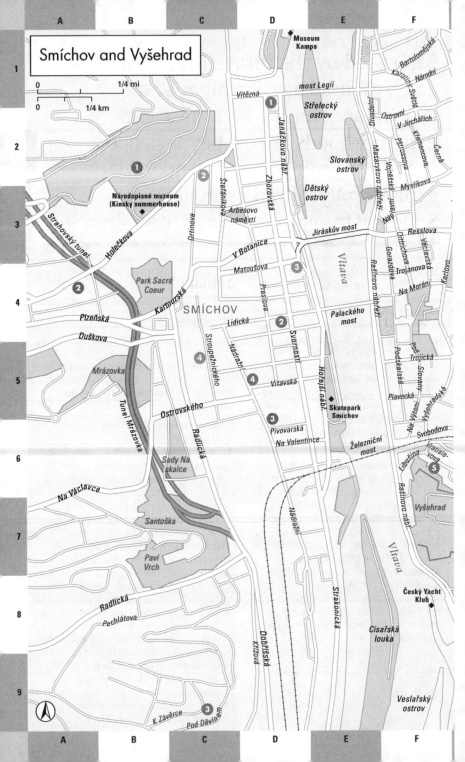

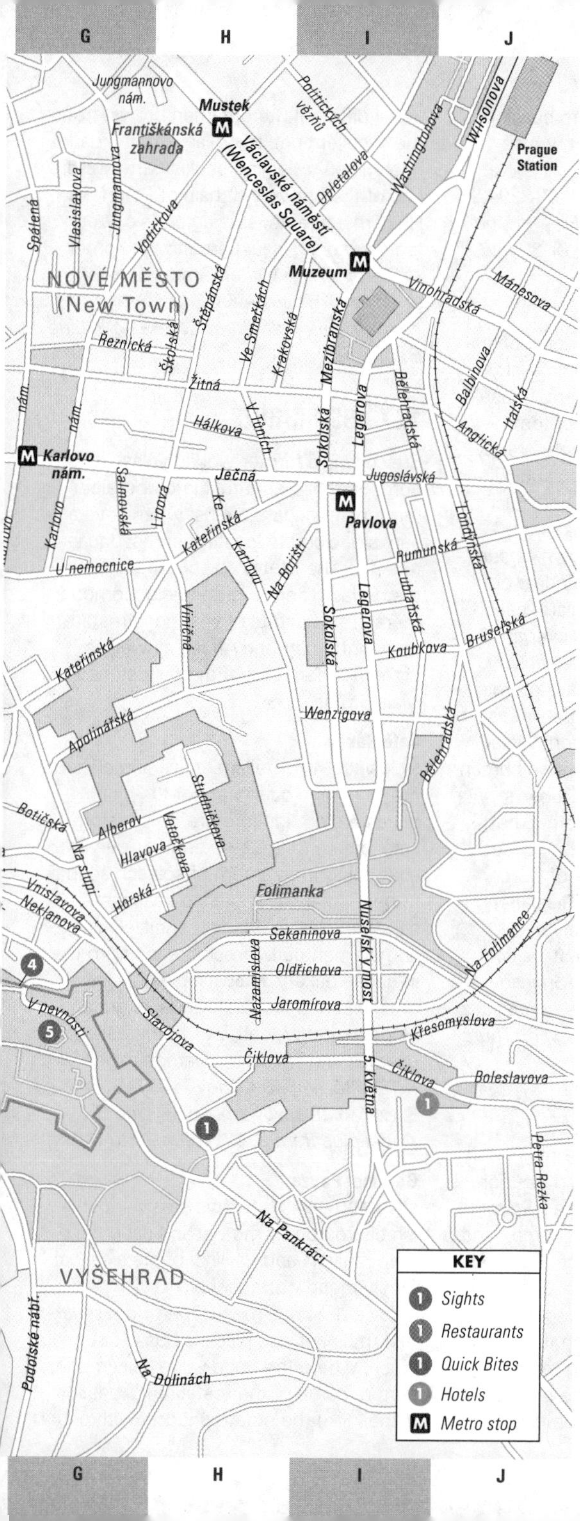

## Sights ▼

1 Chrám sv. archanděla
  Michaela........................... **B2**
2 Gallerie Futura ..................... **A4**
3 Pivovar Staropramen.............. **D5**
4 Vyšehrad Casemates.............. **G6**
5 Vyšehrad Citadel.................. **G7**

## Restaurants ▼

1 Café Savoy ........................ **D1**
2 Gourmet Pauza.................... **D4**
3 Na Kopci............................ **C9**
4 Taro................................. **D5**
5 U Kroka ............................ **F6**

## Quick Bites ▼

1 Caffé Fresco....................... **H8**

## Hotels ▼

1 Corinthia Hotel Prague............. **I7**
2 Hotel Kinsky Garden............... **C2**
3 Mamaison Riverside
  Hotel Prague ...................... **D4**
4 Vienna House Andel's Prague..... **C5**

**7**

Smíchov and Vyšehrad SMÍCHOV

### KEY

1 Sights
1 Restaurants
1 Quick Bites
1 Hotels
M Metro stop

main route up to the museum building, then take the path to its right, which snakes up the hill to the church. ✉ *Na Hřebenkách 60, Smíchov* ☎ *777–329–275* 🌐 *www.parohiapraga.eu* 🎫 *Free* [M] *Line B: Anděl plus Tram 9, 12, 15, or 20 to Švandovo divadlo.*

★ **Galerie Futura**

**MUSEUM** | This free-to-enter (donations welcome) art gallery, set within a labyrinthine, brick-walled basement, houses an eclectic range of quirky, contemporary, and occasionally downright creepy artworks, from oil paintings to audiovisual installations. But it's one particular provocative sculpture that takes the headlines: David Černý's *Brown-Nosers*. Head through the rotating window out into the garden to see two giant, naked, lower halves of bodies, bent over at 90 degrees. Climb one of the two rickety ladders and peer "into" the sculptures to watch a video. In one of the videos—spoiler alert!—former president Václav Klaus is being clumsily spoon-fed human waste to the soundtrack of Queen's "We Are the Champions." In the other, he's the one doing the feeding. The scenes are a metaphor for the state of Czech politics, apparently. ■ **TIP→ The gallery is a 15-minute uphill walk from Anděl Metro station. Ring the buzzer at the door to be let in.** ✉ *Holečkova 49, Smíchov* ☎ *608–955–150* 🌐 *www.futuraproject.cz* 🎫 *Free* ⏲ *Closed Mon., Tues., and Thurs.* [M] *Line B: Anděl.*

**Pivovar Staropramen** (*Staropramen Brewery*)

**FACTORY** | The slogan for this brewery on the riverside in Smíchov could be "For beer, go directly to the source." *Staropramen* literally means "old source," and it's definitely one of the most ubiquitous beers in the city (and beyond). This visitor center offers 50-minute guided tours every day, taking you through the history of the site, the beer brewing method, and how far and wide the beer is exported. It all culminates in a tasting of a few different Staropramen brews, from the excellent unfiltered lager to the dark beer. If you're feeling peckish afterward, one of the brewery's chain of Potrefená Husa restaurants, serving classic Czech food and beer, is just around the corner. ✉ *Staropramen Visitor Center, Pivovarská 9, Smíchov* ☎ *251–553–389* 🌐 *www.centrumstaropramen.cz* 🎫 *269 Kč* [M] *Line B: Anděl.*

## 🍴 Restaurants

Smíchov is a former working-class neighborhood that was thrust into upscale territory in the late 1990s, when several banks decided to locate their headquarters near the Metro station Anděl. Now the de facto center of the neighborhood, there are a handful of very good restaurants dotted around Anděl, as well as in the northern part of the district, near Malá Strana.

**Café Savoy**

**$$** | **EUROPEAN** | Stellar service and elegant meals of high quality at not-too-high prices are de rigueur here. This restored café, dating to the 19th century, serves everything from cream of spinach soups to beef steak tartare, crisp seasonal salads to classic Wiener schnitzel, all complemented by fresh breads from the in-house bakery. **Known for:** extensive breakfast and brunch menus; bright and elegant interior; delicious home-baked pastries and cakes. [$] *Average main: 320 Kč* ✉ *Vítězná 5, Smíchov* ☎ *257–311–562* 🌐 *www.cafesavoy.ambi.cz* [M] *Line B: Anděl plus Tram 9, 12, 15, or 20 to Újezd.*

**Gourmet Pauza**

**$$** | **MEDITERRANEAN** | This small and stylish bistro, run by mother-and-daughter team Zuzana and Pavlína, offers a casual, family-friendly atmosphere in which to enjoy a delicious meal. Open from breakfast to dinner, the place is busiest at lunch, where the good-value daily menus feature some of the restaurant's best dishes (like the potato gnocchi with pork

## Did You Know?

David Černý's risqué sculptures are supposedly a metaphor for Czech politics. Find *Brown-Nosers* at Galerie Futura.

tenderloin and gorgonzola) at half the usual price. **Known for:** stylish but unfussy ambience; quality Mediterannean-inspired food; slightly high prices. $ *Average main: 325 Kč* ✉ *Lidická 19, Smíchov* ☎ *257–312–849* 🌐 *www.gourmetpauza.cz* [M] *Line B: Anděl.*

### ★ Na Kopci

$$ | **CZECH** | Although a little out of the way, this lovely restaurant overlooking Smíchov (the name means "On the Hill") serves exceptional, high-end Czech and international cuisine within a comfortable and casual setting. The menu is completely overhauled every three months, making the best use of seasonal, locally sourced ingredients—from rabbit and wild boar to porcini mushrooms—to create surprising and satisfying dishes. **Known for:** sublime seasonal dishes; warm and welcoming decor; affordable prices. $ *Average main: 400 Kč* ✉ *K Závěrce 20, Smíchov* ☎ *251–553–102* 🌐 *www.nakopci.com* [M] *Line B: Radlická.*

### ★ Taro

$$ | **VIETNAMESE** | This extraordinary Asian fusion restaurant, which consists of just 17 bar stalls arranged around an open kitchen, offers an interactive dining experience combining traditional Vietnamese cuisine with European techniques and flavors. It's a combination inspired by owners Khanh's and Giang's personal experiences as Vietnamese men growing up in Prague. **Known for:** kitchen spectacle with chef interaction; flavor-packed seasonal dishes; great quality-to-value ratio. $ *Average main: 275 Kč* ✉ *Nádražní 100, Smíchov* ☎ *777–446–007* 🌐 *www.taro.cz* ⏲ *Closed Sun. and Mon.* [M] *Line B: Anděl.*

## 🛏 Hotels

With a host of entertainment options on your doorstep, as well as easy access—via tram, Metro, or on foot—to the city's historical center, Smíchov is a great place to stay.

### Hotel Kinsky Garden

$$ | **HOTEL** | You could walk the mile from this pleasant hotel to Prague Castle entirely on the tree-lined paths of Petřín, the hilly park that starts across the street. **Pros:** great parkside location for runners; easy access to airport and city; good value out of season. **Cons:** expensive bar (go out for a drink); short uphill walk from the tram; beds on the firm side. $ *Rooms from: 4500 Kč* ✉ *Holečkova 7, Smíchov* ☎ *257–311–173* 🌐 *www.hotelkinskygarden.cz* 🛏 *62 rooms* 🍴 *Breakfast* [M] *Line B: Anděl plus Tram 9, 12, 15, or 20 to Švandovo divadlo.*

### Mamaison Riverside Hotel Prague

$$ | **HOTEL** | True to its name, the Riverside is situated right above the Vltava across from Frank Gehry's Tančící dům (Dancing House). **Pros:** clever art nouveau design; incredible river views; great value if booked early. **Cons:** no fitness facilities; interior rooms are dark; a little tired in places. $ *Rooms from: 4500 Kč* ✉ *Janáčkovo nabř. 15, Smíchov* ☎ *225–994–611* 🌐 *www.mamaisonriverside.com* 🛏 *80 rooms* 🍴 *Breakfast* [M] *Line B: Anděl.*

### Vienna House Andel's Prague

$$ | **HOTEL** | Located next to one of the city's best shopping malls, this simple, modernist hotel may be built for business, but it's also where many of the young, up-and-coming, and mostly German-speaking trendsetters stay. **Pros:** chic and pared-back interior design; wide choice of foods for breakfast; great tram and Metro connections to the center. **Cons:** breakfast room can be busy; mall area is lacking personality; not walkable to any major sights. $ *Rooms from: 2500 Kč* ✉ *Stroupežnického 21, Smíchov* ☎ *296–889–688* 🌐 *andelsbyviennahouseprague.h-rez.com* 🛏 *239 rooms* 🍴 *Breakfast* [M] *Line B: Anděl.*

# Ⓨ Nightlife

This neighborhood is jam-packed with cool beer and wine bars, cocktail joints, and live music venues. Stroll around and see what takes your fancy.

## BARS AND PUBS
### Bar and Cafe Brothers
BARS/PUBS | This small but stylish American-style bar serves beers, wines, spirits, and a wide range of excellent cocktails. It also has, somewhat unexpectedly, some of Prague's best coffee. Whether serving a Tom Collins or a latte macchiato, the bartenders really know their stuff. ✉ *Lidická 12, Smíchov* ☎ *605–777–206* ⊕ *www.brothersbar.cz* Ⓜ *Line B: Anděl.*

### Craft Beer Spot
BARS/PUBS | This side-street taproom has an enormous, arching bar with an ever-changing selection of 10 Czech and international beers on tap. There are fridgefuls of bottles, too; the enthusiastic and knowledgeable staff will be happy to help you make a selection. Beer-friendly food, from cheddar-smothered nachos to beer-marinated ribs, is served throughout the day. ✉ *Plaská 5, Smíchov* ☎ *257–219–855* ⊕ *www.craftbeerprague.com* Ⓜ *Line B: Anděl plus Tram 9, 12, 15, or 20 to Újezd.*

## JAZZ CLUBS
### ★ Jazz Dock
MUSIC CLUBS | If you missed your boat tour, don't despair. You can still hear notes and beats wafting aross the water while sipping a cocktail in a decadent venue. This extremely cool, glass-enclosed nightclub and jazz bar—built, as the name suggests, on a dock—offers a view of the passing boat traffic and lit-up landmark buildings like the National Theater, while you enjoy the strains of world-class live music acts. There are typically two concerts per night; it's worth reserving a table in advance for weekend shows. ✉ *Janáčkovo nábř. 2, Smíchov* ☎ *774–058–838* ⊕ *www.jazzdock.cz* Ⓜ *Line A: Anděl.*

## LIVE MUSIC CLUBS
### Futurum
MUSIC CLUBS | The decor at this stalwart Smíchov club could be described as odd but cool. Think 1950s sci-fi crossed with art deco, and you're on the right track. It all makes for a fun, casual night out. Video parties, complete with '80s, '90s, and '00s music, draw big crowds every Friday night. There are occasional live performances, too, usually from punk or goth bands, or DJs playing electronic music. ✉ *Zborovská 7, Smíchov* ☎ *257–328–571* ⊕ *futurum.musicbar.cz* Ⓜ *Line B: Anděl.*

### Phenomen Music Bar
DANCE CLUBS | This upmarket dance club has regular themed nights with energetic DJs and, occasionally, live music acts. There's a large dance floor, but also a good-size seating area for enjoying a cocktail, a glass of champagne, or some pick-me-up chicken wings. ✉ *Nádražní 84, Smíchov* ☎ *774–366–636* ⊕ *www.phenomen.cz* Ⓜ *Line B: Anděl.*

# 🎭 Performing Arts

## THEATER AND DANCE
### Švandovo divadlo (*Švanda Theater*)
THEATER | If you want to join the theater-loving masses and there's nothing on in English, Švanda Theater is your best bet. The plays shown here—a rotating mix that can include everything from Shakespeare to Ibsen to contemporary theater—are subtitled above the stage in English. The theater also occasionally hosts live concerts and serves as a major venue for the Prague Pride festival, held every August. ■TIP➜ **Sit in the balcony, on the right side, facing the stage for the best view.** ✉ *Štefánikova 6, Smíchov* ☎ *234–651–111* ⊕ *www.svandovodivadlo.cz* Ⓜ *Line B: Anděl plus Tram 9, 12, 15, or 20 to Švandovo divadlo.*

## VENUES
### Meet Factory
ARTS CENTERS | If you want to take the pulse of Prague's contemporary arts

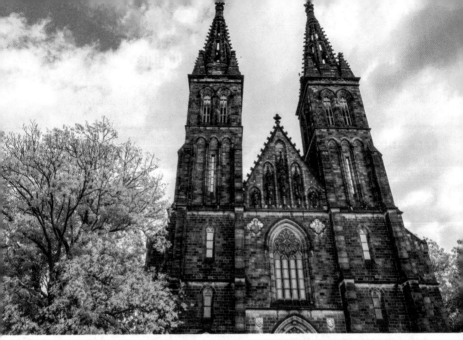

Many of Prague's greats lie buried in the cemetery adjacent to the Basilica of Sts. Peter and Paul. Most notable are the graves of Antonín Dvořák, Bedřich Smetana, and Alfons Mucha.

scene, get yourself down to Meet Factory. This spot really is too cool for school. Established more than a decade ago by leading Czech modern artist David Černý as a place for cultural and artistic collaboration, the space houses a gallery, concert hall, and theater, so it offers regular art, theater, dance, and music performances. To get here, cross over the railway tracks on a little bridge and keep an eye out for the car sculptures driving up the side of the building. ⊠ *Ke Sklárně 15, Smíchov* ☎ *251–551–796* ⊕ *meetfactory.cz* Ⓜ *Line B: Smíchovské nádraží.*

## 👜 Shopping

This area offers a reasonable range of modern shops and international brands. They're mainly within or around Nový Smíchov, the big daddy of shopping centers.

## SHOPPING MALLS AND DEPARTMENT STORES

### Nový Smíchov

**SHOPPING CENTERS/MALLS** | This bright and airy mall is one of Prague's largest, but it's still manageable. It has a convenient mix of shops, including brands like Zara, H&M, Humanic, Levi's, and Clinique. There's also a two-floor Tesco, a multiscreen movie theater, and a varied food court. ⊠ *Plzeňská 8, Smíchov* ☎ *251–101–061* ⊕ *novy-smichov.klepierre.cz* Ⓜ *Line B: Anděl.*

# Vyšehrad

##  Sights

The district of Vyšehrad is dominated by the Vyšehrad Citadel and its many attractions, the most visible of which is the Bazilika sv. Petra a Pavla (Basilica of Sts. Peter and Paul). But the neighborhood also incorporates the area around and below the castle, where there are a handful of other interesting sights.

# A Cubist Walk

Fans of 20th-century architecture should head below the rocky outcropping that's crowned by Vyšehrad Citadel to find a satisfying smattering of cubist gems. Prague's cubist architecture followed a great Czech tradition: embracing new ideas, while adapting them to existing artistic and social contexts to create something sui generis. Between 1912 and 1914, Josef Chochol (1880–1956) designed several of the city's dozen or so cubist projects, and you'll find a number of them in Vyšehrad.

Stroll down the staircase that leads from the citadel to the riverside, then peel off from the crowds by heading left and walking around 200 yards. Here, you'll find an eye-catching three-family house at Rašínovo nábřeží 6–10. This cubist masterpiece was completed early in Chochol's career, when his cubist style was still developing, so you can see a design touched with baroque and neoclassical influences, with a mansard roof and end gables. Cross the road for the best view of properties.

Once you've taken it all in, walk along the riverside back the way you came, then cross back over the road at the second pedestrian crossing. You're now looking into the garden of another great work of cubist architecture, Chochol's villa. The wall and gate of the house use triangular moldings and metal grating to create an effect of controlled energy. Head around to the front of the building (the street address is Libušina 3) to appreciate the property's full, undulating effect, created by smoothly articulated forms.

From here, walk around the corner to Neklanova 2, another apartment house that is attributed to Chochol. It uses pyramidal shapes and a suggestion of Gothic columns. Finally, walk just down the street and you'll come to Chochol's own apartment house. Situated at Neklanova 30 (on the corner of Přemyslova), it's a masterpiece in concrete. The pyramidal, kaleidoscopic window moldings and roof cornices make an expressive link to the baroque yet are wholly novel; the faceted corner balcony column, meanwhile, alludes to Gothic forerunners.

★ **Vyšehrad Casemates**

CAVE | Buried deep within the walls of Vyšehrad Citadel, this series of long, dark passageway was built by the French army in 1742 and later improved by other occupying forces, including the Prussians and the Austrians. A guided tour leads through several hundred meters of military corridors into Gorlice Hall, once a gathering place for soldiers and now a storage site for six of the original, pollution-scarred statues from Charles Bridge. Tours start at the information center, near the Táborská brána entrance gate. ⊠ V

*Pevnosti 5B, Vyšehrad* ⊕ *www.praha-vy-sehrad.cz* ⊠ *60 Kč* Ⓜ *Line C: Vyšehrad.*

★ **Vyšehrad Citadel** (*Vyšehrad Fortress*)

CASTLE/PALACE | Bedřich Smetana's symphonic poem *Vyšehrad* opens with four bardic harp chords that echo the legends surrounding this ancient fortress. Today the flat-top bluff stands over the right bank of the Vltava as a green, tree-dotted expanse showing few signs that splendid medieval monuments once made it a landmark to rival Prague Castle.

The Vyšehrad, or "High Castle," was constructed by Vratislav II (ruled 1061–92), a Přemyslid duke who became the first king of Bohemia. He made the fortified hilltop his capital. Under subsequent rulers it fell into disuse until the 14th century, when Charles IV transformed the site into an ensemble including palaces, the main church, battlements, and a massive gatehouse whose scant remains are on V Pevnosti ulice. By the 17th century royalty had long since departed, and most of the structures they built were crumbling. Vyšehrad was turned into a fortress.

Vyšehrad's place in the modern Czech imagination is largely thanks to the National Revivalists of the 19th century, particularly writer Alois Jirásek. Jirásek mined medieval chronicles for legends and facts to glorify the early Czechs, and that era of Czech history is very much in the popular consciousness today.

Today, the most notable attraction within the fortification walls is the **Basilica of Sts. Peter and Paul,** the landmark neo-Gothic church that can be seen from the riverside. Head inside to see the rich art nouveau decorations, including carvings, mosaics and figural wall paintings. Beside the church is the entrance to **Hřbitov Vyšehrad** (Vyšehrad Cemetery), the final resting place of some of the country's leading artists and luminaries, including composers Antonín Dvořák and Bedřich Smetana.

Traces of the citadel's distant past can be found at every turn and are reflected even in the structure chosen for the visitor center, the remains of a Gothic stone fortification wall known as **Špička,** or Peak Gate, at the corner of V Pevnosti and U Podolského Sanatoria. Farther ahead is the sculpture-covered **Leopold Gate,** which stands next to brick walls enlarged during the 1742 occupation by the French. Out of the gate, a heavily restored **Romanesque rotunda,** built by Vratislav II in the 11th century, stands on the corner of K Rotundě and Soběslavova. It's considered the oldest fully intact Romanesque building in the city. Down Soběslavova are the excavated foundations and a few embossed floor tiles from the late-10th-century **Basilika sv. Vavřince** (St. Lawrence Basilica, closed to the public). The foundations, discovered in 1884 while workers were creating a cesspool, are in a baroque structure at Soběslavova 14. The remains are from one of the few early medieval buildings to have survived in the area and are worth a look.

On the western side of Vyšehrad, part of the fortifications stand next to the surprisingly confined foundation mounds of a medieval palace overlooking a ruined watchtower called **Libuše's Bath,** which precariously juts out of a rocky outcropping over the river. A nearby plot of grass hosts a statue of Libuše and her consort Přemysl, one of four large, sculpted images of couples from Czech legend by J. V. Myslbek (1848–1922), the sculptor of the St. Wenceslas monument.

✉ V Pevnosti 5B, Vyšehrad ☎ 241–410–247 ⊕ www.praha-vysehrad.cz ✒ Grounds and cemetery free, casemates tour 60 Kč, Gothic cellar 50 Kč Ⓜ Line C: Vyšehrad.

## 🍴 Restaurants

Vyšehrad is best enjoyed with a picnic in the park. However, if this doesn't appeal, there are a handful of cafés and pubs dotted around the fortress and more in the streets below.

### ★ U Kroka

**$$ | CZECH |** This traditional pub, which sits below the walls of Vyšehrad Citadel, serves up traditional, meaty Czech fare—think beef goulash, pork knuckle, and duck leg confit—with freshly poured beer. The interior is warm and welcoming, the staff are unfailingly friendly, and the prices are very competitive. **Known for:** good-quality Czech food; pleasant industrial-chic interior; more locals than tourists. Ⓢ Average main: 275 Kč

*Vratislavova 12, Vyšehrad* ☎ *775–905–022* ⊕ *www.ukroka.cz* Ⓜ *Line B: Karlovo náměstí plus Tram 2 or 3 to Výtoň.*

 ## ☕ Coffee and Quick Bites

### Caffé Fresco

**$$ | ITALIAN |** If you're worn out after the long uphill climb to the bluff, Caffé Fresco serves up Italian salads and panini, plus a revivifying set of espresso drinks. It's on the way to or from the Vyšehrad metro stop. Ⓢ *Average main: 280 Kč* ⊠ *Rezidence Vyšehrad, Lumírova 33, Vyšehrad* ☎ *234–724–230* ⊕ *www. caffe-fresco.com* Ⓜ *Line C: Vyšehrad.*

## 🛏 Hotels

Vyšehrad has a very limited choice of accommodations. If you want to stay near the citadel, the Corinthia Hotel Prague is your best option.

### Corinthia Hotel Prague

**$$ | HOTEL |** An ideal accommodation option for business travelers, Corinthia Prague combines modern interiors, spacious rooms, and a choice of good restaurants with a convenient location; it sits on Metro Line C and is right opposite Prague Congress Center. **Pros:** right by Prague Congress Center; top-floor spa with panoramic city views; great value option. **Cons:** rooms a little corporate; reception sometimes understaffed; breakfast room gets busy. Ⓢ *Rooms from: 3300 Kč* ⊠ *Kongresová 1, Vyšehrad* ☎ *261–191–111* ⊕ *www.corinthia.com/ prague* ⊃ *539 rooms* ⦿ *Free Breakfast* Ⓜ *Line C: Vyšehrad.*

##  Performing Arts

### VENUES

**Kongresové centrum Praha** (*Congress Center*)

**ARTS CENTERS |** Somehow, this former Palace of Culture, built in 1981, has never found a place in people's hearts. The large, functionalist, multipurpose building has several performance spaces that can seat thousands, but overall it has a very sterile feel. Plays (usually musicals), stand-up comedians, circus shows, and more come here. As the largest venue in the city, it also hosts the majority of conferences. ⊠ *5. května 65, Vyšehrad* ☎ *261–171–111* ⊕ *www.praguecc.cz* Ⓜ *Line C: Vyšehrad.*

# Chapter 8

# VINOHRADY AND VRŠOVICE

8

Updated by
Joseph Reaney

| ● Sights | 🍴 Restaurants | 🛏 Hotels | 🛍 Shopping | 🍸 Nightlife |
|:---:|:---:|:---:|:---:|:---:|
| ★★★☆☆ | ★★★★☆ | ★★★☆☆ | ★★★★☆ | ★★★★★ |

# NEIGHBORHOOD SNAPSHOT

## TOP EXPERIENCES

■ **Fine Dining:** Enjoy a meal in one of Prague's top-drawer restaurants, such as Vinohrady's Equilibrista or Vršovice's Benjamin.

■ **St. Wenceslas Church:** Stroll around this weird and wonderful 20th-century church, with its sky-high clock tower visible from far and wide.

■ **Craft Beer:** Set off on an epic pub crawl around the countless craft beer bars and microbreweries in this part of town.

■ **Indie Boutiques:** Shop for boho vintage clothes and designer accessories in a host of small, independent boutiques.

■ **Slavia Prague:** Watch one of the country's most famous soccer teams in full flow during a game at the Sinobo Stadium.

## GETTING HERE

Metro Line A bisects Vinohrady, so most sights are within easy reach of three stations: Náměstí Míru, Jiřího z Poděbrad, and Flora. Vršovice does not have any Metro stations, but Tram 22 offers a direct connection to Nové Město (New Town), Malá Strana (Lesser Quarter), and Prague Castle. There is limited (mostly paid) parking available in both neighborhoods.

## PLANNING YOUR TIME

As they are mainly residential, Vinohrady and Vršovice make for pleasant, quiet neighborhoods to visit during weekdays. But if you want to make the most of the restaurants and nightlife—and meet some locals—come during evenings and weekends.

## QUICK BITES

■ **La Focacceria.** Take your pick from dozens of different focaccias, as well as delicious *arancini*, (small balls of rice stuffed with a savory filling) fresh ciabattas, and crispy Italian biscuits. ⊠ *Krymská 30, Vršovice* Ⓜ *Tram 22, 4 to Krymská*

■ **Cafefin.** This popular Vietnamese-Czech coffee shop is the perfect place for people-watching; come on the weekend for the excellent brunch. ⊠ *Nám. Jiřího z Poděbrad, Vinohrady* ⊕ *www.cafefinvpraze.com* Ⓜ *Line A: Jiřího z Poděbrad*

■ **The Conductor.** Famed for its soft and squishy cinnamon rolls (the best in town), this takeout spot also serves perfect pulled-pork sandwiches and lip-smacking vegan wraps. ⊠ *Francouzská 78, Vršovice* ⊕ *www.facebook.com/ streetfoodmaestro* Ⓜ *Tram 22, 4 to Krymská*

■ **Pavilon Grébovka.** This historic pavilion in pretty Havlíčkovy sady (Havlíček Gardens) serves sweet and savory breakfasts, tasty lunches, and all-day snacks. There's also a grill in summer. ⊠ *Havlíčkovy sady 2188, Vinohrady* ⊕ *www. pavilongrebovka.cz* Ⓜ *Tram 13 to Ruská*

Dotted with pretty green parks, charming turn-of-the-20th-century houses, and some of Prague's best cafés and restaurants, Vinohrady and Vršovice are two of Prague's most appealing—yet mercifully crowd-free—neighborhoods.

Vinohrady is centered on Vinohradská, the main street that extends eastward from the top of Václavské náměstí (Wenceslas Square) to a belt of enormous cemeteries. Named for the vineyards that once dominated the area, it retains an air of upper crustiness thanks to its splendid 19th-century apartment buildings, pleasant tree-lined streets, and handsome church- and market-filled squares, as well as its extraordinarily high concentration of upmarket cafés and restaurants. Vinohrady also boasts two of Prague's most popular green spaces: the English garden–style Riegrovy sady (Rieger Park) and the Italian Renaissance–style Havlíčkovy sady (Havlíček Gardens).

Neighboring Vršovice, to the south and east of Vinohrady, is equally charming, if a little rougher around the edges. Its art nouveau town houses may be a little more faded and its hip coffee shops less frequent, but its incredible choice of bars (from craft beer hangouts to down-to-earth *hospody,* or traditional Czech pubs), its quirky modernist churches, and its buzzing atmosphere during Slavia Prague match days more than make up for it.

# Vinohrady

##  Sights

**Havlíčkovy sady** (*Havlíček Gardens*)
**NATIONAL/STATE PARK** | Arguably Prague's prettiest park, Havlíček Gardens is best known for its Italian-style grotto and its rows of verdant vineyards. But the park also manages to pack in plenty of other attractions, from placid lakes to cascading fountains, and expansive green lawns to narrow woodland trails. It also has two excellent drinking and dining options: the charming garden café Pavilon Grébovka and the hilltop gazebo wine bar Viniční Altán. The latter also offers stunning views of the surrounding area. Getting to the park involves a short walk, either from tram stop Krymská (five minutes) or Metro stop Náměstí Míru (10 minutes).
✉ *Vinohrady* ☎ *236–044–111* ⊕ *www. pavilongrebovka.cz* 🎟 *Free* Ⓜ *Line A: Náměstí Míru.*

**Kostel Nejsvětějšího Srdce Páně** (*Church of the Most Sacred Heart*)
**RELIGIOUS SITE** | If you've had your fill of Romanesque, Gothic, and baroque, this church offers a startlingly modernist alternative. Designed in 1927 by Slovenian architect Josip Plečnik (the same architect commissioned to update Prague Castle), the art deco edifice of this church—topped by a tower with an enormous glazed clock—resembles

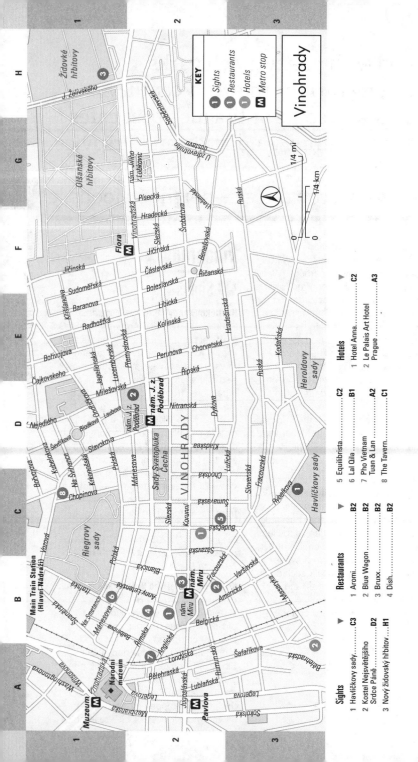

# Vinohrady

**KEY**
- 1 Sights
- 1 Restaurants
- 1 Hotels
- Ⓜ Metro stop

## Sights ▶
1 Havlíčkovy sady ............ **C3**
2 Kostel Nejsvětějšího
  Srdce Páně ............... **D2**
3 Nový židovský hřbitov ... **H1**

## Restaurants ▶
1 Aromi ...................... **B2**
2 Blue Wagon ................ **B2**
3 Bruxx ...................... **B2**
4 Dish ........................ **B2**
5 Equilibrista ............... **C2**
6 Lal Qila .................... **B1**
7 Pho Vietnam
  Tuan & Lan .............. **A2**
8 The Tavern ................ **C1**

## Hotels ▶
1 Hotel Anna ................ **C2**
2 Le Palais Art Hotel
  Prague .................... **A3**

a luxury ocean liner more than a place of worship. The effect was purposeful, as during the 1920s and 1930s the avant-garde imitated mammoth objects of modern technology. The interior decor is equally striking, particularly the altar, overlooked by a 10-foot-high gilded figure of Christ, flanked by six Czech patron saints. It's hard to miss the structure, which looms as you exit the Metro. **■ TIP→ While the front door (with a view of the interior) is open 9 to 5 every day, entrance is allowed only 45 minutes before and after mass.** ✉ *Nám. Jiřího z Poděbrad, Vinohrady* ☎ *222–727–713* 🌐 *srdcepane.cz* 🎟 *Free* [M] *Line A: Jiřího z Poděbrad.*

**Nový židovský hřbitov** (*New Jewish Cemetery*)
**CEMETERY** | In this, the newest of the city's half-dozen Jewish burial grounds, you can find the modest **tombstone of Franz Kafka,** which seems grossly inadequate to Kafka's fame but oddly in proportion to his own modest sense of self. The cemetery is usually open, although guards sometimes inexplicably seal off the grounds. Men may be required to wear a yarmulke (you can buy one here if you need to). Turn right at the main cemetery gate and follow the wall for about 100 yards. Kafka's thin white tombstone lies at the front of section 21. City maps may label the cemetery "Židovské hřbitovy." ✉ *Izraelská 712/1, Vinohrady* ☎ *226–235–248* 🌐 *www.kehilaprag.cz* 🎟 *Free* [M] *Line A: Želivského.*

## 🍴 Restaurants

Vinohrady is home to many of the capital's best restaurants. The neighborhood has two main dining hubs: the area surrounding Náměstí Miru, particularly south along Americká ulice; and the streets around the Metro station Jiřího z Poděbrad. However, you'll find some of the very finest dining experiences tucked away on less well-trodden avenues. For tasty, down-to-earth Czech food, you're better off heading to a pub.

★ **Aromi**
**$$$** | **ITALIAN** | Gracious, gregarious, and extremely confident, Aromi is easily among the top tier of Italian restaurants in the city and proud of it. Classic pastas made in-house and fresh seafood shown off tableside are two of the crowd favorites, as are the superb salads and well-chosen Italian wines. **Known for:** sumptuous seafood dishes; faultless service; cooking courses available. [$] *Average main: 480 Kč* ✉ *Nám. Míru 6, Vinohrady* ☎ *222–713–222* 🌐 *aromi.lacollezione.cz* [M] *Line A: Náměstí Míru.*

**Blue Wagon**
**$$** | **FRENCH** | Open since 2012 and still going strong, this appealing Vinohrady restaurant serves up innovative, high-quality cuisine in a business-casual setting of blond woods, white walls, and inoffensive artworks. The seasonal menu is a little tricky to pin down geographically—expect a mix of contemporary French and Czech dishes, accompanied by mainly Austrian wines—but everything is unfailingly fresh, flavorful, and filling. **Known for:** outdoor seating in summer; phenomenal chocolate fondant dessert; atmosphere a little spoiled by Muzak. [$] *Average main: 400 Kč* ✉ *Uruguayská 19, Vinohrady* ☎ *222–561–378* 🌐 *www.bluewagon.cz* 🕒 *No lunch Sun.* [M] *Line A: Náměstí Míru.*

**Bruxx**
**$$** | **BELGIAN** | Czech beer is facing increasing competition these days as younger Praguers set out to forge new traditions. Belgian ales, often tinged with fruit or nut flavors, served alongside kettles of mussels and golden frites with mayo sauce, are winning over not just locals but an upscale international clientele. **Known for:** Belgian beers on draught; fine fish and seafood dishes; outdoor seating in summer. [$] *Average main: 400 Kč* ✉ *Nám. Míru 9, Vinohrady* ☎ *224–250–404* 🌐 *www.bruxx.cz* [M] *Line A: Náměstí Míru.*

## Dish

**$$ | BURGER |** One of Prague's best burger joints, Dish has a menu of 11 burgers, including the house "Dish" burger with bacon and cheddar cheese, a pulled duck confit burger with red cabbage, and a veggie-friendly portobello mushroom burger with smoked mozzarella and spinach. The interior is warm, with exposed-brick walls, and an appealing terrace blossoms in mild weather. **Known for:** an array of excellent burgers; ironically named "fitness fries" topped with bacon and maple syrup; extensive gin and tonic menu. $ *Average main: 225 Kč* ⊠ *Římská 29, Vinohrady* ☎ *222–511–032* ⊕ *www. dish.cz* Ⓜ *Line A: Náměstí Míru.*

## ★ Equilibrista

**$$$ | ITALIAN |** Simply put, you won't find a better Italian restaurant and wine bar in Prague. Owners Simona and Eric spent 20 years living in Italy and have brought their passion for—and expertise of—the local cuisine to the Czech capital. **Known for:** sumptuous thick-cut tenderloin carpaccio; sophisticated but unconceited ambience; fresh burrata (Italian cow milk cheese). $ *Average main: 495 Kč* ⊠ *Budečská 10, Vinohrady* ☎ *602–228–523* ⊕ *www.equilibrista.cz* ⊘ *Closed Mon. No lunch Tues.* Ⓜ *Line A: Náměstí Míru.*

## Lal Qila

**$$ | INDIAN |** Vinohrady has several very good Indian restaurants, but this corner restaurant along one of the area's prettiest streets may just be the best. Those familiar with Indian cooking can expect all of the standard curries, tandoori dishes, samosas, naans, and other staples of Indian cuisine. **Known for:** delicious lamb dishes; fast and friendly service; lunch buffet available for 150 Kč. $ *Average main: 275 Kč* ⊠ *Italská 30, Vinohrady* ☎ *774–310–774* ⊕ *www.lalqila.cz* Ⓜ *Lines A and C: Muzeum.*

## Pho Vietnam Tuan & Lan

**$ | VIETNAMESE |** Prague's large and long-established Vietnamese community means the city is littered with cheap Southeast Asian dining options, but this cellar restaurant is one of the very best. While it's certainly no-frills—order at the counter and then find a table; in a few minutes someone brings around your food—the dishes are unfailingly fresh and delicious. **Known for:** satisfying fare in big portions; excellent value; can get very warm inside. $ *Average main: 140 Kč* ⊠ *Anglická 15, Vinohrady* ☎ *606–707–880* ⊕ *photuanlan.com* Ⓜ *Line C: I. P. Pavlova.*

## ★ The Tavern

**$$ | BURGER |** A hopping burger bar on the fringe of Riegrovy Park in Vinohrady, the Tavern arguably serves the city's best hamburgers and cheeseburgers. The restaurant began as the dream of an American couple to use classic U.S. combinations, like bacon-cheddar or blue cheese and caramelized onion, and then re-create them with locally sourced beef and toppings. **Known for:** the city's best burgers; intimate cellar setting; extensive cocktail menu. $ *Average main: 220 Kč* ⊠ *Chopinova 26, Vinohrady* ☎ *No phone* ⊕ *www.thetavern.cz* Ⓜ *Line A: Jiřího z Poděbrad.*

# 🛏 Hotels

With its excellent restaurants and pretty tree-lined streets, ideal for meandering after an exhausting day in the center, Vinohrady is the perfect place to stay for those looking to avoid the crowds.

## Hotel Anna

**$ | HOTEL |** The bright neoclassical façade and art nouveau details have been lovingly restored on this 19th-century building on a quiet residential street. **Pros:** top-floor suites have views of the historic district; helpful English-speaking staff; affordable for city center. **Cons:** some guests find walls to be thin; very small elevator; parking fee. $ *Rooms*

## Did You Know?

Havlíčkovy sady, known as Grébovka to locals, is a wonderful park for a stroll, views, and a leisurely glass of wine at the top of the vineyard.

*from: 1750 Kč* ✉ *Budečská 17, Vinohrady* ☎ *222–513–111* ⊕ *www.hotelanna. cz* ⤵ *24 rooms* ❖ *Breakfast* Ⓜ *Line A: Náměstí Míru.*

### ★ Le Palais Art Hotel Prague

$$ | **HOTEL** | This venerable 19th-century mansion served as the home and shop of Prague's main butcher. **Pros:** gorgeous hotel in nice neighborhood; some rooms have fireplaces; excellent breakfast. **Cons:** requires public transit to get anywhere; basic rooms are quite small; beds a little hard for some. Ⓢ *Rooms from: 4500 Kč* ✉ *U Zvonařky 1, Vinohrady* ☎ *234–634– 111* ⊕ *www.lepalaishotel.eu* ⤵ *72 rooms* ❖ *Free Breakfast* Ⓜ *Line C: I. P. Pavlova plus Tram 6 to Zvonařka.*

##  Nightlife

Vinohrady has a great local scene of trendy bars and clubs, as well as laid-back traditional pubs, popular with locals and expats alike.

### BARS AND PUBS
#### ★ BeerGeek Bar

**BREWPUBS/BEER GARDENS** | This popular craft beer bar serves uncommon brews from the Czech Republic, across Europe, and the United States. It has an impressive 32 taps, with the choice of beers changing daily (though usually including at least one from its in-house Sibeeria Brewery label). There's also a good selection of beer snacks; opt for the excellent chicken wings. If you don't have time to stop, there's also a BeerGeek Pivoteka (bottle shop) nearby, which stocks more than 500 bottled beers. ✉ *Vinohradská 62, Vinohrady* ☎ *776–827–068* ⊕ *beer-geek.cz* Ⓜ *Line A: Jiřího z Poděbrad.*

#### Bonvivant's

**BARS/PUBS** | The cocktail maker's cocktail bar of choice in Prague, and still probably one of the absolute best, Bonvivant's has a nostalgic feel and fantastic staff, who ask you what drinks and tastes you like and then whip you up something bespoke. Upmarket but not

pricey, this is a perfect place for for an adventure in mixology and some tasty tapas in a refined setting. ✉ *Máneso-va 55, Staré Mesto* ☎ *604–958–311* ⊕ *www.bonvivantsprague.com* Ⓜ *Line B: Jiřího z Poděbrad.*

#### Vinohradský Parlament

**BARS/PUBS** | Located a short walk beyond Wenceslas Square, Parlament is a modern take on a traditional Czech pub, with everything that implies: tasty food, great beer (they serve Staropramen), and good times. ✉ *Korunní 1, Vinohrady* ☎ *224– 250–403* ⊕ *www.vinohradskyparlament. cz* Ⓜ *Tram 10 to Náměstí Míru.*

#### Vinohradský pivovar

**BREWPUBS/BEER GARDENS** | This popular Vinohrady hangout brews a range of traditional and well-regarded Czech pilsners, including unpasteurized and unfiltered versions, as well as increasing number of IPAs and other ales. You can pop in for a beer or two, or make a whole evening of it with a meal in the restaurant (expect classic Czech pub food at good prices) followed by some live entertainment in the music hall (expect anything from big band concerts to improv comedy). ✉ *Korunní 106, Vinohrady* ☎ *222–760–080* ⊕ *www.vinohradskypivovar.cz* Ⓜ *Line A: Flora.*

### CLUBS
#### Retro Music Hall

**DANCE CLUBS** | With its location just a bit out of the center, this fun club provides an escape from the hassle of downtown. The street-level part is a pleasant functionalist-style café with outdoor seating, and the lower level houses a club with a big dance floor. The name is a bit misleading; there are some '80s nights, but the bulk of the schedule is hip-hop and other more contemporary sounds. ✉ *Francouzská 4, Vinohrady* ☎ *222–510–592* ⊕ *www.retropraha.cz* Ⓜ *Line A: Náměstí Míru.*

## LGBTQ

### Club TERMAX

**DANCE CLUBS** | It claims to be the largest gay club in the Czech Republic, and with three floors that's probably right. There's a disco, multiple bars, seating areas with Wi-Fi, and other attractions for a male crowd. It's open only on Friday and Saturday night, but the party continues right through til 6 am. Not to be confused with the similarly named Club TERMIX, another gay club situated nearby. ✉ *Vinohradská 40, Vinohrady* ☎ *222–710–462* ⊕ *club-max.cz.*

### ★ The Saints

**BARS/PUBS** | This small British-owned pub and cocktail bar is centrally located near several other gay and gay-friendly establishments in Vinohrady. The owners also run a gay-friendly travel and accommodations service. ✉ *Polská 32, Vinohrady* ☎ *222–250–326* ⊕ *www.praguesaints.cz* Ⓜ *Line A: Jiřího z Poděbrad.*

## 🛍 Shopping

As a local neighborhood with less tourist footfall, Vinohrady's shopping scene is less about crystal trinkets and touristy tchotchkes and more about local fashion boutiques.

### CLOTHING

### Pour Pour

**CLOTHING** | Can't bear the thought of leaving Prague without something completely unique? Stop by this little shop filled with eclectic creations—from underwear to funny diaries—by young, up-and-coming Czech designers. With a rotating collection, the shop is all about originality and unexpected fashions, reminding you that getting dressed can be an adventure. ✉ *Vinohradská 74, Vinohrady* ☎ *777–830–078* ⊕ *www.pourpour.cz* ☉ *Closed weekends* Ⓜ *Line A: Jiřího z Poděbrad.*

### Thrift Store

**CLOTHING** | Prague's got good game when it comes to thrift and retro stores, and this emporium in Vinohrady is one of the oldest and best. Moreover, a percentage of the profits goes to charity. ✉ *Budečská 13, Vinohrady* ☎ *608–623–339* ⊕ *www.thriftshop.cz* Ⓜ *Line A: Náměstí Míru.*

# Vršovice

## ◉ Sights

### Kostel sv. Václava (*St. Wenceslas Church*)

**RELIGIOUS SITE** | It's hard to miss this church—a striking constructivist work of art that, at 164 feet high, dominates the Vršovice skyline. Built in 1930 to commemorate 1,000 years since the death of St. Wenceslas, the building's most striking feature is its skyscraping white clock tower, topped by a 23-foot-high gold cross. It's worth a visit to see the exterior alone (and the lovely surrounding park), but for a peek inside, doors are usually open between 8 and 1 on Sunday for services. There are also occasional midweek services; check the website in advance for more information. ✉ *Nám. Svatopluka Čecha 3, Vršovice* ☎ *702–075–417* ⊕ *www.farnostvrsovice.cz* 🎫 *Free* ☉ *Closed Mon.–Sat. (excl. services)* Ⓜ *Line A: Náměstí Miru plus Tram 4, 13, or 22 to Čechovo náměstí.*

## 🍴 Restaurants

The rapidly gentrifying Vršovice has an increasing number of good restaurants and a few excellent ones. The most convenient Metro station for accessing the neighborhood is Náměstí Miru, but from there you'll have to take Tram 4 or 22.

### ★ Benjamin

**$$$$** | **CZECH** | Opened in 2017, Benjamin quickly gained—and has retained—a reputation as one of Prague's most sought-after fine-dining experiences.

**Sights** ▼

1 Kostel sv. Václava ..... **B3**

**Restaurants** ▼

1 Benjamin.... **A2**

2 Osteria Da Clara..... **A2**

**Hotels** ▼

1 Iris Hotel Eden......... **D3**

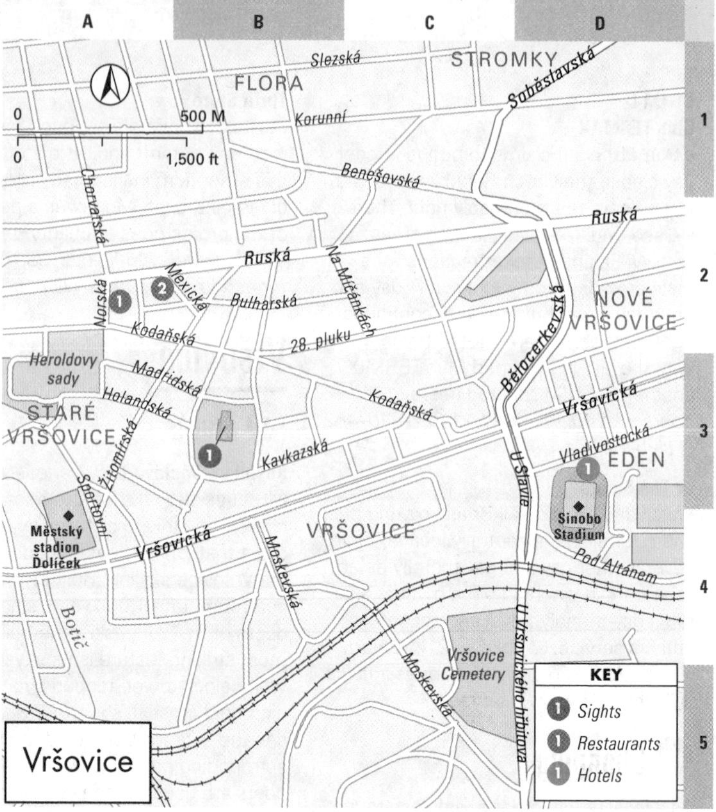


Well, with just 10 seats set around a horseshoe-shaped table, it's a very exclusive ticket. **Known for:** beautifully presented and flavorful dishes; difficulty getting reservations; interactive and communal dining experience. $ *Average main: 1290 Kč* ✉ *Norská 14, Vršovice* ☎ *774–141–432* 🌐 *www.benjamin14.cz* ⏲ *Closed Sun.–Tues. No lunch.* [M] *Line A: Náměstí Míru plus Tram 4, 13, or 22 to Ruská.*

**Osteria Da Clara**

**$$ | ITALIAN** | Osteria Da Clara is an unassuming Italian spot that gets by on the hustle and charm of the staff. When the kitchen isn't overwhelmed—which happens when the austere white dining room gets beyond half full—it serves up lovely, unpretentious Italian cuisine, like crostini with chicken liver, polenta, and tomatoes. **Known for:** giant tiramisu; good food at a great price; tricky location (consider a taxi). $ *Average main: 250 Kč* ✉ *Mexická 7, Vršovice* ☎ *271–726–548* 🌐 *www.daclara.com* ⏲ *Closed Mon.* [M] *Line A: Náměstí Míru plus Tram 4, 13, or 22 to Ruská.*

## 🛏 Hotels

Vršovice has only limited accommodation options, but what's here is generally great value for money. It's also convenient if you're catching an evening soccer match or concert at the Sinobo Stadium.

**Iris Hotel Eden**

**$$ | HOTEL** | Set within the Sinobo Stadium, home of Czech soccer club Slavia Prague and a regular venue for concerts, Iris Hotel Eden is a modern, comfortable city hotel. **Pros:** modern and spacious rooms; great value option; good breakfast buffet. **Cons:** limited dining

Slavia Prague is holder of a world record: since 1892 the players of the club have traditionally been wearing their red and white colors.

options around; Wi-Fi connections can be patchy; a little out of the way. $ *Rooms from: 2500 Kč* ✉ *U Slavie 2A, Vršovice* ☎ *702–033–159* ⊕ *www.irishoteleden.cz* ⇨ *150 rooms* |○| *Free Breakfast* Ⓜ *Line A: Námesti Míru plus Tram 22 to Slavia.*

##  Nightlife

Vršovice has an enjoyable mix of swanky cocktail joints, hipster craft beer bars, and traditional Czech hospody.

### Bad Flash
BREWPUBS/BEER GARDENS | One of Prague's best craft beer bars, Bad Flash has 12 taps serving a constant rotation of brews from its own stable as well as other Czech and international microbreweries. The minimalist, shabby-chic interior and simple menu of beer snacks (try the pickled cheese) attract a young and cosmopolitan crowd. The bar doesn't take reservations, so it's best to come early and stay late. ✉ *Krymská 2, Vršovice* ☎ *273–134–609* ⊕ *www.badflash.cz* Ⓜ *Line A: Námesti Míru plus Tram 4, 13, or 22 to Krymská.*

### ★ Pivnice pivovaru Trilobit
BREWPUBS/BEER GARDENS | From the street, this Vršovice taproom appears entirely unremarkable, but step inside to find one of Prague's true after-dark gems. The beer is exceptional, with four homebrews on tap—the award-winning 12° pale lager plus three seasonal beers—plus always-friendly service and a lovely cozy interior. In the summer, you can enjoy your beer out on the terrace. ✉ *Francouzská 112, Vršov-ice* ☎ *734–525–843* ⊕ *pivovartrilobit. com* Ⓜ *Line A: Námesti Míru plus Tram 4, 13, or 22 to Krymská.*

## 🛍 Shopping

### CLOTHING
### BOHO Vintage Concept Store
CLOTHING | One of Prague's hippest shopping experiences, BOHO has in recent years morphed from perenially popular pop-up to Vršovice mainstay. As well as clothes, there's also a cool café serving brunches and booze. ✉ *Fran-couzská 76, Vršovice* ☎ *222–946–162*

⊕ *boho.cz* ⊙ *Closed Sun. and Mon.*
Ⓜ *Line A: Náměstí Míru plus Tram 4, 13,*
*or 22 to Krymská.*

##  Activities

### SOCCER
**Sinobo Stadium**
**SOCCER** | Home to Slavia Prague, one
of the country's "big two" soccer
teams along with Sparta Prague, the
21,000-seater Sinobo Stadium shows Slavia games throughout the season (July
to May). There are league matches every
other weekend, as well as occasional
midweek European fixtures. Outside
of home games, you can find out more
about the club (and Czech football in general) at the stadium's Slavia Museum. As
one of Prague's biggest seated venues,
the stadium also hosts regular concerts.
⊠ *U Slavie 2A, Vršovice* ☎ *272–118–100*
⊕ *www.slavia.cz* Ⓜ *Line A: Námesti Míru*
*plus Tram 22 to Slavia.*

# Chapter 9

# ŽIŽKOV AND KARLÍN

Updated by
Joseph Reaney

👁 **Sights**
★★★☆☆

🍴 **Restaurants**
★★★★☆

🛏 **Hotels**
★★★☆☆

🛍 **Shopping**
★★★☆☆

🍸 **Nightlife**
★★★★★

# NEIGHBORHOOD SNAPSHOT

## TOP EXPERIENCES

■ **Žižkov Pub Crawl:** Line your stomach and roll up your sleeves for the bar crawl to end all bar crawls in this impossibly pub-packed district.

■ **Karlín Musical Theater:** From *West Side Story* to *Jesus Christ Superstar,* catch a musical theater production at this grand old Karlín venue.

■ **National Monument:** Delve into 20th-century Czech history, from pre–World War II to post–Velvet Revolution, at this Vítkov Hill exhibition.

■ **Žižkov TV Tower:** Take the elevator up to 305 feet for a unique panorama of Prague—or stay at the One Room Hotel to wake up to the view.

■ **Fine Hipster Dining:** Eat your way around Karlín. Hip, high-end restaurants include meat maestro Nejen Bistro and sourdough savant Eska.

## GETTING HERE

Žižkov is not directly served by any Metro line, though the Line A stop at Jiřího z Poděbrad will bring you within about 10 minutes' walking distance. Alternatively, any tram heading east from Hlavní nádraží (just north of the main train station) will take you into the heart of the neighborhood. Karlín, by contrast, has two Metro stops—Florenc (Lines B and C) and Křižíkova (Line B)—as well as trams running the length of Sokolovská ulice.

## PLANNING YOUR TIME

Both Žižkov and Karlín are pretty quiet during weekdays, so this is a good time to come and see the museums. But if you want to make the most of the neighborhoods' after-dark attractions, including restaurants, bars, and theaters, come during evenings and weekends.

## QUICK BITES

■ **Café Pavlač.** This lovely little sit-down spot serves excellent coffee, tasty homemade soups, and an impressive (and all too rare in Prague) choice of vegan dishes. ⊠ *V. Nejedlého 23, Žižkov* ⊕ *www.cafepavlac.cz* Ⓜ Tram 9 to Husinecká

■ **Veltlin.** This modish wine bar offers a wide selection of natural and organic wines by the glass. You can also order cheeses and cured meats to accompany your drink. ⊠ *Křižíkova 115, Karlín* ⊕ *www.veltlin.cz/en* Ⓜ Line B: Křižíkova

■ **Žižkovská štrúdlárna.** This unexpected pastry paradise—essentially, a service hatch set within a regular apartment block— offers WHOLE strudels for a mere 55 Kč. You can choose from three fillings: apple, *tvaroh* (curd cheese), or poppy seed. ⊠ *Jeseniova 29, Žižkov* ⊕ *www.strudl-ziz-kov.cz* Ⓜ Tram 9 to Lipanská

■ **Pivo Karlín.** Pop into this hugely popular neighborhood brewpub for a swift drink (or two) before enjoying a fancy dinner at Eska or a taking in a show at Forum Karlín. ⊠ *Pernerova 42, Karlín* ⊕ *www.pivokarlin.cz* Ⓜ Line B: Křižíkova

For Prague residents, Žižkov and Karlín are synonymous with good times. The two neighborhoods, which border the New Town on its eastern edge, are renowned for their after-dark adventures, from no-nonsense *hospody* (pubs) to sweaty live music clubs. But that's just the beginning of the story.

There are more places to knock back a Pilsner Urquell or a shot of Fernet Stock per square inch along Žižkov's run-down streets than anywhere else in the city (or, according to many, anywhere else in Europe). But alongside these traditional pubs are some of the city's coolest cafés, cinemas, and cocktail joints. The area is also home to the Národní památník na Vítkově (National Monument on Vítkov Hill) and the inescapable Žižkovská televizní věž (Žižkov TV Tower), offering one of the best panoramas in the city—and one of its most exclusive hotel rooms.

In Karlín, the entertainment scene is even more varied, with everything from fine-dining restaurants to craft beer bars and time-honored theaters. Come earlier in the day and you'll also enjoy its lovely parks, decorative churches, and fascinating museums.

## Žižkov

###  Sights

**Národní památník na Vítkově** (*National Monument on Vítkov Hill*)

**MUSEUM** | Vítkov Hill is among the highest points in the city, and is topped by one of the world's largest equestrian statues—a 16½-ton metal sculpture of one-eyed Hussite leader Jan Žižka on horseback. The 20th-century memorial was originally built to honor the war heroes of World War I but was used for a time during the communist period (1953–62) to display the mummified body of the country's first communist leader, Klement Gottwald. Now, the building houses the Národní muzeum (National Museum) permanent exhibition of 20th-century Czech history, with moving displays on the founding of Czechoslovakia in 1918, the Nazi occupation in 1939, the communist coup d'etat in 1948, the Warsaw Pact invasion in 1968, and finally the fall of communism in 1989. There's a great view over the city from the top of the building, or enjoy the view with a drink or snack in the first-floor Café Vítkov. ■TIP→ **To get to the monument, walk from Metro stop Florenc (15 minutes) or from bus stop Tachovské náměstí (10 minutes). Both require a climb. For a longer but gentler approach, walk from tram stop Ohrada (20 minutes).** ⊠ *U Památníku 1900, Žižkov* ☎ *222–781–676* ⊕ *www.nm.cz* ⊠ *120 Kč* ⊗ *Closed Mon.– Wed.* Ⓜ *Lines B and C: Florenc.*

★ **Žižkovská televizní věž** (*Žižkov TV Tower*)

**BUILDING** | Looking like a freakish, futuristic rocket ready to blast off, the Žižkov

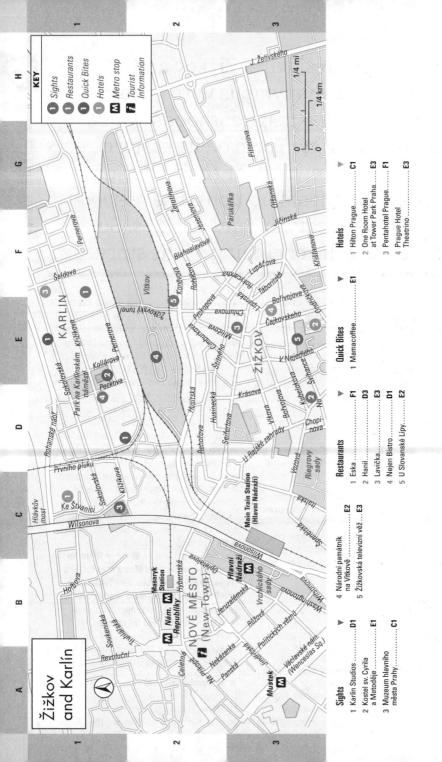

# Žižkov and Karlín

**KEY**

1 Sights
1 Restaurants
1 Quick Bites
1 Hotels
Ⓜ Metro stop
ⓘ Tourist Information

0 ____ 1/4 mi
0 ____ 1/4 km

**Sights** ▶

1 Karlín Studios ............. D1
2 Kostel sv. Cyrila a Metoděje ............. E1
3 Muzeum hlavního města Prahy ............. C1
4 Národní památník na Vítkově ............. E2
5 Žižkovská televizní věž ... E3

**Restaurants** ▶

1 Eska ............. F1
2 Hanil ............. D3
3 Lavička ............. E3
4 Nejen Bistro ............. D1
5 U Slovanské Lípy ............. E2

**Quick Bites** ▶

1 Mamacoffee ............. E1

**Hotels** ▶

1 Hilton Prague ............. C1
2 One Room Hotel at Tower Park Praha ... E3
3 Pentahotel Prague ............. F1
4 Prague Hotel Theatrino ............. E3

TV Tower is easily visible from around the city and commonly makes it onto Top 10 World's Ugliest Buildings lists. The upper-floor observatory platform, reached by a high-speed elevator, gives a bird's-eye view of the numerous courtyards and apartment blocks that make up the city and has a selection of exhibits on the history and architecture of the building. There's also a bar, restaurant, and luxury one-room hotel up there. Once back down on the ground, look up its 709-foot gray steel legs at the bronze statues of babies crawling on the structure, which were created by local provocateur artist David Černý. ⊠ Tower Park Prague, Mahlerovy sady 1, Žižkov ⊕ www.towerpark. cz ⊠ 250 Kč Ⓜ Line A: Jiřího z Poděbrad.

## 🍴 Restaurants

Scruffy Žižkov is better known for its pubs and dives than for fine dining; nevertheless the southern part of the district abutting Vinohrady has some good cafés and restaurants. The best way to get here is to take the Metro to Jiřího z Poděbrad and walk north along Slavíkova.

### Hanil

$$$ | SUSHIKOREAN | A nice counterpoint to the heavy, meaty cuisine found in most Prague diners, Hanil serves good-quality sushi as well as Korean and other Asian dishes at premium but affordable prices. The open, casual setting, which is accented with elegant light and dark woods, burnt-orange chair cushions, and curves galore, attracts a largely local crowd of young professionals who appreciate the blend of high-quality food with a lack of pretension. **Known for:** delicious Korean and Japanese cuisine; elegantly understated interior; slightly high prices for Žižkov. Ⓢ Average main: 440 Kč ⊠ Slavíkova 24, Žižkov ☎ 222–715–867 ⊕ www.hanil.cz Ⓜ Line A: Jiřího z Poděbrad.

### Lavička

$$ | CZECH | A mini-oasis in the heart of Žižkov, this family-owned restaurant sits on a busy street but has a hidden garden terrace and conservatory around the back. The menu features a mix of Czech staples (like beef goulash) and lesser-spotted dishes (like rosemary lamb and tuna steak), as well as lots of vegetarian options. **Known for:** away-from-it-all atmosphere; premium Bernard beer on tap; slightly small portions. Ⓢ Average main: 240 Kč ⊠ Seifertova 77, Žižkov ☎ 222–221–350 ⊕ www.restaurace-lavicka.cz Ⓜ Line C: Hlavní nádraží plus Tram 5, 9, 15, or 26 to Lipanská.

### ★ U Slovanské Lípy

$ | CZECH | One of the oldest pubs in Žižkov, this classic Czech pub offers a warm and inviting setting, great beers, and authentic Czech food. The name means "At the Linden Trees," a Czech and Slovak emblem, and while there are tourists here, it's also a meeting place for locals. **Known for:** typical Czech meals; sharing plates; wooden benches and other period decor. Ⓢ Average main: 195 Kč ⊠ Tachovské náměstí 6, Žižkov ☎ 734–743–094 ⊕ uslovanskelipy.cz Ⓜ Line C: Hlavní nádraží plus Tram 5, 9, 15, or 26 to Lipanská.

## 🛏 Hotels

Although Prague is a safe city where anyone can amble about alone, this is one of its grittier, seedier parts. That said, it's also a great neighborhood for extroverts who like student bars, music clubs, and hangouts where a fashion parade of people with piercings, tattoos, dreadlocks—and sometimes all three—come to socialize. It's also home to one of Prague's most exclusive hotel rooms.

### ★ One Room Hotel at Tower Park Praha

$$$$ | HOTEL | Perhaps the most unique hotel in Prague, a night in this luxuriously decked-out capsule room at the top of the communist-era TV tower is quite an experience. **Pros:** beautiful wood-paneled

interior; amazing city panoramas; Prague's top bucket-list stay. **Cons:** gritty Žižkov an unlikely place for such glamour; incredibly expensive; no view of castle (but see it from the restaurant). $ *Rooms from: 21500 Kč* ✉ *Tower Park Prague, Mahlerovy sady 1, Žižkov* ☎ *210–320–081* ⊕ *towerpark.cz* ⇌ *1 room* ⦿*Breakfast* Ⓜ *Line A: Jiřího z Poděbrad.*

### Prague Hotel Theatrino

**$$ | HOTEL |** This colorful, art nouveau hotel is big on character, but short on real luxury, making it a decent budget choice if you're looking for something original. **Pros:** good breakfast; rooms have individual style; close to lots of bars and nightlife. **Cons:** long walk to the center; no a/c (save for the fifth floor); use of sauna costs extra. $ *Rooms from: 3200 Kč* ✉ *Bořivojova 53, Žižkov* ☎ *227–031–894* ⊕ *www.hoteltheatrino. cz* ⇌ *73 rooms* ⦿*Breakfast* Ⓜ *Line C: Hlavní nádraží plus Tram 5, 9, 15, or 26 to Lipanská.*

##  Nightlife

This edgy neighborhood offers a lot to the discerning, thirsty traveler who ventures out of the city center. It's said to have the densest cluster of pubs in Europe, so if you end up here, it's best to try out the random places that catch your eye.

### BARS AND PUBS
#### Bukowski's Bar

**BARS/PUBS |** This crowd-pleasing drinking establishment, named for the American writer-cum–bar fly Charles Bukowski, serves top-quality cocktails, beer, wine, and spirits. The candlelight makes for a cool (if slightly seedy) atmosphere, and bar staff are unfailingly friendly. In summer, patrons tend to spill out into the street. ✉ *Bořivojova 86, Žižkov* ☎ *773–445–280* ⊕ *facebook.com/bukowskisbar* Ⓜ *Line A: Jiřího z Poděbrad.*

### ★ U Vystřelenýho oka

**BARS/PUBS |** Literally translated as "At the Shot-Out Eye"—it's an homage to the one-eyed Jan Žižka, for whom the neighborhood is named (he's also the guy on the horse atop Vítkov Hill)—this poky, perennially popular pub has been a local favorite for years. As well as perfectly poured Czech beers (always three fingers of foam), the pub does a great line in traditional no-frills food, from cold pickled herring to fried Camembert cheese. Sit inside to enjoy the warm open fire and, often, the live music accompaniment, or head out onto the log-lined terrace. ✉ *U Božích bojovníků 3, Žižkov* ☎ *222–540–465* ⊕ *www.uvoka.cz* Ⓜ *Lines B and C: Florenc plus Bus 133, 175, or 207 to Tachovské náměstí.*

### Vlkova 26

**BARS/PUBS |** The cool kids hang out at this out-of-the-way Žižkov basement bar to drink and chat late into the night. It's cozy, with dim lights, candles, wooden benches, and the bare brick walls. There are DJs and themed music nights, when everyone gets up to dance. ✉ *Vlkova 26, Žižkov* ⊕ *facebook.com/Vlkova26* Ⓜ *Line A: Jiřího z Poděbrad.*

### LIVE MUSIC CLUBS
#### ★ Palác Akropolis

**CAFES—NIGHTLIFE |** Housed in a funky art deco–esque building, this is the city's best live music club. When shows are sold out, the place is pretty packed. While the main room closes at 10 due to noise concerns, DJs play in the two side bars until much later. ✉ *Kubelíkova 27, Žižkov* ☎ *299–330–911* ⊕ *www.palacakropolis.com* Ⓜ *Line A: Jiřího z Poděbrad.*

## 🎭 Performing Arts

Žižkov has a couple of good theaters (including one dedicated solely to the adventures of fictional polymath Jára Cimrman) as well as an excellent indie cinema and arts center.

Palác Akropolis is a palace of entertainment with a café, restaurant, smaller bar upstairs, a theater, and a club with two stages downstairs.

### Kino Aero

**FILM** | Tucked away on a quiet residential street, Kino Aero is one of Prague's best independent movie theaters. It screens a mix of mainstream Hollywood and international fare, indie art-house darlings, and 20th-century cult classics. On site, there's also a cocktail bar and café, which regularly hosts events ranging from stand-up comedy to film quizzes. Kino Aero is part of a minichain of indie Prague cinemas, along with BIO OKO in Holešovice and Kino Světozor off Václavské náměstí (Wenceslas Square). ⊠ *Biskupcova 31, Žižkov* ☏ *271–771–349* ⊕ *www.kinoaero.cz.*

## 🛍 Shopping

This rough-and-tumble area may be most famous for its pubs, but it also has some good shopping, from cool boutiques to one of Prague's largest shopping malls.

## CLOTHING AND ACCESSORIES
### Bliss Farm Gallery

**ART GALLERIES** | Bliss Farm is quintessential Žižkov cool. An "open art studio space" and store, the place is packed with paintings, silkscreen-printed T-shirts, and even stuffed animals, as well as all sorts of other interesting bits and bobs. The products are handmade by local artists, and often recycled. ⊠ *Čajkovského 22, Žižkov* ☏ *775–031–487* ⊙ *Closed Sun.* Ⓜ *Line A: Jiřího z Poděbrad.*

### Bohemian Retro

**CLOTHING** | This vintage clothes shop, tucked down a Žižkov side street, sells retro womenswear, antique jewelry, leather and fabric bags, and more. It also has some random Czechoslovakian curios, from ceramics to clocks. It's only open from 2 to 7, and only five days a week, so plan your visit in advance. ⊠ *Chvalova 8, Žižkov* ☏ *607–914–992* ⊕ *bohemianretro.com* ⊙ *Closed Sun. and Mon.* Ⓜ *Line A: Jiřího z Poděbrad.*

## SHOPPING MALLS

### Atrium Flora

**SHOPPING CENTERS/MALLS** | Home to hundreds of stores, a well-stocked food court, and an IMAX movie theater, the Atrium Flora is hardly the cobble-stoned-street boutique dream you might have in mind. But for shopping junkies, it's a good bet for finding some local and international brands that are hard to hunt down elsewhere. ⊠ *Vinohradská 151, Žižkov* ☏ *255–741–704* ⊕ *www.atrium-flora.cz* Ⓜ *Line A: Flora.*

# Karlín

 Sights

### ★ Karlín Studios

**MUSEUM** | Founded in 2005, this multi-purpose cultural center is at the bleeding edge of what's happening in the Czech art scene. The converted factory building is home to a whole complex of art studios and galleries, but the main focus for visitors is the central, 2,153-square-foot exhibition space. Here, you'll encounter exciting, alternative new creations by up-and-coming Czech and international artists. ⚠ **It's open to visitors only from 2 to 7 on weekends and from 3 to 6 on weekdays.** ⊠ *Prvního pluku 2, Karlín* ☏ *608–955–150* ⊕ *www.futuraproject.cz* Free ⊘ *Closed Mon.* Ⓜ *Lines B and C: Florenc.*

### Kostel sv. Cyrila a Metoděje (Church of Sts. Cyril and Methodius)

**RELIGIOUS SITE** | A Karlín landmark and one of the largest religious buildings in Prague, this unmistakable black-and-white church is dedicated to the Orthodox missionary brothers Cyril and Methodius, who are credited with spreading the Christian faith through the Slavic lands. It was consecrated in 1863, exactly 1,000 years after the brothers started their important work. Head inside the neo-Romanesque basilica to discover decorative pillars, intricately painted ceilings, and an art nouveau baptismal chapel. The church is on the neighborhood's main square, Karlínské náměstí, which regularly hosts farmers' markets, festivals, and cultural events. ⊠ *Karlínské nám., Karlín* ☏ *222–743–517* ⊕ *farnost-karlin.cz* Free Ⓜ *Line B: Křižíkova.*

### Muzeum hlavního města Prahy (City of Prague Museum)

**MUSEUM** | Set inside a grand, turn-of-the-20th-century building, this museum tells the story of Prague through the ages, from the earliest prehistoric settlers, through the city's golden medieval and baroque periods, to the Velvet Revolution of 1989. The big-ticket exhibit is the extraordinary Langweil model of Prague, an intricate, handmade model of the city circa 1826–37. There are more than 2,000 buildings at a scale of 1:480, some of which are still standing today, and some which are long gone (including swathes of the Jewish Town). In fact, this model provides the only proof of how some of these buildings looked. As well as the permanent exhibits, there are also ever-changing temporary exhibitions, often focused on aspects of modern-day Prague. ⊠ *Na Poříčí 52, Karlín* ☏ *221–709–674* ⊕ *www.muzeumprahy.cz* 150Kč ⊘ *Closed Mon.* Ⓜ *Lines B and C: Florenc.*

## 🍴 Restaurants

Once a blighted testament to the fates of state-controlled industry, Karlín is now on the up and up. Nowhere is that more apparent than in its ever-increasing choice of fashionable eating options.

### Eska

**$$$** | **CZECH** | An expensive fine-dining restaurant with a casual carefree vibe, Eska has been a big hit since opening its doors in 2016. The restaurant is located within a converted fabric factory, and it maintains the original industrial aesthetic through bare brick walls and exposed pipework, while also adding modern touches like Scandi-style furniture and a gleaming open kitchen. **Known for:** industrial-chic

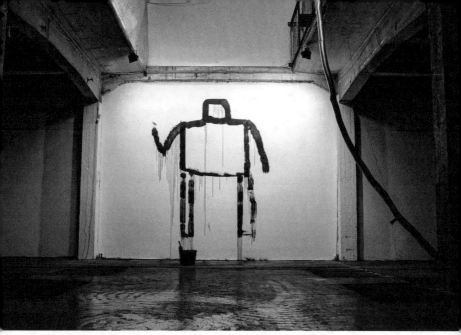

Housed in former military barracks, Karlin Studios is a unique complex of art studios and galleries, showcasing contemporary Czech art.

decor; excellent coffee; sometimes style over substance. $ *Average main: 450 Kč* ⊠ *Pernerova 49, Karlín* ☎ *731–140–884* ⊕ *eska.ambi.cz* Ⓜ *Line B: Křižíkova.*

### Nejen Bistro

**$$ | EUROPEAN |** This trendy bistro, on the corner of the neighborhood's main square, Karlínské náměstí, is all about light and space, with high ceilings, big windows, and an open kitchen, as well as muted colors throughout. It's also about great food, with particular pride taken in its array of meat dishes—from duck breasts to pork loin to sirloin steak—cooked on the charcoal-fueled Josper grill. **Known for:** juicy charcoal-grilled burgers; great wine and beer selection; cool Scandi-chic interior. $ *Average main: 350 Kč* ⊠ *Křižíkova 24, Karlín* ☎ *721–249–494* ⊕ *www.nejenbistro.cz* Ⓜ *Line B: Křižíkova.*

## ☕ Coffee and Quick Bites

### Mamacoffee

**$ | BAKERY |** Of the many café options in this up-and-coming district, Mamacoffee leads the pack with fine brews of fair-trade java. Breakfast business is brisk, with excellent pastries to complement a creamy latte, but many customers linger throughout the afternoon over a well-brewed flat white. **Known for:** tasty well-brewed coffee; selection of crumbly pastries; takeaway beans available. $ *Average main: 120 Kč* ⊠ *Sokolovská 6, Karlín* ☎ *775–568–647* ⊕ *www.mamacoffee.cz* Ⓜ *Line B: Křižíkova.*

## 🛏 Hotels

Karlín has several cheap and cheerful accommodation options. Higher-end hotels are a little thinner on the ground, but they do exist.

### Hilton Prague

**$$ | HOTEL |** From the outside, this gigantic, 11-floor, glass-and-steel building looks like a throwback to communist Czechoslovakia, but step inside and you'll find a pleasant, modern, and stylish business hotel. **Pros:** good selection of restaurants; large indoor swimming pool; quiet part of town. **Cons:** not the most inviting exterior; can get very busy at breakfast; a little out of the action. [$] *Rooms from: 3500 Kč* ✉ *Pobřežní 1, Karlín* ☎ *224–841–111* 🌐 *www.hilton.com* 🛏 *719 rooms* 🍴 *Free Breakfast* [M] *Lines B and C: Florenc.*

**Pentahotel Prague**

**$$ | HOTEL** | Since opening in 2013, this trendy design hotel has been one of Karlín's hippest sleeping options, offering stylish, contemporary rooms with quirky, vintage touches. **Pros:** action-packed common area; nearby Metro and tram stops; parking spaces available. **Cons:** odd mixed hipster-business vibe; only basic Wi-Fi is free (premium can be bought); breakfast not included. [$] *Rooms from: 3750 Kč* ✉ *Sokolovská 112, Karlín* ☎ *222–332–800* 🌐 *www.pentahotels.com* 🛏 *227* 🍴 *No meals* [M] *Line B: Křižíkova.*

## 🍸 Nightlife

It may not be as renowned for nightlife as neighboring Žižkov, but Karlín still has its fair share of good after-dark options, from sky-high cocktail bars to basement brewery bars.

**Cloud 9 Sky Bar**

**BARS/PUBS** | This chic, lounge-style bar, situated on the rooftop of the Hilton Prague hotel, offers glorious views of the Czech capital in all directions. There's an extensive menu of innovative (and occasionally award-winning) cocktails, as well as some beautifully presented snack food; try the sweet potato fries with truffle mayo. ✉ *Hilton Prague, Pobřežní 1, Karlín* ☎ *224–842–999* 🌐 *www.cloud9.cz* [M] *Lines B and C: Florenc.*

**★ Dva Kohouti**

**BREWPUBS/BEER GARDENS** | When it comes to beer buzz, nothing in recent years has come close to Dva Kohouti (translation: "Two Roosters"). Opened in 2018 as a joint brewery and taproom—the beer is brewed there in the mornings then served to thirsty patrons later the same day—it has quickly established itself as a neighborhood favorite. There's only one local beer, but it's excellent: crisp, malty, and incredibly fresh (it's poured from a tank that is filled directly from the brewery). Alternatively, choose from a handful of other Czech lagers and ales on tap. No time to stop? Get a 1-liter can to take away. ✉ *Sokolovská 55, Karlín* ☎ *604–611–001* 🌐 *www.dvakohouti.cz* [M] *Line B: Křižíkova.*

**Pivovarský Klub**

**BARS/PUBS** | With literally wall-to-wall bottles—there are around 250 different brands of beer lining the walls—as well as six ever-changing brews on tap, there's nowhere better to take a deep dive into the Czechs' favorite pastime. The food's good, too. ✉ *Křižíkova 17, Karlín* ☎ *222–315–777* 🌐 *www.pivovarskyklub.com* [M] *Lines B and C: Florenc.*

## 🎟 Performing Arts

Whether you are looking for big-name live music acts or high-quality musical theater, Karlín has you covered.

**Forum Karlín**

**ARTS CENTERS** | This 3,000-seater events space plays host to several touring live music acts. Recent years have seen performances from the likes of Thom Yorke, James Arthur, Keane, Yes, and Simply Red. ✉ *Pernerova 51, Karlín* ☎ *702–203–359* 🌐 *www.forumkarlin.cz* [M] *Line B: Křižíkova.*

**Hudební divadlo Karlín** (*Karlín Musical Theater*)

**THEATER** | **FAMILY** | This beautiful, baroque-revival building plays host to all manner of song-and-dance performances, from high-art operas to cheesy musicals. Shows are usually performed in Czech but with a screen showing English subtitles. ✉ *Křižíkova 10, Karlín* ☎ *221–868–111* 🌐 *www.hdk.cz* [M] *Lines B and C: Florenc.*

Chapter 10

# LETNÁ, HOLEŠOVICE, AND TROJA

Updated by
Jennifer Rigby

| ◉ Sights | 🍴 Restaurants | 🛏 Hotels | 🛍 Shopping | 🍸 Nightlife |
|----------|---------------|----------|-------------|-------------|
| ★☆☆☆☆ | ★★★★☆ | ★☆☆☆☆ | ★★★★★ | ★★★☆☆ |

# NEIGHBORHOOD SNAPSHOT

## TOP EXPERIENCES

■ **Vnitroblock and Veverkova Ulice:** Shop the modern way, in this former factory and cultural collective, or wander along the street currently vying for the title of Prague's coolest, with a handful of shoe, book, design, and cosmetics boutiques.

■ **DOX:** Prague's answer to New York's MoMA.

■ **Mama Shelter:** The city's—and one of Europe's—coolest hotels in this communist-era tower block (and at a reasonable price).

■ **Bistro 8:** Join Prague's growing brunch crowd at this relaxed, impossibly hip little bistro.

■ **Letná Park:** Take a break in this gorgeous hilltop green space, sip a beer at the beer garden, and cast your eyes over to the plain at the back of the park, where historically the city's biggest protests have taken place (after Václavské náměstí, or Wenceslas Square).

■ **Vineyards:** For a break from the city within the city, head to Troja and the beautiful Vinotéka sv. Klára (St. Claire's Vineyard).

## GETTING HERE

By Metro, take Line A to Hradčanská station and then nearly any tram (No. 1, 5, 25, or 26) heading east two stops to Letenské náměstí (Letná Square). For Holešovice, the best Metro stations are both on Line C (Nádraží Holešovice and Vltavská), then various trams take you further into the district (Nos. 1, 2, 6, 12, 14, 15, 17, and 24).

## PLANNING YOUR TIME

Letná is a good place to visit on a weekend, to join Prague's locals in browsing, brunching, and soaking up the park during their downtime, while Troja works better on a weekday, particularly in summer, when there are fewer crowds of families hitting up the zoo or gardens.

## QUICK BITES

■ **Mr. HotDog.** It's almost sacrilegious to describe these U.S.-style dogs as the best sausage in town, but their greatness cannot be denied (make sure you grab a Czech-style *klobasa*, or sausage, while in Prague, too, though). ✉ *Kamenická 24, Letná* ⊕ *mrhotdog.cz* Ⓜ *Line C: Vltavská*

■ **Erhartova cukrárna.** Retro vibes and delicious pastries. ✉ *Milady Horákové 56, Letná/Holešovice* ⊕ *www.erhartovacukrarna. cz* Ⓜ *Line C: Vltavská*

■ **Gelateria Amato.** A perfectly located ice-cream parlor for taking a cold, sweet treat into Letná or Stromovka Park. ✉ *Kamenická 30, Letná* ⊕ *www. gelateriaamato.cz* Ⓜ *Line C: Vltavská*

All three of these neighborhoods are up and coming (and in some cases, particularly genteel Letná, they have up and come already), with new cultural and dining attractions popping up weekly. Come here to get away from the tourist masses and witness the rapid pace of the city's post–Velvet Revolution evolution.

From above the Vltava's left bank, the large, grassy plateau called Letná gives you one of the classic views of Staré Město and the many bridges crossing the river. Beer gardens, tennis, and Frisbee attract people of all ages, while amateur soccer players emulate the professionals of Prague's top team, Sparta, which plays in the stadium just across the road. The Národní technické muzeum (National Technical Museum) is also located near here, as well as a host of new brunch and coffee places.

The rapidly gentrifying former indusrial neighborhood of Holešovice features many urban riches of its own, including perhaps the city's most underrated museum, Veletržní palác (Trade Fair Palace), which houses the National Gallery's permanent exhibition of modern art, as well as the Centrum současného umění DOX (DOX Center for Contemporary Art). It also boasts extremely cool cultural centers, restaurants, and shopping and a recently opened hotel that finally meets the demand from the cool cats to stay somewhere in this neighborhood. Arguably, Letná is part of Holešovice, but the easiest thing to do to fit in with the locals is to refer to both districts as "Prague 7," the postal code that spans both and that

has become the shorthand for Prague's hippest and most creative area.

Troja is a remote, green district situated north of Holešovice on the bank of the Vltava. There are several attractions in this part of town, including the Prague City Gallery's branch at Trojský zámek (Troja Château), the Botanická zahrada (Botanical Gardens), and the zoo. Most visitors are unlikely to make it there on a first trip, but its "day-trip within the city" vibes could entice second- or third-time visitors or those desperate for greenery in the height of summer.

# Letná

 Sights

★ **Letenské sady** (*Letná Park*)
**CITY PARK** | Come to this large, shady park for an unforgettable view of Prague's bridges. From the enormous concrete pedestal at the center of the park—now occupied by a giant working metronome, which some say is marking time since the 1989 Velvet Revolution—the world's largest statue of Stalin once beckoned to citizens on Staroměstské náměstí (Old Town Square) below. The statue was blown up in 1962, just seven years

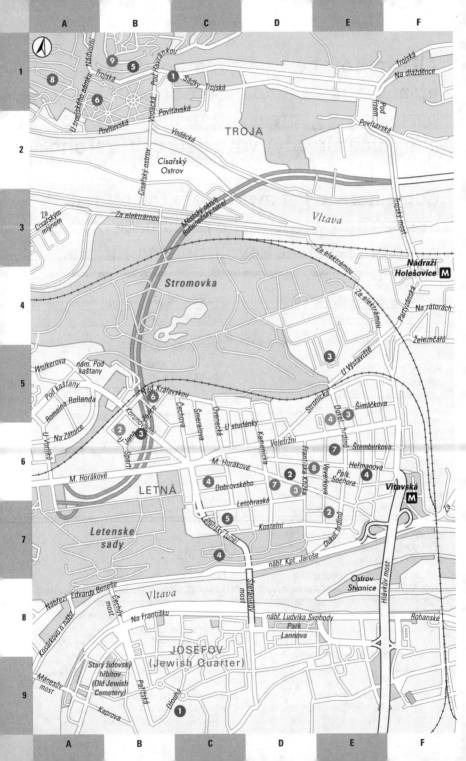

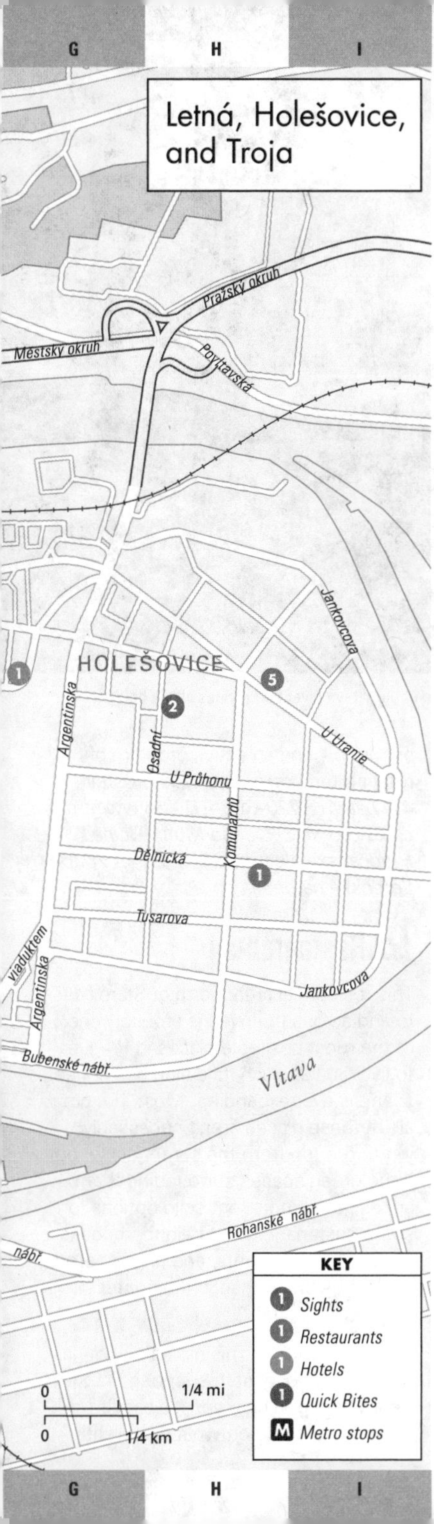

# Letná, Holešovice, and Troja

## Sights ▼

1 Botanická zahrada ......C1
2 Centrum sončasného umění DOX..............H5
3 Lapidárium................E5
4 Letenské sady............C7
5 Národní technické muzeum...................C7
6 Trojský zámek ..........A1
7 Veletržní palác ..........E6
8 Zoologická zahrada v Praze ..................A1

## Restaurants ▼

1 Big Smokers.............H6
2 Bistro 8....................E7
3 Cali Brothers ............E5
4 Curry Palace ............C6
5 The Eatery ...............H4
6 Lokál Nad Stromovkou..............B5
7 Mr. Hotdog...............D6
8 Restaurace Na Mělníku..............D6
9 Salabka .................B1

## Quick Bites ▼

1 Café Domeček ...........C9
2 Dos Mundos.............D6
3 The Farm.................B6
4 Ouky Douky...............E6
5 Vinotéka sv. Klá ........B1

## Hotels ▼

1 Absolutum Boutique Hotel ..........G4
2 Art Hotel .................B6
3 Hotel Belvedere.........D6
4 Mama Shelter Prague ....................E5

HOLEŠOVICE

Pražský okruh

Městsky okruh

Povltavská

Jankovcova

Argentinska

Osadní

U Uranie

U Průhonu

Komunardů

Dělnická

Tusarova

Jankovcova

viaduktem

Argentinska

Bubenské nábř.

Vltava

Rohanské nábř.

nábř.

### KEY

● Sights
● Restaurants
● Hotels
● Quick Bites
Ⓜ Metro stops

0          1/4 mi
0       1/4 km

The expansive Letná Park dominates the northern edge of the Vltava River that divides city in half.

after it was completed. In nice weather, there's a large and popular beer garden at the park's eastern end and Czechs and expats playing games on the grass. Walk east along Milady Horákové ulice after exiting the Metro or take the tram, or head up the hill from Staré Město if you want some exercise. At the back of the park, toward the home of the football club Sparta at the Generali Arena, there's a huge open space that is often used for the Czech Republic's largest protests (it's even bigger than famous Wenceslas Square), including those heralding the end of communism in 1989. ⊠ Letná Ⓜ Line A: Hradčanská plus Tram 1, 25, or 26.

### Národní technické muzeum (National Technical Museum)

**MUSEUM | FAMILY |** This thoroughly renovated and kid-friendly museum is dedicated to the fun aspects of science, technology, and industry. There are full-sized steam locomotives, historic automobiles, and old aircraft on display. There are also engrossing exhibits on photography and astronomy and an active program of rotating temporary shows. ⊠ Kostelní 42, Letná ☎ 220–399–111 ⊕ www.ntm. cz ⊠ 250 Kč ☉ Closed Mon. Ⓜ Line A: Hradčanská plus Tram 1, 5, 25, or 26 to Letenské náměstí.

## 🍴 Restaurants

This residential area, north of Staré Město and across the river, is arguably one of the most desirable places in Prague to live, and as such its dining and coffee scene is ever expanding. Most, but not all, of these places aren't necessarily worth the trip from the center alone, but if the green spaces surrounding them appeal, they represent solid options for some sustenance. The neighborhood is popular with students, and prices here tend to be lower than in the center.

### Bistro 8

**$ | INTERNATIONAL |** This hip little spot has almost legendary status among Prague's trendy young things, and it's easy to see why. Located on what is currently considered to be Prague's coolest street, it combines a retro aesthetic—with black walls, a mix of chairs, and lots of plants—with tasty international food and unique touches, like the bright monster sculptures and cracked pots in the window. **Known for:** good strong coffee; great brunch; cool setting and crowd. $ *Average main: 100 Kč* ⊠ *Veverkova 8, Letná* ☎ *730–511–973* ⊕ *bistro8.cz* Ⓜ *Line C: Vltavská.*

### Curry Palace

**$$** | **INDIAN** | Just behind Letná Park, Curry Palace is a bit off the beaten path, but it's *the* place for Indian and Bangladeshi food. You'll find the usual mix of tandoori dishes and curries, and staff are happy to recommend options if you want to head off the beaten path. **Known for:** excellent rezela, a specialty made with varyingly spicy chicken or lamb, with garlic-ginger paste and yogurt; relaxed family atmosphere; affordable lunch menu. $ *Average main: 250 Kč* ⊠ *Jirečková 13, Letná* ☎ *775–146–252* ⊕ *www.currypalace.cz* Ⓜ *Line A: Hradčanská.*

### Lokál Nad Stromovkou

**$$** | **CZECH** | The same talented team behind Lokál Dlouhááá and Café Savoy refurbished this long-standing Czech pub near Stromovka Park in 2013. Not only did they add a fresh coat of paint to the walls, but, true to form, they refreshed and reintroduced some traditional tavern classics alongside great beer. **Known for:** modern takes on classics, like steak tartare served with toast; convivial vibe; popularity with locals who live in the leafy surrounding area. $ *Average main: 190 Kč* ⊠ *Nad Královskou oborou 31, Letná* ☎ *220–912–319* ⊕ *lokal-nadstromovk-ou.ambi.cz* Ⓜ *Line A: Hradčanská plus Tram 1, 25, or 26 to Letenské náměstí.*

## ☕ Coffee and Quick Bites

### Café Domeček

**$** | **CAFÉ** | This sweet "Little House" perched in a community center in the

other park bordering Letná district, Stromovka, is a very pleasant option for a coffee in summer, particularly ahead of a leafy walk across the park. There are grilled foods, too, some cakes, some sandwiches, homemade ice cream and lemonade, and (of course) beer. **Known for:** decent coffee and cakes; board games; lovely setting in a listed former railway building in Stromovka Park. $ *Average main: 70 Kč* ⊠ *Královská obora 74, Letná* ☎ *736–691–395* ⊕ *www.domusvitae.cz/kavarna* ⊟ *No credit cards* Ⓜ *Tram 1, 2, 8, 12, 25, or 26.*

### Dos Mundos

**CAFES—NIGHTLIFE** | Come for the swings, stay for the coffee: this small coffee shop and local roastery has swing seats (a bit of a gimmick, but actually quite a cute one), lovely cakes, and excellent coffee. It's more of a daytime place than an evening bar, although it is open until 9. ⊠ *Milady Horákové 38, Letná* ☎ *732–243–223* ⊕ *www.dos-mundos.cz* Ⓜ *Line C: Vltavská.*

### The Farm

**$** | **BAKERY** | A great, buzzing café that's all about local produce and is often packed with Czechs from the surrounding refined neighborhood enjoying its generous brunches, breads, and good coffee. Chleba a máslo, next door, is a similarly unpretentious neighborhood bakery that's owned by the same crew. **Known for:** weekend brunch; delicious (but pricey) juices; sister bakery next door. $ *Average main: 120 Kč* ⊠ *Korunovační 923/17, Letná* ☎ *773–626–177* ⊕ *www.facebook.com/Farmletna* Ⓜ *Tram 1, 2, 8, 12, 25, 26 to Sparta.*

##  Hotels

Staying in Letná can offer some bargains in a leafy part of town, with long boulevards, tall trees, and an authentic local feel. It doesn't offer the fairy-tale beauty of Staré Město, but it is a refined, attractive area, and it's a quick tram ride or 20-minute walk over to the main tourist sights (or a pleasant walk through greenery to the area around Prague Castle). Plus, there are increasing numbers of trendy cafés opening up, making it a great spot for brunch.

### Art Hotel

**$ | HOTEL |** This family-run little hotel has art on the walls by the grandfather and great-grandfather of the owner and is otherwise clean, comfortable, and modern. **Pros:** mostly quiet neighborhood; reasonably priced; hotel garden. **Cons:** by Sparta Praha FC stadium so there are crowds after games; showers weirdly low; elevator stops unhelpfully between floors. $ *Rooms from: 1500 Kč* ✉ *Nad Královskou oborou 53, Letná* ☎ *233–101–331* ⊕ *www.arthotel.cz* ⇗ *24 rooms* ❍ *Free Breakfast* Ⓜ *Tram 1, 2, 8, 12, 25, or 26 to Sparta.*

### Hotel Belvedere

**$ | HOTEL |** Located in one of the early-20th-century constructivist-style buildings dotted around this district, the Hotel Belvedere is an unremarkable but reliable hotel with good prices and a prime location, in the middle of Letná and Holešovice (the districts kind of blend into one around here). **Pros:** surrounded by hip cafés and restaurants; decent hotel restaurant and breakfast; still only 20 minutes' walk from Old Town Square. **Cons:** away from the main sights; some street noise; a little dated. $ *Rooms from: 1400 Kč* ✉ *Milady Horákové 19, Letná* ☎ *220–106–111* ⊕ *www.hotelbelvedereprague.cz* ⇗ *149 rooms* ❍ *Free Breakfast* Ⓜ *Line C: Vltavská.*

##  Nightlife

Once a sleepy part of town, Letná now has a burgeoning coffee and bar scene, and the whole of Prague 7 is probably one of the best districts to visit as a tourist if you want to drink with cool young Czechs.

## BARS AND PUBS

### Café Letka

**CAFES—NIGHTLIFE |** This gorgeous café-bar, all distressed walls and high ceilings, is open from 8 am til midnight, and manages to transition nicely from coffee stop by day to funky bar by night. The owners reclaimed an old Austro-Hungarian café space for their modern version, and the update is pitched perfectly, with tasty food as well as drinks, including beer from the well-regarded Matuška brewery. ✉ *Letohradská 44, Letná* ☎ *777–444–035* ⊕ *www.cafeletka.cz* Ⓜ *Line A: Hradčanská plus Tram 1, 5, 25, or 26 to Letenské náměstí.*

### ★ Cobra

**CAFES—NIGHTLIFE |** The owners set up this exceedingly cool bar when bemoaning the fact that Letná used to be entirely dead after midnight. Almost single-handedly, they've changed that, with cool, modern food, a brilliant cocktail list, a disco ball or two, no sign (of course: the right people know where to come), industrial-chic decor, and a welcoming attitude at all hours of the day and late into the night. A gem. ✉ *Milady Horákové 8, Letná* ☎ *777–355–876* ⊕ *barcobra.cz* Ⓜ *Line C: Vltavská.*

### ★ Letenské sady

**BREWPUBS/BEER GARDENS |** You can pay a lot for a pint and great views in Prague, or you could go to this cunningly located beer garden at the top of Letná Park and pay hardly anything for cold, crisp pints while you gaze over the river and the breathtaking rooftops of Staré Město. It's a truly great beer garden, even if its other facilities (food choices, toilets) are a little basic. ✉ *Letná* ☎ *233–378–200* ⊕ *www.letenskyzamecek.cz* Ⓜ *Line A: Hradčanská.*

## CLUBS

### ★ Stalin parties

**GATHERING PLACES |** This free, open-air party at the top of Letná Park in summer is the hottest ticket in town. There are concerts on Wednesday, film screenings on Thursday, electronic music shindigs on Friday and Saturday, and a "musical siesta" on Sunday. The bar and DJs are located right next to the huge metronome monument, which marks the spot that once housed the world's largest statue of Stalin. Chill vibes, a young, international crowd, and great views over the sparkling city lights make this a cool option on warm nights. Beer is for sale, but lines can be long—good thing bringing a can of your own is acceptable. Currently it's open only May–September and is overseen by an art collective that also runs a container bar in Stromovka Park. ✉ Letenské sady, Letná ☎ 774–573–251 ⊕ containall.cz/stalin Ⓜ Line A: Hradčanská.

# 🛍 Shopping

Both Letná and Holešovice have a lot to offer shoppers, from high-concept design stores to warren-like traditional hardware shops. While the boundaries of the districts blur a bit, we've included most of the shops on the main streets here, with a few farther-afield markets and the amazing Vnitroblock in Holešovice. The main treat in Letná is a wander down Veverkova ulice, currently one of the holders of the unofficial title of Prague's coolest street: it's a small strip, and there are cool new additions all the time.

## BEAUTY
### ★ Liška Mazaná
PERFUME/COSMETICS | A unique, 100% natural, zero-waste, ecofriendly cosmetics shop that not only sells products, from lotions to lip balms, but also runs classes teaching customers how to make their own. From the moss growing in the cupboard (for decoration) to the friendly owners, Petra and Tereza, who are happy to help with any queries, it's a delight. ✉ Veverkova 10, Letná ☎ 607–726–676 ⊕ liskamazana.cz Ⓜ Line C: Vltavská.

## BOOKS
### Page Five
BOOKS/STATIONERY | Remember when people thought bookshops were doomed? This wonderful modern bookshop specializing in art books, magazines, and prints, from gorgeous coffee-table photography books to Czech poetry, shows why they have bounced back: there's something special about the printed word, particularly when it is produced as beautifully as this. Page Five is also a publishing house, with a few of its own books available, as well as a meeting place and exhibition space. Plus, there's a dog. ✉ Veverkova 5, Letná ☎ 735–852–693 ⊕ www.pagefive.com Ⓜ Line C: Vltavská.

## CLOTHING
### Sisters Conspiracy
CLOTHING | This light-filled boutique in a historic building, with a gorgeous tiled floor, showcases clothes that are easily as lovely as the surroundings. Chic, light, and individual, for men and women, this is modern Czech fashion at its most understated and elegant. Call or email to make an appointment if you want to visit on a day it isn't open. ✉ Dobrovskeho 24, Letná ☎ 732–644–122 ⊕ sistersconspiracy.cz ⊙ Closed Sun., Mon., Wed., and Fri., except by appointment Ⓜ Line A: Hradčanská plus Tram 1, 5, 25, or 26 to Letenské náměstí.

## HOME
### Coverover
HOUSEHOLD ITEMS/FURNITURE | The shop logo (it looks more like (C)over than Coverover) should give you a clue: this is an interiors shop with design chops that's not afraid to have fun. Set up by a French man and his Czech wife, products are available from across Europe and are varied and interesting, from the fig room scent by Geodesis that also gives the boutique its fragrance to the psychedelic gold jewelry by Juana Benta, among the other cool bags, coasters, rugs, and

cushions. ⊠ *Milady Horákové 24, Letná* ☎ *222–096–011* ⊕ *www.coverover.cz* ⊙ *Closed weekends* Ⓜ *Line C: Vltavská.*

## SHOES

### Sneaker Barber/Garage

**SHOES/LUGGAGE/LEATHER GOODS** | The Sneaker Barber guys take their sneakers seriously (their website proclaims, "Sneakers are like alchemy"), so there's a great selection and it's fun spot to browse. Even better, the shop is connected to the record store next door, Garage, and regularly hosts small cultural events, including vinyl release parties. ⊠ *Veverkova 6, Letná* ☎ *720–074–004* ⊕ *www.sneakerbarber.com* Ⓜ *Line C: Vltavská.*

# Holešovice

 **Sights**

### ★ Centrum současného umění DOX (*DOX Center for Contemporary Art*)

**MUSEUM** | Alongside the Trade Fair Palace and the Academy of Fine Arts college next to Stromovka Park, this giant modern art hub makes up the trio of big-beast artistic institutions in Prague 7 that have seen the district christened the city's most creative. Depending on your tastes, this one is arguably the most fun, from its witty slogans (emblazoned on the building and sold as postcards) to its often flamboyant modern art collection, via a discussion space located in a life-size suspended airship. DOX, in a former factory, is more than just a brilliant modern art gallery, though; it is also a cultural center aiming to put art at the forefront of modern ways of thinking about the world. ⊠ *Poupětova 1, Holešovice* ☎ *295–568–123* ⊕ *www.dox.cz* 🆓 *Free* ⊙ *Closed Tues.* Ⓜ *Line C: Nádraží Holešovice.*

### Lapidárium

**MUSEUM** | A fascinating display of 11th- to 19th-century sculptures rescued from torn-down buildings (or the vicissitudes of Prague's weather) is sheltered here, in this fine building in its own right. Original Charles Bridge statues can be found here, along with a towering bronze monument to Field Marshal Radetzky, a leader of the 19th-century Austrian army. Pieces of a marble fountain that once stood in Old Town Square now occupy most of one room. For horse lovers, there are several fine equestrian statues inside. ⊠ *Výstaviště 422, Holešovice* ☎ *702–013–372* ⊕ *www.nm.cz* 🖼 *50 Kč* ⊙ *Closed Mon. and Tues.* Ⓜ *Line C: Vltavská.*

### ★ Veletržní palác (*Trade Fair Palace*)

**MUSEUM** | This sometimes overlooked gallery, boasting the National Gallery's collection *Art of the 19th, 20th, and 21st Centuries,* has a real claim to being the city's best. Touring the vast spaces of this 1920s functionalist exposition hall filled to the brim with quirky, stimulating, comprehensive modern and contemporary local art is the best way to see how Czechs surfed the forefront of the avant-garde wave until the cultural freeze following World War II. Keep an eye out for works by František Kupka, credited as one of the first-ever abstract artists, and other Czech giants like Josef Čapek. Also on display are works by Western European—mostly French—artists from Delacroix to the present, with paintings by Gauguin, Picasso, and Braque an unexpected bonus. But painting is only the beginning—also occupying the many levels of the museum are collages, cubist sculptures, vintage gramophones, futuristic architectural models, art deco furnishings, and an exhaustive gathering of work from this new century, some of which is just as engrossing as the older stuff. Also, watch the papers and posters for information on traveling shows and temporary exhibits. ✉ *Dukelských hrdinů 47, Holešovice* ☎ *224–301–122* 🌐 *www.ngprague.cz* 🎟 *220 Kč* 🕒 *Closed Mon.* [M] *Line C: Vltavská or Tram 6 or 17 to Veletržní palác.*

## 🍴 Restaurants

This is a gentrifying, formerly scruffy area that is becoming something of a dining mecca. As well as the new clutch of hip places, though, there are still plenty of low-cost pizzerias and pubs that serve food at an acceptable level of quality at prices that are much lower than in areas more popular with tourists.

**Big Smokers**
$$ | **BARBECUE** | This recently opened joint brings modern barbecue to the Czech capital, in a big way. The meats are glorious, the vibe is industrial-cool, and the welcome is friendly. **Known for:** trays of perfectly flamed meat; piquant accompaniments; cheap sandwich-based lunch menu. [$] *Average main: 180 Kč* ✉ *Dělnická 40, Holešovice* ☎ *737–070–373* 🌐 *www.facebook.com/bigsmokersprague* 🕒 *Closed Sun. and Mon.* [M] *Tram 1, 2, 7, 11, 12, 14, or 25 to Dělnická.*

**Cali Brothers**
$$ | **DINER** | Run by two close American friends who have been in Prague since the '90s and have already put their stamp on the Prague food scene with Bohemia Bagel and the Mexican chain Burrito Loco, among other openings, this newly revamped restaurant celebrates their Californian heritage, with a distinctly U.S. vibe and good meats and mussels. **Known for:** dry-aged steaks; quality mussels and oysters; beers from Žatecký pivovar. [$] *Average main: 250 Kč* ✉ *Dukelských hrdinů 48, Holešovice* ☎ *731–655–851* 🌐 *calibrothers.cz* 💳 *No credit cards* 🕒 *Closed Sun. and Mon.* [M] *Line C: Vltavská.*

**★ The Eatery**
$$ | **CZECH** | This fantastic destination restaurant, with thoughtful, delicate twists on modern Czech food in a shiny-steel-and-concrete industrial setting, is certainly the district's best and even holds its own against the rest of the city. Run by the former Michelin-starred chef at Alcron, in the center of town, the Eatery is a more informal but no less delicious venture, with all the extras you'd expect from an establishment of this quality, from a chef's table to delicious wines, all local ingredients, and an open kitchen. **Known for:** Czech dishes like traditional garlic soup or carp; theatrical cooking in the open kitchen; popularity (reservations are recommended). [$] *Average main: 350 Kč* ✉ *U Uranie 18, Holešovice* ☎ *603–945–236* 🌐 *www.theeatery.cz* 🕒 *Closed Sun. and Mon. No lunch Sat.* [M] *Line C: Nádraží Holešovice.*

**Restaurace Na Mělníku**
$$ | **CZECH** | This pub is perfect for cool, global travelers who want to eat authentic local cuisine with locals when they visit a place, in this case in a properly authentic pub alongside Czechs working and living in the neighborhood. And because it isn't in the city center, the kitsch factor is dialed down, along with the prices. **Known for:** great schnitzel; cheap beer; down-to-earth, historic atmosphere. [$] *Average main: 175 Kč* ✉ *Františka Křížka 745/28, Holešovice* ☎ *233–378–731* 🌐 *namelniku.cz* [M] *Line C: Vltavská, Tram 6 or 17 to Veletržní palác, or Tram 26 to Kamenicka.*

## ☕ Coffee and Quick Bites

**Ouky Douky**
$ | **CAFÉ** | A Prague original, this combination Czech bookstore and coffeehouse draws a lively mix of students, intellectuals, and vagabonds from around the neighborhood. The coffee is very good, as are the homemade daily soups and breakfast specials. **Known for:** eclectic setting; always lively; homemade soups.

Mama Shelter Prague offers well-designed rooms, excellent service and amenities, and a bar and a lobby you'll want to hang out in.

§ *Average main: 140 Kč* ⊠ *Janovského 14, Holešovice* ☎ *266–711–531* ⊕ *www. oukydouky.cz* Ⓜ *Line C: Vltavská.*

##  Hotels

Holešovice used to be a cheap, slightly grimy alternative to staying in the city center. That is still available; but now that the area has sealed its reputation as Prague's most arty neighborhood, the accommodation options are catching up.

### Absolutum Boutique Hotel
$ | **HOTEL** | This modern hotel in a somewhat industrial part of town doesn't exactly live up to its "boutique" name, but it's not a bad option nevertheless. **Pros:** Finnish sauna, aromatic baths, and massages on-site; clean and comfortable; very close to Nádraží Holešovice for getting around the city. **Cons:** breakfast could be better; uninspiring exterior; little to do in the immediate surroundings. § *Rooms from: 1500 Kč* ⊠ *Jablonského 4, Holešovice* ☎ *220–874–253* ⊕ *www.*

*absolutumhotel.cz* ⇌ *45 rooms* ⦿ *Free Breakfast* Ⓜ *Line C: Nádraží Holešovice.*

### ★ Mama Shelter Prague
$ | **HOTEL** | Stand up and take a bow, Mama Shelter: finally, this hip district has the hip lodging it deserves, in this revitalized communist-era tower block right by the National Gallery. **Pros:** cool rooms with large windows and fun design touches, like Looney Tunes lamps; huge bar and terrace to see and be seen; reasonable prices. **Cons:** no gym; breakfast can get packed; not central to main attractions. § *Rooms from: 1635 Kč* ⊠ *Veletržní 1502/20, Holešovice* ☎ *225–117–862* ⊕ *www.mamashelter. com/en/prague* ⇌ *238 rooms* ⦿ *Free Breakfast* Ⓜ *Line C: Vltavská, Tram 6 or 17 to Veletržní palác, or Tram 26 to Kamenicka.*

##  Nightlife

Going out in Holešovice, whether to a bar listed below or an experimental art performance listed in the Performing Arts section, is often a uniquely memorable, distinctly Czech event. Shake off your apprehensions and get involved.

## BARS

### Kavárna Liberál

CAFES—NIGHTLIFE | This very traditional, welcoming gathering spot offers a convivial drinking place from morning to midnight, following in the tradition of the grand cafés of Prague's past, where literary greats would gather and debate til morning. To get a hit of that vibe, head in, take a seat at one of the dark wood tables, order a beer, and start setting the world to rights. There are dance, art, and theater performances, too. ⊠ *Heřmanova 6, Holešovice* ☎ *732–355–445* ⊕ *www. facebook.com/kavarnaliberal* Ⓜ *Line C: Vltavská.*

### Pivovar Marina

BREWPUBS/BEER GARDENS | An old-school Czech microbrewery with views of the river in summer and a cozy beer-hall vibe in the winter. There's also some surprisingly fancy Italian food at the restaurant. Try the wheat beer in particular. ⊠ *Jankovcova 1059, Holešovice* ☎ *220–571–183* ⊕ *www.pivovarmarina.cz* Ⓜ *Line C: Nádraží Holešovice plus Tram 6 to Maniny.*

## CLUBS

### Cross Club

DANCE CLUBS | If you're a fan of alternative culture and really memorable nights, Cross Club will not let you down. It's a glorious mixture of many different things: otherworldly metal sculptures; floors and floors of different music, including lots of drums and bass; interesting artistic happenings, such as poetry readings, theater shows, film screenings, author readings, and an afternoon kids' theater; and a gorgeous garden lit in a variety of bright colors. But, it all comes together for a great night out, if not one for the fainthearted. Its closing hours are listed as "??," which should give you some idea of its general ethos. ⊠ *Plynární 1096/23, Holešovice* ☎ *736–535–010* ⊕ *www.*

*crossclub.cz* Ⓜ *Line C: Nádraží Holešovice, Tram 6, 12, or 17, or Night Tram 53 or 54.*

### SaSaZu

DANCE CLUBS | A restaurant and nightclub and music venue in a warehouse in the middle of a market isn't really the place you'd expect to draw Prague's high-heeled glitterati, but SaSaZu often does. The gorgeous restaurant serves delicious and inventive pan-Asian fusion cuisine, and the vast club can be fun, too: it hosts performances by big international names, from Kesha to Public Enemy, and diners get their own doorway to the club, making an evening here—involving dinner and tickets to see a global music star—a pleasingly swanky experience. ⊠ *Pražská tržnice, Bubenské nábř. 306/13, Holešovice* ☎ *778–054–054* ⊕ *www.sasazu.com* Ⓜ *Line C: Vltavská.*

## 🎭 Performing Arts

For modern, experimental performances, this neighborhood is the place to be.

### THEATER AND DANCE

#### Divadlo Alfred ve dvoře (*Alfred in the Courtyard Theater*)

DANCE | Most of the programming for this small, out-of-the-way theater is physical, nonverbal theater and dance, along with some music. It's a great place to see cutting-edge, unconventional productions; each year has a different theme. It's also home to Motus, a not-for-profit organization, set up by young local artists, producers, and presenters to promote and produce interesting and inventive new art. ⊠ *Fr. Křížka 36, Holešovice* ☎ *233–376–985* ⊕ *www.alfredvedvore.cz* Ⓜ *Line C: Vltavská.*

#### Jatka78

DANCE | An experimental theater based in a market hall, complete with a cavernous bar and bistro bisected by a huge, twisting plywood sculpture, it's worth checking out Jatka78's program online to see what new and often thrilling Czech

10

Letná, Holešovice, and Troja HOLEŠOVICE

or European performances are on, from comedy to cabaret to circus. ✉ *Pražská tržnice, Bubenské nábř. 306/13, Halls 7 and 8, Holešovice* ⊕ *Inside market, toward back* ☎ *775–402–027* ⊕ *www. jatka78.cz* Ⓜ *Line C: Vltavská.*

### Studio Alta

**ARTS CENTERS** | A creative hub that in some ways defies description, combining theater, dance, teaching, artists' studios, and a "living room" café. Nestled among the warehouses so typical of this district, Alta is an artistic, exciting place to spend a few hours or take in some cutting-edge contemporary dance. ✉ *U Výstaviště 21, Holešovice* ☎ *605–439–612* ⊕ *www. altart.cz* Ⓜ *Tram 17 to Výstaviště Holešovice.*

#  Shopping

Shopping in this district, once you have exhausted the boutiques at the Letná end of town, can be a bit hit or miss, but a wander is often rewarding (particularly around the market and the area near the DOX gallery), and Vnitroblock in particular is a must-see.

### Pražská tržnice (*Prague Market*)

**OUTDOOR/FLEA/GREEN MARKETS** | This large, industrial-style market by the river offers some great deals and scope for bargaining, as well as a pleasant art nouveau market hall selling fruits, vegetables, and fresh flowers (hall 22). Known locally as Holešovická tržnice, there are also some restaurants, bars, and bakeries, including a Slovakian deli, plus the experimental theater Jatka78. ■**TIP→ There's an Asian market section here, too, but if you are looking for Prague's famous Vietnamese market, head to Sapa, or "Little Hanoi," on the edge of town (Metro Line C to Chodov, then Bus 197).** ✉ *Bubenské nábř. 306/13, Holešovice* ☎ *220–800–592* ⊕ *www. prazska-trznice.cz* ⊘ *Closed Sun.* Ⓜ *Line C: Vltavská.*

### ★ Vnitroblock

**SHOPPING CENTERS/MALLS** | A cultural center in a former factory that's also a foodie mecca with a cinema, plus a hub for workshops, galleries, and hip boutiques, Vnitroblock resembles a shopping center as imagined by the coolest kids on the block. From the pop-up selling falafel and rosé wine, to the sneaker shop, the gorgeous reclaimed industrial spaces, and the chill café vibe at the heart of the project, it's worth a trip here regardless of where in Prague you are based. ✉ *Between Tusarova 31 and Dělnická 32, Holešovice* ☎ *770–101–231* ⊕ *vnitroblock. cz* Ⓜ *Line C: Vltavska or Nádraží Holešovice plus Tram 1, 12, 24, or 25 to Tusarova or Dělnická.*

# Troja

##  Sights

**Botanická zahrada** (*Botanical Gardens*)
**GARDEN** | Not far from Zoologická zahrada v Praze (Prague Zoo), the public garden has a path in a greenhouse that first takes you through a semidesert environment, then through a tunnel beneath a tropical lake and into a rain forest; you end up cooling off in a room devoted to plants found in tropical mountains. Sliding doors and computer-controlled climate systems help keep it all together. The impressive Fata Morgana, a snaking 429-foot greenhouse that simulates the three different environments, has been drawing large crowds since it opened in 2004. There are lots of other areas in the huge outdoor gardens to explore, too, including beehives, a Japanese ornamental garden, and hilly areas with good views. The trails, including a scented trail and a nature trail, are pleasant as well. And don't miss the vineyard. ✉ *Trojská 196, Troja* ☎ *234–148–122* ⊕ *www.botanicka.cz* 🎟 *Garden and Fata Morgana 50 Kč, outside areas 100 Kč, free Dec.–Feb.*

Trojský zámek (Troja Château) is a luxurious baroque château surrounded by beautiful gardens and vineyards in Prague's northwest borough.

Ⓜ Line C: Nádraží Holešovice plus Bus 112.

**Trojský zámek** (*Troja Château*)
**BUILDING** | Built in the late 17th century for the Czech nobleman Count Šternberg, this sprawling summer residence, modeled on a classical Italian villa, had the first French-style gardens in Bohemia. Inside, rich frescoes that took more than 20 years to complete depict the stories of emperors. Outside, there's plenty of pomp and ceremony, with a red-and-white baroque façade and a sweeping staircase adorned with statues of the sons of Mother Earth. ■**TIP**➔ **The château is closed from early November through March.** ✉ U trojského zámku 1, Troja ☎ 283–851–614 ⊕ ghmp.cz/zamek-troja ☜ 120 Kč ⊙ Closed Mon. and Nov.–Mar. Ⓜ Line C: Nádraží Holešovice plus Bus 112.

**Zoologická zahrada v Praze** (*Prague Zoo*)
**ZOO** | **FAMILY** | Flora, fauna, and fresh air are the main things you can find in Prague's zoo. Hit hard by the floods in 2002, when some 134 animals perished, and again in 2013, when much of the zoo's grounds were inundated with water, Prague's zoo gets a periodic cleanup and offers a welcome break from the bustle of the city, particularly for those traveling with kids. Covering 160 acres on a slope overlooking the Vltava River, the zoo has thousands of animals representing 500 species. Take the chairlift for an outstanding view of the area, and look into arriving via boat: either, in summer, on a steamboat from the center of town or on the simple daily passenger ferry between Podbaba and Podhoří. ✉ U trojského zámku 3, Troja ☎ 296–112–230 ⊕ www.zoopraha.cz ☜ 200 Kč Ⓜ Line C: Nádraží Holešovice plus Bus 112.

## 🍴 Restaurants

### Salabka
**$$$** | **EUROPEAN** | Residential, semirural-seeming Troja is hardly a dining hot spot, but this vineyard restaurant with rooms is a real treat if you are in the area or looking for something a bit different for a special-occasion lunch or dinner.

High-end dining, a stylish setting, and delicious wines combine to make visitors forget, or maybe remember, that they are in the bustling Czech capital. **Known for:** excellent wines, particularly the historic Riesling; inventive tasting menus (no à la carte), with standout freshwater fish dishes; exclusive feel. [$] *Average main: 600 Kč* ✉ *K Bohnicím 2, Troja* ☎ *778–019–002* 🌐 *www.salabka.cz* 🕓 *Closed Mon. and Tues.* [M] *Line C: Nádraží Holešovice plus Bus 112.*

## Coffee and Quick Bites

**Vinotéka sv. Klára** (*St. Claire's Vineyard*) **$** | **CZECH** | This vineyard perched on a hill within the Botanical Gardens is a rewarding stop on a visit to Troja's zoo, the gardens, or the château. Well priced and lively, with delicious hyperlocal vintages, of course, it's a beautiful and relaxed spot for sunset among the vines. **Known for:** affordable local wines; stunning views; relaxing spot. [$] *Average main: 80 Kč* ✉ *Botanická zahrada , Trojská 196, Troja* ✥ *Entrance through Botanical Gardens* ☎ *234–148–153* 🌐 *www.facebook.com/vinotekasvklara/?rf=241071755920015* 🎟 *100 Kč* 💳 *No credit cards* [M] *Line C: Nádraží Holešovice plus Bus 112.*

Chapter 11

# DAY TRIPS
# FROM PRAGUE

Updated by
Joseph Reaney

| 👁 Sights | 🍴 Restaurants | 🏨 Hotels | 🛍 Shopping | 🍸 Nightlife |
|-----------|---------------|-----------|-------------|-------------|
| ★★★★★ | ★★★☆☆ | ★★★★☆ | ★★☆☆☆ | ★★☆☆☆ |

# WELCOME TO
# DAY TRIPS FROM PRAGUE

## TOP REASONS TO GO

★ **Find a storybook come to life:** A true medieval castle—babbling brook and all—can be found in Karlštejn.

★ **Take a historic tour:** The home of Archduke Franz Ferdinand, whose assassination started World War I, is remarkably well preserved in Konopiště; look for the bear living in the moat.

★ **Visit spooky Sedlec:** The *kostnice* (ossuary) outside of Kutná Hora is a mesmerizing church decorated with human bones.

★ **Sample the wine:** It's not all about beer. Try the locally produced wine at pretty Mělník.

★ **Pay remembrance to the past:** In Terezín, a baroque fortress turned into a concentration camp is both powerful and chilling.

**1** **Český Šternberk.** An enormous family-owned fortification perched high over the river.

**2** **Karlštejn.** The quickest castle excursion ticks all the European fairytale fortress boxes.

**3** **Konopiště Castle.** A castle with a moat of bears, a hall of horns, and an untamed park.

**4** **Křivoklát.** An evocative 12th-century fortress, complete with a torture-chamber tour.

**5** **Kutná Hora.** Home to a macabre bone church and a majestic cathedral.

**6** **Lidice.** A haunting memorial to the horrors of World War II.

**7** **Litomyšl.** This pretty town is dominated by a UNESCO-listed Renaissance château.

**8** **Mělník.** Toast this beautiful medieval town with a glass (or two) of delicious local wine.

**9** **Terezín.** A glimpse into a former World War II Jewish ghetto and concentration camp.

**10** **Czech Switzerland.** Excellent hiking opportunities in mystical landscapes.

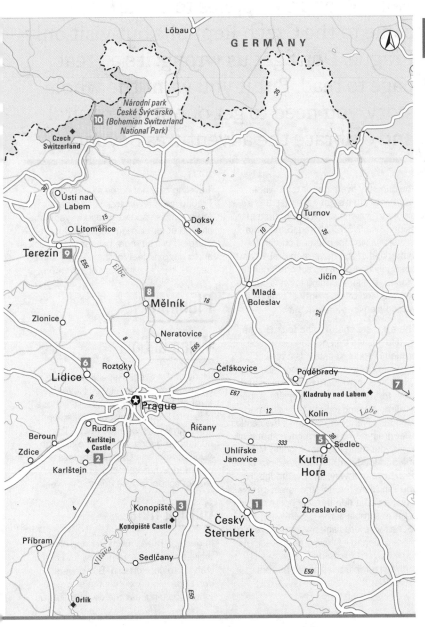

As the saying goes, the world is a book, and those who don't travel read only one page. The same applies to visitors who come to the Czech Republic but visit only Prague. Don't get us wrong: it's a great page to read. But if you want the whole story, you need to get out of the capital and embrace the adventures beyond.

You can stay overnight or for a whole weekend, but it's not essential; there's plenty to do with just a few hours set aside. The UNESCO-listed Kutná Hora is worth a visit for its bone church alone; one of the most memorable, and strangely beautiful, attractions close to Prague. The surrounding town is charming, too, and offers plenty of options if you do plan an overnight stay.

There's more charm to be found in the myriad castles that dot the landscape around Prague. Karlštejn is a typical fairy-tale château atop a mountain; Křivoklát is a wonderfully secluded and quiet fortification; and Konopiště is the onetime hunting lodge of the doomed Archduke Franz Ferdinand. All the castles offer great hiking opportunities, but if hiking is your thing, it's worth going farther afield to the breathtaking Pravčická brána (Pravčická Archway), or rock bridge. Here, you can roam through the forest or take a guided boat ride through gorges. If you want to sample some Czech wine, Mělník has vineyards aplenty. And there are more sobering—in every sense—sights, too, such as Lidice and Terezín, which both tell terrible tales of the horrors of World War II.

Traveling may not come as easy as in Prague, with fewer tourist facilities, fewer English speakers, and fewer nightlife and entertainment options. But the trade-off will be more bang for your buck and a genuine feel for the country and its people, plus a real sense of adventure.

# Planning

## When to Go

Many of the Czech Republic's castles and monuments are closed November through March. Some, especially those closer to Prague, stay open year-round although with shortened hours. The busiest time for a visit is June through August; April and October are less crowded. When school is in session, expect school groups during the week.

## Getting Here

In general, buses are faster and cheaper, while trains are easier to navigate and a bit more comfortable. Bus drivers don't typically announce the stops, so when boarding, ask the driver to let you know when you should get off. If you are planning a trip, it's worth it to know your options ahead of time; visit ⊕ www.idos. cz for an online timetable (an English version is available). If you are taking a bus from Florenc, go to the station a day or two before your trip and purchase your tickets. People with tickets board first, and you'll get an assigned seat (and not have to stand). The ticket will be printed with the platform number. There's a computer terminal in Florenc station where you can check bus times as well.

# Guided Tours from Prague

Guided bus tours are available from several companies for Karlštejn, Konopiště, Kutná Hora, Český Šternberk, and Terezín. The ease of booking and traveling (compared with figuring out the train and bus schedules or renting a car) are often worth the time constraints and extra cost. Wittmann Tours specializes in tours to Terezín as well as to Jewish sites all over the country. If you are looking for something more specialized, Avantgarde Prague offers tailor-made tours.

### Biko Adventures Prague

**BICYCLE TOURS | FAMILY |** Biko offers a gentle and family-friendly full-day tour by e-bike through small villages (with stops for beer and baked goods) to Hrad Karlštejn (Karlštejn Castle). It's around 65 km (40 miles) there and back. Other options include a bike tour through huge blocks of flats ending in a lush national park. ⊠ Vratislavova 3, Vyšehrad ☎ 733–750–990 ⊕ www.bikoadventures. com Ⓜ Line B: Karlovo náměstí.

### Premiant City Tour

**GUIDED TOURS |** This company has knowledgeable guides and a wide range of day trips, from Karlštejn to Kutná Hora. Standard tours, which are available in several languages, are in small groups,

but individual or private groups are also available on request. Book online or at the easy-to-find booths on Na příkopě. ⊠ Na příkopě 23, Nové Mesto ☎ 606–600–123 ⊕ www.premiant.cz.

### Wittmann Tours

**GUIDED TOURS |** Interesting and informative trips with a particular focus on Jewish sites and history. As well as offering day trips to the former Jewish ghetto of Terezín (with an optional add-on of Lidice) the company has a full day tour to Kutná Hora and Kolín, once the country's second main Jewish center. ⊠ Novotného lávka 5, Staré Mesto ☎ 222–252–472 ⊕ www.wittmann-tours.com.

# Restaurants and Hotels

In general, food and lodging should be cheaper than in Prague, but some restaurants, especially those close to the center or near a tourist attraction, can be just as pricey. You won't find the same range of options either, and be prepared for fewer English speakers—but people will probably be friendlier than in the big city. Anyway, that's all part of the adventure.

*Restaurant and hotel reviews have been shortened. For full information, visit Fodors.com.*

## What it Costs In koruny

| | $ | $$ | $$$ | $$$$ |
|---|---|---|---|---|
| **RESTAURANTS** | | | | |
| | under 150 Kč | 150 Kč–300 Kč | 301 Kč–500 Kč | over 500 Kč |
| **HOTELS** | | | | |
| | under 3,500 Kč | 3,500 Kč–5,000 Kč | 5,001 Kč–7,000 Kč | over 7,000 Kč |

# Český Šternberk

*48 km (30 miles) southeast of Prague.*

A real-deal Czech castle, complete with descendants of its 13th-century founders still living inside. Český Šternberk may not be the easiest day trip from Prague, but for history, atmosphere, and authenticity, it's hard to beat.

## GETTING HERE

There are daily trains to Český Šternberk, but it isn't the easiest trip. Trains leave from Hlavní nádraží (Prague's main train station) and stop in many small towns on the way; you have to change trains in Čerčany, about one hour out of Prague. The good news is that the last leg, which runs alongside the Sázava River, is very scenic. Also, in summer you may be lucky enough to score a ride on an old-fashioned steam train; ask at the main station for the *parní vlak* (steam train). Whichever trains you end up taking, expect a two-hour journey time.

If you're driving, you will take the D1 highway out of Prague (the main highway to Brno) and take the turnoff to Český Šternberk, following Route 111 to the castle, which perches over the highway. The drive takes around 45 minutes.

## TIMING

Summer sees the most tourists at Český Šternberk, and it can get very busy June through August. Nevertheless, the daily falconer displays can make a peak-time visit worthwhile. May and September are a little quieter yet still warm, while October has a historical festival that features "live" characters from the castle's history. From November to March, as well as midweek in April and October, the castle is open only by appointment.

##  Sights

### Český Šternberk

**CASTLE/PALACE** | Dramatic Český Šternberk looms over the Sázava River and surrounding countryside and looks positively forbidding at night. Perched on an outcropping of rock, this 13th-century castle is not only striking from the exterior; it has the period interiors to match.

Founded in 1241 by Zdeslav of Divišov, it was originally built as a fortress. Amazingly, descendants of Zdeslav have remained in the castle, making it their residence through the centuries and up to the present day. Šternberk is the Czech spelling of the German composite word Sternberg (it was customary to use German names at the time), which roughly translates to "star on the hill." Look out for the eight-pointed gold star on the family coat of arms, which can be found throughout the property.

The exterior of the castle retains a late Gothic look, while the interiors were mainly redone in a baroque style. The latest major work was done in 1911, when electricity and water were added. Guided tours lasting around 45 minutes are required to see the interior, but the rooms are gorgeous and the guides are excellent. There are regular English-language tours in summer, but out of peak season it's best to call or email in advance to book your place.

Furnishings date back to the Renaissance and are either original from the castle or brought from other Šternberk properties around Europe. Beautiful frescoed walls and stucco ceilings can be found throughout, including the Knight's Hall lined with paintings. You'll see items in the rococo and Czech baroque style, Louis XVI furnishings, and an amazing collection of copper engravings dating back to the 17th century.

Česky Šternberk, or the "Star on the Hill," lives up to its name.

Look out for a (literal) family tree, with portraits of generations of the Šternberk family. Its members included scientists, bishops, officers, and government employees, all of whom left their mark on aspects of the country's history. One even helped found the Národní muzeum (National Museum) in Prague.

During the nationalization period under communism, the castle was seized and became government property; however Jiří Šternberk agreed to stay on as caretaker and guide, thus keeping the family's connection to the castle. The Šternberks received the property back in 1992, and Jiří's son Zdeněk still lives in four rooms on the second floor.

There are some lovely walks in the woodlands around the castle. One route leads to Hladomorna, a stand-alone fortress tower you can climb during the summer for a fine view of the castle, river, and surrounding forest. ✉ *Český Šternberk 1* ☎ *317–855–101* 🌐 *www.hradceskysternberk.cz* 🎟 *Guided tour in English 230 Kč, night tour 300 Kč* 🕒 *Closed Mon. Closed weekdays in Apr. and Oct. Nov.–Mar. by appointment only.*

## 🛏 Hotels

**Parkhotel Český Šternberk**

**$ | HOTEL** | The Parkhotel—on the opposite side of the river from the castle—doesn't have much competition; it's one of the only hotels in town. **Pros:** magnificent view of the castle; quality seasonal food in restaurant; incredibly good value. **Cons:** not all rooms face the castle; breakfast not included; can only book by email or phone. [$] *Rooms from: 750 Kč* ✉ *Český Šternberk 46* ☎ *774–443–854* 🌐 *www.phcs.cz* 🕒 *Closed Oct.–Mar., except for group bookings* 🛏 *19 rooms* 🍴 *No meals.*

# Karlštejn

*29 km (18 miles) southwest of Prague.*

If you've only a few hours to spend outside of Prague, going to Karlštejn is an easy and delightful day trip. The town itself seems to exist mainly to support visitors to the castle, so if you are looking for some Czech authenticity this probably isn't the one to choose. But for castle lovers and nature lovers, it's a lovely outing.

## GETTING HERE

There's no bus service to Karlštejn from Prague, but it's a quick, simple, and scenic train journey (around 65 Kč) from the main station. Many trains leave every day from Hlavní nádraží—look on the schedule for trains heading to Beroun. When you arrive at Karlštejn station, simply follow the crowds across the river and up to the castle. On the very rare occasions where there's no one else around, here's what you need to do: Exit the station, turn right, and walk back along the small lane parallel to the railway tracks to find the town. Follow the signs reading "Hrad." After a few minutes, cross a bridge over the river, and turn right onto the main road, which resembles a small highway (the absence of a pedestrian sidewalk doesn't bother the locals). Be wary of traffic, but continue for another two or three minutes until you reach a road going up the hill to your left. This is the main road up to the village and castle.

A visit to Karlštejn can also be combined with a challenging 13-km (8-mile) hike through beautiful forests and along a small wooded waterfall from Beroun. Get off at Beroun train station, walk toward town, and make a right just before an underpass. Follow the red-marked trail through the hills and dales, passing through the tiny village of Svatý Jan pod Skalou before arriving in Karlštejn—just above the village—about three hours later. Don't set out without water, good shoes, and, above all, a decent local hiking map, available at the visitor center.

By car from Prague, take Highway 4—on the western side of the Vltava—to the edge of the city, then go right on Highway 115, southwest through Radotín.

Take the Karlštejn exit, which puts you on Highway 116, and after a few more minutes you end up beside the Berounka River. You can find a large parking lot at the bottom of the hill below Karlštejn. No vehicles are allowed on the road up to the castle.

## TIMING

It's possible to visit Karlštejn all year round, but peak season is from Easter to October. In September, there's a wine festival, complete with tastings, craft booths, artistic displays, and a visit from Charles IV himself (sort of). December is also a good time to visit, as there are often Christmas concerts on weekends–and far fewer crowds than in summer.

 # Sights

★ **Hrad Karlštejn** (*Karlštejn Castle*)
**CASTLE/PALACE** | If it's a picture-book European castle you're after, look no further. Perched atop a wooded hillside, Karlštejn comes complete with battlements, turrets, and towers. Once Charles IV's summer palace, Karlštejn was originally built to hold and guard the crown jewels (which were moved to Prague Castle's Katedrála sv. Víta, or St. Vitus Cathedral, in 1619). There is a fairly strenuous hike up to the castle—lined with souvenir stands and overpriced snack bars—but it's worth the journey. Once you've reached the top, take time to walk the ramparts and drink in the panorama of the village and countryside below. There's a slightly bewildering list of different interior tours, but the pick of the bunch is Tour 2, which includes the castle's greatest treasure, the Chapel of the Holy Cross, which once held the crown jewels. Tours of the chapel are limited (and more expensive than the other tour route), so you must book in advance. There's an exterior tour, too, if it's a sunny day, or you can poke your head around the exterior courtyards at no cost. Because of its proximity

Karlštejn Castle is a 45-minute train ride from Prague, and one of the most convenient and popular escapes from the Czech capital city.

to Prague, it is the most-visited site outside of the Czech capital, so be prepared for crowds, especially in the high summer months. Email for tour reservations. ✉ *Karlštejn 18* ☎ *311–681–617* 🌐 *www.hrad-karlstejn.cz* 🎫 *Tours from 1320 Kč* ⏱ *Tower closed Oct.–Apr., chapel closed Nov.–Apr.*

## 🍴 Restaurants

**Pod dračí skálou**

**$$ | CZECH** | This traditional hunting lodge–style restaurant is the most rustic and fun of Karlštejn's eateries. To find it, follow the main road uphill out of the village about a third of a mile from town. **Known for:** large portions of good food; hit-or-miss service; accommodation also available. [$] *Average main: 220 Kč* ✉ *Karlštejn 130* ☎ *311–681–177* 🌐 *www.poddraciskalou.eu.*

**U Janů**

**$ | CZECH** | The best of the many touristy restaurants in the town proper, this spot is just on the upper edge of the village, not far from where the castle path starts. It also offers a nice big terrace with slight views of the castle. **Known for:** good food at a reasonable price; location right on the main street; option of three suites and a double room. [$] *Average main: 130 Kč* ✉ *Karlštejn 28* ☎ *725–805–965* 🌐 *www.ujanukarlstejn.cz.*

## 🛏 Hotels

**Hotel Karlštejn**

**$ | HOTEL** | The best "proper" hotel in town, the Karlštejn offers 11 modern but pared-down rooms. **Pros:** clean and modern rooms; outdoor pool with view of castle; free parking spaces. **Cons:** no restaurant for dinner; some rooms are poky; lacking an elevator. [$] *Rooms from: 2400 Kč* ✉ *Karlštejn 7* ☎ *311–600–900* 🌐 *www.hotel-karlstejn.cz* 🛏 *11 rooms* 🍽 *Free breakfast.*

# Konopiště Castle

*45 km (27 miles) southeast of Prague.*

Bears, hunting trophies, and history are found at the country residence of the doomed Archduke Franz Ferdinand, whose 1914 assassination ignited World War I and changed the course of modern history.

### GETTING HERE

For being so close to Prague, Konopiště can feel a little remote. Trains leave from Hlavní nádraží to Benešov u Prahy and cost around 80 Kč. However, there's still another 2½ km (1½ miles) from here to Zámek Konopiště (Konopiště Castle). You can either walk the last leg (simply follow the signs), hop on a bus (438 or 455; 18 Kč) or take a taxi (though this will take longer than the bus). By car, take the D1 highway southwest toward Brno, and exit following the signs to Benešov. Signs on this road lead you to Konopiště.

### VISITOR INFORMATION

**CONTACTS Turistické informační centrum.** (*Tourist Information Center*) ✉ *Konopiště, Benešov* ☎ *317–705–681 for main tourist office in Benešov.*

## Sights

**Zámek Konopiště** (*Konopiště Castle*)
**CASTLE/PALACE** | Set in a huge, beautiful park, Konopiště Castle dates to the 14th century and is best known as the hunting lodge of the ill-fated Archduke Franz Ferdinand, whose assassination sparked World War I. He no doubt had a whale of a time hunting on the grounds before he met his untimely end, and now visitors can wander the forests, gaze at the lake, and even watch plays in summer, as well as muse on the archduke's global significance. In a suitably historic touch, there's also bear who lives in the castle moat; he's a bit shy so you might not see him.

The castle itself is also worth a look, with a carefully preserved interior including many original furnishings from Ferdinand's time. The rooms reflect his incredible opulence as well as his fondness for hunting—there are animal trophies and weapons everywhere. For a properly immersive experience, you can even stay inside the castle walls at a little pension.

Getting to the castle usually involves a ⅓-mile walk through the woods. It can be seen only on a guided tour; book in advance for an English-speaking guide. If one isn't available, ask for an English text to accompany the tour. An atmospheric night tour is also offered. ✉ *Benešov* ☎ *317–721–366* 🌐 *www.zamek-konopiste.cz* 🎫 *Tours 300 Kč* 🕒 *Closed Mon. and Dec.–Mar.*

## Hotels

**Pension Konopiště**
**$ | B&B/INN** | Konopiště is near enough to Prague that you don't really need to stay overnight, but if you fancy a night in the countryside, this pension inside the castle walls and attached to a motorcycle museum is a lovely option. **Pros:** great location; free activities like table tennis and pétanque; surrounded by nature. **Cons:** no restaurant; narrow staircases; some rooms small. [$] *Rooms from: 2200 Kč* ✉ *Konopiště 30, Benešov* ☎ *317–702–658* 🌐 *www.penzion-konopiste.cz* 🛏 *6 apartments* 🍴 *Free breakfast.*

# Křivoklát

*43 km (27 miles) west of Prague.*

One of the most evocative castles in the country, Křivoklát is the real deal. A brisk walk up the hill to the top feels like a trip back in time as you leave the trappings of modern life behind.

### GETTING HERE

A train is the best, and prettiest, way to reach Křivoklát. Trains depart from Hlavní nádraží, and a change in Beroun is required. The scenic ride will take about

1½ hours and cost around 100 Kč. Trains aren't all that regular, so check your return options before setting off. If you plan to visit over a summer weekend, the heritage train "Rakovnický rychlík" offers irregular but direct services from Prague; check ⊕ *kzc.cz* for details and timetables.

If you're driving, the fastest way to Křivoklát is to follow Route 6 from Prague toward Karlovy Vary, and after Jeneč turn onto Route 201 via Unhoště to Křivoklát. The trip is about an hour. For a beautiful drive (and an extra 15 minutes) take the E50 Highway from Prague toward Plzeň, then exit at Křivoklát to Route 116. Follow this highway, which goes along a river before veering up into the hills, to Route 201, which winds back south toward Křivoklát. There's free parking just beneath the castle or paid parking just above it.

### TIMING

In summer you'll see cyclists zooming around the region and locals visiting the castle in swarms. At the beginning of December, Křivoklát holds an Advent fair, complete with musicians, performances, and lots of crafts.

### VISITOR INFORMATION

**CONTACTS Křivoklát Tourist Information.**
✉ *Nám. Svatopluka Čecha 82* ☎ *313– 558–101* ⊕ *www.is-krivoklat.cz.*

##  Sights

### ★ Křivoklát

**CASTLE/PALACE** | A man dressed as a monk asleep in the corner; children practicing archery; traditional craftsmen offering their wares—close your eyes in Křivoklát's strangely atmospheric courtyard and you can easily imagine the scene with hunters clattering back atop their horses. Because the castle is a little farther from Prague, it's much less crowded and more authentic, so you can let your imagination run wild as you wander the walls and gaze out on the surrounding forest and the Berounka

# A Pagan Spring

Spirits swing to life in Křivoklát on April 30, when many Czech villages celebrate something called Čarodejnice. Roughly translated as "witch-burning"—a pagan-rooted festival to ward off the winter spirit and welcome the bounty of spring— it turns Křivoklát into a gleeful scene of Slavic festivities and mock Celtic battles. Hundreds of Czechs from all over come to enjoy the music, merriment, and cheap wine into the wee hours.

River winding lazily by below. The evocative name helps as well, even if it's a little hard to pronounce (it means "twisted branches" in Czech). There also aren't many signs, which helps with the feeling that you are having an adventure. You'll meet a lot of locals, rather than tourists, enjoying the castle, mainly because it's a national favorite thanks to its many romantic references in Czech literature. The river area is also popular with hikers and cyclists.

Křivoklát began life as a humble hunting lodge back in the 12th century. Greater things were to come, thanks to King Wenceslas I, who commissioned the first castle here. Future inhabitants expanded and beautified the place, including Charles IV and his son, Wenceslas IV. A number of fires significantly damaged the buildings, and toward the end of the 16th century it lost its importance and fell into disrepair. Following the Thirty Years' War, the Schwarzenbergs took over and revived it. It's been in state hands since 1929.

Take a tour of the castle and you'll pass through the Great Hall (one of the largest Gothic halls in Central Europe, second only to one in Prague Castle) plus another hall, both loaded with Gothic paintings and sculpture; a beautiful chapel (another highlight of the interior tour), the castle library, a castle prison complete with torture instruments, and lots of hunting trophies. It's truly one of the more interesting castle tours around. Tours, which last from 20 minutes to 1 hour and 40 minutes, are offered regularly in Czech, and in the summer there are also tours available in English; there's no need to prebook, but check the website for times. Out of season, you can join a Czech tour and purchase a pamphlet with information in English.

Even without a tour, the castle is well worth a visit. You can walk along the castle ramparts, climb the tower (for great views of the surrounding countryside), or simply sit and nurse a beer in the beautiful courtyard. There's also a lovely 2-km (1-mile) woodland walk from the castle to a viewpoint above the river; follow the path marked with yellow paint, which starts across the road from the castle entrance. ✉ *Křivoklát 47* ☎ *313–558–440* 🌐 *www.hrad-krivoklat.cz* 🎫 *Full castle tour 400 Kč, Gothic palace long/short tour 340/240 Kč, ramparts tour 80 Kč* 🕒 *Closed Mon. Closed weekdays Nov.–Mar. (except festivals; check website for details).*

## 🍴 Restaurants

**U Jelena**

**$$** | **CZECH** | The pleasant riverside setting and the hearty hunting theme—as well as proximity to the castle itself—are the main draws here, while the food, from the familiar *svíčková* (slices of beef loin in cream sauce) to more elaborate dishes like venison steak with Cumberland sauce, is decent if unspectacular. If you'd like to stay overnight, there are a few rooms upstairs, outfitted simply but with a cozy feeling thanks to wooden furnishings and pleasant lighting. **Known for:** riverside terrace; Czech dumplings; hunting lodge decor. $ *Average main: 180 Kč* ✉ *Hradní 53* ☎ *313–558–235* 🌐 *www.ujelena.eu.*

# Kutná Hora

*70 km (44 miles) east of Prague.*

Kutná Hora is a UNESCO World Heritage Site, and the town proudly boasts of its "10 centuries of architecture" that run the gamut from Gothic to cubist. The town is worth a visit any time, but the tourist season really starts in April. Historic peddlers, dancers, and fencers celebrate the city's silver-mining history at the Královské stříbření (Royal Silvering) festival held every June. There are also some traditional Czech eateries, a great silver-mining museum, and the stunning Chrám sv. Barbory (St. Barbara's Cathedral), which dates from 1388.

Nearby, Sedlec Ossuary, or the "Bone Church," is one of the Czech Republic's most famous sights. The small chapel is decorated floor to ceiling with human bones. The shapes, chandeliers, and sculptures are strangely, hauntingly beautiful, adding up to a breathtaking and morbid memento mori.

### GETTING HERE

Both buses and trains make the short trip to Kutná Hora, but the train is a better bet. The journey takes less than an hour and a ticket costs around 115 Kč. You will most likely be dropped off at the Kutná Hora main station, which is in the suburb of Sedlec, about 2 km (1 mile) away. If you are given a ticket that says *město* (city), that means you'll be going to the train station in town. However, since you are in Sedlec anyway, take advantage of the fact and walk about 10 minutes (signs point the way and there's a map in the station) to the bone church. You can then walk into town—about 25 minutes. It's an easy straight shot but not the most scenic.

Bus 381 leaves from Háje at the end of Metro Line C (red). It's a little cheaper than the train, but takes almost twice as long. By car, follow Vinohradská třída west out onto the E65, then take the D11

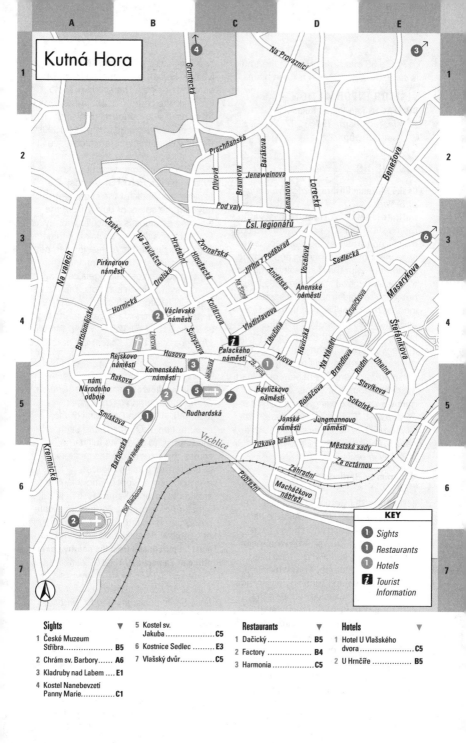

# Kutná Hora

to Route 38 into Kutná Hora. If the traffic is clear, the drive should take an hour.

## VISITOR INFORMATION
**CONTACTS Info-Centre Kutná Hora.**
✉ *Palackého nám. 377* ☎ *327–512–378* ⊕ *www.kutnahora.cz.*

#  Sights

**České Muzeum Stříbra** (*Czech Museum of Silver*)
**FACTORY | FAMILY |** A silver mine is a little more romantic than a run-of-the-mill coal mine, and this silver museum combines all manner of period mining and minting equipment with the real deal: the chance to tour a medieval silver mine. It's fun, but if you're claustrophobic it's worth noting that the tunnel is a bit tight and you're underground for about 30 minutes. The city boasted some of the deepest mines in the world back in the 16th century, and the trek nowadays will probably make you glad you weren't a miner. Tours start every half hour; last admission is 90 minutes before closing. ✉ *Barborská ul. 28* ☎ *327–512–159* ⊕ *www.cms-kh.cz* 🎟 *From 70 Kč, foreign-language explanation 20 Kč* ⊗ *Closed Dec.–Mar. and possibly in bad weather.*

★ **Chrám sv. Barbory** (*St. Barbara's Cathedral*)
**RELIGIOUS SITE |** Getting to this beautiful cathedral is nearly as pleasurable as a visit to the Gothic church itself. It's about a 10-minute walk from the main Palackého náměstí along a road lined with baroque statues, from which you can gaze at the surrounding countryside and watch the massive shape of the cathedral come closer. From afar, the church resembles a grand circus tent more than a religious center. As the jewel in Kutná Hora's crown, it's a high point of Gothic style, although through the centuries there have been alterations and improvements. St. Barbara's was started in the late 1300s; it drew on the talents of the Peter Parler workshop as well as

two luminaries of the late 15th century, Matyáš Rejsek and Benedikt Ried. Upon entering, look up. The soaring ceiling is one of the church's most impressive features. It was added in 1558 and replaced and restored in the late 1800s. If you walk to the western façade, you'll see a lovely view over the town and the visibly leaning tower of the Kostel sv. Jakuba (Church of St. James). Do explore the whole of the church—gazing down at the splendor below from the elevated sections is particularly lovely. St. Barbara is the patron saint of miners, and glimpses of this profession can be seen throughout the interior, including Gothic frescoes of angels carrying shields with mining symbols. There's also a special Mintner's Chapel, which holds a statue of a miner, a novelty for its time. ✉ *Barborská ul.* ☎ *327–515–796* ⊕ *www. khfarnost.cz* 🎟 *120 Kč, combo ticket 220 Kč (incl. Sedlec Ossuary and Church of the Assumption).*

**Kostel Nanebevzetí Panny Marie** (*Church of the Assumption of the Virgin*)
**RELIGIOUS SITE |** The Cathedral of the Assumption of Our Lady and Saint John the Baptist, to give it its full name, sits across the street from the ossuary at the former Sedlec Monastery. It exemplifies the work of one-of-a-kind architect Giovanni Santini (1667–1723), a master of expressive line and delicate proportion who fathered a bravura hybrid of Gothic and baroque. ■TIP→ **Tickets must be purchased from the nearby ticket office at Zámecká 279.** ✉ *U Zastávky, Sedlec* ☎ *326–551–049* ⊕ *www.sedlec. info* 🎟 *50 Kč, combination ticket 220 Kč (incl. Sedlec Ossuary and St. Barbara's Cathedral).*

**Kostel sv. Jakuba** (*Church of St. James*)
**RELIGIOUS SITE |** If you've already been to St. Barbara's, you'll have seen the tilting tower of this church next to the old mint. It doesn't keep normal operating hours, but go ahead and try the door anyway. It was originally built in the Gothic style,

The looming St. Barbara's Cathedral is a tribute to Kutná Hora's miners.

but a massive baroque transformation occurred in the 17th and 18th centuries; the onion dome was added in 1737. The baroque paintings on the wall are Czech masterpieces. ⊠ *Jakubská* ☎ *327–515–796* ⊕ *khfarnost.cz* ✉ *Free.*

★ **Kostnice Sedlec** (*Sedlec Ossuary*)
**RELIGIOUS SITE** | This is the reason many people outside the Czech Republic have heard of, and make the trip to, Kutná Hora. Forget all that beautiful baroque architecture and descend into the darkness with some bones. The skeletal remains of around 40,000 people have been lovingly arranged in the Kaple Všech svatých (All Saints Chapel), more commonly called the Bone Church. Built in the 16th century, this church forced the movement of a nearby graveyard. Monks from the nearby Sedlec Monastery decided to use the displaced cemetery bones to decorate the church with beautiful, weird, and haunting results. ■TIP→ **Check out the chandelier, as it's made with every bone in the human body. It's downright spooky.** ⊠ *Zámecká,*

*Sedlec* ☎ *326–551–049* ⊕ *www.sedlec. info* ✉ *90 Kč, combination ticket 220 Kč (incl. Church of the Assumption and St. Barbara's Cathedral).*

★ **Národní hřebčín Kladruby nad Labem**
(*National Stud at Kladruby nad Labem*)
**HISTORIC SITE** | This national stud farm, established in the 16th century to breed and train ceremonial horses for the Habsburg court, was named a Unesco World Heritage site in 2019. Located 56 miles east of Prague and about a half-hour drive from Kutná Hora, in the town of Kladruby nad Labem, the Kladruby Stud is the first stud farm in the world to be be listed. The Kladruber is a rare breed that is one of the oldest in the world with a population of only 1,200. Since the late 18th century, the Kladruber horses have come in two colours, grey and black. The former were used for royal ceremonies and the latter for high-ranking clergy. The Kladruby farm occupies 1,310 hectares (3,240 acres) of flat, sandy land and fenced pastures near the Elbe. The site, whose size has changed little since the

16th century, includes fields and forests along with its classic stables, indoor and outdoor training grounds, all designed with the main objective of breeding and training kladruber horses. Visitors can enjoy a guided tour of the stables, of the coach room with the Kladruber Horse Exhibit, and of the Chateau. You can also tour the forester's lodge, climb up a hill to a viewing tower offering a unique view of the stud and its surroundings, and take a coach ride. ✉ *Kladruby nad Labem č.p. 1* ☎ *601–191–580* 🌐 *www.nhkladruby.cz/en* 🎟 *From 157 Kč* 🕒 *Closed Nov.–Mar.; Closed Mon.*

**Vlašský dvůr** (*Italian Court*)
**MUSEUM** | Coins were first minted here in 1300, made by Italian artisans brought in from Florence—hence the mint's odd name. The Italian Court was where the Pražský groš (Prague groschen), one of the most widely circulated coins of the Middle Ages, was minted until 1726. There's a **coin museum,** where you can see the small, silvery groschen being struck and buy replicas. ✉ *Havlíčkovo nám. 552* ☎ *327–512–873* 🌐 *www.pskh.cz* 🎟 *From 85 Kč.*

## 🍴 Restaurants

**★ Dačický**
**$$** | **CZECH** | A medieval tavern feel and big plates of Czech food make Dačický a warm, authentic experience. The yellow walls decorated with cartoon-style murals, long, shared wooden tables, and the massive chandelier also add to the ambience. **Known for:** popularity with locals; good choice of draft beers; giant kebab with meat skewered on a sword. [$] *Average main: 220 Kč* ✉ *Rakova 8* ☎ *603–434–367* 🌐 *www.dacicky.com.*

**Factory**
**$$** | **AMERICAN** | This popular, modern bistro-café serves fairly standard European-American fare, but everything is freshly and expertly made. That means pizzas cooked crispy Neapolitan style, steaks that have been matured for 14 days, and fresh pasta that's cooked al dente. **Known for:** cozy cellar setting; friendly English-speaking waitstaff; phenomenal French fries. [$] *Average main: 190 Kč* ✉ *Česká 1* ☎ *721–323–145* 🌐 *www.factorybistro.cz* 🕒 *Closed Mon.*

**Harmonia**
**$$** | **CZECH** | A charming spot just off Komenského náměstí near the Church of St. James, Harmonia serves good food at good prices. The small back patio is relatively secluded and the perfect place for an espresso and quiet conversation. **Known for:** generous portions; lovely quiet patio area; slow service. [$] *Average main: 220 Kč* ✉ *Husova 104* ☎ *327–512–275* 🌐 *www.restauranthamonia.cz.*

## 🛏 Hotels

**Hotel U Vlašského dvora**
**$** | **HOTEL** | Lovely views from this hotel make it a nice option for an overnight stay in Kutná Hora. **Pros:** great views from room; nice breakfast; convenient central location. **Cons:** lots of steps; lack of a/c makes rooms hot in summer; some furniture a bit dated. [$] *Rooms from: 1800 Kč* ✉ *28. října 511* ☎ *327–514–618* 🌐 *www.vlasskydvur.cz* 🛏 *10 rooms* 🍴 *Free breakfast.*

**U Hrnčíře**
**$** | **B&B/INN** | If you are looking for a more rustic stay, head over to U Hrnčíře, where you will find basic decor but a good restaurant and a view of the Church of St. James. **Pros:** old picturesque building; good restaurant; exceptional value. **Cons:** steep stairs and no elevator; rooms are no-frills; no private parking. [$] *Rooms from: 850 Kč* ✉ *Barborská 24* ☎ *722–222–578* 🌐 *www.hoteluhrncire.cz* 🛏 *5 rooms* 🍴 *Free breakfast.*

# Lidice

*18 km (11 miles) northwest of Prague.*

No more than a speck on the map to the northwest of Prague, this tiny village became a part of the tragic history of World War II. Adolf Hitler ordered Lidice to be razed to the ground as a lesson to the Czechs and a representation of what would happen to anyone who opposed his rule. The act was a retaliation for the assassination of the Nazi leader Reinhard Heydrich by Czech patriots. On the night of June 9, 1942, a Gestapo unit entered Lidice. The entire adult male population was shot, nearly 200 men; about the same number of women were sent to the Ravensbrück concentration camp. The children were either sent to Germany to be "Aryanized" or accompanied the women to the death camp. By June 10, the entire village was completely wiped out.

The name Lidice soon became an example around the world of the brutality of Nazi rule. A group of English miners from Stoke-on-Trent took up the cause and formed Lidice Must Live, an initiative to build a new village of Lidice. The city is adjacent to the memorial, which is an amazing and beautiful site, albeit one that is usually visited only by school groups. For most tourists, and even Czechs, heartbreaking Lidice still doesn't seem to be on the map. If you are driving and plan to go to Terezín, make Lidice a short stop on your way.

## GETTING HERE

It's a shame that an important memorial so close to Prague can be a bit tricky to reach by public transportation, although it's a quick trip once you are on board. There's no train service to Lidice, but there is a regular bus service from Zličín, at the end of the Metro Line B (yellow)—the same place you can get the airport bus. Tickets (24 Kč) are purchased directly from the driver. You can also get Bus 300, Prague–Kladno, from the stop above Metro station Nádraží Veleslavín (Line A). Either way, the trip takes about 20 minutes, and you'll be let off at an intersection across from the memorial itself.

By car, Lidice is an easy 30-minute journey. From the Dejvice area, follow Evropská třída out of Prague past the airport, then continue west on D7 until you see the well-marked memorial, with a parking lot, beside the highway. If you're driving, it's ideal to combine this with a trip to Terezín, about 30 km (18 miles) farther along in the same direction from Prague.

## ◉ Sights

★ **Památník Lidice** (*Lidice Memorial*)
**MEMORIAL** | There is an eerie silence at Lidice. The lovely green rolling hills, small pond, babbling brook, and groves of trees are typical of the Czech countryside, but somehow the events that happened here remain in the air. It's incredibly moving to walk around the empty area, constantly reminding yourself that within living memory, this was a thriving village before the Nazis effectively erased it from the map.

You'll first enter the colonnade that houses a small museum. Inside you're introduced, through a series of films and photographs, to the original inhabitants of the city. German documentation from the time describes the horror of the mass murder in a disturbingly straightforward fashion. From here, the grounds of the memorial are free to wander, or you can secure an English-speaking guide to escort you around the entire area for 500 Kč (book in advance through the website).

The most visited and evocative sight in Lidice is the Monument to Child Victims of War. This life-size sculpture of the 82 children gassed by the Nazis is haunting in its detail, particularly the delicate facial expressions. Sculptor Marie Uchytilová dedicated two decades of her life to the project. On the opposite side of the path is a stark cross, which marks the place where the men were executed.

Walk to the end of the field to see the former location of the town's cemetery, or head back toward the entrance to a vast rose garden; the west portion of the garden is planted with light-color roses to honor the children.

The museum entrance fee also includes access to Lidická galerie, home to a permanent exhibition of contemporary art donated by artists from around the world, and Rodinný dům č. 116, an example of the typical 1950s houses that make up the new, thriving village of Lidice. Both are around a 10-minute walk west of the rose garden. ⊠ Tokajická 152 ☎ 312–253–088 ⊕ www.lidice-memorial.cz ☞ 90 Kč, guided tour (in English) 500 Kč.

# Litomyšl

*160 km (100 miles) east of Prague.*

This small Eastern Bohemian city is renowned for its picture-perfect, UNESCO-listed arcade castle. It also has one of the country's prettiest town squares, as well as the annual summer opera festival **Smetanova Litomyšl** (⊕ *www.smetanovalitomysl.cz*), named for renowned composer and local boy Bedřich Smetana.

### GETTING HERE

It's possible to get from Prague to Litomyšl with public transport, but it's a little complicated. You'll need to take a *rychlík* (fast train) from Prague's main station to Česká Třebová (about 1½ hours), then switch to a local bus (23 or 25, about 30 minutes). The whole journey will cost around 220 Kč. For drivers, it's even more complicated. Take the E67 east, then follow the signs to Pardubice (you'll join Route 35, then 37). Take the 324 exit off Route 37 (signed Hrobice), then follow a number of small roads—namely 2987,

2985, and 2984—to connect to Route 36. After around 10 km (6 miles), turn right at the roundabout onto Route 35 (signed Olomouc) and follow this all the way into Litomyšl. The journey takes just more than two hours on a clear day.

# Sights

**11**

**Day Trips from Prague** LITOMYŠL

★ **Státní zámek Litomyšl** (*Litomyšl Castle*) **CASTLE/PALACE** | Built in 1568, this towering Renaissance château is a rare example of the "arcade" castle style in northern Europe. As you approach, the white-walled exterior appears to be made from thousands of bricks, but on closer inspection, it becomes clear the pattern has been achieved through intricate *sgraffito*. Each "brick" is etched into the plaster and has its own design, often incorporating imagery from the Old Testament or from classical mythology. Head into the courtyard to find even grander and more elaborate wall frescoes. While the exterior has remained largely unchanged for the last 450 years, the interior has a number of high baroque architectural additions. To see them, two guided tours are available: the first takes in a set of 12 castle rooms plus the perfectly preserved 18th-century baroque theater, complete with original stage machinery and decorations; the second takes in another set of 12 rooms as well as the elegant, vaulted castle chapel. Each tour lasts just 50 minutes, but if you have time for only one, choose the first. Tours are in Czech, but an English transcript is provided. It's also possible to visit the castle cellars—home to a permanent exhibition of contemporary sculptures by Olbram Zoubek—for a wine tasting and to stroll around the pretty castle gardens. ⊠ Jiráskova 93 ☎ 461–615–067 ⊕ www.zamek-litomysl.cz ☞ Tours 150 Kč each ⊙ Closed Mon. and Oct.–Mar.

# Mělník

*40 km (23 miles) north of Prague.*

This pretty town, on the confluence of the Vltava and Elbe Rivers, is the closest place to Prague to go for homegrown Czech wine. Every autumn, usually in late September, the town celebrates what is likely the region's best Vinobraní, an autumn festival held when barrels of young, still fermenting wine, called *burčak,* are tapped. If you happen to come at this time, look for the rare red-wine version. Even outside of wine season, Mělník has plenty of reasons to visit, with a historic center featuring a hilltop château, a baroque church with bone-filled crypt, and a hidden underground network.

## GETTING HERE

The only direct route to Mělník is by bus. Nos. 349 and 369 depart from Ládví on Metro Line C (red) and take between 35 and 50 minutes. Tickets cost around 35 Kč and can be bought from the driver. You'll be dropped off at the bottom of the hill, and it's a short, signposted walk up to the town center with all the sights. If you're coming by car, take Highway 9 from Prague's northern tip, which heads all the way to Mělník. Park on the small streets just off the main square (head in the direction of the towers to find it).

In the summer, an all-day boat trip along the Vltava River is a lovely option. Check out Prague Steamboat Company's website for sailing times.

**BOAT TRAVEL Prague Steamboat Company.** ✉ *Rašínovo nábř., Staré Mesto* ☎ *734–761–003* ⊕ *www.praguesteamboats. com.*

## VISITOR INFORMATION

**CONTACTS Turistické informační centrum Mělník.** (*Tourist Information Center Mělník*) ✉ *Legionářů 51* ☎ *315–627–503* ⊕ *ticmelnik.cz.*

#  Sights

**Chrám sv. Petra a Pavla** (*Church of Sts. Peter and Paul*)
**RELIGIOUS SITE** | With origins dating back around 1,000 years, this is one of the oldest churches in Bohemia, with a dramatic Gothic interior. But it's what lies beneath, and what rises above, that's really of interest. Below the church is a crypt with an ossuary, containing the skeletal remains of 10,000 to 15,000 people. Like a smaller-scale version of Kostnice Sedlec in Kutná Hora (but without the tourist hordes), bones and skulls are arranged into various sculptures, including an anchor, a cross, and a heart to symbolize hope, faith, and love. The remains date from between the 13th and 18th centuries, and have been used by academics to learn about diseases in medieval Europe.

Above the church soars the 127-foot tower. Climb to the top, through rooms of exposed stone walls and wooden beams, past the three 15th-century bells and the intricate clock mechanism, and you'll emerge onto an open-air platform. From here, you can enjoy the best panorama in Mělník, with views of the town in one direction and vistas of the rivers, vineyards, and rolling hills in the other.

If you are visiting outside of summer, email to arrange access to the crypt and tower. ✉ *Na Vyhlídce* ☎ *731–518–750* ✉ *farnostmelnik@seznam.cz* ⊕ *www.farnostmelnik.cz* ✉ *Church free, ossuary 40 Kč, tower 50 Kč* ⊗ *Closed Mon. Closed Nov.–Mar. except by appointment.*

★ **Mělnické podzemí** (*Underground Mělník*)
**LOCAL INTEREST** | Under the historic center of Mělník lies a secret: a network of underground passages leading to a medieval well. Half-hour guided tours from the Tourist Information Center take you down into the tunnels, which were dug out of the sandstone rock in the 13th and 14th century and used as storage rooms,

The town of Mělník lies on a high ridge overlooking the junction of Bohemia's two greatest rivers, the Labe and the Vltava.

wine cellars, and shelters during times of war. After a short walk, you'll come to the beautiful and unique medieval well. At 184 feet deep and 15 feet wide, it's the largest well in the Czech Republic—yet from above ground in the main square, you wouldn't even know it exists. ✉ *Turistické informační centrum Mělník, Legionářů 51* ☎ *315–627–503* ⊕ *ticmelnik.cz* ✆ *Free*.

**Zámek Mělník** (*Mělník Château*)
**CASTLE/PALACE** | The town's castle may be petite but it hovers grandly over the confluence of the Labe (Elbe) and Vltava Rivers. On entering, the courtyard's three dominant architectural styles jump out at you, reflecting alterations to the castle over the years. On the north side, note the typical arcaded Renaissance balconies, decorated with *sgraffiti*. To the west, a Gothic touch is still easy to make out. The southern wing is clearly baroque (although also decorated with arcades).

Inside the castle, you can walk through 10 ornate rooms filled with paintings, furniture, and porcelain belonging to the old aristocratic Lobkowicz clan, as well as a vestry chapel. In particular, look out for the Big Hall, which is decorated with 17th-century European maps and *vedute* (views) of cities including London, Paris, and Madrid.

Day-tripping wine lovers can also tour the wine cellars under the castle and book a wine tasting. The town is known best for its special Ludmila wines made from these grapes. As the locals tell it, Emperor Charles IV was responsible for bringing wine production to the area. Having a good eye for favorable growing conditions, he encouraged vintners from Burgundy to come here and plant their vines.

The castle also has a good restaurant, looking out on the vineyards, river, and fields beyond, as well as a café and wine bar. ✉ *Svatováclavská 16* ☎ *315–622–127* ⊕ *www.lobkowicz-melnik.cz* ✆ *Castle 110 Kč, wine cellar tour 50 Kč, wine tasting from 140 Kč*.

## 🍴 Restaurants

### Němý Medvěd

**$$ | BURGER |** Although billing itself primarily as a microbrewery and beer bar, this lovely cellar restaurant also serves the city's best burgers. Choose your beer (there are usually eight options on tap: a mix of home brews and beers from other Czech breweries), then dive into the extensive burger menu, including delicious vegetarian and vegan options. **Known for:** atmospheric cellar with vaulted ceilings; great selection of Czech beers; monster 21-oz. "Grizzly Daddy Burger". $ *Average main: 250 Kč* ✉ *Nám. Míru 27* ☎ *773–898–122* ⊕ *www. nemymedved.cz.*

## 🛏 Hotels

### Pension Hana

**$ | B&B/INN |** Most of the better accommodation options in the town are on the outskirts, but this small home with a garden is a 10-minute walk from the center. **Pros:** tasty breakfast; cyclist friendly; public swimming pool nearby. **Cons:** a little basic for the refined visitor; Wi-Fi can be patchy; no toiletries supplied. $ *Rooms from: 1300 Kč* ✉ *Fügnerova 714* ☎ *603–512–485* ⊕ *www.penzion-melnik.cz* ⤴ *11 rooms* ⦿ *Free breakfast.*

# Terezín

*48 km (30 miles) northwest of Prague.*

Just the word "Terezín" (Theresienstadt in German) immediately recalls the horrors of the Jewish Holocaust for Czechs. Originally built as a military city in the 18th century, Nazis quickly saw its potential and removed the 7,000 original inhabitants to turn the city into a Jewish ghetto and the fortress into a prison. Terezín was the main Nazi concentration camp in Bohemia, but it wasn't designed as a death camp, even though in the end more than 38,000 people died in either the ghetto or the prison. The city was supposed to be a "model" Jewish settlement, part of a humane façade the Nazis presented to the Red Cross in 1944.

## GETTING HERE

There's no train service directly to Terezín. Several buses leave the Nádraží Holešovice station daily, and weekends offer a bit more choice. The trip lasts almost an hour and typically costs 105 Kč each way.

If you're driving, take the E55 north out of Prague (this is the main highway going to Dresden and Berlin) and head toward Lovosice. You can either take Exit 35 at Doksany and follow the country road straight to Terezín or continue to Lovosice, and from there turn right; the road leads directly into Terezín. There's a large parking lot next to the Malá Pevnost. The trip takes about 50 minutes. To visit Střekov, follow the road signs from Terezín to Litoměřice, then take Highway 261 to Ústí nad Labem.

## VISITOR INFORMATION

**CONTACTS Terezín Tourist Information.** ✉ *Nám. ČSA 179* ☎ *775–711–881* ⊕ *www.terezin.cz.*

## 👁 Sights

### Památník Terezín – Magdeburská kasárna (*Terezín Memorial – Magdeburg Barracks*)

**MUSEUM |** Under the Nazis, this unassuming building was primarily used for administration offices, but today it is a fascinating and important education facility. There's an excellent re-creation of how a former dormitory would have looked, plus exhibits detailing the arts in Terezín. Inspiring displays show how people in the ghetto continued to hold literary, musical, theatrical, and artistic happenings. ✉ *Tyrsova 204* ☎ *416–782–225* ⊕ *www.pamatnik-terezin.cz* 🎟 *180 Kč (incl. Ghetto Museum), combination ticket 220 Kč (also incl. Small Fortress).*

★ **Památník Terezín – Malá pevnost**
(*Terezín Memorial – Small Fortress*)
**MUSEUM** | The most powerful aspect of Terezín is that you don't need much imagination to visualize how it looked under Nazi rule. When it was a Jewish ghetto, more than 59,000 people were crammed into this camp. Terezín was actually an exception among the many Nazi concentration camps in Central Europe. The Germans, for a time, used it as a model city in order to deflect international criticism of Nazi policy toward the Jews. In the early years of the war—until as late as 1944—detainees had a semblance of a normal life, with limited self-rule, schools, a theater, and even a library. (Pictures drawn by the children at Terezín are on display in Prague's Jewish Museum.) As the Nazi war effort soured, the conditions for the people in Terezín worsened. Transports to Auschwitz and other death camps were increased to several times a week, and eventually 87,000 Jews were murdered in this way. Another 35,000 died from starvation or disease.

The enormity of Terezín's role in history is most starkly illustrated at this former military fortress. From 1940 to 1945, it functioned as a jail, mainly for political prisoners and others resisting the German occupation, holding them in abject conditions. Around 30,000 prisoners came through here during the war. A tour through the fortress is chilling; you'll first visit the administrative area, where new prisoners were brought, and then glimpse their cells, crudely furnished with stone floors and long wooden beds. Not much has been done to spruce up the place for visitors, leaving the original atmosphere intact. As a military prison, 150 people could be held in the cells; under the Nazis, it was typical to have 1,500 prisoners held in the same space. There was no gas chamber here, but the appalling hygienic conditions led to many deaths, and about 300 prisoners were

executed. Many of the juxtapositions are deeply cruel, such as the swimming pools for guards and their families, which prisoners would pass on their way to their execution.

Those who did not die in detention were shipped off to other concentration camps. Above the entrance to the main courtyard stands the horribly false motto "Arbeit macht Frei" (Work Brings Freedom). At the far end of the fortress, opposite the main entrance, is the special wing built by the Nazis when space became tight. These windowless cells display a brutal captivity.

✉ *Principova alej 304* ☎ *416–782–225* ⊕ *www.pamatnik-terezin.cz* 🖫 *180 Kč, combination ticket 220 Kč (incl. Ghetto Museum and Magdeburg Barracks)* ⊙ *Crematorium closed Sat.*

**Památník Terezín – Muzeum ghetta** (*Terezín Memorial – Ghetto Museum*)
**MUSEUM** | Told in words and pictures, the town's horrific story is depicted at the Museum of the Terezín Ghetto, just off the central park in town. A short documentary is also shown in many languages. Tell the staff that you speak English; they'll let you roam the building and flag you down when the next English-language video is being shown. ✉ *Komenského 148* ☎ *416–782–225* ⊕ *www.pamatnik-terezin.cz* 🖫 *180 Kč (incl. Magdeburg Barracks), combination ticket 220 Kč (also incl. Small Fortress).*

# 🍴 Restaurants

Terezín has very little in the way of services for visitors. There are a couple of depressing haunts, serving mostly inedible pub standards from menus run off on mimeograph machines. Duck out of town to nearby Litoměřice down the road about 2 km (1 mile). Buses run regularly from the main square, and it's barely a five-minute ride. After the heavy atmosphere of Terezín, it's refreshing to walk down the tree-lined main street between colorful buildings bustling with shops and people.

**Radniční Sklípek**
$$ | **CZECH** | This spot is a local favorite, and it's easy to see why. Here the setting, a Gothic cellar with arched ceilings, is as pleasant as the food. **Known for:** deliciously hearty Czech food; summer terrace on lovely city square; hosts occasional wine-tasting events. [$] *Average main: 225 Kč* ✉ *Mírové nám. 13, Litomerice* ☎ *731–422–013* 🌐 *www.radnicni-sklipek.cz.*

# Czech Switzerland

*110 km (68 miles) northwest of Prague.*

Czech Switzerland, also known as Bohemian Switzerland, is a picturesque region with towering sandstone cliffs, fairy-tale landscapes, quaint villages, and excellent hiking and biking opportunities, all just 90 minutes' drive from Prague. It lies on the Czech side of the Elbe Sandstone Mountains north of Děčín on both sides of the Elbe River. Confusingly, you are not in Switzerland; the name was inspired by the Swiss artists Adrian Zingg and Anton Graff, who were reminded of their homeland by the geography of northern Bohemia. While you cannot cross into Switzerland here, you may find yourself in Narnia—several scenes of *The Chronicles of Narnia: The Lion, the Witch and the Wardrobe* were filmed at the Pravčická Archway here.

### GETTING HERE

Czech Switzerland may seem like a bit of a hike from Prague, but it can be done in a day with some forward planning. Take the train to Děčín, which takes just more than 90 minutes (and costs just under 200 Kč), followed by the local bus to Hřensko, the nearest village, which takes another 35 minutes or so. The driver, or the tourists getting off, will let you know where the best stop is for the hike to Pravčická Archway. If you're driving, head north on the E55 to Ústí nad Labem, then switch to Route 62. There are plenty of paid parking lots in Hřensko.

## 👁 Sights

★ **Pravčická Brána** (*Pravčická Archway*)
**NATURE SITE** | The largest natural rock bridge in Europe, Pravčická Archway is the symbol of the gorgeous national park that is Czech Switzerland, which sits on the border with Germany. To reach the archway, you can either start walking from Hřensko (follow the red hiking route) or take a local bus to a stop called Tři Prameny. From here, it's a lovely and atmospheric walk up through the forest to reach the rock formation, which comes complete with a museum and restaurant called Falcon's Nest—supplies are brought in via pulley. This being the Czech Republic, there's also a pub where you can order fine beer in the shadow of the bridge itself. For an entrance fee of 75 Kč, you can scramble around nearby rock formations, which have a similarly alien appeal, for a better vantage point.

A series of gentle, well-marked hikes on pretty forest trails and mossy gorges will take you on a circular route back, ending up in Hřensko. The highlight of these trails is being punted along the river—when the paths run out—in a precarious boat with a ferryman who tells you (in German and Czech and hand gestures) how the rocks over your head look like different animals and monsters. Each boat trip costs around 50 Kč.

✉ *Hrensko* ☎ *412–554–286 for local tourist information* 🌐 *www.pbrana.cz* 🕒 *Closed weekdays Nov.–Mar.*

# Chapter 12

# SOUTHERN BOHEMIA

Updated by
Raymond Johnston

| ⊙ Sights | 🍴 Restaurants | 🛏 Hotels | 🛍 Shopping | 🍸 Nightlife |
|----------|--------------|----------|------------|-------------|
| ★★★★★ | ★★★☆☆ | ★★★★☆ | ★★☆☆☆ | ★★☆☆☆ |

# WELCOME TO SOUTHERN BOHEMIA

## TOP REASONS TO GO

★ **Sense the enchantment:** Feel like a storybook character strolling through Český Krumlov.

★ **Loop around the streets:** Get lost among the tiny streets of Tábor.

★ **Take the bike lane to lunch:** Bike around and eat the fresh carp caught from the fishponds of Třeboň.

★ **Go for baroque:** Experience rustic baroque with a visit to the 19th-century living-museum village of Holašovice.

★ **Sip the suds:** Drink the local brew in České Budějovice, Český Krumlov, or Třeboň.

Southern Bohemia is one of the most popular regions in the Czech Republic. Chock-full of castles and pretty cities with well-preserved squares, it's a favorite weekend getaway for many Prague locals. Well-marked hiking and biking trails encourage lots of sporty times, and it's easy for visitors to take part, since even some of the train stations rent bicycles. The towns themselves are active, too, and many hold a variety of festivals throughout the year.

Being so close to Prague, several of these cities can be done in a day-trip; but to get a true flavor of the town and its inhabitants, it's worth your time to stay over or spend a couple of days jumping between a few of the outer areas. The attractiveness of the landscape combined with cultural pursuits makes Southern Bohemia an amazing place to explore.

**1 Český Krumlov.** A fanciful city with a stunning castle and gardens: Český Krumlov is *the* must-see in Southern Bohemia.

**2 Tábor.** With streets designed to thwart invading armies, Tábor will lose you in its beauty and friendliness.

**3 Písek.** Strung along the river, the city with the oldest Gothic bridge in the country is also home to some great museums.

**4 Třeboň.** The spas of Southern Bohemia can be found in Třeboň. Peat-moss bath, anyone?

**5 Jindřichův Hradec.**
Authentic and attractive, Jindřichův Hradec is the perfect example of a true Southern Bohemian town: interesting castle, beautiful architecture, and real people.

**6 Hluboká nad Vltavou.**
A castle to die for. The fairy-tale hulk of turreted white can be seen for miles around.

**7 České Budějovice.**
Southern Bohemia's largest city, with a beautiful medieval square and lots of outdoor activities.

Southern Bohemia calls itself the "pearl of the Czech Republic," and it's not just a clever nickname. The richness and beauty of this corner of the country bordering Germany and Austria are undisputable.

The natural landscape is lovely—soft rolling hills crisscrossed with rivers and dotted with ponds mark most of the territory—and the Šumava Mountains to the southwest are a popular ski destination. Coming from Prague, you'll cross the border somewhere north of Tábor; heading east, the indiscernible crossing to Moravia comes near to Telč. Forestry and fishing make up most of the area's important industry, with tourism and beer brewing more fun runners-up.

The history of the cities is intertwined with many an aristocratic name. The Habsburgs, Rosenbergs, and Schwarzenbergs all had a large influence on the region, and their nobility is reflected in the area's many castles and beautifully preserved historic squares. The 15th century saw the territory wrapped up in the religious wars sparked by Jan Hus, whose reformist ways angered the Catholic Church and eventually led to his martyrdom. Evidence of the Hussite Wars in the mid-1400s is visible in Tábor.

Český Krumlov is the one must-see destination and often the only stop for visitors, which means huge crowds on summer weekends. The castle here rivals any monument in Prague.

# Planning

## When to Go

Southern Bohemia is a nature lover's paradise, and in nice weather it seems that the whole country heads here for cycling and hiking trips. Most of the main attractions are closed November through March, as well as Monday year-round, so winter is quiet but no less lovely in its snowy way. Many towns host weekend Christmas markets, so December is a particularly pretty time. Note: roads get congested with weekenders on Friday and Sunday.

## Getting Here

Trains from Prague normally depart from the Hlavní nádraží main station, while buses leave from either the main Florenc station or the southern Roztyly station, accessible from a Metro stop on Line C (red). When exploring your transport options, look into private bus lines like RegioJet (formerly called Student Agency, but its services are not just for students). It offers more direct routes, plus free hot drinks and videos on board. Tickets must be purchased ahead of time; the company has a window at the Florenc station.

# Guided Tours to Southern Bohemia

Guided bus tours are available from several companies covering several of the destinations in Southern Bohemia. Most need to be booked at least a day in advance. These are only two of many organizers.

### Čedok

The country's original tour operator offers a variety of longer trips through the region. Experiences include Český Krumlov, a spa visit in Třeboň, and combinations of other cities and even regions. ⊕ www.cedok.com.

### Martin Tours

Information can be found at the company's booths at Staroměstské náměstí (Old Town Square) and Republiky náměstí. It offers a bus tour to Český Krumlov. ⊕ www.martintour.cz.

# Restaurants and Hotels

Outside of Prague, prices for food and hotels are lower, but service—especially in functional English—sometimes lags behind. With Austria so close, you are much more likely to find German-language menus in restaurants and German-speaking staff in both restaurants and hotels.

*Restaurant and hotel reviews have been shortened. For full information, visit Fodors.com.*

## What It Costs in Koruny

| | $ | $$ | $$$ | $$$$ |
|---|---|---|---|---|
| **RESTAURANTS** | | | | |
| | under 150 Kč | 150 Kč–350 Kč | 351 Kč–500 Kč | over 500 Kč |
| **HOTELS** | | | | |
| | under 2,200 Kč | 2,200 Kč–4,000 Kč | 4,001 Kč–6,500 Kč | over 6,500 Kč |

# Český Krumlov

*48 km (29 miles) southwest of Třeboň; 186 km (112 miles) south of Prague.*

It's rare that a place not only lives up to its hype but exceeds it. Český Krumlov, the official residence of the Rožmberk (Rosenberg) family for some 300 years, is such a place. It's the only must-see in Southern Bohemia, with a storybook landscape so perfect it resembles a movie set. Hordes of other tourists pass through, but if you stay overnight you can experience the city after the tour buses have departed, and in the evening when quiet descends, the town is twice as spellbinding.

Český Krumlov's lovely looks can be put down to a castle and a river. Hrad Český Krumlov (Český Krumlov Castle) is one of the most gorgeous in the country, perched on a hill and watching over its quaint village with the Vltava River doing its picturesque winding best. The castle area offers plenty of sightseeing, and the extensive gardens are worth an hour or two. Down in the town, the medieval streets are beyond charming.

As in the rest of Southern Bohemia, outdoor activities are plentiful here. Check with the local tourist information office about places to rent bikes or rafts, or pick up an area hiking map.

## GETTING HERE

A direct bus to Český Krumlov leaves Prague from both the Florenc and the Na Knížecí stations. The trip lasts a hair under three hours, and costs 171 Kč. There's no direct train; with a change at České Budějovice, a train trip clocks in at usually more than three hours and costs around 169 Kč. Note that the train station is a 20-minute hike from the main square, while the bus station is much closer. Your best choice would be to purchase a bus ticket at least a day or two before travel; Český Krumlov is a popular destination.

Car travel from Prague is fairly straightforward and takes three hours. Simply follow the directions to České Budějovice, and once there follow the signs to Český Krumlov. When you arrive in Český Krumlov you'll be confronted by a confusing array of public parking areas, with no indication of how close the parking lot is to the Old Town. One safe bet is to use Parking Lot No. 2, which, if you follow the tiny lanes as far as they go, will bring you to just behind the town brewery and an easy 10-minute walk from the main square.

## TIMING

Wintertime can be lonely in Český Krumlov, and most of the sites are closed, including the castle. On the flip side, avoid weekends in the summer; hordes of tourists, both Czech and German, flood the streets. Also, midday when the tour buses arrive can be a bit overwhelming. The city holds a Renaissance festival called the Five-Petaled Rose Celebration every June; an Early Music Festival and an International Music Festival in July; an Autumn Fair at the end of September; and a number of holiday events in December.

## VISITOR INFORMATION

Český Krumlov's tourist information office is on the main square. Well versed and extremely helpful, the staff can assist you in everything from what to see to where to go. They can recommend restaurants and hotels as well as book tickets and assist with bus and train schedules, or even boat and bike travel.

The Vltava travel agency is a solid bet if you're considering outdoor activities. It will rent boats and bikes as well as arrange excursions.

A discount pass called **Český Krumlov Card** is available at information centers and offers reduced admission to several attractions.

**INFORMATION Infocentrum Český Krumlov.** ✉ *Nám. Svornosti 2* ☎ *380–704–622* ⊕ *www.ckrumlov.cz.* **Vltava.** ✉ *Hradební 60* ☎ *380–711–988* ⊕ *www.ckvltava.cz.*

 # Sights

### Egon Schiele Center

**MUSEUM** | A large and rambling former brewery now showcases the work of Austrian painter Egon Schiele, along with other modern and contemporary Czech and European artists. The Renaissance building, built in three phases in the early 1600s, is a wonder, with soaring ceilings in some places and wooden-beamed rooms in others. Schiele often painted landscapes of Český Krumlov from the castle's bridge. The museum does close unexpectedly on occasion in winter but is one of the only sites in town normally open year-round. ✉ *Široká 71* ☎ *380–704–011* ⊕ *www.schieleartcentrum.cz* 🎫 *200 Kč; discount with Český Krumlov Card* ☉ *Closed Mon.*

### ★ Hrad Český Krumlov (*Český Krumlov Castle*)

**CASTLE/PALACE | FAMILY** | Like any good protective fortress, the castle is visible from a distance, but you may wonder how to get there. From the main square, take Radniční ulice across the river and head up the staircase on your left from Latrán ulice. (Alternatively, you can continue on Latrán and enter via the main gateway, also on your left.)

You'll first come across the oldest part of the castle, a round 13th-century **tower** renovated in the 16th century to look something like a minaret, with its delicately arcaded Renaissance balcony. Part of the old border fortifications, the tower guarded Bohemian frontiers from the threat of Austrian incursion. It's now repainted with an educated guess of its Renaissance appearance, since the original designs have long been lost. From dungeon to bells, its inner secrets can be seen climbing the interior staircase. Go ahead and climb to the top; you'll be rewarded with a view of the castle grounds and across the countryside.

Next up is the moat, fearlessly protected by a pair of brown bears—truthfully not really much help in defending the castle; their moods range from playful to lethargic. But bears have been residents of this moat since 1707. In season, the castle rooms are open to the public. Crossing the bridge, you enter the second courtyard, which contains the ticket office. The Route 1 tour will parade you past the castle chapel, baroque suite, and Renaissance rooms. The highlights here are the 18th-century frescoes in the delightful **Maškarní sál** (Masquerade Hall). Route 2 takes you through the portrait gallery and the seigneurial apartments of the Schwarzenbergs, who owned the castle until the Gestapo seized it in 1940. (The castle became state property in 1947.) In summer you can visit the Lapidarium, which includes statues removed from the castle for protection, and the dungeon.

A succession of owners all had the same thing in mind: upgrade the castle a bit more opulently than before. Vilém von Rožmberk oversaw a major refurbishment of the castle, adding buildings, heightening the tower, and adding rich decorations—generally making the place suitable for one of the grandest Bohemians of the day. The castle passed out of the Rožmberks' hands, however, when

Vilém's brother and last of the line, the dissolute Petr Vok, sold both castle and town to Emperor Rudolf II in 1602 to pay off his debts. Under the succeeding Eggenbergs and Schwarzenbergs the castle continued to be transformed into an opulent palace. The Eggenbergs' prime addition was a **theater,** which was begun in the 1680s and completed in 1766 by Josef Adam of Schwarzenberg. Much of the theater and its accoutrements—sets, props, costumes, stage machinery—survive intact as a rare working display of period stagecraft. Theater buffs will appreciate a tour, and tickets should be reserved in advance.

Continuing along outside, the third courtyard bears some beautiful Renaissance frescoes, while the fourth contains the Upper Castle, whose rooms can be visited on the tours. From here you'll arrive at a wonderfully romantic elevated passageway with spectacular views of the huddled houses of the Old Town. The Austrian expressionist painter Egon Schiele often stayed in Český Krumlov in the early 1900s and liked to paint this particular view over the river; he titled his Krumlov series *Dead City*. The middle level here is the **most Na plášti** (Cloaked Bridge), a massive construction spanning a deep ravine. Below the passageway are three levels of high arches, looking like a particularly elaborate Roman viaduct. At the end of the passageway you come to the theater, then to the nicely appointed **castle garden** dating from the 17th century. A cascade fountain, groomed walking paths, flower beds, and manicured lawns are a restful delight. The famed open-air **Revolving Theater** is here, as is the **Musical Pavilion**. If you continue walking away from the castle, the park grows a bit wilder and quieter. Unlike the castle, the courtyards and passageways are open to the public year-round. ■TIP➔ If visiting between October and April, check the website for detailed opening hours, as these vary for different parts of the castle and for different tours. ✉ Zámek 59

**12**

**Southern Bohemia** ČESKÝ KRUMLOV

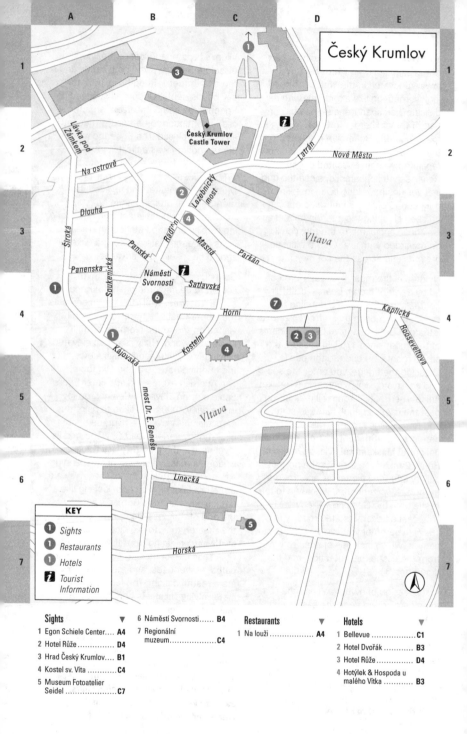

# Český Krumlov

## Sights ▼

1 Egon Schiele Center.... **A4**

2 Hotel Růže .............. **D4**

3 Hrad Český Krumlov.... **B1**

4 Kostel sv. Víta ............ **C4**

5 Museum Fotoatelier
  Seidel .................... **C7**

6 Náměstí Svornosti...... **B4**

7 Regionální
  muzeum.................. **C4**

## Restaurants ▼

1 Na louži ................. **A4**

## Hotels ▼

1 Bellevue ................. **C1**

2 Hotel Dvořák ............ **B3**

3 Hotel Růže .............. **D4**

4 Hotýlek & Hospoda u
  malého Vítka ............ **B3**

### KEY

- **①** Sights
- **①** Restaurants
- **①** Hotels
- **ℹ** Tourist Information

☎ *380–704–721* 🌐 *www.castle.ckrumlov.cz* 🎫 *Castle tours (in English) from 230 Kč, theater tour (in English) 380 Kč, castle museum and tower 150 Kč (discount only on museum and tower with Český Krumlov Card), garden free* 🕓 *Garden closed and no tours Nov.–Mar.*

**Hotel Růže**

**HOTEL—SIGHT** | Gorgeous *sgraffiti* façades decorate this former Jesuit school, now the Hotel Růže. Abundant Renaissance flourishes point to the fact that the city used to be on the Bavarian-Italian trade route. Be sure to visit the parking area (really!); the view is perfect. ✉ *Horní 154* 🌐 *www.hotelruze.cz.*

**Kostel sv. Víta** (*Church of St. Vitus*)

**RELIGIOUS SITE** | This neo-Gothic church with its octagonal tower provides a nice contrast with the castle's older tower across the river. Step inside to see the elaborate baptismal font and frescoes. Much reconstruction took place in the 17th and 18th centuries but some earlier features remain; the Gothic entrance portal dates to 1410. ✉ *Kostelní ul.* 🌐 *www.farnostck.bcb.cz.*

**Museum Fotoatelier Seidel** (*Seidel Photographic Studio Museum*)

**MUSEUM** | Head across the other side of the river from the castle and explore a more lived-in side of the city. This refurbished home used to belong to photographer Josef Seidel and is now a museum dedicated to his work and the history of photography. The exhibit is a fascinating mix of home and workplace, with period furnishings plus a photographic studio. The building itself is lovely and includes a picturesque garden, and photography lovers will enjoy the historic camera collection plus samples of Seidel's work. ✉ *Linecká 272* ☎ *380–712–354* 🌐 *www.seidel.cz* 🎫 *120 Kč; discount with Český Krumlov Card* 🕓 *Closed Mon. Oct.–Mar.*

**Náměstí Svornosti** (*Unity Square*)

**PLAZA** | A little oddly shaped, yes, but a "square" nonetheless; Náměstí Svornosti should be home base for your explorations. Pick a street and head off into the tiny alleys that fan out in all directions. There's no real sense in "planning" your route, simply choose a direction and go—you'll end up where you started eventually. Each turn seems to bring a new charming vista, and cute buildings and shops will amuse and keep shutterbugs busy. Don't forget to look up in the direction of the castle every once in a while; it pokes through in some amazing places. The actual square has a couple of notable buildings, including the town hall with its Renaissance friezes and Gothic arcades. ✉ *Ceský Krumlov.*

**Regionální muzeum** (*Regional Museum*)

**MUSEUM** | From the main square, a street called Horní ulice leads off toward the regional museum. A quick visit gets you acquainted with the history of the region from prehistoric times. A ceramic model of the city is one of the highlights. ✉ *Horní 152* ☎ *380–711–674* 🌐 *www.ckrumlov.info/docs/en/atr2.xml* 🎫 *60 Kč; discount with Český Krumlov Card.*

## 🍴 Restaurants

**★ Na louži**

**$$** | **CZECH** | Czech comfort food is served up every day and every night at Na louži. Lovingly preserved wood furniture and paneling lend a traditional touch to this warm, inviting, family-run pub. **Known for:** hearty traditional food; lovely wood-paneled interior; occasionally brusque service. $ *Average main: 300 Kč* ✉ *Kájovská 66* ☎ *380–711–280* 🌐 *www.nalouzi.cz* 💳 *No credit cards.*

## 🛏 Hotels

It seems you can't walk two blocks in Český Krumlov without stumbling over a pension or place offering private rooms. Even with this plethora, you'll need to book ahead May through September, when it's high season. Prices can be on a level with some Prague hotels and

# Spooky Side Trip

About 20 km (12 miles) south of Český Krumlov, the sprawling Hrad Rožmberk (Rosenberg Castle) overlooks the Vltava River. Inside, on the main tour, you'll see a mix of Romantic and Renaissance interiors; portraits of crusaders; and the Rosenberg Hall, dedicated to the family's history. The second route shows the apartments of aristocrats. The English Tower is a 200-step climb and rewards with beautiful vistas of the countryside. English-language tours on Routes 1 and 2 are available for groups only. The basement has a Museum of Capital Justice, but the information is only in Czech. Buses run from Český Krumlov's main depot but are infrequent on weekends. Legend has it that the ghost of a White Lady appears from time to time. ⊕ *www.hrad-rozmberk.cz/en*

definitely more expensive than in neighboring cities.

### Bellevue

**$$** | **HOTEL** | The façade of a 16th-century bakery gives way to a modern hotel with all the standard accessories. **Pros:** close to the castle; sauna and massage service; good restaurant and wine cellar. **Cons:** small breakfast room; rooms a bit cramped; no air conditioning since it is a historical building. ⓢ *Rooms from: 2995 Kč* ✉ *Latrán 77* ☎ *380–720–177* ⊕ *www. bellevuehotelkrumlov.cz* ⇱ *65 rooms* ⍥ *Free breakfast.*

### Hotel Dvořák

**$$$** | **HOTEL** | Wonderful views of the castle and river are the main selling points of this centrally located and quaint hotel. **Pros:** nice views; smack-dab-central location; large rooms. **Cons:** old-fashioned interior design; elevator does not reach fifth floor; noise from street performers. ⓢ *Rooms from: 4085 Kč* ✉ *Radniční 101* ☎ *380–711–020* ⊕ *www.hoteldvorak. com* ⇱ *22 rooms, 4 apartments* ⍥ *Free breakfast.*

### ★ Hotel Růže

**$$$** | **HOTEL** | Converted from a Jesuit school, this excellent centrally located hotel with spacious rooms is a two-minute walk from the main square. **Pros:** central location; magnificent castle views; quality restaurant. **Cons:** inconsistent bed layouts; baroque decorations are a bit overdone; service doesn't always come with a smile. ⓢ *Rooms from: 4823 Kč* ✉ *Horní 154* ☎ *380–772–100* ⊕ *www.hotelruze.cz* ⇱ *71 rooms* ⍥ *Free breakfast.*

### Hotýlek & Hospoda u malého Vítka

**$** | **HOTEL** | Rooms are cleverly named after Czech fairy tales, with simple wooden furniture and fittings, and the folklore spirit extends throughout this hotel located between the main square and the castle. **Pros:** whimsical spirit; great value for the money; great location and views. **Cons:** limited in-room amenities; rooms are simple and pared down; cramped bathrooms. ⓢ *Rooms from: 2005 Kč* ✉ *Radniční 27* ☎ *380–711–925* ⊕ *www.vitekhotel.cz* ⇱ *20 rooms* ⍥ *Free breakfast.*

## 🍸 Nightlife

### Cikánská jizba

**BARS/PUBS** | If you're in town on a Friday night, head over to this tiny Romany-owned pub; the name translates to Gypsy Tavern. Romany musicians play, and Czechs pack the place for locally made cold beer. It can get very crowded, but there are no reservations. ✉ *Dlouhá*

*31* ☎ *380–717–585* ⊕ *www.cikanskajizba. cz.*

##  Performing Arts

Český Krumlov is a hotbed of cultural activity in summer. Events range from Renaissance fairs to music festivals. Activities to note include the International Music Festival held at the castle in July and August and summer performances at the open-air Revolving Theater. Opera and theater companies from České Budějovice perform here. Tickets can be prebooked (almost a necessity) by visiting ⊕ *www.otacivehlediste.cz* or check with the tourist information offices in either Český Krumlov or České Budějovice. The website also has information on an app called Overtekst that allows people to follow a translation of the show's dialogue on a phone or tablet that runs an Android OS. The Český Krumlov office can also tell you about any other concerts or events happening while you are in town.

# Tábor

*90 km (54 miles) south of Prague.*

Looking at Tábor now, it's hard to believe that this was once a counterculture utopia and fortress. Lucky for visitors a few centuries later, the town has retained all this turbulent history in its design and buildings.

In the 15th century the town began as an encampment for religious reformers centered on the teachings of the anti-Catholic firebrand preacher Jan Hus. After Hus was burned at the stake in Constance, his followers came here by the thousands to build a society opposed to the excesses of Rome and modeled on the primitive communities of the early Christians. Tábor quickly evolved into the Hussites' symbolic and spiritual center and, along with Prague, served as the bulwark of the religious reform movement.

The 1420s in Tábor were heady days for the reformers. Private property was denounced, and the many poor who made the pilgrimage to Tábor were required to leave their possessions at the town gates. Some sects rejected the doctrine of transubstantiation (the belief that the Eucharistic elements become the body and blood of Christ), turning Holy Communion into a bawdy, secular feast of bread and wine. Other reformers considered themselves superior to Christ—who by dying had shown himself to be merely mortal.

War fever in Tábor ran high, and the town became one of the focal points of the Hussite Wars (1419–34), which pitted reformers against an array of foreign crusaders, Catholics, and noblemen. Military general Jan Žižka led the charge fairly successfully, but the Church proved to be stronger and wealthier. Many of the reformists' victories were assisted by the strategic location of Tábor, which with its hilltop position and river boundary made it virtually impregnable. And what nature didn't provide, the residents did. The town was well fortified and there was an ingenious system of underground tunnels (whether they were used to hide in or to store food in is disputed). The streets were purposely laid out in a crooked and confusing manner to thwart invaders. Glimpses of this past can still be seen and make Tábor one of the more interesting places to visit.

### GETTING HERE
Direct buses and trains to Tábor are available, and both take about 1½ hours. Buses from Prague leave from the Florenc station and cost about 88 Kč; trains cost about 119 Kč and depart from Hlavní nádraží station. By car, the distance is about 90 km (56 miles) and should take a little more than an hour. You'll take the E55 heading south toward České Budějovice.

### TIMING

Tábor is rarely overrun with tourists, which makes it a relaxing place to see. It's a popular spot with cyclists, and summers always bring a few more people. The South Bohemian Music Festival is held each July. There's also a Christmas market in December. The big event is the Tábor Meeting Days, held at the beginning of September. This fun medieval festival is incredibly popular. Crafts, music, entertainers, and food all pack into the main square; there's even a parade.

### VISITOR INFORMATION

**CONTACTS Tábor Tourist Information.** ✉ *Žižkovo nám. 2* ☎ *381–486–230* 🌐 *www.visittabor.eu.*

## Sights

**Hrad Kotnov** (*Kotnov Castle*)
**CASTLE/PALACE** | Rising above the river in the distance, this castle dates to the 13th century and was part of Tábor's earliest fortifications. After a fire in the early 1600s the castle was rebuilt as a brewery. You can visit the tower, which the Hussites used for storing artillery, as well as Bechyňská brána (Bechyně Gate). This is the last city gate still standing and has been preserved in its original High Gothic style. Inside is a new permanent exhibition of the history of Tábor opened in early 2020. ✉ *Klokotská* ☎ *381–252–242* 🌐 *www.husitskemuzeum.cz* 🎫 *Tower and gate 30 Kč* 🕒 *Closed Oct.–Apr.*

**Husitské muzeum** (*Hussite Museum*)
**MUSEUM** | You can find out all you ever wanted to know about the Hussite movement and the founding and history of the city. The museum is housed in the Old Town Hall, a building that dates back to the early 1500s. You can also enter the extensive labyrinth of tunnels below the Old Town here. A tour of the tunnels takes about 20 minutes. The Gothic Hall was renovated in 2018–20. ✉ *Žižkovo nám. 1* ☎ *381–252–242* 🌐 *www.husitskemuzeum.cz* 🎫 *Museum tour 70 Kč, tunnel tour 60 Kč, combined tour 100 Kč* 🕒 *Closed Sun.–Tues. Oct.–May.*

**Pražská ulice**
**NEIGHBORHOOD** | The main route to the newer part of town, this street is delightfully lined with beautiful Renaissance façades. If you turn right at Divadelní and head to the Lužnice River, you can see the remaining walls and fortifications of the 15th century, evidence of the town's function as a vital stronghold. ✉ *Tábor.*

**Žižkovo náměstí** (*Žižka Square*)
**PLAZA** | There's no doubt who this square belongs to—a bronze statue of Jan Žižka dominates the area and clearly points to its Hussite past. The stone tables in front of the Gothic town hall and the house at No. 6 date to the 15th century, used by the Hussites to give daily communion to the faithful. Many fine houses that line the square bear plaques describing their architectural style and original purpose. Be sure to stroll the tiny streets around the square, as they curve around, branch off, and then stop; few lead back to the main square. This bemusing layout, created in the 15th century, was designed to thwart incoming invaders. ✉ *Tábor.*

## Restaurants

**Havana**
**$$ | AMERICAN** | Right on the square, this café-bar has a superb atmosphere, if oddly resembling an English pub, and serves up tasty plates of steaks, grilled meat, burgers, and chicken. **Known for:** outdoor seating; set on historic town square; good burgers and beers. [$] *Average main: 200 Kč* ✉ *Žižkovo nám. 17* ☎ *381–253–383* 🌐 *www.kafehavana.cz.*

## Hotels

**Dvořák**
**$ | HOTEL** | A bit outside the city center, this former brewery building has been thoroughly renovated into one of the

nicest places in town. **Pros:** modern rooms; free parking; on-site beer spa. **Cons:** can be busy during conferences; weak Wi-Fi at times; swimming pool very small. $ *Rooms from: 2130 Kč* ✉ *Hradební 3037* ☎ *381–212–221* ⊕ *www.lhdvoraktabor.cz* ⇥ *84 rooms* ¶⊚¶ *Free breakfast.*

### ★ Nautilus

**$$ | HOTEL |** This tasteful boutique hotel on the edge of Tábor's charming central square exhibits touches of Bohemian craftsmanship in the architecture, beautiful antiques in the rooms, and elegant, original art on the walls (think shells). **Pros:** great eats; best address in town; rooms with genuine Bohemian flair. **Cons:** some rooms are a little dark; breakfast spread not as great as the food at the restaurant; paid parking is separate from hotel. $ *Rooms from: 2729 Kč* ✉ *Žižkovo nám. 20* ☎ *380–900–900* ⊕ *www.hotelnautilus.cz* ⇥ *22 rooms* ¶⊚¶ *Free breakfast.*

# Písek

*44 km (28 miles) west of Tábor; 103 km (62 miles) south of Prague.*

Písek is a bit of a surprise. It used to be that people came for one thing: Písek's 700-year-old Gothic bridge peopled with baroque statues. But an infusion of European Union funds has introduced some beautiful upgrades. The former mill and power station is now a museum dedicated to electricity, and a former malt house is a cultural house and art museum. There's a promenade that runs along the river beside the old city wall, and the square around the church is nothing short of lovely. They've changed the former Gothic moat into a tiny park, and even the city museum displays some interesting finds.

## GETTING HERE

Buses leave from Prague's Na Knížecí station and will take you there for around 119 Kč in approximately 90 minutes. Trains leave from Prague's Hlavní nádraží and cost 119 Kč, with the trip taking more than 2½ hours. If you drive, the trip should take no more than 90 minutes.

## TIMING

Písek means "sand," and back before the city was a city, people used to pan for gold in the river. From mid-May to the beginning of June the city displays sand sculptures honoring its namesake. There's a town festival every June and a folklore festival at the end of August.

## VISITOR INFORMATION

**CONTACTS Písek Tourist Information.** ✉ *Velké nám. 113* ☎ *387–999–999* ⊕ *www.pisek.eu.*

 **Sights**

### Gothic Bridge

**BRIDGE/TUNNEL |** Once the city's only claim to fame, this bridge is a site to see. It was built in the 1260s—making it the oldest bridge in the Czech Republic, surpassing Prague's Charles Bridge by 90 years. Not too shabby. Přemysl Otakar II commissioned it, seeking a secure crossing for his salt shipments over the difficult-to-ford Otava River. As early as the 9th century, Písek stood at the center of one of the most important trade routes to the west, linking Prague to Passau and the rest of Bavaria. In the 15th century it became one of five major Hussite strongholds. The statues of saints weren't added to the bridge until the 18th century. During the devastating floods of 2002 one of the statues was damaged, and all the paving stones washed away, but divers recovered most of the lost pieces. The statues on the bridge are not the originals. You can reach the bridge from třída Národní svobody on the left bank or Karlova ulice from the right bank. ✉ *Karlova ul.*

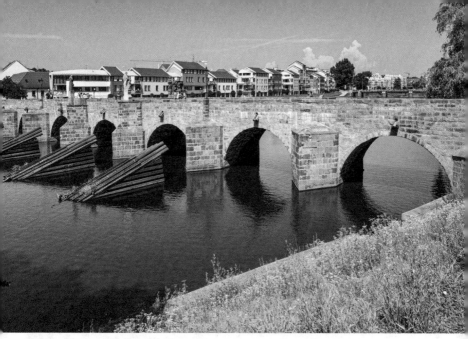

Písek's stone bridge crosses the Otava River and was built before the end of the 13th century.

**Mariánský chrám** (*Church of the Virgin*)
**RELIGIOUS SITE** | Just off the main square, this church is the highlight of the recently renovated Bakaláře náměstí. You can't miss the 240-foot tower, which is open for a climb. Construction began in the late 1200s, about the time the bridge was built. The lone surviving tower was completed in 1487. On the inside, look for the *Madonna of Písek*, a 14th-century Gothic altar painting. On a middle pillar is a rare series of early-Gothic wall paintings dating from the end of the 13th century. ■ **TIP→ Ask about a tower visit at the Písek Tourist Information Center.** ⊠ *Bakaláře at Leoše Janáčka* ⊕ *www.farnostpisek.cz* ✉ *Free.*

**Prácheňské muzeum**
**MUSEUM** | Inside a 13th-century castle's frescoed medieval halls, this museum documents the history of Písek and its surroundings, including the Czech fishing industry (with the additional original touch of live fish in a large aquarium) and the history of local gold panning and mining in the nearby hills. There are two galleries devoted to temporary exhibits. Everything is in Czech, but ask for an info sheet in English. ⊠ *Velké nám. 114* ☎ *382–201–111* ⊕ *www.prachenskemuzeum.cz* ✉ *40 Kč, photography fee 20 Kč* ⊗ *Closed Mon. and Jan. and Feb.*

**Sladovna**
**MUSEUM | FAMILY** | Písek has a brewing history dating back to the Middle Ages. This malt house was built in the 19th century and continued producing malt for 100 years. In 2008 the city opened Sladovna, a cultural facility that houses two permanent exhibitions and five showrooms for temporary ones. There's a spot for inspired kids to color, a reading area, plus an igloo that shows fairy tales. It's all in Czech, but children should appreciate the bright colors and great graphics. ⊠ *Velké nám. 113* ☎ *387–999–999* ⊕ *www.sladovna.cz* ✉ *140 Kč* ⊗ *Closed Mon.*

##  Hotels

### Hotel Biograf

$ | **HOTEL** | A design-conscious hotel with an award-winning restaurant is a rare find in Písek. **Pros:** large rooms; good location; all amenities. **Cons:** exterior low on charm; not a lot in the area to keep you overnight; near church bells that ring in the night. $ *Rooms from: 1800 Kč* ✉ *Gregorova 124* ☎ *380–425–510* ⊕ *www.hotelbiograf.com* ☐ *47 rooms* 🍽 *Free breakfast.*

# Třeboň

*48 km (28 miles) south of Tábor; 138 km (83 miles) south of Prague.*

Třeboň, like Tábor, is off the international tourist trail, but it's a favorite with cyclists. And the town offers an appealing mix of adorable old buildings and authentic workaday local life.

Třeboň itself is a charming jewel box of a town. It was settled during the 12th century by the Wittkowitzes (later called the Rožmberks, or Rosenbergs), once Bohemia's noblest family. You can see their emblem, a five-petal rose, on castles, doorways, and coats of arms all over the region. Their official residence was 40 km (25 miles) to the southwest, in Český Krumlov, but Třeboň was an important second residence and repository of the family archives, which still reside in the town's château. The main square, Masarykovo náměstí, is a pleasing arrangement of baroque and Renaissance structures. Various markets pop up here all through the summer, and the Town Hall has notable frescoes.

To Czechs, Třeboň and carp are almost synonymous. If you're in the area in late autumn, you may be lucky enough to witness the great carp harvests, when tens of thousands of the glittering fish are netted from ponds in the surrounding area. Traditionally, they are served breaded and

## Authentically Ancient

In a country overrun with castles, Zvíkov lays claim to being the most famous early Gothic one. Everyone needs its marketing hook, but Zvíkov is interesting enough thanks to its location on two rivers and its authenticity. Unlike many other castles in Bohemia, this one survived the 18th and 19th centuries without renovation and still looks exactly as it did 500 years ago. If you have the time, you can cycle here from Písek or jump on a boat and float downriver to another nearby castle, Orlík. ⊕ *www.hrad-zvikov.cz/en*

fried as the centerpiece of Christmas Eve dinner. But regardless of the season, you'll find carp on every menu in town. Don't be afraid to order it; the carp here are not the notorious bottom-feeders they are elsewhere but are raised in clean ponds and served as a fresh catch with none of that muddy aftertaste.

One of the most pleasant activities here is a walk around the **Rybník Svět** (World Pond), an easy 12-km (7½-mile) trail that takes you through grassy fields and forests. When taking the walk (or as a destination itself), visit the Schwarzenberg Family Vault. Built in English Gothic style; it's a bit startling at first but then seems to blend into its woody environs. If you'd rather not walk, 45-minute boat tours go around the lake about once an hour (in season and weather permitting). There's a variety of other walks and lots of cycle paths in the region; ask at the tourist information office for recommended routes and maps.

## GETTING HERE

Direct bus service to Třeboň is infrequent but costs around 130 Kč and departs from the Roztyly Metro stop in Prague. Trains depart from the main station, and a change is required in Veselí; trains cost around 190 Kč. Be sure to ask to go to the Třeboň lázné station and not the main Třeboň station, and save yourself a 20-minute walk into town.

## VISITOR INFORMATION

**CONTACTS Třeboň Tourist Information.**
⊠ *Masarykovo nám. 103* ☏ *384–721–169*
⊕ *www.itrebon.cz.*

#  Sights

**Bílý koníček** (*Little White Horse*)
**HOTEL—SIGHT** | Look for the Little White Horse, the best-preserved Renaissance house on the square, dating to 1544. It's now a modest hotel and restaurant—the perfect spot to enjoy some excellent local beer. ⊠ *Masarykovo nám. 97* ☏ *792–314–606* ⊕ *bilykonicekhotel.cz.*

**Kostel sv. Jiljí** (*Church of St. Giles*)
**RELIGIOUS SITE** | The Gothic style of South Bohemia is exemplified in this curious church. The unassuming exterior gives no clue to the vastness inside or the treasures it holds. Paintings in the Czech Gothic style can be found by the main altar, along with other artwork and frescoes dating as far back as the late 15th century. ⊠ *Husova* ☏ *Free.*

**Zámek Třeboň** (*Třeboň Château*)
**CASTLE/PALACE** | The entrance to this château lies at the southwest corner of the square. From the outside the white walls make it appear restrained, but the inner courtyard is covered with *sgraffito*. There's a variety of tours of the interior, which boasts sumptuous re-creations of the Renaissance lifestyle enjoyed by the Rožmberks and apartments furnished in late-19th-century splendor. The gardens adjacent to the castle are well maintained and free to stroll in. The last of the

Rožmberks died in 1611, and the castle eventually became the property of the Schwarzenberg family, who built their family tomb in a grand park on the other side of Svět Pond. It's now a monumental neo-Gothic destination for Sunday-afternoon picnickers. It's well worth the easy stroll along the lake to visit this tomb; summer concerts are held here occasionally. In the summer you can tour a kitchen for preparing dogs' meals, a stable, and casemates (part of the fortifications) with tunnels. The dogs' kitchen is a rarity and was for the noble family's pampered pets and working dogs. ⊠ *Masarykovo nám.* ☏ *384–721–193* ⊕ *www.zamek-trebon. cz* ☏ *Tours from 70 Kč* ⊙ *Closed Mon. and Nov.–Apr. Stable, dogs' kitchen, and casemates closed Sept.–June.*

## SPAS

Along with its ponds, the Třeboň area is known for its peat bogs. This has given rise to a local spa industry, and wellness weekends are popular attractions at the city's two main spas. A variety of treatments are on offer, but both do peat massages. A dip in the iron-rich squishy substance is supposed to help with arthritis and other joint problems. Be prepared: the sensation and smell are acquired tastes.

### Bertiny Lázně

**FITNESS/HEALTH CLUBS** | Treatments with peat at Bertiny Lázně began in 1883, though the current modern facility, sporting a pool, sauna and wellness center, is much more recent, and was renovated in the first half of 2020. People can stay at the spa for multiday programs or a spa weekend. Services include baths with peat, herbs, Dead Sea salt, and iodine, among others. Massages and various types of motion therapy are also offered. The spa is located close to Třeboň's historical center, next to a park and small waterway. ⊠ *Tylova 171* ☏ *384–754–111* ⊕ *www.berta.cz.*

## Lázně Aurora

**FITNESS/HEALTH CLUBS** | The socialist-style high-rise complex at the western edge of Třeboň may not be inviting at first glance, but inside it has a spa for treatment stays and relaxation weekends. The mud baths in peat are the main attraction. A range of other baths, massages, and therapies can also be found. There a saltwater pool, an aqua center, and a sauna. ✉ *Lázeňská 1001* ☎ *384–750–333* ⊕ *www.laznetrebon.cz/en/spa-houses/aurora-spa.*

 Restaurants

## Šupinka

**$$ | MODERN EUROPEAN** | In a city full of fish, this is where the locals come to enjoy theirs. A stylish interior with floor-to-ceiling wooden arches and a small terrace serve as the backdrops to some creative cooking. **Known for:** fresh carp dishes from nearby fisheries; rustic vibe; locally made Regent beer. $ *Average main: 310 Kč* ✉ *Valy 56* ☎ *384–721–149* ⊕ *www.supina.cz* ⊗ *Closed Mon.–Wed. Šupina closed Mon. and Tues.*

## 🛏 Hotels

The tourist information center on the square is very helpful when it comes to booking rooms. It also offers a catalog of hotel options that includes amenities and prices to help narrow your choices.

## Romantick

**$ | HOTEL** | "Flower power" is the theme at this boutique hotel, as each room is named and designed after a flower; some also offer nice views of the city. **Pros:** lots of amenities for this area; lovely views from some rooms; water heated with solar energy. **Cons:** on the outskirts of the city, in an unattractive area; not all rooms have air-conditioning; some rooms very small. $ *Rooms from: 1990 Kč* ✉ *K Bertě 183* ☎ *725–135–888* ⊕ *www.romantick.cz* ➷ *26 rooms* ¶⊙¶ *Free breakfast.*

# Jindřichův Hradec

*28 km (17 miles) southwest of Třeboň; 158 km (95 miles) south of Prague.*

The ancient town of Jindřichův Hradec, which dates to the end of the 12th century, is mirrored in the reflective waters of the Vajgar Pond right in the town's center. Originally a market colony near the border between Bohemia and Moravia, the town acquired a castle to protect it, and it's the main attraction here as the third-largest castle in the country. (The interior, now an administrative center, is less interesting.) Other attractions include a town square with Gothic, Renaissance, and some baroque aspects, a regional museum, and excursions into the countryside.

Like other Southern Bohemian towns, this region is a popular spot for cyclists and hikers. If the countryside appeals to you but you're lacking the footpower to explore it, hitch a ride on the Narrow Gauge Railway (⊕ *www.jhmd.cz*). Trains depart daily in July and August from the city's main train station. The rails are a mere 30 inches apart, and the route winds south nearly to the border with Austria.

### GETTING HERE

Jindřichův Hradec is about three hours from Prague. The train from Prague's Hlavní nádraží station requires a change at Veselí. It costs about 150 Kč. There is no good direct bus connection.

### TIMING

A laid-back vibe flows through Jindřichův Hradec. Winter feels isolated, but summer brings lots of cyclists to the area. The Day of the City festival is held at the castle every June, while the big summertime festivities happen during the Folk Rose Festival in mid-July.

## VISITOR INFORMATION

**CONTACTS Jindřichův Hradec Tourist Information.** ✉ *Panská 136* ☎ *384–363–546* ⊕ *infocentrum.jh.cz.*

 ## Sights

**Kostel Nanebevzetí Panny Marie** (*Church of the Ascension of Our Lady*)

**RELIGIOUS SITE** | Dating to the second half of the 14th century, this church and its tower are the other dominating features of the city's skyline besides the castle. It's a Gothic triple-nave church with some interesting elements, including a Gothic Madonna from the beginning of the 15th century. By coincidence, the church straddles the 15th meridian, and you'll see a line marking the point. The city tower is also open for those wishing to scale 157 steps for an extensive view of the surrounding area. ✉ *Za kostelem* ☜ *Church free, tower 20 Kč* ⊙ *Tower closed Oct.–Mar. and weekdays Apr., May, and Sept.*

**Kostel sv. Jana Křtitele** (*Church of St. John the Baptist*)

**RELIGIOUS SITE** | The oldest church in town, built between the 13th and 16th centuries, this is an excellent example of Bohemian Gothic architecture. Inside, extensive frescoes in the clerestory date to the first half of the 14th century and portray scenes from the lives of Christ, the Apostles, and various Czech saints. They also demonstrate the medieval necessity for pictorial narratives in educating the illiterate population. On the south side of the sanctuary you can see the Chapel of St. Nicholas, built in 1369. The vaulted ceiling is supported by a single central pillar; this is one of the earliest buildings using this construction in Bohemia. The church and monastery are part of the municipal museum and sometimes have exhibitions. ✉ *Štítného* ☎ *384–363–660* ⊕ *www.mjh.cz* ☜ *Church and cloister 30 Kč, exhibitions 20 Kč* ⊙ *Closed Oct.–May.*

**Muzeum Jindřichohradecka**

**MUSEUM** | Founded in 1882, this museum's big draw is its impressive Nativity scene. The huge, mechanical créche was built by one committed craftsman, Mr. Krýza, who dedicated more than 60 years to its creation in the latter part of the 19th century. The old mechanism has now been replaced with an electrical system, but the primitive charm of the moving figures remains. Amazingly, the scene contains 1,398 figures. Other exhibitions in the former Jesuit seminary include an apothecary. ✉ *Balbínovo nám. 19* ☎ *384–363–660* ⊕ *www.mjh. cz* ☜ *60 Kč, exhibitions 20 Kč* ⊙ *Closed Jan. 6–Mar., Mon. Apr.–June, and Mon. Sept.–mid-Dec.*

**Národní muzeum fotografie** (*National Photography Museum*)

**MUSEUM** | This former Jesuit college now houses the foremost photography institution in the country. Reconstructed interiors rival the photos on display—the wall and ceiling frescoes have been lovingly restored. The permanent collection includes more than 200 photos donated by Czech photographers. Attached to the museum is the Chapel of St. Mary Magdalene, which occasionally hosts concerts. ✉ *Kostelní 20* ☎ *384–362–459* ⊕ *www.mfmom.cz* ☜ *90 Kč* ⊙ *Closed weekends Jan.–Mar., Mon. Apr.–June, and Mon. Sept.–Dec.*

**Zámek v Jindřichově Hradci** (*Jindřichův Hradec's Castle*)

**CASTLE/PALACE** | As the third-largest castle in the Czech Republic, this is the dominant structure in town, holding 300 rooms and 10,000 pieces of art. Behind the courtyard and its elegant Italian arcades, the castle's core is pure Gothic splendor, reflected not only in its thick defensive walls and round tower but also in the **frescoes** covering interior corridors. Colorful examples of medieval coats of arms and a panorama depicting the legend of St. George date to 1338. Over the course of centuries, buildings of an

**Jindřichův Hradec has a cluster of historic buildings including a castle that features the European mannerism style.**

adjoining Renaissance-era château were added to the early Gothic castle, together forming a large complex. There are three different marked routes through the castle for visitors to follow. Tour A is best for design lovers: you'll visit the Adam building, which includes glimpses of Renaissance, baroque, rococo, Empire, and classical styles, as well as see numerous paintings from a previous owner's vast collection. Tour B takes you to the castle's Gothic and medieval core, the Chapel of the Holy Spirit, and the Royal Hall. Tour C offers the opportunity to visit 18th- and 19th-century apartments as well as the Rondel, a bit of an architectural oddity set in this Gothic scene, designed by an Italian in the 16th century. The official term for the decor is "European mannerism," but it really resembles a big pink cake with confectionary images of aristocratic dancers and musicians. Built as a ballroom, this space still hosts the occasional concert. Wander the exterior courtyards for free, or simply climb the Black Tower for a view of the castle and surrounding area. ✉ *Dobrovského 1* ☎ *384–321–279* 🌐 *www.zamek-jindrichuvhradec.cz/en* 🎟 *Castle tours (in Czech): from 60 Kč; exhibitions from 100 Kč* 🕒 *Closed Mon. and Nov.–Apr.*

## 🛏 Hotels

**Hotel Bílá paní**

$ | **HOTEL** | Situated next to the castle, this cozy hotel takes its name (The White Lady) from a ghost legend—and its otherwise comfortable rooms are alleged to be haunted. **Pros:** cheap and cheerful; castle views; historical building. **Cons:** rooms are sweet but spare; bathroom size and placement is a bit unorthodox; the promised ghost never appears. [$] *Rooms from: 1440 Kč* ✉ *Dobrovského 5* ☎ *384–363–329* 🌐 *www.hotelbilapani.cz* 🛏 *11 rooms* 🍴 *Free breakfast.*

**Hotel Concertino**

$ | **HOTEL** | Right on the town square, this historical-looking hotel with a modern interior lets you spring directly into sightseeing action. **Pros:** near the town square; expressive furnishings; plentiful services for business travelers. **Cons:** decor is expressive but not necessarily cohesive; restaurant is hit or miss; rooms can be noisy in summer due to open windows. $ *Rooms from: 1500 Kč* ⊠ *Nám. Míru 141* 🕾 *384–362–320* ⊕ *www.concertino.cz* 💬 *37 rooms* |❂| *Free breakfast.*

# Hluboká nad Vltavou

*17 km (11 miles) southwest of Třeboň; 155 km (94 miles) south of Prague.*

Yes, Hluboká has a massive fairy-tale castle that can be seen for miles around. But active outdoorsy types should come here for the excellent sport center that offers tennis, golf, an adrenaline center, and more. Cycling is easy for a brief nature break.

## GETTING HERE

The journey from Prague to Hluboká—either by train from the Hlavní nádraží station or by bus from the Florenc station—is 2½ hours unless you get one of the local connections that stops in every small town (in which case the trip takes 3½ hours). The train ticket costs about 170 Kč, the bus ticket 190 Kč; both require a change in České Budějovice. You may find it more convenient to stay overnight in České Budějovice and see the castle in the morning after a 10-minute train trip. Alternatively, there's a 10-km (6-mile) cycle path.

## VISITOR INFORMATION

**CONTACTS Hluboká nad Vltavou Tourist Center.** ⊠ *Zborovská 80* 🕾 *387–966–164* ⊕ *www.hluboka.cz.*

 Sights

**Galerie Mikoláše Alše** (*Aleš Art Gallery*)
**MUSEUM** | Located near the château, the region's museum for art history displays a variety of works including sculpture, paintings, and porcelain. It's one of the most extensive collections of Gothic art in the country, and temporary exhibitions range from modern to contemporary. ⊠ *Hluboká nad Vltavou 144* 🕾 *387–967–120* ⊕ *www.ajg.cz* 💬 *130 Kč.*

**Lovecká chata Ohrada** (*Ohrada Hunting Lodge*)
**MUSEUM | FAMILY** | Care for a brisk walk? Follow the yellow trail signs 2 km (1 mile) to the Lovecká chata Ohrada, which houses a museum of hunting and fishing and is near a small children's zoo. ■ **TIP→ The lodge and the zoo have the same entrance.** ⊠ *Zamék Ohrada 1, off Rte. 105* 🕾 *728–328–304* ⊕ *www.nzm.cz/en/ohrada* 💬 *110 Kč (incl. zoo)* 🕙 *Closed Nov.–Mar.*

**Sportovně relaxačni areál** (*Sport-Relax Area*)
**SPORTS VENUE** | Hluboká is working hard to offer visitors something beyond its castle, and this extensive sports complex is a complete change of pace. Here you can golf, play tennis or volleyball, rent Rollerblades or other sports equipment, test your bravery (and fitness level) in the "adrenaline park" (think a massive ropes course, unicycles, and a bungee trampoline), watch the local hockey team play in the stadium, or even catch a baseball or soccer game. The park offers a playground for kids, plus a restaurant with a huge terrace. It backs up to the woods, so you can take off for a short hike as well. There's also a hotel. ⊠ *Sportovní 1276* 🕾 *606–096–326 restaurant and accommodations* ⊕ *www.areal-hluboka. cz* 🕙 *Some parts closed Nov.–Feb.; weekdays Mar., Apr., and Oct.; and Mon. May, June, and Sept.*

★ **Státní zámek Hluboká** (*State Château Hluboká*)
**CASTLE/PALACE** | Hluboká's main focus is its castle, with a cluster of white towers flanking its walls, and tour groups pop in and out regularly. Although the structure dates to the 13th century, what you see is pure 19th-century excess, perpetrated by the wealthy Schwarzenberg family attempting to prove their good taste. If you think you've seen this castle

Endear yourself to locals by referring to the city of České Budějovice as "Budějce," pronounced "boo-dyay-tse."

somewhere before, you're probably thinking of Windsor Castle, near London, which served as the template. Take a tour; the happy hodgepodge of styles in the interior reflects the no-holds-barred tastes of the time. On Tour A you'll see representative rooms, including the stunning morning salon and library. Tour B brings you into the private apartments and hunting salon, while Tour C takes in the kitchen. Tour D is available daily only in July and August, and weekends only in June and September, and shows off the tower and chapel. Check out the wooden Renaissance ceiling in the large dining room, which was removed by the Schwarzenbergs from the castle at Český Krumlov and brought here. Also look for the beautiful late-baroque bookshelves in the library. The gardens are free to wander in. ✉ *Zamek 142* ☎ *387–843–916* ⊕ *www.zamek-hluboka. eu* ✉ *Tours from 100 Kč (tours with English commentary, audio headsets also available)* ☾ *Closed Mon. Sept.–June.*

# České Budějovice

*26 km (16 miles) southwest of Třeboň; 164 km (99 miles) south of Prague.*

České Budějovice is the largest city in Southern Bohemia, but it's more of a transportation hub and not nearly as charming as the neighboring towns. Still, a couple of interesting spots ensure that you won't be bored if you have a stopover, and you probably will. Schedule a couple of extra hours for a wander through the Old Town and a lunch break, and pause to sip the locally brewed Budvar.

The enormously proportioned main square, named after King Přemysl Otakar II, is lined with arcaded houses. The stunning Old Town Hall is from the 16th century. Designed by an Italian, it has bells in the tower that chime old Southern Bohemian tunes at the top of every hour. Another attraction is the central fountain from the 18th century. Be sure to look for the "magic stone," the lone cobblestone in the brick-covered square. Legend has it that if you step on this stone after 10 pm, you'll become lost. But the town's real claim to fame is its beer—the slightly sweetish Budvar.

### GETTING HERE

The trip from Prague takes about two hours by either bus or train. Be careful to choose a *rychlík* (express train), not an *osobní* (passenger train), which would make your journey four hours. Trains leave from Prague's Hlavní nádraží station and cost about 170 Kč; buses leave from both Florenc and Na Knížecí stations and cost 99 Kč–190 Kč. Car travel (about 2½ hours) affords the greatest ease and flexibility. České Budějovice lies on the main artery through the region, the two-lane E55 south from Prague, which, though often crowded, is in relatively good shape.

### VISITOR INFORMATION

**CONTACTS České Budějovice Tourist Center.** ⊠ *Nám. Přemysla Otakára II 2* ☏ *386–801–413* ⊕ *www.budejce.cz/en/ information-center*.

##  Sights

### Budějovický Budvar Brewery

**SPECIAL-INTEREST** | Tours of the brewery start at the modern glass-enclosed visitor center. On the 60-minute route, you'll see the wells that source the water, the brew house, and other parts of the process up to the bottling plant. A beer tasting is included at the end of the tour. Advanced booking (online) is required. ⊠ *Karolíny Světlé 4* ☏ *387–705–347* ⊕ *www.visit-budvar.cz* ⊠ *150 Kč* ⊙ *Closed Sun. and Mon. in Jan. and Feb.*

### Černá věž (*Black Tower*)

**BUILDING** | To get a good view over the city, climb the 225 steps up to the Renaissance gallery of the Black Tower at the northeast corner of the square next to St. Nicholas's Cathedral. Don't look for a black tower; it's actually white but

got the nickname after a fire left some charred marks. ⊠ *Nám. Přemysla Otakara II* ⊠ *30 Kč* ⊙ *Closed Nov.–Mar., Mon. Apr.–June, and Mon. Sept. and Oct.*

### Holašovice

**HISTORIC SITE** | Peppered with small country homes and farmsteads, this traditional Czech village is so well preserved it's been designated a UNESCO World Heritage Site. Hardly touched by reconstruction or modern meddling, some of the houses date back to the town's founding in the 13th century. Don't expect grand châteaus or extensive decoration; this is "rural baroque" but every bit as picturesque with custard-yellow façades. The information center at No. 43 has a small exhibit about rural life. Budget about an hour for a visit or longer if you'd like to enjoy traditional fare at **Špejchar u Vojty** (Holašovice 3 ☏ *777–621–221*). Every July a "peasant" festival, Selské slavnosti, is held with traditional crafts and entertainment. ⊠ *Holašovice* ☏ *387–982–145 for tourist office* ⊕ *www.holasovice.eu* ⊙ *Tourist Information Office closed Nov.– Mar. and Mon. and Tues. Apr.–Oct.*

### Jihočeské muzeum (*Museum of Southern Bohemia*)

**MUSEUM** | You can't miss the imposing neo-Renaissance building of the Museum of Southern Bohemia. It was originally founded in 1877 in a small building next to the town hall, but generous donors flooded the facility with so many artifacts that the space had to be expanded. The major exhibits include theme collections portraying the history of the town and the region through an extensive variety of artifacts including metalwork, ceramics, glass, and furniture. A fascinating large-scale model shows the Old Town and its picturesque medieval walls and towers. A regular series of temporary exhibits also runs alongside the permanent ones. ⊠ *Dukelská 1* ☏ *391–001–531* ⊕ *www. muzeumcb.cz* ⊠ *70 Kč* ⊙ *Closed Mon.*

**Koněspřežka**

**BUILDING** | A source of pride for České Budějovice, Koněspřežka is the oldest railway station on the continent. Designed to transport salt to Bohemia from Linz in Austria, a horse-drawn railway was built between 1825 and 1832. One of the first major industrial developments in Europe, it reduced the journey between Linz and České Budějovice from two weeks to four days. Public transport was introduced soon afterward. The station is now a part of the city museum and houses an exhibit dedicated to the horse-drawn railroad. You can also pick up a brochure from the tourist office that details other buildings throughout town that played a role in the transport. ✉ *Mánesova 10* ☎ *386–354–820* 🌐 *www.muzeumcb.cz* 🎫 *30 Kč* 🕒 *Closed Oct.–Apr. and Mon. May–Sept.*

## 🍴 Restaurants

**Masné krámy**

**$$** | **CZECH** | Operated by the Budvar brewery, the restaurant—a former butcher's market—aims for an upscale yet casual atmosphere with reasonably priced food and is now one of the best restaurants in town. It specializes in great Czech food and serves unpasteurized Budvar beer; fish and game are also on the menu. **Known for:** fresh tank beer; relaxed atmosphere; locally sourced trout. [$] *Average main: 225 Kč* ✉ *Krajinská 13* ☎ *387–201–301* 🌐 *www.masne-kramy.cz.*

## 🛏 Hotels

**Hotel Budweis**

**$$** | **HOTEL** | Situated next to the river in a former mill, this beautifully restored grand hotel has exposed wooden beams, polished floors, and loads of natural light. **Pros:** nicest hotel in town; central location with good views; rooms adapted for people with disabilities. **Cons:** cheaper options available; modern room design doesn't match historical exterior; showers are a bit tricky to use. [$] *Rooms from: 2990 Kč* ✉ *Mlýnská 6* ☎ *389–822–111* 🌐 *www.hotelbudweis.cz* 🛏 *60 rooms* 🍴 *Free Breakfast.*

## 🎫 Performing Arts

The city has its own theater, ballet, opera, and orchestra that put on a variety of performances throughout the year. The Jihočeské divadlo (South Bohemian Theater) is also the group that organizes the July and August performances at the Revolving Theater in Český Krumlov. Tickets sell out fast. You can reserve online at 🌐 *www.cbsystem.cz.* ✉ *Dr. Stejskala 23* ☎ *386–356–925* 🌐 *www.jihoceske-divadlo.cz*

# Chapter 13

# WESTERN
# BOHEMIA

Updated by
Raymond Johnston

| ◉ Sights | 🍴 Restaurants | 🛏 Hotels | 🛍 Shopping | 🍸 Nightlife |
|----------|---------------|----------|-------------|-------------|
| ★★★★★ | ★★☆☆☆ | ★★★★★ | ★★★★★ | ★☆☆☆☆ |

# WELCOME TO WESTERN BOHEMIA

## TOP REASONS TO GO

★ **Take the waters:** Wind through the Vřídlo Colonnade, where adventurous souls can sip the waters.

★ **Book a spa day:** Try the spa treatments, either old-school health-oriented treatments or more familiar pampering.

★ **Catch the stunning view:** Head up to Stag's Leap for a sweeping vista.

★ **Walk the "main streets":** Picturesque spa towns Františkovy Lázně and Mariánské Lázně make a quaint stroll.

★ **Drink a Pilsner Urquell:** Try this brew in the town where it was born—Plzeň.

The natural springs of hot mineral water that dot the lands of Western Bohemia have made this region one of Europe's most important spa centers. These facilities near neighboring Germany have been renovated inside to meet international expectations during the last 25 years, but the exteriors of the colonnades and pavilions still reflect the styles of the 19th century. Because access to much of the border area was highly restricted in the communist era, the hills and forests still provide unspoiled natural settings for hiking and biking. The area also has a rich history of manufacturing luxury glassware and porcelain, which can be seen in downtown shops and factory stores. Farther south is the city of Plzeň, famous for inventing pilsner.

**1** **Karlovy Vary.** Better known to many as Karlsbad, the largest of the spa towns also hosts the country's biggest film festival every July.

**2** **Cheb.** Proximity to the German border brings many bargain hunters for shopping, while castle ruins and a historical center add some diversion.

**3** **Františkovy Lázně.** The smallest of the spa towns in West Bohemia offers a quiet escape to hotels with mud baths and old-world pampering.

**4** **Mariánské Lázně.** In this town's heyday, everyone from Thomas Edison to Czar Nicholas II came to take the waters. Today visitors can also enjoy golf and hiking.

**5** **Plzeň.** The only major Czech city to have been liberated by U.S. forces at the end of World War II, it's also home to the country's largest brewery.

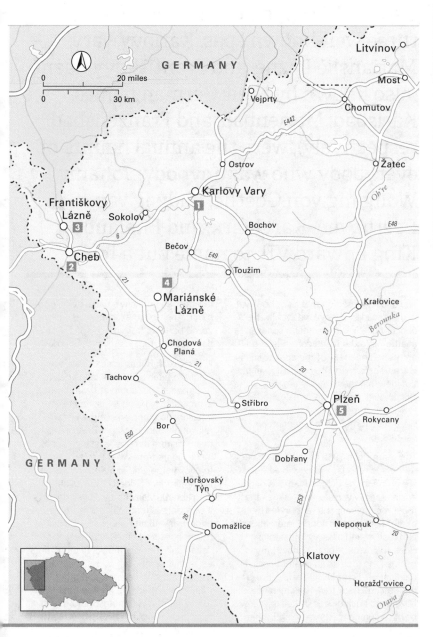

Once upon a time, Western Bohemia was known as the playground of Central Europe's rich and famous. Its three well-known spas, Karlovy Vary, Mariánské Lázně, and Františkovy Lázně (also known by their German names, Karlsbad, Marienbad, and Franzensbad, respectively), were the annual haunts of everybody who was anybody: Johann Wolfgang von Goethe, Ludwig van Beethoven, Karl Marx, and England's King Edward VII, to name but a few.

The spas suffered dramatically, however, in the decades after World War II. The concept of a luxurious health spa was anathema to the ruling communist government, and many of the spa facilities were transformed into hospitals—in fact, the idea that these towns are where the sick should recuperate remains today. Pre-1989, some of the nicest properties were transformed into recuperation centers for workers.

The years since 1989 have been kinder to the spa resorts, and now the cities are home to the rich and famous once again. Karlovy Vary, as always, has the most recognition, and rebounded best of all. Helped by its annual international film festival and a heavy infusion of Russian private capital, Karlovy Vary is back on the map as an international spa destination. Františkovy Lázně, too, is on the comeback trail. The city officials have used bucketloads of Kaiser-yellow paint to spruce up those aging Empire facades, and the city's parks have gotten a much-needed makeover. Mariánské Lázně benefits from hordes of German day-trippers from just over the border.

In the Czech Republic spas have traditionally been seen as serious health treatments first, complete with physical examinations, blood tests, and various infusions to complement the waters, relaxation, and massage. This means for many visitors that the local concept of a spa differs from what they are used to back home (and explains in part the large number of elderly tourists shuffling about). Many hotels have added treatments—from Thai massages to pedicures—that fit the modern concept of a spa resort. For many places, though, "spa" still primarily means doctors, nurses, and lab coats, but this is changing as beer spas, wine spas, and other less traditional places pop up. The best place to inquire is at your hotel or the tourist information center.

Aside from the spas, the area is full of historic features stemming from the wealth it accrued as the district's important trade route into Germany and Italy. A strong Germanic influence can still be seen, particularly in towns like Cheb and Mariánské Lázně. Everywhere in the region you'll see Germans, mostly pensioners on coach tours dropping by for a walk around town and a slice of apple strudel before hitting the road back to Deutschland.

# Planning

## When to Go

The region's key cultural event is the Karlovy Vary International Film Festival, held in the first week in July. As strolling on the promenades of the spa towns is de rigueur, the summer months are the season. The winter months are fine if you want to spend all your time indoors getting massages and other luxury treatments. Most hotels do stay open during this season. But promenading around the colonnade will be a bit of a letdown in the cold, and there's less hobnobbing with fellow spa goers due to much smaller crowds.

## Getting Here

By car, the D5 (E50) highway leads directly to Plzeň, while the R6 (E48) goes to Karlovy Vary and the spa towns in the northern part of the region. Some towns, lack direct train connections, making a direct bus a better choice. Buses to major hubs such as Plzeň are also faster and less expensive than trains.

# Guided Tours from Prague

Guided one-day bus tours from Prague are available from several companies to the larger spa towns.

### Martin Tours
One of the country's larger tour operators, Martin Tours offers regular trips to Karlovy Vary, including a glass factory, and the brewery in Plzeň for 1,500 Kč and 1,200 Kč each. The Plzeň trip includes beer tasting. ⊕ *www.martintour. cz.*

### Tip Top Travel
Tip Top Travel offers a combined Karlovy Vary–Mariánské Lázně tour for 2,100 Kč. The tour lasts about 10 hours and the price includes a pickup at your hotel. ⊕ *www.tiptoptravel.cz.*

# Restaurants and Hotels

The quality of hotels in Western Bohemia is on a par with those in Prague (something that can't be said about some other parts of the country) and three- and four-star establishments have standard amenities, including satellite TV, room phones, and private bathrooms (and sometimes even Wi-Fi). One difference from the hotels in Prague: the peak season is shorter, running from May through September. Another difference: the staff tend to speak a very limited amount of English—German and Russian (particularly in Karlovy Vary) are much more common, in keeping with the majority of visitors. Prices have risen dramatically in recent years, making private accommodations a more attractive offer. ■ TIP→ **Be sure to read the fine print, as many spa hotels quote rates per person per night, rather than for double occupancy.** The local tourist offices usually keep lists of pensions and private rooms. In addition to value-added tax (V.A.T.), there is also a "spa tax" of about 15 Kč per day for accommodations in spa facilities.

*Hotel reviews have been shortened. For full information, visit Fodors.com.*

## WHAT It Costs in Koruna

|  | $ | $$ | $$$ | $$$$ |
|---|---|---|---|---|
| **RESTAURANTS** | | | | |
| | under 150 Kč | 150 Kč–350 Kč | 351 Kč–500 Kč | over 500 Kč |
| **HOTELS** | | | | |
| | under 2,200 Kč | 2,200 Kč–4,000 Kč | 4,001 Kč–6,500 Kč | over 6,500 Kč |

# Karlovy Vary

*132 km (79 miles) west of Prague on R6 (E48).*

Karlovy Vary—often known outside the Czech Republic by its German name, Karlsbad—is the most famous of the Bohemian spas. It's named for the omnipresent Emperor Charles IV, who allegedly happened upon the springs in 1358 while on a hunting expedition. As the story goes, the emperor's hound fell into a boiling spring and was scalded. Charles had the water tested and, familiar with spas in Italy, ordered the village of Vary to be transformed into a haven for baths. The spa reached its golden age in the 19th century, when aristocrats from all over Europe came for treatments. The long list of those who "took the cure" includes Peter the Great, Goethe, Schiller, Beethoven, and Chopin. Even Karl Marx, when he wasn't decrying wealth and privilege, spent time at the wealthy and privileged resort; he wrote some of *Das Kapital* here between 1874 and 1876.

Pulling off an extraordinary comeback after decades of communist neglect that left many buildings crumbling into dust behind beautiful facades, Karlovy Vary drips with luxury once again. Much of the reconstruction was led not by Czechs,

but by Russians. Since the days of Peter the Great, Karlovy Vary has held a deep fascination for Russians, and many of them poured their newly gained wealth into properties here—so much so that Karlovy Vary's sleepy airport boasts non-stop service from Moscow several times a week, and four-fifths of the properties are actually Russian-owned. Don't be surprised to hear Russian spoken widely in the streets or see it used as the second language, after Czech, on restaurant menus.

Karlovy Vary's other vehicle in luring attention and investment has been its international film festival, which began in 1946. Every year during the first week of July, international stars and film fans flock here. Recent attendees include Oliver Stone, John Travolta, and Helen Mirren. If you're planning on visiting during the festival, line up your hotel room well in advance. Unless you're a true film buff, you're better off coming on a different week.

Whether you're arriving by bus, train, or car, your first view of the town approaching from Prague will be of the run-down section on the banks of the Ohře River. Don't despair: continue along the main road, following the signs to the Grand-hotel Pupp, until you are rewarded with a glimpse of the lovely main street in the older spa area, situated gently astride the banks of the little Teplá ("Warm") River. (Drivers, note that driving through or parking in the main spa area is allowed only with a permit obtained at your hotel.) The walk from the new town to the spa area is about 20 minutes.

The Historická čtvrt (Historic District) is still largely intact. Tall 19th-century houses, with decorative and often eccentric façades, line the spa's proud riverside streets. Throughout, you can see colonnades full of people sipping the spa's hot sulfuric water from funny drinking cups with piped spouts.

## GETTING HERE

Frequent bus service between Prague and Karlovy Vary makes the journey only about two hours each way, and the ticket costs about 160 Kč. The Prague–Karlovy Vary run takes longer—more than three hours by the shortest route—and costs about 170 Kč. If you're driving, you can take the E48 directly from Prague to Karlovy Vary, a drive of about 1½ hours in light traffic.

**VISITOR INFORMATION Karlovy Vary**
**Tourist Information.** ⊠ *Husovo nám. 2* ☎ *355–321–171* ⊕ *www.karlovyvary.cz.*

 **Sights**

**Hotel Thermal**
**HOTEL—SIGHT** | Built in the late 1960s as the communist idea of luxury, this oversize modern hotel is the main venue of the Karlovy Vary International Film Festival in early July. Many people, though, consider it an eyesore that's out of step with the rest of the city. ⊠ *I. P. Pavlova 11* ☎ *359–001–111* ⊕ *www.thermal.cz.*

★ **Jelení skok** (*Stag's Leap*)
**VIEWPOINT** | From Kostel svatého Lukáše, take a sharp right uphill on a redbrick road, then turn left onto a footpath through the woods, following signs to Jelení skok (Stag's Leap). After a while, steps lead up to a bronze statue of a deer looking over the cliffs, the symbol of Karlovy Vary. From here a winding path threads toward a little red gazebo opening onto a mythical panorama that's worth the strenuous hike to the top. ⊠ *Sovava trail in Petrova Výšina park.*

**Kostel Maří Magdaleny** (*Church of Mary Magdalene*)
**RELIGIOUS SITE** | To the right of the Vřídlo Colonnade, steps lead up to the white Church of Mary Magdalene. Designed by Kilian Ignaz Dientzenhofer (architect of the two churches of St. Nicholas in Prague), this is the best of the few baroque buildings still standing in Karlovy

Vary. ■**TIP→** If it's open, try to visit the crypt. ⊠ *Moravská ul.* ⊕ *www.farnost-kv.cz.*

**Kostel svatého Lukáše** (*St. Luke's Church*)
**RELIGIOUS SITE** | A five-minute walk up the steep Zámecký vrch from the Market Colonnade brings you to the Victorian, redbrick St. Luke's Church, once a gathering point for the local English community. ⊠ *Zámecký vrch at Petra Velikého.*

**Kostel svatých Petra a Pavla** (*Church of Sts. Peter and Paul*)
**RELIGIOUS SITE** | Six domes top this splendid Russian Orthodox church. It dates to the end of the 19th century, and is decorated with paintings and icons donated by wealthy Russian visitors. ■**TIP→** You can usually peek inside, daily 9–6. ⊠ *Třída Krále Jiřího 26.*

**Mlýnská kolonáda** (*Mill Colonnade*)
**BUILDING** | This neo-Renaissance pillared hall, along the river, is the town's centerpiece. Built from 1871 to 1881, it has four springs: Rusalka, Libussa, Prince Wenceslas, and Millpond. ⊠ *Mlýnské nábř.*

**Rozhledna Diana**
**VIEWPOINT** | Give your feet a rest. You won't need to walk to one of the best views of the town. Even higher than Stag's Leap sits this observation tower, accessible by funicular from behind the Grandhotel Pupp. There's an elevator to the top of the tower, and a restaurant at the tower's base. ⊠ *Výšina přátelství* ⊕ *www.dianakv.cz* 🚡 *Funicular from 45 Kč; tower free.*

**Sadová kolonáda** (*Park Colonnade*)
**BUILDING** | Laced with white wrought iron, this elegant colonnade at the edge of Dvořákovy sady was built in 1882 by the Viennese architectural duo Fellner and Helmer, who sprinkled the Austro-Hungarian Empire with many such edifices during the late 19th century. They also designed the town's theater, the quaint wooden Tržní kolonáda (Market Colonnade) next to the Vřídlo Colonnade, and one of the old bathhouses. ⊠ *Dvořákovy sady.*

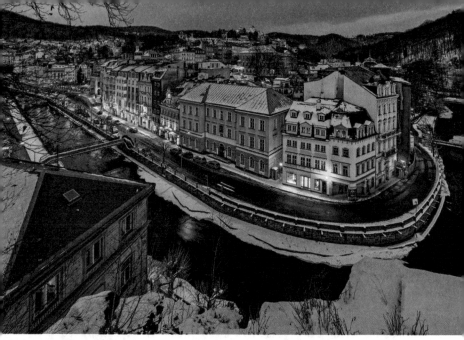

Like Prague, Karlovy Vary also has a central river: the swirling Teplá.

### Vřídelní kolonáda (*Vřídlo Colonnade*)

**HOT SPRINGS** | Shooting its scalding water to a height of some 40 feet, the Vřídlo is indeed Karlovy Vary's hottest and most dramatic gusher. Built around it is the jarringly modern Vřídlo Colonnade. Walk inside the arcade to watch patients take the famed Karlsbad drinking cure. The waters (30°F–72°F) are said to be especially effective against diseases of the digestive and urinary tracts. They're also good for gout (which probably explains the spa's former popularity with royals). If you want to join the crowds and take a sip, you can buy your own spouted cup from one of the souvenir vendors throughout the town. ⊠ *Vřídelní ul., near Kosterní nám.*

## 🍽 Restaurants

The food in Karlovy Vary has improved due to the influx of Russians with money to spend. Pork and beer pubs are still the rule, though. Hotel food tends to be better.

### Pizzeria Capri

**$$** | **ITALIAN** | This "riverfront" pizzeria became an institution during the annual film festival. The walls are decked out with photos of the owner smiling next to Hollywood stars. $ *Average main: 250 Kč* ⊠ *Stará Louka 42* ☎ *353–236–090* ⊕ *www.pizzeriacapri.cz.*

### Promenáda

**$$$** | **CZECH** | Although it's pricey, Promenáda is unquestionably the best place to eat in Karlovy Vary. The starchy vibe is "'70s French fussy," and meals are on the heavy side. $ *Average main: 400 Kč* ⊠ *Trziste 31* ☎ *353–225–648* ⊕ *hotel-promenada.cz.*

### U Švejka

**$$** | **CZECH** | Usually when a restaurant has the name "Schweik" in it—from the novel *Good Soldier Schweik*—it means one thing: tourist trap. But this local Schweik incarnation is a cut above its brethren. $ *Average main: 250 Kč* ⊠ *Stará Louka 10* ☎ *353–232–276* ⊕ *www.svejk-kv.cz* ⊟ *No credit cards.*

## Coffee and Quick Bites

**Elefant**
**RESTAURANT—SIGHT** | On one of the town's main shopping streets is this resolutely old-fashioned, sophisticated coffeehouse, connected to Hotel Elefant. The apple strudel and coffee are quite good, and the outdoor terrace is a prime location for people-watching. ✉ *Stará louka 30* ☎ *353–229–270* 🌐 *www.hotelelefant.cz.*

**Jelení skok**
**RESTAURANT—SIGHT** | After reaching the summit of Stag's Leap, reward yourself with a light meal at the nearby restaurant Jelení skok. There may be a cover charge if a live band is playing (prepare yourself for smooth rock by a synth-guitar duo). If you don't want to walk up, you can drive up a signposted road from the Victorian church. ✉ *Pod Jelením skokem 884/2.*

## Hotels

**Carlsbad Plaza**
**$$$** | **HOTEL** | A luxury hotel a stone's throw from the Grandhotel Pupp, Carlsbad Plaza is aimed at Karlovy Vary's wealthiest visitors. **Pros:** everything you could ever want; great wellness center. **Cons:** lots of things you probably don't—and you're paying for it all; some might find it fussy or distant. [$] *Rooms from: 6325 Kč* ✉ *Mariánskolázeňská 23* ☎ *352–441–111* 🌐 *www.carlsbadplaza.cz* 🛏 *126 rooms, 26 suites* 🍴 *Breakfast.*

**★ Grandhotel Pupp**
**$$$** | **HOTEL** | The granddaddy of them all, this is one of Central Europe's most famous resorts, going back some 200 years. **Pros:** large rooms; living history; a sleek casino. **Cons:** costly extras; rooms are opulent but not that modern. [$] *Rooms from: 5100 Kč* ✉ *Mírové nám. 2* ☎ *353–109–631* 🌐 *www.pupp.cz* 🛏 *Grandhotel Pupp de Luxe: 111 rooms; Grandhotel Pupp First Class: 117 rooms* 🍴 *Breakfast.*

**Hotel Dvořák**
**$$** | **HOTEL** | The Austrian-owned hotel, which opened in 1990, occupies three renovated houses that overlook Nová louka and the Teplá River. **Pros:** efficient staff; large spa for the price point. **Cons:** some rooms are cramped. [$] *Rooms from: 2675 Kč* ✉ *Nová Louka 11* ☎ *353–224–145* 🌐 *www.hotel-dvorak.cz* 🛏 *126 rooms* 🍴 *Breakfast.*

**★ Hotel Embassy**
**$$** | **HOTEL** | On a peaceful bend in the river, this family-run hotel includes spacious, well-appointed rooms. **Pros:** perfect for duffers; rooms offer a great value. **Cons:** small; no spa. [$] *Rooms from: 2950 Kč* ✉ *Nová Louka 21* ☎ *353–221–161* 🌐 *www.embassy.cz* 🛏 *29 rooms* 🍴 *Breakfast.*

**Hotel Heluan**
**$$** | **HOTEL** | A clean, safe bet if you've arrived in town without reservations and don't want to spend your savings on a room. **Pros:** inexpensive; friendly staff; completely no-smoking hotel. **Cons:** a bit of a hike uphill. [$] *Rooms from: 3000 Kč* ✉ *Tržíště 41* ☎ *353–321–111* 🌐 *www.heluan.eu* 🛏 *25 rooms* 🍴 *Breakfast.*

**Promenáda**
**$$** | **HOTEL** | The family-operated hotel is another good last-minute option right in the center of town, with pastel yellow rooms that are brightened by the occasional exposed wooden beam or windowsill flower box. **Pros:** beautiful pool; American-style spa; great restaurant; large rooms. **Cons:** dated fixtures; street noise on weekends. [$] *Rooms from: 3550 Kč* ✉ *Trziste 31* ☎ *353–225–648* 🌐 *www.hotel-promenada.cz* 🛏 *22 rooms* 🍴 *Breakfast.*

**Růže Hotel**
**$$** | **HOTEL** | More than adequately comfortable and well-priced given its location in the center of the spa district, the Růže also offers an array of modern spa services like bubble baths and Thai massage. **Pros:** nice views; good for large groups;

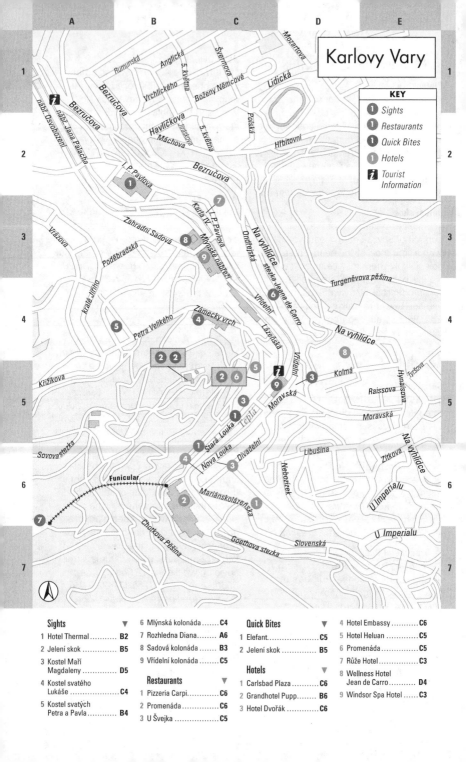

# Karlovy Vary

**KEY**

- **1** Sights
- **1** Restaurants
- **1** Quick Bites
- **1** Hotels
- 🛈 Tourist Information

The town of Karlovy Vary is famed for bubbling hot springs and spa experience and for its cast-iron colonnade.

new rooms. **Cons:** the modern interior lacks character. [$] *Rooms from: 3200 Kč* ✉ *I. P. Pavlova 1* ☎ *353–221–846, 353–221–853* 🌐 *www.hotel-ruze.com* 🛏 *54 rooms* 🍴 *Breakfast.*

**Wellness Hotel Jean de Carro**

**$$** | **HOTEL** | Framed on a hilltop off a side street above the spa, the Jean de Carro sits comfortably above the fray. **Pros:** great views; friendly staff. **Cons:** a bit of a hike; small rooms. [$] *Rooms from: 2990 Kč* ✉ *Stezka Jeana de Carro 4–6* ☎ *353–365–160* 🌐 *www.jeandecarro.com* 🛏 *32 rooms* 🍴 *Breakfast.*

**Windsor Spa Hotel**

**$** | **HOTEL** | Neo-Gothic in style—on the outside, anyway—this spa hotel has fairly spartan rooms and a slight hospital vibe (it takes treatment rather seriously), but the location is excellent and treatments are gently priced. **Pros:** beautiful building; great location. **Cons:** austere rooms; limited amenities; medical feel. [$] *Rooms from: 1675 Kč* ✉ *Mlýnské nábř. 5* ☎ *353–242–569* 🌐 *windsor-carlsbad.cz* 🛏 *36 rooms* 🍴 *Breakfast.*

## Performing Arts

**Lázně III**

**MUSIC** | If you're looking to get your high-culture fix, the Karlovy Vary Symphony Orchestra plays regularly at this hotel, a spa facility that doubles as an important cultural center for the town. Head to the Antonín Dvořák Music Hall on the first floor of the building to catch the concerts. The same building is also now home to Windsor Spa Hotel. ✉ *Mlýnské nábř. 5* ☎ *353–242–500* 🌐 *www.lazneiii.cz.*

**Městské divadlo**

**THEATER** | Restored to its opulent 1890s glory, the Municipal Theater is home to live concerts of many kinds as well as theater performances. Interior paintings were done by well-known artists including a young Gustav Klimt. ✉ *Divadelní nám. 21* ☎ *353–225–621* 🌐 *www.karlovarske-divadlo.cz.*

##  Nightlife

**Grandhotel Pupp**

CASINOS | This upscale funhouse consists of the two nightclubs and the casino of the biggest hotel in town. You don't have to be James Bond to get in, so gamble the night away within the mirrored walls and under the glass ceiling of the Pupp Casino Club, or settle into a cocktail and some live music at the English-themed Becher's Bar. ☒ *Mírové nám. 2* ☎ *353–109–111* ⊕ *www.pupp.cz.*

## Shopping

A cluster of exclusive stores huddles around the Grandhotel Pupp and back toward town along the river on Stará Louka. Lesser-known, high-quality makers of glass and porcelain can also be found on this street. If you're looking for an inexpensive but nonetheless singular gift from Karlovy Vary, consider a bottle of the bittersweet (and potent) Becherovka, a liqueur produced by the town's own Jan Becher distillery. Another thoughtful gift would be one of the pipe-shape ceramic drinking cups used to take the drinking cure at spas; you can find them along the colonnades. Boxes of tasty *oplatky* wafers, with various sweet fillings, can be found at shops in all the spa towns. (The most famous, Kolonáda, is actually made in Mariánské Lázně.) The challenge is stopping yourself from eating it all before you give it as a gift.

**Moser**

CERAMICS/GLASSWARE | To glass enthusiasts, Karlovy Vary is best known as the home of Moser, one of the world's leading producers of crystal and decorative glassware. ☒ *Tržiště 7* ☎ *353–235–303* ⊕ *www.moser-glass.com.*

**Moser Visitors Center**

CERAMICS/GLASSWARE | For people who want to see more of the process of glassmaking, the Moser Visitors Center has a museum and offers factory tours

along with shopping. ☒ *Kapitána Jarose 19* ☎ *353–416–242* ⊕ *www.moser.cz* ☞ *180 Kč combined admission for museum and glassworks.*

##  Activities

Karlovy Vary is a town made for staying active in the outdoors. Exercise was often part of the treatment during the heyday of the resort, and the air quality here is markedly superior to that of Prague or other industrialized towns in the Czech Republic. Hiking trails snake across the beech-and pine-covered hills that surround the town on three sides. If you walk past the Grandhotel Pupp, away from the center, and follow the paved walkway that runs alongside the river for about 10 minutes, you'll discover a Japanese garden.

**Karlovy Vary Golf Club**

GOLF | This course, opened in 1904, has been extensively modernized since 2004 to include a new clubhouse and redesigned holes, including two water traps. The clubhouse has a relaxation center and an indoor golf simulators. The club requires a golf association membership and a minimum handicap of 36 to make a reservation to use the course. Electric carts and clubs can be rented. The European ground squirrel, listed as a vulnerable species, lives on the course.

✉ *Pražská 125* ☎ *353–331–001* ⊕ *www. golfresort.cz* ✉ *1200 Kč for 9 holes; 2000 Kč for 18 holes* ⚲ *18 holes; 6773 yards; par 72* ☉ *Closed Nov.–Mar.*

# Cheb

*42 km (26 miles) southwest of Karlovy Vary; 174 km (105 miles) southwest of Prague.*

Known for centuries by its German name of Eger, the old town of Cheb tickles the German border in the far west of the Czech Republic. The town has been a fixture of Bohemia since 1322 (when it was handed over to King Jan as thanks for his support of a Bavarian prince), but as you walk around the beautiful medieval square it's easy to forget you're not in Germany. The tall merchants' houses surrounding the main square, with their long, red-tile, sloping roofs dotted with windows like droopy eyelids, are more Germanic in style than anything else in Bohemia. You will also hear a lot of German on the streets from the day-trippers coming here from across the border.

Germany took possession of the town in 1938 under the terms of the notorious Munich Agreement. Following World War II, virtually the entire German population was expelled, and the Czech name of Cheb was officially adopted. During the Cold War, Cheb suffered as a communist outpost along the heavily fortified border with West Germany. Since then, thanks to German tourist dollars, Cheb has made an obvious economic comeback. The town center, with a lovely pedestrian zone, merits a few hours of strolling.

## GETTING HERE

The journey from Prague to Cheb is about 3½ hours each way, whether you are taking the bus or the train; expect to pay more for the ride by train. The price for the bus trip is 200 Kč; the price for the train ride 300 Kč. The high-speed Pendolino train service goes to Cheb in 2½ hours, but seat reservations are required. Look for special deals on the Czech Railways website (⊕ *www.cd.cz*) that sometimes make the seat reservations free. If you're driving, you can take the E50 and then the 21 from Prague to Cheb, a drive of about 2½ hours, though traffic can sometimes be heavy.

**VISITOR INFORMATION Tourist Info Cheb.** ✉ *Jateční 2* ☎ *354–440–302* ⊕ *www.tic. mestocheb.cz.*

 **Sights**

**Chebské muzeum** (*Cheb Museum*)
**MUSEUM** | The building that houses this museum is just as interesting at its collection; it's known as the Pachelbel House, the setting for a murder during the Thirty Years' War. In 1634, General Albrecht von Wallenstein was executed in this house on the orders of Hapsburg emperor Ferdinand II. He was provoked by Wallenstein's increasing power and rumors of treason. According to legend, Wallenstein was on his way to the Saxon border to enlist support to fight the Swedes when his own officers barged into his room and stabbed him through the heart with a stave. Wallenstein's stark bedroom has been left as it was with its four-poster bed and dark red velvet curtains. (The story also inspired playwright Friedrich Schiller to write the *Wallenstein* trilogy; he planned the work while living at the top of the square at No. 2.) The museum is also interesting in its own right, with a Wallenstein family picture gallery, a section on the history of Cheb, and a collection of minerals (including one discovered by Goethe). There's also the stuffed remains of Wallenstein's horse. ✉ *Nám. Krále Jiřího z Poděbrad 4* ☎ *354–400–620* ⊕ *www.muzeumcheb. cz* ✉ *Full museum: 70 Kč; Wallenstein route only: 40 Kč; exhibition hall: 40 Kč* ☉ *Closed weekdays in Jan. and Feb., Mon. and Tues. in Mar., Apr., and Oct.– Dec., and Mon. May–Sept.*

**Chebský hrad** (*Cheb Castle*)

**CASTLE/PALACE** | Built with blocks of lava taken from the nearby Komorní Hůrka volcano, this castle stands on a cliff overlooking the Ohře River. The castle—now a ruin—was built in the late 12th century for Holy Roman Emperor Frederick Barbarossa. Redbrick walls are 17th-century additions. Inside the castle grounds is the carefully restored double-decker **Romanesque chapel,** notable for the many lovely columns with heads carved into their capitals. The rather dark ground floor was used by commoners. A bright, ornate top floor was reserved for the emperor and his family, who entered via a wooden bridge leading to the royal palace. ✉ *Dobrovského 21* ☎ *354–422–942* 🌐 *www.hrad-cheb.cz* 🎟 *80 Kč* 🕒 *Closed weekdays in Nov.–Mar., and Mon. Apr.–June, Sept., and Oct.*

**Komorní Hůrka**

**NATURE SITE** | Red markers indicate a path from Cheb's main square westward along the river and then north past this extinct volcano, now a tree-covered hill. Excavations on one side have laid bare the rock, and one tunnel remains open. Goethe instigated and took part in the excavations, and you can still—barely—make out a relief of the poet carved into the rock face. ■ **TIP→ The volcano is about 2 miles out of town.** ✉ *Komorní dvůr.*

**Kostel svatého Mikuláše** (*Church of St. Nicholas*)

**RELIGIOUS SITE** | The plain but imposing Church of St. Nicholas was begun in 1230, when the church belonged to the Order of Teutonic Knights. You can still see Romanesque windows on the towers; tinkering over the centuries added an impressive Gothic portal and a baroque interior. Just inside the Gothic entrance is a wonderfully faded plaque commemorating the diamond jubilee of Hapsburg emperor Franz Joseph in 1908. ✉ *Kostelní nám.* ☎ *354–422–458* 🌐 *www.farnostcheb.cz.*

**"Roland" Statue**

**PUBLIC ART** | In the middle of the central square, náměstí Krále Jiřího z Poděbrad, this statue is similar to other Roland statues seen throughout Bohemia, attesting to the town's royal privileges. (Roland is a figure in medieval and Renaissance literature; his statues are found throughout Europe.) This one represents the town hero, Wastel of Eger. Look carefully at his right foot, and you can see a small man holding a sword and a head—this shows the town had its own judge and executioner. ✉ *Nám. Krále Jiřího z Poděbrad.*

**Špalíček**

**NEIGHBORHOOD** | In the lower part of náměstí Krále Jiřího z Poděbrad stand two rickety-looking groups of timbered medieval buildings (11 houses in all) divided by a narrow alley. The houses, forming the area known as Špalíček, date to the 13th century, and were once home to many Jewish merchants. **Židovská ulice** (Jews' Street), running uphill to the left of the Špalíček, served as the actual center of the ghetto. The small, unmarked alley running to the left off Židovská is called ulička Zavražděných (Lane of the Murdered). It was the scene of an outrageous act of violence in 1350: pressures had been building for some time between Jews and Christians. Incited by an anti-Semitic bishop, the townspeople chased the Jews into the street, closed off both ends, and massacred them. Now only the name attests to the slaughter. ✉ *Nám. Krále Jiřího z Poděbrad.*

## 🍴 Restaurants

**Kavárna-Restaurace Špalíček**

**$$** | **CZECH** | The sameness of the restaurants lining the square can be a bit numbing, but this one offers a reasonably priced selection of standard pork and chicken dishes, with the added charm of being in the ancient Špalíček complex. [$] *Average main: 200 Kč* ✉ *Nám. Krále Jiřího z Poděbrad 50* ☎ *736–759–409* 🌐 *restaurace-spalicek.cz* 💳 *No credit cards.*

## Hotels

**Barbarossa**

$ | **HOTEL** | One block from the main square, this charming family-run hotel is a favorite among visiting Germans, so book ahead, especially on weekends. **Pros:** near the main square; friendly staff. **Cons:** gets crowded; few amenities. [$] *Rooms from: 1800 Kč* ✉ *Jateční 7* ☎ *354–423–446* 🌐 *www.hotel-barbarossa.cz* 🛏 *21 rooms with bath* 🍴 *Breakfast.*

# Františkovy Lázně

*6 km (4 miles) north of Cheb; 180 km (109 miles) southwest of Prague.*

Františkovy Lázně, or Franzensbad, is the smallest of the three main Bohemian spas. It isn't really in the same league as Karlovy Vary. The main spa area is only a few blocks, and aside from a dozen or so cafés in which to enjoy an apple strudel or ice cream, there isn't much to see or do. That said, the charm of its uniform, Kaiser-yellow Empire architecture grows on you. Gardens surrounding the main spa area—both the manicured "French" gardens and the wilder "English" parks—grow on you, too. They're as perfect for strolling now as they were 200 years ago. Summer is particularly pleasant, when a small orchestra occupies the gazebo in the Městské sady (City Park) and locals and visitors sit in lawn chairs and listen.

The healing properties of the waters here were recognized as early as the 15th century, but Františkovy Lázně came into its own only at the start of the 19th century. Like Bohemia's other spas, Františkovy Lázně drew from the top drawer of European society, including one Ludwig Van Beethoven, who came here in 1812. But it remained in Cheb's shadow, and the spa stayed relatively small. In the years following World War II the spa declined. Most of the buildings were given over to factories and organizations to use as convalescent centers. Františkovy Lázně also developed a reputation for helping women with fertility problems, and Milan Kundera used it as the humorous, small-town backdrop for his novel *The Farewell Party.* Since 1989 the town has worked hard to restore the yellow facades to their former glory.

The best way to approach Františkovy Lázně is simply to find **Národní ulice,** the main street, and walk.

### GETTING HERE

Expect to spend about four hours each way traveling between Prague and Františkovy Lázne via bus or train. As with other destinations, you'll pay more for riding the rails, and also make a few changes as there is little direct service. Costs are about 215 Kč one-way for the bus, about 310 Kč for a train with a change or 400 Kč without a change. Frequent buses run to and from Cheb. If you're driving, you can take the E50 and then the 21 from Prague to Františkovy Lázne, a drive of about three hours.

**VISITOR INFORMATION Františkovy Lázně Tourist Information.** ✉ *Tři Lilie Hotel, Národní 3* ☎ *354–201–170* 🌐 *www.franzensbad.cz.*

## Sights

**Františkův pramen**

**HOT SPRINGS** | Under a little gazebo filled with brass pipes sits the town's main spring. The colonnade to the left once displayed a bust of Lenin that was replaced in 1990 by a memorial to the American liberation of the town in April 1945. To the right, in the garden, you'll see a statue of a small cherub holding a fish. The oval neoclassical temple just beyond the spring (amazingly, *not* painted yellow and white) is the **Glauberova dvorana** (Glauber Pavilion), where several springs bubble up into glass cases. ✉ *Národní ul. at nám. Miru.*

**Městské muzeum** (*Town Museum*)
**MUSEUM** | A fascinating peek into spa culture is housed in this small museum, just off Národní ulice. There's a wonderful collection of spa-related antiques, including copper bathtubs and a turn-of-the-20th-century exercise bike called a Velotrab. The guest books provide insight into the cosmopolitan world of pre–World War I Central Europe. The book for 1812 contains the entry "Ludwig van Beethoven, composer from Vienna." There are also rotating exhibitions of graphic arts. ✉ *Dlouhá 4* ☎ *354–542–344* 🌐 *www.muzeum-frantiskovylazne.cz* 🎟 *35 Kč* 🕒 *Closed Mon., and mid-Dec.–mid-Jan.*

## Hotels

Most of the lodging establishments in town depend on spa patients, who generally stay for several weeks. Spa treatments usually require a medical checkup and cost substantially more than the normal room charge. Walk-in treatment can be arranged at some hotels or at the information center. Signs around town advertise massage therapy and other treatments for casual visitors.

**Rossini**
**$ | HOTEL** | An alternative to the upscale spa hotels in the center, this small family-operated pension is in a more residential area and offers nine rooms, two with balconies. **Pros:** affordable and clean; free coffee throughout the day. **Cons:** no spa; outside of the town's main area. [$] *Rooms from: 1100 Kč* ✉ *Lidická 5* ☎ *603–156–760* 🌐 *www.rossini.cz* 🛏 *9 rooms* 🍴 *Breakfast.*

**★ Tři Lilie**
**$$$ | HOTEL** | "Three Lilies" is thoroughly elegant, from its brasserie to its guest rooms, some of which have balconies with French doors. **Pros:** glorious a/c; rooms with balconies; extremely efficient service. **Cons:** if you don't want spa services, much of its appeal is lost. [$] *Rooms from: 5800 Kč* ✉ *Národní 3* ☎ *354–208–900* 🌐 *www.frantiskovy-lazne.cz/cs/hotel-tri-lilie* 🛏 *31 rooms* 🍴 *Breakfast.*

### Mother and Child

Františkovy Lázne has long been known as a refuge for women seeking help in fertility problems. Evidence of that can be seen in the main spring's statue of a small cherub holding a fish. In keeping with the fertility theme, women are encouraged to touch the fish to ensure their own fertility. You'll notice the statue is shiny from so many years of being rubbed.

# Mariánské Lázně

*30 km (18 miles) southeast of Cheb; 47 km (29 miles) south of Karlovy Vary.*

Once Bohemia's star spa town, Mariánské Lázně now plays second fiddle to Karlovy Vary. Whereas the latter, with its glitzy international film festival and wealthy "New Russian" residents, has succeeded in luring investors, Mariánské Lázně seems to survive largely on the decidedly less glamorous (and much older) crowd coming over from Germany. Busloads of German retirees arrive daily. They walk the promenades and repair over ice cream and cake before boarding the coach to head back home. This trade keeps the properties in business but hardly brings the capital influx needed to overhaul the spa facilities.

The grounds have remained lush and lovely, especially the upper part of the town's spa area near the Grandhotel Pacifik. Here you'll find the colonnades and fountains and river walks you expect from

a once-world-famous spa. And the woods surrounding the town are magnificent.

A hundred years ago Mariánské Lázně, or Marienbad as it was known, was one of Europe's finest resorts. It was a favorite of Britain's King Edward VII. Goethe and Chopin also came. Mark Twain, on a visit in 1892, couldn't get over how new everything looked. Twain—who had a natural aversion to anything too salubrious—labeled the town a "health factory."

The best way to experience the spa—short of signing up for a weeklong treatment—is simply to buy a spouted drinking cup (available at the colonnades) and join the rest of the sippers taking the drinking cure. Be forewarned, though: the waters from the Rudolph, Ambrose, and Caroline springs, though harmless, all have a noticeable diuretic effect. For this reason they're used extensively in treating disorders of the kidney and bladder. Unlike Karlovy Vary, the springs here are all cold water, and may be easier to stomach.

Walking trails of varied difficulty surround the resort in all directions, and one of the country's best golf courses lies about 3 km (2 miles) to the east of town. Hotel staff can also help arrange activities such as tennis and horseback riding. For the less intrepid, a simple stroll around the gardens, with a few deep inhalations of the town's clean air, is enough to restore a healthy sense of perspective.

### GETTING HERE

Regular bus and train service between Prague and Mariánské Lázně makes the journey about three hours each way. Although similar in travel time, the train costs more than the bus. Expect to pay 184 Kč one-way for the bus, 255 Kč for the train. However, from Karlovy Vary, there is hourly train service for about 63 Kč. If you're driving, you can take the E50 and then the 21 from Prague to Mariánské Lázně, a drive of about two hours.

**VISITOR INFORMATION Mariánské Lázně Tourist Information.** (*Cultural and Information Center*) ✉ *Hlavní 47* ☎ *354–622–474* 🌐 *www.marianskelazne.cz.*

## 👁 Sights

**Chodová Planá**

**SPA—SIGHT** | Need a break from the rigorous healthiness of spa life? Chodovar Beer Wellness Land is a few miles south of Mariánské Lázně and offers a wellness hotel, two restaurants, and an underground complex of granite tunnels that have been used to age beer since the 1400s. Generous servings of Czech dishes can be ordered to accompany the strong, fresh Chodovar beer tapped directly from granite storage vaults. You can tour the brewery, but don't expect much English commentary. The brewery also offers a beer bath, massage and, unlimited consumption starting at 1290 Kč. The brewery promises it will cause a mild and gradual rise in heart activity and "scour away any unhealthy substances that may have accumulated." ■ **TIP→ There are brewery tours daily at 2 pm.** ✉ *Pivovarská 107, Chodová Planá* ☎ *374–617–100* 🌐 *www.chodovar.cz* 🎟 *Tour 85 Kč.*

## 🍴 Restaurants

**Churchill's**

**$$** | **BRITISH** | Dark-wood paneling, a serpentine bar, and a mixture of tables and booths give this restaurant a comfy British-pub vibe. It's in the same building as the Excelsior hotel, but with a separate entrance. [$] *Average main: 215 Kč* ✉ *Hotel Excelsior, Hlavní 121* ☎ *354–697–111* 🌐 *www.excelsiormarienbad.com.*

**Koliba**

**$$** | **CZECH** | An excellent alternative to the hotel restaurants in town, Koliba serves grilled meats and shish kebabs, plus tankards of Moravian wine (try the dry, cherry-red Rulandské červené), with traditional gusto. Occasionally fiddlers play rousing Moravian folk tunes. $ *Average main: 250 Kč* ✉ *Hotel Koliba, Dusíkova 592* ☎ *354-625-169* ⊕ *www.hotel-koliba.cz.*

 **Hotels**

Hotel prices have risen in recent years, and many properties are terribly overpriced for what is offered. Despite the glorious Empire and neoclassical facades of many of the hotels and spas, the rooms are a bit on the blah side—typical Central European bland for the most part—with a few exceptions listed below. Most of the hotels have ready-made packages with treatments, and if you plan to indulge in the spas anyway, they can offer some level of savings. Check the hotel's website for current offers. Private accommodations are usually cheaper than hotels, although with more limited amenities. The best place to look for a private room is along Paleckého ulice and Hlavní třída, south of the main spa area, or look in the neighboring villages of Zádub and Závišín.

### Centrální Lázně

$$$ | HOTEL | Near the colonnade and Ambrose Spring, this eggshell-white spa hotel offers unusual treatments such as magnetotherapy and peat packs. **Pros:** extensive therapies; central location (hence the name). **Cons:** not exactly a jumping scene; rooms are a bit spartan. $ *Rooms from: 5250 Kč* ✉ *Goethovo nám. 1* ☎ *354-634-111* ⊕ *marianske-lazne.danubiushotels.cz* ➲ *99 rooms* ⦿ *Breakfast.*

### Grandhotel Pacifik

$$$ | HOTEL | This regal hotel at the top of Hlavní Street has been thoroughly renovated and now may be the best of the bunch, with a full range of spa and wellness facilities including a pool and a sauna. **Pros:** great views; prime location; extensive treatments. **Cons:** pricey; common areas a bit down at the heels. $ *Rooms from: 4860 Kč* ✉ *Mírové nám. 84* ☎ *354-651-111* ⊕ *www.danubiushotels.com* ➲ *102 rooms* ⦿ *Breakfast.*

### Hotel Bohemia

$$ | HOTEL | As a cheaper alternative to some of the posher places in town, this late-19th-century hotel feels pleasantly down-to-earth. **Pros:** inexpensive compared with the other properties in town; friendly staff; beautiful fixtures. **Cons:** rooms a bit dark and grim; no spa. $ *Rooms from: 3513 Kč* ✉ *Hlavní třída 100* ☎ *354-610-111* ⊕ *www.orea.cz/bohemia* ➲ *Bohemia: 76 rooms; Dependence: 12 rooms* ⦿ *Breakfast.*

### Hotel Grand Spa Marienbad

$$$ | HOTEL | The new kid on the block, this Austrian-owned hotel, made up of three interconnected buildings, boasts the most rooms and the biggest wellness center in Mariánské Lázně. **Pros:** huge spa; sleek rooms. **Cons:** officious staff; overly Teutonic vibe. $ *Rooms from: 4380 Kč* ✉ *Ruska 123* ☎ *354-929-397* ⊕ *www.falkensteiner.com/en/hotel/marienbad* ➲ *174 rooms* ⦿ *Some meals.*

### ★ Hotel Koliba

$ | HOTEL | This hunting-style lodge is a perfect choice if you're here for just a day or two, puttering around town without an interest in lavish spa treatments. **Pros:** authentic charm; friendly staff. **Cons:** outside the center of town; a bit rustic. $ *Rooms from: 1500 Kč* ✉ *Dusíkova 592* ☎ *354-625-169* ⊕ *www.hotel-koliba.cz* ➲ *12 rooms* ⦿ *Breakfast.*

### Hotel Nové Lázně

$$$ | HOTEL | This neo-Renaissance hotel and spa—opened in 1896—boasts an opulent façade and public spaces, but these give way to slightly austere rooms. **Pros:** beautiful façade; ideal for spa-fiends. **Cons:** not so ideal for the casual visitor; maintains a slight institutional feel. $ *Rooms from: 6100 Kč* ✉ *Reitenbergerova 53* ☎ *354-644-111* ⊕ *www.danubiushotels.com* ➲ *98 rooms* ⦿ *Breakfast.*

##  Performing Arts

The West Bohemian Symphony Orchestra performs regularly in the New Spa (Nové Lázně). The town's annual Chopin Festival each August brings in pianists from around Europe to perform the Polish composer's works.

## ▼ Nightlife

#### Casino Bellevue

CASINOS | Open nonstop for those who want to try their luck, Casino Bellevue also caters to buses of tourists on shopping and gambling trips from Germany. ✉ Anglická 281 ☎ 354–628–628 ⊕ www. casino-bellevue.cz.

# Plzeň

*92 km (55 miles) southwest of Prague.*

Plzeň—or Pilsen in German, as it's better known abroad—is the industrial heart of Western Bohemia and the region's biggest city. To most visitors the city is known as a beer mecca. Anyone who loves the stuff must pay homage to the enormous Pilsner Urquell brewery, where modern Pils-style beer was first developed more than 150 years ago. Brewery tours are available and highly recommended. There's even a brewing museum here for intellectual beer aficionados.

Another item of interest—particularly for Americans—is historical. Whereas most of the Czech Republic was liberated by Soviet troops at the end of World War II, Plzeň was liberated by the U.S. Army, led by General George S. Patton. Under the communists this fact was not widely acknowledged. But since 1989 the liberation week celebrations held in May have gotten bigger and bigger each passing year. If you're traveling in the area at this time, it's worth stopping by to take part in the festivities. To this day Plzeň retains

## Marienbad with  a French Twist

If the name "Marienbad" rings a bell, it may recall the groundbreaking 1961 French film *Last Year at Marienbad*. A collection of surreal vignettes, the movie explores the possible affair one French couple had in Marienbad through new-wave tricks like jarring jump cuts. But don't expect the manicured lawns and estates of this movie to reflect the landscape of the real Marienbad; it was shot in southern Germany.

a certain "pro-American" feeling that other towns in the Czech Republic lack. There's even a big statue here emblazoned with an enthusiastic "Thank You, America!" written in both English and Czech. You'll find it, naturally, at the top of Americká Street near the intersection with Klatovská. You can learn all about the liberation at the Patton Memorial Museum.

### GETTING HERE

Frequent bus and train service between Prague and Plzeň makes the journey about 1 hour 15 minutes each way. Expect to pay about 100 Kč for the bus, 105 Kč for the train. If you're driving, you can take the E50 directly to Plzeň, a drive of about one hour.

**VISITOR INFORMATION Plzeň City Information Centre.** ✉ Nám. Republiky 41 ☎ 378–035–330 ⊕ www.pilsen.eu/tourist.

##  Sights

#### Na Spilce

RESTAURANT—SIGHT | After a visit to the Pilsner Urquell Brewery, you can carry on drinking and find some cheap traditional grub at the large Na Spilce beer hall just inside the brewery gates. The pub is open weekdays and Sunday from 11 am to 10 pm, Friday and Saturday from 11 am to 11 pm. ⊠ *U Prazdroje 7* ⊕ *www. naspilce.com.*

**Náměstí Republiky** (*Republic Square*)
PLAZA | The city's architectural attractions center on this main square. Dominated by the enormous Gothic **Chrám svatého Bartoloměje** (Church of St. Bartholomew), the square is one of the largest in Bohemia. The church, at 335 feet, is among the tallest in the Czech Republic, and its height is rather accentuated by the emptiness of the square around it. There are a variety of other architectural jewels around the perimeter of the square, including the town hall, adorned with *sgraffiti* and built in the Renaissance style by Italian architects during the town's heyday in the 16th century. The **Great Synagogue,** which claims to be the second-largest in Europe, is a few blocks west of the square, just outside the green strip that circles the Old Town. Three very modern gold-color fountains were added to the square in 2011; however, not everyone is a fan, as the fountains don't really mesh with the historic surroundings. ⊠ *Náměstí Republiky.*

★ **Pilsner Urquell Brewery**
WINERY/DISTILLERY | This is a must-see for any beer lover. The first Pilsner beer was created in 1842 using the excellent Plzeň water, a special malt fermented on the premises, and hops grown in the region around Žatec. (Hops from this area remain in great demand today.) Guided tours of the brewery, complete with a visit to the brewhouse and beer tastings, are offered daily. The brewery is near the railway station. The tour can be combined with a tour of the nearby Gambrinus brewery, the city's underground tunnels, and the Brewery Museum. ⊠ *U Prazdroje 7* ☎ *377–062–888* ⊕ *www.prazdrojvisit. cz* ⊠ *200 Kč (in English); 25% discount available for combined tours and Brewery Museum.*

**Plzeň Historical Underground**
BUILDING | Dating to the 13th century, this is a web of multilevel tunnels. Used for storing food and producing beer and wine, many of the labyrinthine passageways are dotted with wells and their accompanying wooden water-pipe systems. Tours last about 50 minutes. The entrance is in the Brewery Museum. ⊠ *Veleslavínova 6* ☎ *377–235–574* ⊕ *www.plzenskepodzemi.cz* ⊠ *120 Kč (in English); 25% discount available for combined tours and Brewery Museum.*

**Pilsen Beer Spa & Wellness Hotel Purkmistr**
HOT SPRINGS | While Plzeň lacks the bitter thermal waters that are a draw in the spa region, it is better known for bitter Pilsner-style beer. So the opening of a beer spa was inevitable. You can bathe in a custom-made larchwood tub filled with warm beer for a 60-minute treatment. Potable beer is available from a barrel at the same time. The room is lined with stone tiles, and relaxing music plays in the background. The treatment can be combined with a beer massage, or a honey or chocolate massage. Other procedures are also available. The spa is a bit outside of the city center. ⊠ *Selská náves 21/2* ☎ *377–994–311* ⊕ *www. pilsenbeerspa.cz.*

**Pivovarské muzeum** (*Brewery Museum*)
MUSEUM | In a late-Gothic malt house, this museum sits one block northeast of náměstí Republiky. All kinds of fascinating paraphernalia trace the region's brewing history, including the horse-drawn carts used to haul the kegs. ■TIP➔ **A phone app is available in place of an audio guide.** ⊠ *Veleslavínova 6* ☎ *377–062–888* ⊕ *www.prazdrojvisit.cz* ⊠ *90 Kč unguided (with English text), 30 Kč for audio guide, 25% discount when combined with brewery tour and underground.*

**U.S. General George S. Patton Memorial**
MUSEUM | With exhibits and photos, this memorial tells the story of the liberation of Plzeň from the Nazis by U.S. soldiers on May 6, 1945. As the story goes,

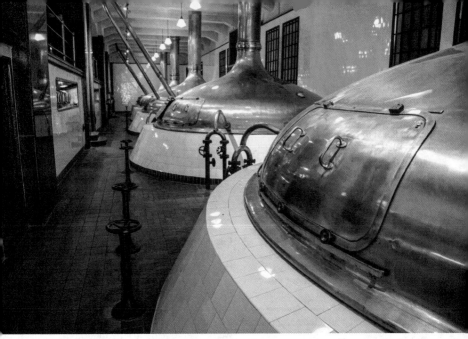

The Pilsner Urquell Brewery is the birthplace of the world renowned lager Pilsner Urquell and the biggest brewery in the Czech Republic.

Patton wanted to press on from Plzeň to liberate Prague, but was prevented from doing so by the Yalta agreement between the United States and the Soviet Union that said Czechoslovakia was to remain under Soviet influence. U.S. aid to Czechoslovakia is also documented. The museum was dedicated in 2005 on the 60th anniversary of Plzeň's liberation. ✉ Pobřežní 10 ☎ 378–037–954 ⊕ www.patton-memorial.cz 🎫 60 Kč 🕑 Closed Mon.

## 🍴 Restaurants

### Anděl Café

$ | CAFÉ | In the evenings, this café, which offers affordable lunches and snacks, becomes a trendy bar. The emphasis is on fair trade items and food from local farmers who follow ecological practices. $ Average main: 110 Kč ✉ Bezručova 7 ☎ 777–022–235 ⊕ www.andelcafe.cz.

### Caffe Fellini

$ | CAFÉ | This dessert spot is right across from St. Bartholomew Church. With an outdoor patio overlooking the square, it's a great place to cool down. $ Average main: 80 Kč ✉ Nám. Republiky 7 ☎ 776–151–429 ⊕ www.caffefellini.cz 🚫 No credit cards.

### El Cid

$$ | SPANISH | Strawberry-infused mojitos wash down excellent tapas dishes at this Spanish-style restaurant along the old town walls, just across from the Continental hotel. Pictures of bullfighters line the yellow walls, while a large patio overlooks the sprawling Křižíkovy Park. $ Average main: 300 Kč ✉ Křižíkovy sady 1 ☎ 377–224–595 ⊕ www.elcid.cz.

### Pizzerie Paganini

$ | PIZZA | Just off the main square on Rooseveltova, this cheery spot with red-and-white checked tablecloths serves up above-average thin-crust pies and pastas. Still, you're better off sticking with the simpler menu items rather than getting too fancy. $ *Average main: 120 Kč* ✉ *Rooseveltova 12* ☎ *377–326–604* ⊕ *pizza-paganini.cz.*

### Rango

**$$ | MEDITERRANEAN** | Part of a hotel of the same name, the interior of Rango is a mash-up of medieval, baroque, and modern style—think Gothic arched ceilings and '60s modern light fixtures. Similarly, the cuisine ranges from Italy to Greece; in addition to pizzas and panini, they serve excellent mussels in white wine, and pork fillet in cream sauce with Parmesan and lemon. $ *Average main: 200 Kč* ✉ *Pražská 10* ☎ *377–329–969* ⊕ *www.rango.cz.*

### Slunečnice

**$$ | INTERNATIONAL** | The sunny interior here echoes its name, which means "sunflower." This café bills itself as a health restaurant and offers some (but not exclusively) organic and vegetarian menu items in a variety of styles, from Indian to Italian. $ *Average main: 170 Kč* ✉ *Jungmannova 4* ☎ *377–236–093* ⊕ *www.slunecniceplzen.cz.*

### U Mansfelda

**$$ | CZECH** | Fresh Pilsner Urquell and variations on classic Czech dishes draw diners to this Pilsner Urquell–sponsored restaurant. A gleaming copper hood floats above the taps in traditional pub style, and the patio invites visitors to spend the evening sipping cold beer and enjoying treats such as boar guláš with dumplings or roasted duck with red cabbage. $ *Average main: 200 Kč* ✉ *Dřevěná 9* ☎ *377–333–844* ⊕ *umansfelda.cz* ⊙ *Wine bar closed Mon. and Sat.*

 Hotels

### Courtyard Pilsen

**$$ | HOTEL** | A surprising addition to the hotel scene in Plzeň, this sleek new property offers all the amenities a visiting

American could hope for, right down to the flat-screen televisions and ice machines in the hallways on each floor. **Pros:** great amenities; a trusted name. **Cons:** doesn't feel especially local; extras such as breakfast are pricey. $ *Rooms from: 2650 Kč* ✉ *Sady 5. kvetna 57* ☎ *373–370–100* ⊕ *www.marriott.com* ➥ *195 rooms* ❍ *No meals.*

### Hotel Central

**$ | HOTEL** | This angular 1960s structure is recommendable for its sunny rooms, friendly staff, and great location, right on the main square. **Pros:** superlative staff; beautiful views of the main square; no-smoking restaurant; free Wi-Fi. **Cons:** the square can echo noise at night; very small bathrooms. $ *Rooms from: 1566 Kč* ✉ *Nám. Republiky 33* ☎ *377–226–757* ⊕ *www.central-hotel.cz* ➥ *77 rooms* ❍ *No meals.*

### Hotel Gondola

**$$ | HOTEL** | A superb choice, the Gondola is clean and quiet with cozy brick-walled rooms and modern facilities, including air-conditioning—all just a few steps away from the central square. **Pros:** incredible value; chockablock with add-ons. **Cons:** slightly odd location; limited business facilities. $ *Rooms from: 2390 Kč* ✉ *Pallova 12* ☎ *377–994–211* ⊕ *www.hotelgondola.cz* ➥ *20 rooms* ❍ *Breakfast.*

### Parkhotel Plzeň

**$ | HOTEL** | A 10-minute tram ride from the center, this large hotel built in 2004 near the Borský Park is perfect for anyone passing through town with a car. **Pros:** sleek new rooms; free Wi-Fi; golf course. **Cons:** outside the center; breakfast options rather limited. $ *Rooms from: 1490 Kč* ✉ *U Borského parku 31* ☎ *378–772–977* ⊕ *en.parkhotel-czech.eu* ➥ *150 rooms* ❍ *Breakfast.*

#  Nightlife

### House of Blues

**MUSIC CLUBS** | House of Blues, related to the American chain in name only, showcases live blues and rock acts. Ignore the mirrored disco ball on the ceiling—ashtrays on every table let you know you're in a real joint. ⊠ *Černická 10* ☎ *608–777–606* ⊕ *www.houseofblues.cz* ⊘ *Closed Aug.*

### Jazz Rock Cafe

**MUSIC CLUBS** | Jazz Rock Cafe gives you a license to party. Drop by on Wednesday to catch some live blues or jazz music. ⊠ *Sedláčkova 18* ☎ *377–224–294* ⊕ *jazz.magicpoint.cz.*

### Zach's pub

**MUSIC CLUBS** | Zach's pub highlights various live acts, including Latin and blues, outdoors on its summer patio. The pub also serves reasonably priced Mexican food, and pets are welcome. ⊠ *Palackého nám.* ☎ *377–223–176* ⊕ *www.zachspub.cz.*

# Chapter 14

# MORAVIA

14

Updated by
Raymond Johnston

| 👁 Sights | 🍴 Restaurants | 🛏 Hotels | 🛍 Shopping | 🍸 Nightlife |
|-----------|---------------|-----------|-------------|-------------|
| ★★★★★ | ★★★☆☆ | ★★★★☆ | ★★☆☆☆ | ★★☆☆☆ |

# WELCOME TO MORAVIA

## TOP REASONS TO GO

★ **Circle the square:** In a country of town squares, Telč's is far and away the most impressive.

★ **See a classic castle:** When people think of castles, they imagine something like Hrad Bouzov (Bouzov Castle).

★ **Spot colossal columns:** Olomouc's Morový sloup (Trinity Column) is so amazing, it's under UNESCO protection.

★ **See the Château Lednice:** A delightful castle, with huge gardens and even a minaret out back!

★ **Uncover some history:** It's exciting to watch Třebíč and Mikulov embrace their past by renovating and promoting their Jewish Quarters.

The most obvious difference between Bohemia and Moravia is that the former is beer country and the latter is wine country. The divisions, while amicable, run much deeper. The people are also more in touch with their past, embracing folk costumes and music for celebrations. In smaller towns some older women still wear embroidered scarves and dresses, something you never see in Bohemia. The pace is also much slower, as agriculture and not industry has always been the driving force of life.

The castles and châteaus attest to the fact that the area was once quite wealthy, but in recent times development has been limited, leaving many areas still unspoiled. And because it's so far off the beaten path of Prague, you'll see far fewer tourists.

**1 Třebíč.** With one of the best-preserved Jewish Quarters in Central Europe, with a number of synagogues and a cemetery, this small town finds itself on the UNESCO World Heritage list. The city's dominant

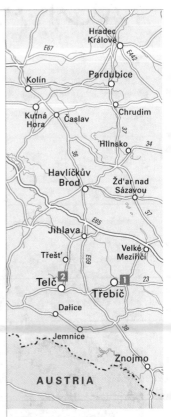

feature, however, is a looming Catholic basilica.

**2 Telč.** Time seems to have stopped several centuries ago in this town, almost unchanged since the Renaissance. Beautiful frescoes adorn the exteriors of most of the buildings in pastel colors or ornate black and white.

**3 Mikulov.** Moravia is wine country, and Mikulov is at its center. Castles,

POLAND

SLOVAKIA

châteaus, and sculpted parks dot the area, and vineyards cover many of the hills. Small wine cellars serve the best of the local beverages plus regional cuisine.

**4 Brno.** The capital of Moravia, Brno is a busy hub and the modern counterpoint to Prague's Old World charm. That said, Brno also has a castle, a cathedral, and an Old Town Hall that are on par with attractions in other European capitals.

**5 Olomouc.** The central city of Moravia was a major base for occupying Russian soldiers. Parts still have an abandoned feel, but the city is slowly waking up. The main square offers a truly monumental baroque column not far from a curious socialist-realist town clock built after World War II.

The Czech Republic's other half, Moravia, is frequently overlooked by visitors. No cities here can compare with the noble beauty of Prague, and Moravia's gentle mountains suffer in comparison with the more rugged Tatras in Slovakia just to the east. Yet Moravia's colorful villages and rolling hills do merit a few days of exploration. Come here for good wine, good folk music, friendly faces, and the languid pace.

Despite sharing a common political union for more than 1,000 years with Bohemians, Moravians still consider themselves distinct from "Czechs" (though it must be said that those differences are not always apparent to visitors). The Moravian dialect of Czech is softer and—as Moravians insist—purer than that spoken in Bohemia. It's hard to generalize, but in a word the Moravians are "earthier" than their Bohemian cousins. They tend to prefer a glass of wine—or even better, fiery *slivovice* (plum brandy)—to beer. Folk music, all but gone in Bohemia, is still very much alive in Moravia. And Catholicism is still a part of life here—particularly in cities like Olomouc—in a way that died out long ago in much of Bohemia.

Historically, Olomouc is one of Moravia's main centers. And it is still impressive today. Long a bastion of the Austro-Hungarian Empire—the city boasts two enormous central squares, a clock tower, and the country's largest Trinity column. In addition, southern Moravia has many small cities, including Mikulov, and a lovely wine region.

If your time is limited or you're just passing through, be sure to at least plan a stopover in the town of Telč in the south. Its enormous central square is like the backdrop of a film set.

# Planning

## When to Go

Wine harvest festivals, with the opportunity to taste the barely fermented young wine, hear folk songs, and eat local delicacies, are mainly in September. For some towns it is the only time they are truly crowded. But the summer months offer pleasant relaxation at outdoor cafés in an unhurried atmosphere. For cyclists, many trails have opened up in the wine region, with spring and early summer being ideal for a tour, but beware that intoxicated cycling is illegal. Winter should be avoided, especially in smaller towns, as many sights are closed, and many shops still close for the weekend throughout the year.

## Getting Here

Bus and train service makes much of Moravia easily accessible. A high-speed train to Olomouc makes it possible to go to there for a day trip from Prague, in just over two hours each way. And while trains do serve the smaller towns and cities, buses are usually more direct and faster. The D1 highway from Prague also leads into South Moravia and loops back up to end near Olomouc, but it gets heavy traffic at the start and end of the weekend.

## Guided Tours

Only a few tour providers offer day trips from Prague to Moravia, as it is farther than places in Bohemia. Guided tours are often available from tourist information centers in individual towns but without transportation to and from Prague.

**Wittmann Tours**
Wittmann Tours focuses on Jewish culture and offers a private trip to Třebíč. The trip starts at 9,000 Kč for a group, plus entrance fees, and goes up depending on the group size. ⊕ *www.wittmann-tours. com.*

## Restaurants and Hotels

Compared with Prague, change has been slow to arrive in Moravia since 1990, especially beyond the major towns. The good news: food and hotels are priced lower. Service has improved but still lags behind Prague's. Older hotel staff might not be proficient in English, but the younger generation has a functional level. And you might find menus in Czech and German, rather than English, especially

in the south near the border. On the plus side, hotel and restaurant workers tend to be friendlier in Moravia and a bit more attentive than they are in Prague.

Cuisine in Moravia leans toward the heavy and the old-fashioned. Choices are sometimes limited to pork, chicken, and duck dishes, usually with lots of gravy. Slowly, a few places with healthier food and modern international cuisine are opening. Pizza places are also widespread. In mountainous areas, inquire locally about the possibility of staying in a *chata* (cabin). These are abundant, and they often carry a bit more of the Moravian spirit than faceless modern hotels. Many lack modern amenities, though, so be prepared to rough it a bit.

*Restaurant and hotel reviews have been shortened. For full information, visit Fodors.com.*

### What it Costs in koruny

|  | $ | $$ | $$$ | $$$$ |
|---|---|---|---|---|
| **RESTAURANTS** | | | | |
|  | under 150 Kč | 150 Kč–350 Kč | 351 Kč–500 Kč | over 500 Kč |
| **HOTELS** | | | | |
|  | under 2,200 Kč | 2,200 Kč–4,000 Kč | 4,001 Kč–6,500 Kč | over 6,500 Kč |

## Třebíč

*35 km (21 miles) east of Telč; 151 km (91 miles) southeast of Prague.*

UNESCO declared both the looping streets of the Židovská čtvrt' (Jewish Quarter) and an ornate basilica in Třebíč World Heritage Sites in 2003. The town is first mentioned in 1101, but it was almost completely destroyed in a war in 1468 and then rebuilt. Although known for its historic buildings, Třebíč also has a few modern ones in the art nouveau, cubist, and functionalist styles. Guided tours of the town are available in English from the information center at Karlovo náměstí 53. As in all small towns, very few shops are open on weekends.

If you arrive by bus or train from Prague, keep an eye out for the 19th-century windmill at the west edge of town. The town's tower, **Městská věz,** on Martinské náměstí provides a nice view of the whole city.

### GETTING HERE
Ideally, you should combine Třebíč with a visit to Telč. Direct bus travel to Třebíč from Prague takes around 2½ hours and costs around 160 Kč. Train connections are not direct and are more expensive. Bus travel with a change in Jihlava, which has a nice square and town wall, is also possible; from Telč the bus trip takes less than 45 minutes and costs around 25 Kč.

Car travel from Telč is direct on Route 23 and takes about 20 minutes. From Prague it's fastest to get back on Highway E50 and go east to Velké Meziříčí. Then go south on Route 360; the trip should take less than three hours.

### TIMING
Out of respect for Jewish traditions, some sites are closed on Saturday.

### VISITOR INFORMATION
**CONTACTS Třebíč Tourist information.**
✉ *Karlovo nám. 47* ☎ *568–610–021* ⊕ *www.visittrebic.eu.*

 ## Sights

**Bazilika sv. Prokupa** (*St. Procopius Basilica*)
**RELIGIOUS SITE** | The late Romanesque and early Gothic St. Procopius Basilica remains true to its original layout from 1260. New sections were added as recently as the 1950s, but the oldest parts are easy to spot. Look for a very heavy style, with lots of stone and few windows. Two baroque towers at the front were added in the early 1700s by

architect F. M. Kaňka. One of the oldest sections is the crypt, with Romanesque pillars and arches. Tours of the connected Benedictine Abbey are available for groups of five or more in July and August but must be booked two days in advance. The château next door has been fully renovated and houses the Vysočina Museum Třebíč. ✉ *Zámek 1* ☎ *568–610–022* ⊕ *www.visittrebic.eu/ sights/basilica-of-st-prokopius* 🎫 *Basilica 100 Kč, museum 120 Kč, Benedictine Abbey 110 Kč* ⊘ *Museum closed Mon. Sept.–June.*

**Rear Synagogue**
**RELIGIOUS SITE** | The Rear Synagogue has an exhibition of Jewish religious items and a wooden model of the ghetto as it was in the 1800s. A touch screen attached to the model provides audio information about the various buildings, with English as an option. Guided tours to the synagogue are available and include a tour of the house of Seligmann Bauer. ✉ *Subakova 44* ☎ *568–610–023* ⊕ *www.visittrebic.eu/sights/rear-syna- gogue-and-seligmann-bauer-apos-s-house* 🎫 *Synagogue from 50 Kč.*

**Židovská čtvrť** (*Jewish Quarter*)
**NEIGHBORHOOD** | A spiraling maze of winding streets, the Jewish Quarter has two synagogues and other buildings formerly used by the town's Jewish community. The **Front Synagogue** on Tiché náměstí is now used for Protestant services. Several houses in the district are intriguing, including a pink Renaissance house with an overhanging second floor at Pokorný 5. A trail of signs in English points out the remarkable spots. Remember your manners—most houses in this area are not museums, and people actually live in them. ✉ *Tiché nám.* ⊕ *www.visittrebic.eu* 🎫 *Guided tour (in English) 170 Kč.*

**Židovský hřbitov** (*Jewish Cemetery*)
**CEMETERY** | The Jewish Cemetery has 3,000 tombstones dating from the Renaissance up to the 20th century. It's free to enter, but guided tours can

be arranged. The cemetery is closed on Saturday, but almost all of it can be seen from the gate and the low wall. ⊠ *Hrádek 14* ☎ *737–180–813* ⊕ *www.visittrebic.eu/ sights/jewish-cemetery* 🖪 *Free* 🕙 *Closed Sat.*

# Telč

*35 km (21 miles) west of Třebíč; 154 km (94 miles) southeast of Prague via Rte. 406.*

Don't be fooled by the dusty approach to the little town of Telč or the unpromising, unkempt countryside surrounding the place. Telč is a knockout. What strikes the eye most here is not just its size but the unified style of the buildings. On the lowest levels are beautifully vaulted Gothic halls, just above are Renaissance floors and façades, and all the buildings are crowned with rich Renaissance and baroque gables.

## GETTING HERE

A car is your best option and makes it easy to combine a trip to Telč with a stop in Třebíč. From Prague, take Highway E50 and E59 south to Route 23 and then west to Telč. The trip takes about two hours without stops. Třebíč is east on Route 23.

Direct bus service leaves from Prague's Florenc bus station and takes just under three hours; the fare is approximately 195 Kč. From Třebíč a direct bus can take 42 minutes and costs around 25 Kč.

Train service from Prague requires several changes and takes more than four hours, so it isn't a practical option. It's recommended only for those who want the scenic route.

## VISITOR INFORMATION

**CONTACTS Telč Tourist Information.**
⊠ *Nám. Zachariáše z Hradce 10* ☎ *567– 112–407* ⊕ *www.telc.eu.*

# ◉ Sights

**Kostel sv. Ducha** (*Church of the Holy Spirit*)
**RELIGIOUS SITE** | A tiny street leading off the main square takes you to the 160-foot Romanesque tower of the Church of the Holy Spirit, a solid tower finished off in conical gray peaks. This is the oldest standing structure in Telč, dating to the first quarter of the 13th century. The interior, however, is a confused hodgepodge, as the style was fiddled with repeatedly, first in a late-Gothic makeover and then refashioned again because of fire damage. ■ **TIP→ In the summer months, the tower is open for a small entrance fee.** ⊠ *Palackého ul.* ☎ *567–112–407 tower information* ⊕ *www.telc.eu/vez_sv_ducha* 🖪 *Free.*

**★ Náměstí Zachariáše z Hradce**
**PLAZA** | This main square is so perfect you feel like you've stepped into a painting, not a living town. Zacharias of Neuhaus, the square's namesake, allegedly created the architectural unity. During the 16th century, so the story goes, the wealthy Zacharias had the castle—originally a small fort—rebuilt into a Renaissance château. But the town's dull buildings clashed so badly that Zacharias had the square rebuilt to match the castle's splendor.

From the south side of town, walk through the **Great Gate,** part of the original fortifications dating to the 13th century. As you approach on Palackého ulice, the square unfolds in front of you, graced with the château at the northern end and beautiful houses bathed in pastel ice-cream shades. Fans of Renaissance reliefs should note the *sgraffito* corner house at No. 15. The house at No. 61, across from the Černý Orel Hotel, also bears intricate details. ⊠ *Telc.*

**Statní zámek Telč** (*Telč Château*)
**CASTLE/PALACE** | This Gothic castle was transformed into a refined Renaissance château by Italian masters between 1553

A unified style is what makes Telč so lovely.

and 1568. Grouped in a complex with the former **Jesuit college** and **Kostel sv. Jakuba** (Church of St. James), the castle was built during the 14th century, perhaps by King John of Luxembourg, the father of Charles IV. In season you can tour the castle and admire the rich Renaissance interiors. The chastising *sgraffito* relief in the dining room depicting gluttony (in addition to the six other deadly sins) seems oddly placed. Other interesting rooms with *sgraffiti* include the Treasury, the Armory, and the Blue and Gold Chambers. There are two tours: the first, Tour A, goes through the Renaissance chambers and is available in English; the second, Tour B, displays the rooms that were used as recently as 1945 but is available only in Czech. The castle basment and gardens are also accessible. ⊠ *Nám. J. Kypty* ☎ *567–243–943* ⊕ *www.zamek-telc.eu* ✉ *Tours from 20 Kč* ⊘ *Closed Mon. No Tour B Oct.–Apr.*

##  Coffee and Quick Bites

### Cukrárna u Matěje

$ | **CAFÉ** | Indulge in good, freshly made cakes or an ice-cream cone at Cukrárna u Matěje, a little café and pastry shop at Na baště 2, on the street leading past the château to a small lake. **Known for:** good coffee; fresh ice cream; smoking permitted. Ⓢ *Average main:* ⊠ *Na baště 2* ☎ *777–162–160.*

## 🛏 Hotels

### Celerin

$ | **HOTEL** | Occupying a tiny corner of the square on the opposite side from the castle, this is the nicest hotel in town. **Pros:** central location on square; historical details in rooms; children's playground. **Cons:** some rooms have limited views due to small (but historically accurate) windows; no elevator; limited parking. Ⓢ *Rooms from: 1520 Kč* ⊠ *Nám. Zachariáše z Hradce 1/43* ☎ *567–243–477* ⊕ *www.hotelcelerin.cz* ⇲ *12 rooms* ⊙ *Free breakfast.*

### Hotel U Černého orla

**$ | HOTEL |** A decent older lemon-yellow baroque hotel on the main square has suitably high standards. **Pros:** restored historic building right on the main square; romantic ambience; pets can stay for free. **Cons:** lacks modern features such as a/c; limited parking; only one room has barrier-free entrance. $ *Rooms from: 1849 Kč* ✉ *Nám. Zachariáše z Hradce 7* ☎ *567–243–222* ⊕ *www.cernyorel.cz* 🛏 *33 rooms* ❍ *Free breakfast.*

# Mikulov

*60 km (37 miles) south of Brno; 283 km (174 miles) southeast of Prague.*

In many ways Mikulov is the quintessential Moravian town, with pastel pink-and-yellow buildings and green rolling hills. For centuries it was one of the most important towns in the region—the seat of the Liechtenstein family in the late Middle Ages and then later the home to the powerful Dietrichstein family. The castle's size and splendor demonstrate Mikulov's onetime crucial position astride the traditional border between Moravia and Austria.

But Mikulov began an extended decline in the 19th century, when the main railroad line from Vienna bypassed the town in favor of Břeclav. Historically, Mikulov was the center of Moravia's Jewish community, growing to a population of several thousand at one point, but many Jews left to seek out life in bigger cities. The 20th century was especially cruel to Mikulov. The Nazis Aryanized many of the industries and deported remaining Jews. After the war, many local industries—including the all-important wineries—were nationalized. Mikulov stagnated as a lonely outpost at the edge of the Iron Curtain.

Recent years have seen a slow revival. Much of the wine industry is back in private hands, and standards have been raised, thanks in part to European Union wine regulations. Day-trippers from Austria have spurred development of a nascent tourist industry. And after many decades of decline, the old Jewish Quarter is getting overdue attention. Although the Jewish community is still tiny—numbering just a handful of people—work is under way to try to preserve some of the remaining houses in the quarter. You can tour the quarter, where many of the houses are now marked with plaques explaining their significance. The Jewish cemetery is one of the largest in Central Europe and a must-see if you're passing through.

Grape-harvesting time in October provides an ideal moment to visit and enjoy the local pastoral delights. Head for one of the many private *sklípky* (wine cellars) built into the hills surrounding the town. If you visit in early September, try to hit Mikulov's renowned wine-harvest festival that kicks off the season with traditional music, folk dancing, and much guzzling of local Riesling.

### GETTING HERE

Mikulov is easily reached by bus from Prague with a change at Brno's Zvonařka bus station. The trip takes a little more than four hours and costs about 242 Kč.

Train service from Prague requires a change at Břeclav. It takes about 4½ hours and costs about 315 Kč.

By car, the trip is south of Brno on Highway E65 to Břeclav and then east on Route 40 and takes a little more than 30 minutes from Brno.

### VISITOR INFORMATION

**CONTACTS Mikulov Tourist Information.**
✉ *Nám. 1* ☎ *519–510–855* ⊕ *www.mikulov.cz.*

#  Sights

★ **Státní zámek Lednice na Moravé** (*Château Lednice na Moravé*)

**CASTLE/PALACE** | The Château Lednice na Moravé, 12 km (7 miles) east of Mikulov, is a must-see. The dining room alone, with resplendent blue-and-green silk wall coverings embossed with the Moravian eagle, makes the visit memorable. The grounds have a 200-foot-tall minaret and a massive greenhouse filled with exotic flora. The minaret halls have been recently restored. A horse-drawn carriage ride and a romantic boat ride are available and are a great way to see the grounds. The absolute splendor of the palace and gardens contrasts sharply with the workaday reality of the town of Lednice. ⊠ *Zámek 1, Lednice* ☎ *519–340–128* ⊕ *www.zamek-lednice.com* 🖭 *Tours from 180 Kč; Museum of Marionettes from 180 Kč; greenhouse 80 Kč; minaret 80 Kč; minaret halls 150 Kč; castle ruin 100 Kč* ⊙ *Closed weekdays Nov.–May and Mon. June–Sept.*

**Zámek Mikulov** (*Mikulov Château*)

**CASTLE/PALACE** | The château holds the **Regionální Muzeum** (Regional Museum), exhibiting period furniture and local wine-making items, including a remarkable wine cask, made in 1643, with a capacity of more than 22,000 gallons. Built as the Gothic-era residence of the noble Liechtenstein family in the 13th century, this château later served as the residence of the powerful Dietrichsteins. Napoléon Bonaparte also stayed here in 1805 while negotiating peace terms with the Austrians after winning the Battle of Austerlitz (Austerlitz is now known as Slavkov, near Brno). Sixty-one years later, Bismarck used the castle to sign a peace treaty with Austria. At the end of World War II, retreating Nazi SS units set fire to it. Much of what you see today was rebuilt after World War II. ■**TIP➔ There are several different tours that can be combined in various ways.** ⊠ *Zámek 5* ☎ *519–309–019* ⊕ *www.rmm.cz* 🖭 *Tours from 30 Kč* ⊙ *Closed Dec.–Mar.; Mon.–Thurs. in Apr., Oct., and Nov.; and Mon. in May, June, and Sept.*

**Zámek v Moravském Krumlově** (*Moravský Krumlov Château*)

**CASTLE/PALACE** | Admirers of art nouveau master Alfons Mucha may want to take a 40-km (31-mile) detour off the main road linking Mikulov to Brno to visit the Moravský Krumlov Château, which will once again be home to one of Mucha's most celebrated works, his 20-painting *Slav Epic*. This enormous work took almost two decades to complete and tells the history of the Slav nation. The city of Prague won ownership of the paintings in a long legal battle but is lending them back until a new exhibition space is ready in Prague. The paintings will reside here from summer 2020 until 2025. The château, built as a castle in the 13th century, also hosts other exhibits and has a large park with a plague column (a monument built in thanksgiving for the end of a plague). ⊠ *Zámecká 2* ☎ *515–321–064* ⊕ *www.mkrumlov.cz/zamek-v-moravskem-krumlove/d-5009* 🖭 *80 Kč* ⊙ *Closed Mon.*

**Židovská čtvrť** (*Jewish Quarter*)

**RELIGIOUS SITE** | What's left of Mikulov's once-thriving Jewish Quarter can be seen on a stroll down Husova ulice, which was once its center. An information board near the corner with Brněnská ulice explains the significance of the community and what happened to it. The most important building still standing is the 16th-century Altschul. The community once numbered several thousand people, and the town was the seat of the chief rabbi of Moravia from the 17th to the 19th century. Several respected Talmudic scholars, including Rabbis Jehuda Loew and David Oppenheimer, lived and taught here. ⊠ *Husova ul. 11* ⊕ *www.rmm.cz/index_en.html* 🖭 *Synagogue 50 Kč* ⊙ *Synagogue closed Dec.–Feb.; Mon.–Thurs. in Apr., Oct., and Nov.; and Mon. in May and June.*

Main Square with the fountain and Holy Trinity Statue in Mikulov

★ **Židovský hřbitov** (*Jewish Cemetery*)
**CEMETERY** | Mikulov's massive cemetery with 4,000 tombs is not far from Husova ulice, just off Brněnská. The cemetery dates to shortly after 1421 when Jews were forced to leave Vienna and Lower Austria. The oldest legible stone is from 1605 and the most recent are from the 19th century, giving a wide range of stylistic flourishes. Step into the ceremonial hall to view an exhibit of the cemetery's history. Visits outside of opening hours and guided tours can be arranged at least two days in advance. ✉ *Off Brněnská ul.* 🌐 *www.jewishheritagemikulov.org* 🎟 *30 Kč* 🕒 *Closed Nov.–Mar. and Mon. in Apr. and Oct.*

## 🛏 Hotels

**Hotel Tanzberg**
**$** | **HOTEL** | Prim and nicely renovated, this hotel sits in the middle of the Jewish Quarter, on Husova ulice. **Pros:** central location; historic building; wine cellar for tastings. **Cons:** very narrow stairs and no elevator; parking lot distant from the hotel; furniture is basic and a bit worn. [$] *Rooms from: 1950 Kč* ✉ *Husova ul. 8* ☎ *519–510–692* 🌐 *www.hotel-tanzberg.cz* 🛏 *17 rooms* 🍴 *Free breakfast.*

# Brno

*202 km (122 miles) southeast of Prague via Hwy. E65.*

Nicknamed the "Manchester of Moravia," Brno (pronounced *burr*-no) has a different feel from other Czech or Moravian cities. Beginning with a textile industry imported from Germany, Holland, and Belgium, Brno became a leading industrial center of the Austro-Hungarian Empire during the 18th and 19th centuries. Some visitors search in vain for an extensive Old Town, pining for the traditional arcaded storefronts that typify other historic Czech towns. Instead, you'll see fine examples of the Empire and neo-Renaissance styles, their formal, geometric façades more in keeping with the conservative tastes of the 19th-century middle class.

In the 1920s and '30s, the city became home to some of the best young architects working in the early-modern, Bauhaus, and "international" styles. The architectural rivalry with Prague continues to this day, with Brno now claiming the country's tallest building. The AZ Tower beats Prague's City Tower by a mere six feet. When Prague roundly rejected a modern library designed by famed architect Jan Kaplický, a scale model of the façade was built as a bus stop on Okružní ulice in Brno's Lesná district.

Experimentation wasn't restricted to architecture. Leoš Janáček, an important composer of the early modern period, lived and worked in Brno, as did Austrian novelist Robert Musil. That artistic support continues today, and the city is considered to have some of the best theater and performing arts in the country, as well as a small but thriving café scene. It has also become a high-tech development hub, with numerous software companies, several good science-oriented schools, and a government-backed support center.

And while the city has been reaching new heights with skyscrapers in its "Little Manhattan" area, it has also been reaching new depths by opening up an underground labyrinth as well as Europe's largest ossuary—a subterranean collection of human bones from several centuries.

Allow a couple of hours to fully explore the Hrad Špilberk (Spielberg Castle). Museum enthusiasts could easily spend a half day or more browsing through the city's many collections. Brno is relatively busy on weekdays and surprisingly slow on weekends. Avoid the city at trade-fair time (the biggest are in early spring and early autumn), when hotel and restaurant facilities are strained. If the hotels are booked, the tourist information center at the town hall will help you find a room.

## GETTING HERE AND AROUND

Bus connections from Prague's Florenc terminal to Brno are frequent, and the trip is a half hour shorter than the train route. Most buses arrive at the main bus station, a 10-minute walk from the train station. Some buses stop next to the train station. Bus and train lines connect Brno and Vienna and run several times a day.

Brno—within easy driving distance of Prague, Bratislava, and Vienna—is 196 km (122 miles) from Prague and 121 km (75 miles) from Bratislava. The E65 highway links all three cities.

Comfortable EuroCity or InterCity trains run six times daily, making the three-hour run from Prague to Brno's station. They depart either from Prague's main station, Hlavní nádraží, or the suburban Nádraží Holešovice. Trains leaving Prague for Bratislava, Budapest, and Vienna normally stop in Brno (check timetables to be sure).

Trams are the best way to get around the city. Tickets start at 10 Kč for one zone with no transfer and go up to 86 Kč, depending on the time and zones traveled, and are available at newsstands and yellow ticket machines. A 25 Kč ticket allows for an hour of travel with changes. Tickets from the driver cost more. Single-day, three-day, and other long-term tickets are available. Most trams stop in front of the main station (Hlavní nádraží). Buses to the city periphery and nearby sights such as Moravský Kras in northern Moravia congregate at the main bus station, a 10-minute walk behind the train station. To find it, simply go to the train station and follow the signs to *čsad*.

The tourist card **Brnopas,** available at tourist information centers, also works as a public transportation pass and allows entry to five main attractions, plus a chance to get last-minute tickets to Villa

# Saved by the Bell

During the Thirty Years' War, Brno faced a fierce attack by Swedish troops. Brno's resistance was determined, and the Swedish commander decided that if the town couldn't be taken by noon the next day, they would give up the fight. Word of this reached the cathedral's bell ringer, and just as the Swedish troops were preparing their final assault, they rang the noon bells—an hour early. The ruse worked, and the Swedes decamped. The cathedral bells proved to be the final defensive strategy that saved the town from being taken. The new bullet-shaped clock at Náměstí Svobody commemorates this by dropping a glass ball into a hole at 11 am every day.

Tugendhat. The pass can be valid for between one and three days.

The nominal taxi fare is about 30 Kč per km (½ mile), on top of a 60 Kč initial fee. There are taxi stands at the main train station, at the Výstaviště exhibition grounds, on Joštova ulice at the north end of the Old Town, and at other locations. Brush up on your Czech—dispatchers sometimes don't understand English.

**INFORMATION Hlavní nádražní.**
✉ *Nádražní 1* ☎ *221–111–122* ⊕ *www.idos.cz.* **Main bus station.** (*ÚAN Zvonařka*)
✉ *Zvonařka 1* ☎ *543–217–733* ⊕ *idos.cz.*

## VISITOR INFORMATION
**CONTACTS Brno Tourist Information.** ✉ *Old Town Hall, Radnická 8* ☎ *542–427–150* ⊕ *ticbrno.cz/en.*

### Sights
**Chrám sv. Petra a Pavla** (*Cathedral of Sts. Peter and Paul*)
**RELIGIOUS SITE** | Best admired from a distance, the silhouette of slim neo-Gothic twin spires—added in the 20th century—give the cathedral a touch of Gothic dignity. Up close, the interior is light and tasteful but hardly mind-blowing. The treasury and tower can be visited for a fee. The crypt can be visted on request if it is closed. This is the church pictured on the face of the 10 Kč coin. ✉ *Petrov at Petrská ul.* ⊕ *www.katedrala-petrov.*

*cz* ✉ *Free, treasury and tower 40 Kč* ⊙ *Crypt closed weekdays.*

**Hrad Špilberk** (*Spielberg Castle*)
**CASTLE/PALACE** | Once among the most feared places in the Habsburg Empire, this fortress-cum-prison still broods over Brno behind menacing walls. The castle's advantageous location brought the early lords of the city, who moved here during the 13th century from neighboring Petrov Hill. Successive rulers gradually converted the old castle into a virtually impregnable fortress. It withstood the onslaughts of Hussites, Swedes, and Prussians over the centuries; only Napoléon, in 1809, succeeded in occupying the fortress. But the castle's fame comes from its gruesome history as a prison for enemies of the Austro-Hungarian monarchy and later for the Nazis' prisoners during World War II. The hardest offenders were shackled day and night in dank, dark catacombs and fed only bread and water. The castle complex is large, and the various parts generally require separate admission. The **casemates** (passages within the walls of the castle) have been turned into an exhibition of the late-18th-century prison and their Nazi-era use as an air-raid shelter. You can see the entire castle grounds as well as the surrounding area from the **observation tower**. Aboveground, a **museum** in the fortress starts off with more displays on the prison era with detailed

Booming Brno, with its creativity, history, and subterranean mystery, is the perfect antidote to tourist-filled Prague.

English texts. Included in the tour of the museum are exhibitions of objects from Brno's history and art from the Renaissance to modern times from the city's collection. ■ TIP→ **Admission and opening hours vary according to what you want to see and where you want to go, that is, the entire complex, various combinations of exhibits, or individual castle sections.** ✉ *Špilberk 1* ☎ *542–123–611* ⊕ *www. spilberk.cz* ✉ *From 50 Kč* ⊙ *Closed Mon. Oct.–Mar.*

**Kostel Nalezení sv. Kříže** (*Church of the Holy Cross*)

**RELIGIOUS SITE** | Formerly part of the Capuchin Monastery, the Church of the Holy Cross combines a baroque form with a rather stark façade. Enter the *krypta* (crypt) in the basement, and the mummified remains of some 200 nobles and monks from the late 17th and 18th centuries are displayed, ingeniously preserved by a natural system of air circulating through vents and chimneys. The best-known mummy is Col. František Trenck, commander of the brutal Pandour

regiment of the Austrian army, who, at least in legend, spent several years in the dungeons of Spielberg Castle before finding his final rest here in 1749. A note of caution about the crypt: the graphic displays can be frightening to children (and even some adults), so ask at the admission desk for a small brochure (60 Kč) with pictures that preview what's to come, or look at the postcards for sale. Locals refer to the building simply as the Capuchin Church. ✉ *Kapucínské nám. 5* ☎ *511–140–053* ⊕ *www.kapucini.cz* ✉ *80 Kč, photography fee 30 Kč.*

**Kostnice u sv. Jakuba** (*St. James Ossuary*)

**CEMETERY** | Several basement rooms in the tunnels next to the St. James Church are filled with neatly stacked bones, making it one of the largest ossuaries in Europe. Sealed up since the late 1700s, its contents were unearthed in 2001 and were cleaned after years of neglect before being opened to the public in 2012. Remains of some 50,000 people are estimated to be in the rooms, including victims of plagues, epidemics, and wars from the 13th to 18th centuries. It is much larger than the famous ossuary in Kutná Hora in Central Bohemia, which has bones in decorative designs. At one of the upper windows of the church, as seen from the street, there is a sculpture of a monk exposing his backside toward a rival church across town. ⊠ Jakubské nám. ☎ 515–919–793 ⊕ www.ticbrno.cz/en/podzemi/kostnice-u-sv-jakuba ☜ 140 Kč, video fee 50 Kč ⊘ Closed Mon.

**Labyrint pod Zeleným trhem** (Labyrinth under the Cabbage Market)
ARCHAEOLOGICAL SITE | Some 2,296 feet of underground passages are filled with exhibits relating to alchemy, medicine, medieval punishment, and the more mundane aspects of life—like storing wine. Some of the old passages were rediscovered in the 1970s and have undergone years of archeological research before opening to the public in 2011. Unfortunately, explanatory plaques are only in Czech. ⊠ Zelný trh 21 ☎ 542–212–892 ⊕ www.ticbrno.cz ☜ 160 Kč, video fee 50 Kč ⊘ Closed Mon.

**Mincmistrovský sklep** (Mint Master's Cellar)
ARCHAEOLOGICAL SITE | The project to open up some of Brno's medieval underground includes access to the Mint Master's Cellar, which is under the house of Bruno, one of the city's coin makers. The basement opened to the public in 2010 after being discovered during excavations in 1999. An exhibition in the vaulted rooms shows historical minting techniques. ⊠ Dominikánské nám. 1 ☎ 602–128–124 ⊕ www.ticbrno.cz ☜ 100 Kč, video fee 50 Kč ⊘ Closed Tues.

**Místodržitelský palác** (Governor's Palace)
CASTLE/PALACE | Moravia's strong artistic ties to Austria can be seen in the impressive collection of painting and sculpture found in this splendid palace. The museum is divided into sections, but the most impressive part—art from the Gothic period to the 19th century—is on the first floor. The short-term exhibits are often a bit disappointing. ⊠ Moravské nám. 1A ☎ 532–169–130 ⊕ www.moravska-galerie.cz ☜ Permanent exhibits free, temporary exhibits vary ⊘ Closed Mon. and Tues.

**Muzeum romské kultury** (Museum of Romani Culture)
MUSEUM | A small but singular museum devoted to the culture of the Roma, as Gypsies prefer to be called, is halfway between Brno's historical center and the high-rise housing projects. To foster crosscultural understanding (as Roma people are often the victims of discrimination), this museum is dedicated to their culture and history. Exhibits deal with traditional occupations, dress, and lifestyles. A study room has documents and photographs. ⊠ Bratislavská 67 ☎ 545–581–206 ⊕ www.rommuz.cz ☜ 80 Kč, English audio guide 80 Kč ⊘ Closed Mon. and Sat.

**Náměstí Svobody** (Freedom Square)
PLAZA | The best place to start any walking tour, this is the focal point of the city and a centerpiece for the massive effort to modernize the area. The square underwent extensive renovation in 2006, and adjoining streets feature some of the city's best shopping. Anyone who has been to Vienna might experience déjà vu here, as many of the buildings were designed by 19th-century Austrian architects. Especially noteworthy is the stolid Klein Palace at No. 15, built by Theophil Hansen and Ludwig Foerster, both prominent for their work on Vienna's Ringstrasse. A highly controversial clock—it's supposed to look like a bullet and remind people of a battle that happened in 1645—was added in 2010; most people, however, say it looks more like—ahem—a sex toy than a bullet. Also, you need a pamphlet to explain how to read the time on it. The clock drops a glass ball on the hour, which people try to catch. ⊠ Brno.

**Pražákův palác** (*Pražák Palace*)
MUSEUM | The largest collection of modern and contemporary Czech art outside of Prague lines the walls of this handsome, 19th-century neo-Renaissance building. If you've already seen these same artists represented in Prague's major galleries, you may be tempted to adopt a been-there-done-that attitude. But the emphasis here is on Moravian artists, who tended to prefer rural themes—their avant-garde concoctions have a certain folksy flavor. Modern and contemporary art is on the second floor; other sections have temporary exhibits. ✉ *Husova 18* ☎ *532–169–111* ⊕ *www.moravska-galerie.cz* ✒ *Permanent exhibits free, temporary exhibits vary* ⊘ *Closed Mon. and Tues.*

**Stará radnice** (*Old Town Hall*)
GOVERNMENT BUILDING | Just inside the door of the oldest secular building in Brno, dating to the 13th century, are the remains of two famous Brno legends, the **Brno Dragon** and the **wagon wheel.** The dragon—actually an alligator—apparently turned up at the town walls one day in the 17th century and began eating children and livestock. As the story goes, a gatekeeper came up with the idea of stuffing a freshly slaughtered goat with limestone. The dragon devoured the goat, swallowing the limestone as well, and when it drank at a nearby river, the water mixed with the limestone and burst the dragon's stomach (the scars on the preserved dragon's stomach are still clearly visible). The story of the wagon wheel, on the other hand, concerns a bet placed some 400 years ago that a young wheelwright, Jiří Birek, couldn't chop down a tree, form the wood into a wheel, and roll it from his home at Lednice (53 km [33 miles] away) to the town walls of Brno—all between sunup and sundown. The wheel stands as a lasting tribute to his achievement. (The townspeople, however, became convinced that Jiří had enlisted the help of the devil to

## Old Refueling Spot

After climbing to Spielberg Castle and touring several museums, stop and relax awhile with a cold beer at Stopkova pivnice; if you're hungry, try the house *guláš* (goulash). Now part of the Kolkovna chain, there has been a pub on this site since the late 19th century. Its name comes from Jaroslav Stopka, who took over the existing pub in 1910. ⊕ *www.kolkovna.cz*

win the bet, so they stopped frequenting his workshop; poor Jiří died penniless.)

No longer the seat of the town government, the Old Town Hall holds exhibitions and performances and the town's tourist information office. To find out what's on, ask in the information center just inside Pilgram's portal. The view from the top of the tower is one of the best in Brno, but the climb (five flights) is strenuous. ✉ *Radnická 8* ⊕ *ticbrno.cz* ✒ *Tower 70 Kč* ⊘ *Tower closed Jan.–Mar.*

### 10-Z Fallout Shelter
ARCHAEOLOGICAL SITE | A Cold War–era relic, this highly classified (hence the "10-Z" code name) shelter was designed to protect the political elite of the region in the event of a nuclear attack. Built during the Nazi occupation in World War II as a bomb shelter, between 1945 and 1948 it was used by a wine wholesaler, after which it served as a secret shelter until 1989. Up to 500 people could have stayed inside if needed, but fortunately no one had to. It was declassified and opened to the public in 2015. There is an exhibition about the Cold War at the entrance with English text. Guided group tours of the whole complex with a flashlight (provided) take place as well, with some at night. On the tour you can see

underground offices, a phone switchboard, heavy doors, and other curious infrastructure. The entrance is across the street from Husova 12. Tour tickets are available at the Tourist Information Center at Panenská 1. ✉ *Husova* ⊕ *ticbrno.cz* 🎫 *Tours from 150 Kč* ⊗ *Closed Mon.*

### Villa Tugendhat

**HOUSE** | Designed by Ludwig Mies van der Rohe and completed in 1930, this austere, white Bauhaus villa counts among the most important works of the modern period and is now a UNESCO World Heritage Site. Function and the use of geometric forms are emphasized. The Tugendhat family fled before the Nazis, and their original furnishings vanished. Replicas of Mies's cool, functional designs have been installed in the downstairs living area. Some of the original exotic wood paneling and an onyx screen remain in place. The best way to get there is to take a taxi or Tram 3, 5, or 11 to the Dětská nemocnice stop and then walk up unmarked Černopolní ulice for 10 minutes or so; you'll be able to see the modernist structure up on the hill. ■ **TIP→ Reservations for tours are highly recommended at least three months in advance and can be made online.** Holders of the Brnopas have access to a limited number of last-minute tickets at the Tourist Information C enter at Panenská 1 and can skip to the front of the line at the villa. The extended tour shows some of the building's infrastructure. ✉ *Černopolní 45* 📷 ⊕ *www.tugendhat.eu* 🎫 *Tours 350 Kč* ⊗ *Closed Mon.*

### Zelný trh (Cabbage Market)

**FOUNTAIN** | Only in this Cabbage Market could Brno begin to look like a typical Czech town—not just for the many stands from which farmers still sell vegetables but also for the flamboyant **Parnassus Fountain** that adorns its center. This baroque outburst (inspiring a love-it-or-hate-it reaction) couldn't be more out of place amid the formal elegance of most of the buildings on the square. But when Johann Bernhard Fischer von Erlach created the fountain in the late 17th century, it was important for a striving town like Brno to display its understanding of the classics and of ancient Greece. Therefore Hercules slays a three-headed dragon, and Amphitrite awaits the arrival of her lover—all incongruously surrounded by farmers hawking turnips and onions. What could be more Czech? ✉ *Brno.*

## 🍽 Restaurants

### Atelier Cocktail Bar and Bistro

**$$** | **CONTEMPORARY** | The menu is on the decidedly short side but offers a constantly changing list of modern takes on fish, meat, and pasta dishes, served in a relaxed but trendy environment. Tasting menus with seasonal dishes include a vegetarian option. **Known for:** seasonal tasting menus; modern casual dining; trendy cocktails. $ *Average main: 250 Kč* ✉ *Kobližná 2* 📷 *739–401–086* ⊕ *www.atelierbar.cz.*

### Pavillon

**$$$** | **CZECH** | A contemporary re-creation of a landmark 1920s coffeehouse (the original was razed by the communists to make way for a theater), this spot is high on flapper flair. Everything from the light fixtures to the furniture was faithfully copied from the original interior. **Known for:** modern Bauhaus architecture; tasting menus; vegan options. $ *Average main: 450 Kč* ✉ *Jezuitská 6, between Za Divadlem and Koliště* 📷 *541–213–497 for large events* ⊕ *www.restaurant-pavillon.cz.*

### Restaurace Špalíček

**$$** | **CZECH** | This homey pub has a terrific central location right on the edge of the Cabbage Market. The menu features the standard "roast pork and dumplings" kind of thing but in a comfortable and merry setting. **Known for:** old-fashioned Czech atmosphere; good view on a main square; reasonable prices for a restaurant with a view. $ *Average* *main: 150 Kč* ⊠ *Zelný trh 12* ☎ *542–211–526* ▭ *No credit cards.*

### Výčep Na stojáka

$$ | CZECH | It is always standing room only, as this pub has no chairs—just high tables. This keeps the line at the tap moving. **Known for:** no seats; friendly vibe; glass of beer foam for a discount. $ *Average main: 195 Kč* ⊠ *Behounska 16* ☎ *702–202–048* ⊕ *www.vycepnastojaka.cz/en/v/vycep-na-stojaka-jakubak.*

 ## Hotels

### Grandhotel Brno

$$ | HOTEL | The hotel dates to 1870 but got a thorough face-lift in the late 1980s and another upgrade in recent years, making it both comfortable and convenient, especially if you're traveling to Brno by train, as it's just across the street from the station. **Pros:** close to main transportation hub; air-conditioning; sauna and fitness room. **Cons:** parking at the hotel is limited; breakfast costs extra; location can be noisy. $ *Rooms from: 2527 Kč* ⊠ *Benešova 18/20* ☎ *542–518–111* ⊕ *www.grandhotelbrno.cz* ↪ *105 rooms* |◎| *No meals.*

### Hotel Pegas

$$ | HOTEL | A little inn with a reasonable price and central location, Pegas has plain rooms that are snug and clean, with wood paneling and down comforters. **Pros:** on-site brewery; central location; air-conditioning. **Cons:** parking is separate from hotel and costs extra; elevator does not reach ground floor; rooms are very plain. $ *Rooms from: 2500 Kč* ⊠ *Jakubská 4* ☎ *542–210–104* ⊕ *www.hotelpegas.cz* ↪ *14 rooms* |◎| *Free breakfast.*

### ★ Royal Ricc

$$ | HOTEL | Lovingly restored from a baroque town house, this boutique hotel retains period details, like exposed-beam ceilings. **Pros:** fine detail in furniture; stained-glass windows; historical

wooden ceilings in some rooms. **Cons:** hard to access by car since it's at the edge of a pedestrian zone; busy street is noisy at night; hotel bar is very small. $ *Rooms from: 3318 Kč* ⊠ *Starobrněnská 10* ☎ *542–219–262* ⊕ *www.royalricc.cz* ↪ *30 rooms* |◎| *Free breakfast.*

### Slavia

$ | HOTEL | The century-old Slavia, just off the main Česká ulice, feels a little dated, but the prices here are lower than at the comparable Grandhotel Brno and the location is excellent. **Pros:** central location; wheelchair accessible, with one room for people with disabilities; inexpensive. **Cons:** rooms lack character; bathrooms very old-fashioned; street parking costs extra. $ *Rooms from: 1349 Kč* ⊠ *Solniční 15/17* ☎ *542–321–249* ⊕ *www.slaviabrno.cz* ↪ *84 rooms* |◎| *Free breakfast.*

 ## Nightlife

### Klub Alterna

**MUSIC CLUBS** | A few blocks north of the city center, Klub Alterna hosts good Czech jazz and folk performers. ⊠ *Kounicova 48* ☎ *541–212–091* ⊕ *www.alterna.cz.*

 ## Performing Arts

Brno is renowned throughout the Czech Republic for its theater and performing arts. Jacket-and-tie cultural events take place at a few main venues slightly northwest of the center of town, a five-minute walk from Náměstí Svobody. Check posted schedules at the theaters or on their websites.

### TICKETS

#### Předprodej vstupenek

**TICKETS** | In Brno you can buy tickets for performing arts productions at individual theater box offices or at the central Předprodej vstupenek. ⊠ *Panenská 1* ⊕ *vstupenky.ticbrno.cz.*

## VENUES

**Divadlo Husa na provázku** (*Goose on a String Theater*)

**THEATER** | One of the country's best-known fringe theater companies, the Goose on a String Theater, has its home in Brno. ✉ *Zelný trh 9, at Petrská ul.* ☎ *542–211–630* ⊕ *www.provazek.cz.*

**Janáčkovo divadlo** (*Janáček Theater*)

**THEATER** | Opera and ballet productions are held at the modern Janáček Theater. ✉ *Rooseveltova 7* ☎ *542–158–111* ⊕ *www.ndbrno.cz.*

**Mahenovo divadlo** (*Mahen Theater*)

**THEATER** | The Mahen Theater is the city's principal venue for dramatic theater. Some productions have projected English subtitles. ✉ *Rooseveltova 1* ☎ *542–158–111* ⊕ *www.ndbrno.cz.*

## 🛍 Shopping

Bright red, orange, and yellow flower patterns are the signature folk-pottery look in Moravia. You can find these products in stores and hotel gift shops throughout the region.

The shopping mall **Vaňkovka** (✉ *Ve Vaňkovce 1* ☎ *533–110–111*), linking the main rail station and main bus station, has several restaurants and stores for clothing.

### Antikvariát Alfa

**ANTIQUES/COLLECTIBLES** | For rare books, art monographs, old prints, and a great selection of avant-garde 1920s periodicals, stop by Antikvariát Alfa. ✉ *Veselá 39* ☎ *542–211–947* ⊕ *www.antikalfa.cz* ⊘ *Closed weekends.*

### Galerie AmbrosianA

**ART GALLERIES** | For sophisticated artwork, including paintings and photography, stop by Galerie AmbrosianA. ✉ *Jezuitská 11* ☎ *542–214–439* ⊕ *www.ambrosiana.cz* ⊘ *Closed weekends.*

# Olomouc

*77 km (48 miles) northeast of Brno; 275 km (165 miles) east of Prague.*

Olomouc (pronounced oh-loh-moats) is a handsome district capital, with some beautifully restored baroque houses along its broad central squares and the country's largest Trinity column, another UNESCO World Heritage Site. Its laid-back, small-town feel and the presence of a charming, inexpensive pension right in town make it an easy choice for an overnight stay.

Olomouc owes its relative prosperity to its loyalty to the Austro-Hungarian Empire. In the revolutionary days of the mid-19th century, when the rising middle classes throughout the empire were asserting their independence from the nobility, the residents of Olomouc remained true to the ruling Habsburgs. During the revolutions of 1848, the royal family even fled here from Vienna for protection. Mozart, Mahler, and other famous composers stopped by on occasion, leaving behind a musical heritage that is still alive today with an active classical music scene.

The most prominent open space in Olomouc is the triangular Horní náměstí (Upper Square). Four of the city's half dozen renowned **baroque fountains,** depicting Hercules (1687), Caesar (1724), Neptune (1695), and Jupiter (1707), dot the square and the adjacent other large square, Dolní náměstí (Lower Square) to the south.

A discount card called the **Olomouc Region Card** is valid for most tourist sights in and around the city, and for public transportation in the city, and is available for 240 Kč for 48 hours and 480 Kč for five days. Admission to the town hall tower, botanical gardens, zoo, Hrad Bouzov (Bouzov Castle), Hrad Šternberk, and other sites is included. The card also provides discounts at some restaurants, pools, fitness centers, and hotels. You can buy the card—and get more information on discounts and deals—at the main tourist information center at Horní náměstí 1 and at many hotels, travel agencies, and tourist venues. The information center also can tell you about local tour operators that organize half-day outings to the area's castles.

## GETTING HERE

Traveling from Prague, in addition to driving, you can take either a train or a bus. By car, follow the D1 motorway south to Brno and then follow the signs and turnoffs to Olomouc from Brno. The trip will take about three hours in moderate traffic.

Direct train travel from Prague takes at least 2¾ hours and costs around 220 Kč for the 250-km (150-mile) trip. High-speed Pendolino trains also serve Olomouc from Hlavní nádraží (the main train station); seat reservations are required, often at no additional fee. Privately operated trains by Leo Express also travel here, with tickets starting at 169 Kč.

Bus travel requires a change at Brno and takes over four hours.

## VISITOR INFORMATION

**CONTACTS Olomouc Tourist Information.** ⊠ *Radnice, Horní nám.* ☎ *585–513–385* ⊕ *www.tourism.olomouc.eu.*

 Sights

**Arcidiecézní muzeum** (*Archdiocesan Museum*)
**HOUSE** | This ornate complex is home to treasures from the collections of the archdiocese, including golden monstrances, religious paintings, carved ivory objects, and a full-sized gilded coach. Modern art is also displayed in part of the building complex and included in the same admission, but it is often a bit disappointing in comparison. In 1767 the young musical prodigy Wolfgang Amadeus Mozart, age 11, spent six weeks recovering from a mild attack of chicken pox and completed his Sixth Symphony here. The 16-year-old King Wenceslas III suffered a much worse fate here in 1306, when he was murdered, putting an end to the Přemyslid dynasty. ⊠ *Václavské nám. 3* ⊕ *www.muo.cz/en/olomouc-archdiocesan-museum* ☎ *100 Kč (free Sun.), incl. Romanesque Bishop's Palace* ⊗ *Closed Mon.*

**Chrám sv. Mořice** (*Church of St. Maurice*)
**RELIGIOUS SITE** | Nothing is left of the original Church of St. Maurice that stood just north of Horní náměstí in 1257. This is a new church started in 1412 on the same site and remodeled many times. Its current fierce, gray exterior dates to the middle of the 16th century. A sculpture of Christ on the Mount of Olives dates to the 15th century. The baroque organ inside, the largest in the Czech Republic, originally contained 2,311 pipes until it was expanded in the 1960s to more than 10,000 pipes. An international organ festival takes place in the church every September. The tower is sometimes open to the public, depending on the weather. ⊠ *8. května* ⊕ *www.moric-olomouc.cz* ☎ *Free.*

**Dóm sv. Václava** (*Cathedral of St. Wenceslas*)
**RELIGIOUS SITE** | Between the main square and this cathedral lies a peaceful neighborhood given over to huge buildings, mostly belonging either to the university or the archbishop. The church itself is impressive, but its Gothic appearance comes only from a 19th-century makeover. A shrine has an ornate case with the relics of St. Jan Sarkander, a 17th-century priest who was tortured. A plaque marks the fact that Pope John Paul II celebrated mass there in 1995. The crypt, open in the summer and fall, has a marble box with the heart of an archduke who otherwise is buried in Vienna. Some ecclesiastical treasures are also on display.

## Did You Know?

Within Olomouc's Trinity Column is a secret chapel that is closed to the public, featuring highly-detailed stone reliefs depicting events from the bible.

# Off the Beaten Path

**Hrad Bouzov***Bouzov Castle* One of Moravia's most impressive castles, 30 km (18 miles) west of Olomouc, has been featured in several fairy-tale films. Its present romanticized exterior comes from a remodeling at the turn of the 20th century, but the basic structure dates back to the 1300s. Owned by the Order of Teutonic Knights from the late 1600s up to the end of World War II, it was later confiscated by the state. Inside, the knights' hall has extensive carved-wood decorations and wall paintings that look old, even if many are reconstructions. Other rooms have collections of period furniture. The castle kitchen, which was used until 1945, is one of the best-preserved examples. The castle offers several tours, some aimed at children and one that shows off the wedding hall and knights' hall. You can easily arrange a tour from the tourist information office in Olomouc; the castle is included in the Olomouc Region Card. ⊠ *Bouzov 8, Bouzov* ☎ *775–888–960* ⊕ *www.hrad-bouzov.cz* ✉ *Classic tours from 150 Kč, other tours from 60 Kč.*

⊠ *Václavské nám.* ✉ *Free* ⊙ *Crypt closed Oct.–Apr.*

**Kostel sv. Michala** (*Church of St. Michael*)
RELIGIOUS SITE | The interior of this triple-domed church casts a dramatic spell. The frescoes, the high and airy central dome, and the shades of rose, beige, and gray trompe-l'oeil marble on walls and arches work in concert to present a harmonious whole. The decoration followed a fire in 1709, only 30 years after the original construction. Another renovation took place in the 1890s. The architect and builder are not known, but it's surmised they are the same team that put up the Church of the Annunciation on Svatý Kopeček (Holy Hill), a popular Catholic pilgrimage site just outside Olomouc. ⊠ *Žerotínovo nám.* ✛ *1 block uphill from Horní nám., along Školní ul.* ⊕ *www. svatymichal.cz.*

★ **Morový sloup** (*Trinity Column*)
BUILDING | In the northwest corner of Horní náměstí, the eccentric Trinity Column is one of the best surviving examples of the Olomouc baroque style, which was prevalent in this region of Moravia after the Thirty Years' War in the 17th century. At 115 feet, it's the tallest column devoted to victims of the plague in the Czech Republic. The column alone (not the rest of the square) is a UNESCO World Heritage Site. Its construction began in 1717, but it was not completed until 1754, long after the death of its principal designer, Václav Render, who left all his wealth to the city of Olomouc so that the column could be finished. Inside is a small chapel that, unfortunately, is never open. ⊠ *Horní nám.*

**Radnice** (*Town Hall*)
GOVERNMENT BUILDING | Olomouc's central square is marked by the bright, spire-bedecked Renaissance Town Hall with its 220-foot tower. The tower was constructed in the late 14th century. The modern socialist-realist mosaic decorations of the current clock on the face of the tower date to 1955. It replaced an astronomical clock built in 1422 that once rivaled the one in Prague. It was mostly destroyed by an artillery shell on the last two days of World War II. Be sure to look inside the Town Hall at the beautiful stairway. You can also visit a large Gothic banquet room in the main building, with scenes from the city's history, and a late-Gothic

chapel. The Town Hall was renovated in late 2019 and early 2020, and the wooden interior of the tower was completely rebuilt. Tours of the tower are given several times daily; tours of the rest of the building are by appointment. An audio guide to the city can be borrowed from the information center in the Town Hall. ✉ *Horní nám.* ☎ *585–513–385 for tourist office* 🌐 *www.tourism.olomouc.eu* 🎟 *Tower tour 30 Kč* ⏲ *Tower closed Jan. and Feb.*

**Románský biskupský palace** (*Romanesque Bishop's Palace*)

**MUSEUM** | Next to the Cathedral of St. Wenceslas is a complex of buildings that for centuries were the center of the archdiocese. The oldest, commonly called Palác Přemyslovců (Přemyslid Palace), houses a museum where you can see early-16th-century wall paintings decorating the Gothic cloisters and, upstairs, a wonderful series of Romanesque windows and displays of sculpted stonework fragments. This part of the building was used as a schoolroom some 700 years ago, and you can still make out drawings of animals engraved on the walls by young vandals. ✉ *Václavské nám. 4* 🎟 *100 Kč, incl. Archdiocesan Museum* ⏲ *Closed Mon. and Oct.–Mar.*

## 🍴 Restaurants

**Hanácká Hospoda**

**$$** | **CZECH** | A low-key, relatively cheap dining option, this popular local pub serves staples like pork, chicken, and duck but nicely turned out. The restaurant is located on the side of a palace but has an uncluttered, modern look inside. **Known for:** historical building; outdoor seating on a main square; above-standard food for a pub. [$] *Average main: 180 Kč* ✉ *Dolní nám. 38* ☎ *774–033–045* 🌐 *www.hanackahospoda.com.*

**Moravská restaurace a vinarná**

**$$** | **CZECH** | Traditional Moravian dishes like roast duck with cabbage, chicken breast stuffed with almond butter, roast piglet, or fried Olomouc cheese are served in a rustic interior. The wine cellar, open weekdays, is a bit homier than the street-level restaurant. **Known for:** folkloric atmosphere; traditional Moravian dishes; local wines. [$] *Average main: 320 Kč* ✉ *Horní nám. 23* ☎ *585–222–868* 🌐 *www.moravskarestaurace.cz.*

## ☕ Coffee and Quick Bites

**Café Mahler**

**$** | **CAFÉ** | Wooden paneling and floral upholstery in the Café Mahler recall the taste of the 1880s, when Gustav Mahler briefly lived around the corner while working as a conductor at the theater on the other side of Horní náměstí. It's a good spot for ice cream, cake, or coffee or simply for sitting back and taking in the lovely view. **Known for:** palačinke (crepes); leisurely spot for coffee; views of the main square. [$] *Average main:* ✉ *Horní nám. 11.*

## 🛏 Hotels

**Arigone Hotel and Restaurant**

**$$** | **HOTEL** | A renovated historic building blends a nice façade with modern rooms that have modern furnishings. **Pros:** a good blend of historical and modern architecture; relaxation studio offering several types of massage; sauna and wellness facilities in some suites. **Cons:** parking is 300 yards away; hotel is three buildings, so reception and breakfast can require a trip; no elevator. [$] *Rooms from: 2290 Kč* ✉ *Universitní 20* ☎ *585–232–351* 🌐 *www.arigone.cz* 🛏 *59 rooms* 🍴 *Free breakfast.*

**Hotel Flora**

$ | **HOTEL** | The words "traditional communist-era hotel" don't generally evoke images of comfort, but this one was made much more inviting by a thorough makeover of the lobby and public areas. **Pros:** close to the main highways; lots of parking; barrier-free and allergy-free rooms. **Cons:** hotel might not suit modern tastes; relatively far from the center in a commercial zone; rooms have an institutional feel. [$] *Rooms from: 1357 Kč* ✉ *Krapkova 34* ☎ *585–422–200* 🌐 *www.hotelflora.cz* 🛏 *144 rooms* 🍴 *Free breakfast.*

**U Dómu**

$ | **HOTEL** | Each of the rooms in this quiet, family-run pension just off Vaclavské náměstí sleeps up to four and has a small kitchenette. **Pros:** quiet; near the center; breakfast is cooked to order. **Cons:** on a steep street; furniture has a 1980s vibe; parking is around the corner in a lot. [$] *Rooms from: 1800 Kč* ✉ *Dómská 4* ☎ *585–220–502* 🌐 *www.hoteludomu.cz* 🛏 *6 rooms* 🍴 *Free breakfast.*

# Index

# Photo Credits

**Front Cover:** Chan Srithaweeporn [Description: The Bridges of Prague in Czech Republic]. **Back cover, from left to right:** DaLiu/Shutterstock, kps1664/Shutterstock, Marcin Catarina Belova/Shutterstock. **Spine:** AlexAnton/Shutterstock. **Interior, from left to right:** Alberto Zamorano/Shutterstock (1). Anton Aleksenko/iStockphoto (2). **Chapter 1: Experience Prague:** Prague City Tourism (6-7). Shutterstock. com (8). Petr Bonek/Shutterstock (9). David Marvan/CzechTourism (9). Jiri Alexander Bednar (10). Libor Svacek/CzechTourism (10). Prague City Tourism (10). CzechTourism (10). Jiří Kružík/CzechTourism (11). Seqoya/Shutterstock (11). Irena Brozova/CzechTourism (12). Jakub Kynčl/ CzechTourism (12). Prague City Tourism (12). Plzeňský Prazdroj (12). Michal Vitásek/CzechTourism (13). Lukas Zentel/CzechTourism (14). Libor Svacek/CzechTourism (14). Filip Fuxa/Shutterstock (14). Michal Fic/CzechTourism (14). Dagmar Veselková/CzechTourism (15). Prague City Tourism (15). Ladislav Renner/CzechTourism (22). Rhombur/Dreamstime (22). Kletr/Shutterstock (22). Aleš Motejl/CzechTourism (23). Zámek Loučeň (23). The First Beer Spa Carlsbad (24). Fotokon/Shutterstock (25). Ingrid Prats/Shutterstock (26). Paolo Gallo/Shutterstock (27). Courtesy_Stefanik Observatory (28). KDEBUDEMEBYDLET_RADEK_HABADA (28). www.filipvido.com (28). Courtesy of Pragulic (29). Courtesy of Mr. Jan Kolman (29). frantic00/Shutterstock (30). hsunny/Shutterstock (31). **Chapter 3: Staré Město (Old Town) and Josefov:** Zoltan Gabor/Dreamstime (57). Marco Brivio/Dreamstime (63). Dmitry Agafontsev/Shutterstock (68-69). rglinsky/iStockphoto (72). Israel dlrg/Flickr (75). Gabor Kovacs Photography/Shutterstock (89). Warren LeMay/Flickr (90). **Chapter 4: Malá Strana:** RossHelen/Shutterstock (97). Dorinmarius/Dreamstime (98). Millafedotova/Dreamstime (99). Adisa/Shutterstock (99). Mistervlad/Shutterstock (104). courtyardpix/Shutterstock (106-107). Nataliya Hora/Shutterstock (112). Cafe Savoy (114). Kirillm/iStockphoto (119). **Chapter 5: Prague Castle and Hradčany:** NaughtyNut/Shutterstock (121). dimbar76/Shutterstock (125). Grisha Bruev/Shutterstock (127). Tatiana Dyuvbanova/Shutterstock (129). **Chapter 6: Nové Město:** PytyCzech/iStockphoto (133). mikecphoto/Shutterstock (138). Vladimir Sazonov/Shutterstock (143). AL CASE ASHLAND DAILY PHOTO (150). **Chapter 7: Smíchov and Vyšehrad:** Radomír Režný/Dreamstime (157). National Geographic Image Collection / Alamy (163). PhotoFires/Shutterstock (166). Jan Pohunek/Shutterstock (169). **Chapter 8: Vinohrady and Vršovice:** Gabriel Prehn Britto/ Shutterstock (171). islavicek/Shutterstock (177). Juanlu Fajardo/Shutterstock (181). **Chapter 9: Žižkov and Karlín:** Ekrystia/Dreamstime (183). Julien Chatelain/Flickr (189). Pavel Matejicek/Flickr (191). **Chapter 10: Letná, Holešovice, and Troja:** DaLiu/Shutterstock (193). Larysa Uhryn/Dreamstime (198). FRANCIS AMIAND (204). Alexey Osokin/Shutterstock (207). **Chapter 11: Day Trips from Prague:** rpeters86/iStockphoto (209). Nikolai Sorokin/Dreamstime (215). Iakov Filimonov/Shutterstock (217). muratart/Shutterstock (223). Lindrik/ Dreamstime (224). Honzik7/Dreamstime (229). **Chapter 12: Southern Bohemia:** Nataliia Budianska/Shutterstock (233). Sergey Fedoskin/ Dreamstime (242). Kaprik/Dreamstime (247). Jens Hertel/Dreamstime (252). Botond Horvath/Shutterstock (254). **Chapter 13: Western Bohemia:** Zdenek Bedus/Dreamstime (257). marchello_/Shutterstock (264). lavendertime (267). Lukas Gojda/Shutterstock (271). vanGeo/ Shutterstock (274-275). guteksk7/Shutterstock (280). **Chapter 14: Moravia:** Martin Mecnarowski/Shutterstock (283). Jirik V/Shutterstock (290). Prosiaczeq/Dreamstime.com (293). Steven Hatton/Dreamstime (296). nektofadeev/Shutterstock (303). **About Our Writers:** All photos are courtesy of the writers.

*Every effort has been made to trace the copyright holders, and we apologize in advance for any accidental errors. We would be happy to apply the corrections in the following edition of this publication.*

# Notes

# Notes

# Notes

# Notes

# Notes

# Fodor's PRAGUE

**Publisher:** Stephen Horowitz, *General Manager*

**Editorial:** Douglas Stallings, *Editorial Director*; Jill Fergus, Jacinta O'Halloran, Amanda Sadlowski, *Senior Editors*; Kayla Becker, Alexis Kelly, Rachael Roth, *Editors*

**Design:** Tina Malaney, *Director of Design and Production*; Jessica Gonzalez, *Graphic Designer;* Mariana Tabares, *Design and Production Intern*

**Production:** Jennifer DePrima, *Editorial Production Manager*; Elyse Rozelle, *Senior Production Editor,* Monica White, *Production Editor*

**Maps:** Rebecca Baer, *Senior Map Editor*; David Lindroth, Mark Stroud (Moon Street Cartography), *Cartographers*

**Photography:** Viviane Teles, *Senior Photo Editor;* Namrata Aggarwal, Ashok Kumar, Carl Yu, *Photo Editors;* Rebecca Rimmer, *Photo Intern*

**Business and Operations:** Chuck Hoover, *Chief Marketing Officer*; Robert Ames, *Group General Manager*; Devin Duckworth, *Director of Print Publishing*; Victor Bernal, *Business Analyst*

**Public Relations and Marketing:** Joe Ewaskiw, *Senior Director Communications and Public Relations*; Esther Su, *Senior Marketing Manager*

**Fodors.com:** Jeremy Tarr, *Editorial Director;* Rachael Levitt, *Managing Editor;* Teddy Minford, *Editor*

**Technology:** Jon Atkinson, *Director of Technology;* Rudresh Teotia, *Lead Developer*; Jacob Ashpis, *Content Operations Manager*

**Writers:** Raymond Johnston, Joseph Reaney, Jennifer Rigby

**Editor:** Jacinta O'Halloran

**Production Editor:** Jennifer DePrima

3rd edition

ISBN 978-1-64097-278-0

ISSN 1554–3447

**SPECIAL SALES**
This book is available at special discounts for bulk purchases for sales promotions or premiums. For more information, e-mail SpecialMarkets@fodors.com.

PRINTED IN CANADA

10 9 8 7 6 5 4 3 2 1

# About Our Writers

**Raymond Johnston** has worked in media for all of his professional career, hosting a popular radio show in the Midwest in the early 1990s before moving to New York to work for a company that published critical guide-books on the Internet. In 1996 he moved to Prague, where he has worked as a film critic, a historical and linguistic consultant for TV programs, and a newspaper and magazine journalist and editor. Currently, he works for several websites with news, cultural and historical information about Prague. For this edition he updated the Western Bohemia, Southern Bohemia, Moravia, and Travel Smart chapters

**Joseph Reaney** is an experienced British travel writer and editor based in Prague and specializing in Central and Eastern Europe. As well as writing for international publications like *National Geographic* and *The Guardian*, he also runs his own travel content writing agency, World Words. When he has the time, Joseph also writes and directs comedy productions, from short films to live sketch shows. For this edition, he updated Žižkov and Karlín, Vinohrady and Vršovice, Smíchov and Vyšehrad, and the Prague Castle and Hradčany neighborhood chapters as well as Day Trips from Prague.

**Jennifer Rigby** is a British journalist who first came to live in Prague in 2012 and in her heart, she has never really left. Via a stint in Myanmar, she and her young family now split their time between London and Prague. She has worked for a number of leading international newspapers and broadcast-ers all over the world, writing about anything from heavy metal to women's rights, but makes time whenever she's in Prague to appreciate the city's sheer heart-stopping beauty as well as its delicious beer.

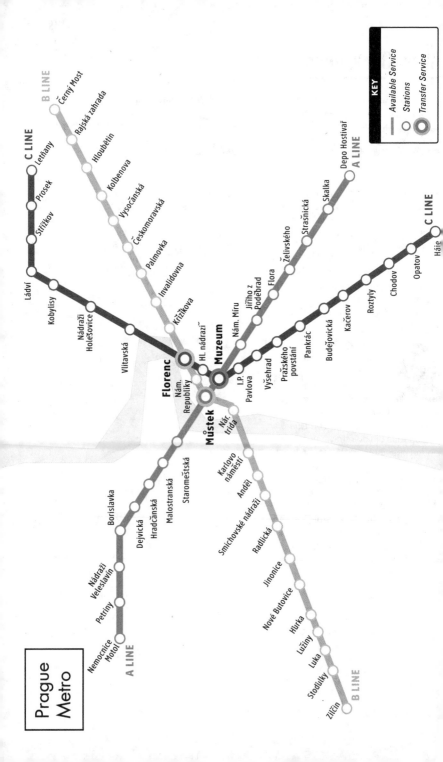